"*Captive Genders* is an exciting assemb... ...tings—analyses, manifestos, stories, interviews—that traverse the complicated entanglements of surveillance, policing, imprisonment, and the production of gender normativity. Focusing discerningly on the encounter of transpersons with the apparatuses that constitute the prison industrial complex, the contributors to this volume create new frameworks and new vocabularies that surely will have a transformative impact on the theories and practices of twenty-first century abolition."

—*Angela Y. Davis, professor emerita, University of California, Santa Cruz*

"The purpose of prison abolition is to discover and promote the countless ways freedom and difference are mutually dependent. The contributors to *Captive Genders* brilliantly shatter the assumption that the antidote to danger is human sacrifice. In other words, for these thinkers: where life is precious life is precious."

—*Ruth Wilson Gilmore, author of* Golden Gulag: Prisons, Surplus, Crisis, and Opposition in Globalizing California

"*Captive Genders* is at once a scathing and necessary analysis of the prison industrial complex and a history of queer resistance to state tyranny. By analyzing the root causes of anti-queer and anti-trans violence, this book exposes the brutality of state control over queer/trans bodies inside and outside prison walls, and proposes an analytical framework for undoing not just the prison system, but its mechanisms of surveillance, dehumanization, and containment. By queering a prison abolition analysis, *Captive Genders* moves us to imagine the impossible dream of liberation."

—*Mattilda Bernstein Sycamore, author of* So Many Ways to Sleep Badly *and editor of* Nobody Passes: Rejecting the Rules of Gender and Conformity

CAPTIVE GENDERS

Trans Embodiment and the Prison Industrial Complex

EDITED BY ERIC A. STANLEY
AND NAT SMITH

AK
PRESS
EDINBURGH · OAKLAND · BALTIMORE

Captive Genders: Trans Embodiment and the Prison Industrial Complex
Edited by Eric A. Stanley and Nat Smith

All essays © 2011 by their respective authors

This edition © 2011 AK Press (Edinburgh, Oakland, Baltimore)

ISBN-13: 978-1-84935-070-9
Library of Congress Control Number: 2011920478

AK Press
674-A 23rd Street
Oakland, CA 94612
USA
www.akpress.org
akpress@akpress.org

AK Press UK
PO Box 12766
Edinburgh EH8 9YE
Scotland
www.akuk.com
ak@akdin.demon.co.uk

The above addresses would be delighted to provide you with the latest AK
Press distribution catalog, which features several thousand books, pamphlets,
zines, audio and video recordings, and gear, all published or distributed by AK
Press. Alternately, visit our websites to browse the catalog and find out
the latest news from the world of anarchist publishing:
www.akpress.org | www.akuk.com
revolutionbythebook.akpress.org

Printed in the United States on FSC®certified paper.

Cover image: Marie Ueda, photo from the White Night riots,
San Francisco, CA 1979
Courtesy of the Gay, Lesbian, Bisexual, Transgender Historical Society.

Cover by Kate Khatib | www.manifestor.org/design
Interior by Michelle Fleming with Kate Khatib

CONTENTS

PRISON BEYOND THE PRISON: CRIMINALIZATION OF THE EVERYDAY

WALLED LIVES: CONSOLIDATING DIFFERENCE, DISAPPEARING POSSIBILITIES

ACKNOWLEDGEMENTS

Like all struggle we have not acted alone. We would like to acknowledge the labor, support, and guidance of the following people: Ralowe T. Ampu, Ryan Conrad, Angela Y. Davis, Jay Donahue, Jason Fritz, Ruth Wilson Gilmore, Donna Haraway, Rachel Herzing, Rebecca Hurdis, Kentaro Kaneko, Colby Lenz, Matt Luton, Toshio Meronek, José Muñoz, Yasmin Nair, Isaac Ontiveros, Julia Chinyere Oparah, Adam Reed, Andrea Ritchie, Chris Smith, the late Will Smith, Dean Spade, Mattilda Bernstein Sycamore, Chris Vargas, and Ari Wohlfeiler.

Working with organizations, collectives, and with unaffiliated people is essential to grounding the analysis put forth by this book. While central to the project of abolition, writing must always be produced within the context of action. Similarly, action devoid of analysis often makes for shaky ground upon which to build.

AK Press has been supportive of this project from its beginning many years ago. We are also grateful for the people who have and continue to organize with the Bay Area NJ4 Solidarity Committee, Critical Resistance, Gay Shame, the Sylvia Rivera Law Project, Transgender, Gender Variant, and Intersex Justice Project, and the amazing people who organized Transforming Justice, the groundbreaking conference held in 2007.

Captive Genders is evidence of a collective dedication to abolishing the prison industrial complex (PIC). When we first started talking about a possible writing project in 2006 we wanted to push the LGBT movement towards a deeper understanding of the role the PIC plays in our lives. Specifically we wanted to focus on the ways in which the LGBT mainstream, through its racist logic, relies on the PIC and is used by the PIC to criminalize transgender, gender variant, and queer people. We also wanted to push the anti-prison and PIC abolition movements to more centrally incorporate and foreground the struggles of transgender, gender variant, and queer people.

We started by making it clear that we wanted to emphasize writing from folks currently inside as well as former prisoners. Importantly, discussions of exploitation, inclusion without tokenization, and risking prisoner safety due to the content of our correspondence were in the forefront. We attempted to contact all of the members of Transgender, Gender Variant, and Intersex Justice Project's contact list as well as our personal contacts. The Sylvia Rivera Law Project and additional organizations encouraged members to contribute.

Of the hundred or so letters sent out and ads posted in prisoner publications, we received relatively few responses. This makes sense because prison mail is "unreliable" as guards will often tamper with or simply destroy it, whether it is considered contraband or they just don't feel like sorting mail that day. Furthermore, guards sometimes hold a vendetta against activist and/or "othered" prisoners and frequently "disappear" their mail. While our letters explained openly and honestly what we were attempting to accomplish, some folks inside were understandably wary from being burned by supposed claims of support by others in the past and declined to submit. While we recognize that access to writing resources, supporting documents, and editorial assistance are limited if not completely absent inside, only a small number of the submissions were editable within our timeframe and our own limited resources. Additionally and unfortunately, authors of a few pieces we had chosen for publication were un-locatable as their housing had changed (and a few folks were released on parole!) and thus we could no longer contact them (though we tried). Because of these and other reasons related to mail communication and the busyness of our lives, it took a long time to gather pieces that we felt demonstrated a broad and essential scope.

Finally, a few contributions (from both within and outside prison) we were holding out for never materialized and there are definitely some important ideas and voices missing. However, we collectively covered a lot of important ground that will make room for even more organizing and writing in the future, and we invite you to join or continue your participation in both. Ultimately, *Captive Genders* is a powerful offering of struggle, innovation, comeuppance and sorrow; a call to arms and a cry for true, self-determined justice.

FUGITIVE FLESH:

Gender Self-Determination, Queer Abolition, and Trans Resistance

Eric A. Stanley

We always felt that the police were the real enemy.
—Sylvia Rivera

Bright lights shattered the dark anonymity of the dance floor. The flicker warned of the danger of the coming raid. Well experienced, people stopped dancing, changed clothing, removed or applied makeup, and got ready. The police entered, began examining everyone's IDs, and lined up the trans/gender-non-conforming folks to be "checked" by an officer in the restroom to ensure that they were wearing the legally mandated three pieces of "gender appropriate clothing." Simultaneously the cops started roughing up people, dragging them out front to the awaiting paddy wagon. In other words, it was a regular June night out on the town for trans and queer folks in 1969 New York City.

As the legend goes, that night the cops did not receive their payoff or they wanted to remind the patrons of their precarious existence. In the shadows of New York nightlife, the Stonewall Inn, like most other "gay bars," was owned and run by the mafia, which tended to have the connections within local government and the vice squad to know who to bribe in order to keep the bar raids at a minimum and the cash flowing. As the first few captured queers were forced into the paddy wagon, people hanging around outside the bar began throwing pocket change at the arresting officers; then the bottles started flying and then the bricks. With the majority of the patrons now outside the bar, a crowd of angry trans/queer folks had gathered and forced the police to retreat back into the Stonewall. As their collective fury grew, a few people uprooted a parking meter and used it as a battering ram in hopes of knocking down the bar's door and escalating the physical confrontation with the cops. A tactical team was called to rescue the vice squad now barricaded inside the Stonewall. They eventually arrived, and the street battle raged for two more nights. In a blast of radical collectivity, trans/gender-non-conforming folks, queers of color, butches, drag queens, hair-fairies, homeless street youth, sex workers, and others took up arms and fought back against the generations of oppression that they were forced to survive.[1]

Forty years later, on a similarly muggy June night in 2009, history repeated itself. At the Rainbow Lounge, a newly opened gay bar in Fort Worth, Texas, the police staged a raid, verbally harassing patrons, calling them "faggots" and beating a number of customers. One patron was slammed against the floor, sending him to the hospital with brain injuries, while seven others were arrested. These instances of brutal force and the administrative surveillance that trans and queer folks face today are not significantly less prevalent nor less traumatic than those experienced by the Stonewall rioters of 1969, however the ways this violence is currently understood is quite different. While community vigils and public forums were held in the wake of the Rainbow Lounge raid, the immediate response was not to fight back, nor has there been much attempt to understand the raid in the broader context of the systematic violence trans and queer people face under the relentless force of the prison industrial complex (PIC).[2]

Captive Genders is in part an attempt to think about the historical and political ideologies that continually naturalize the abusive force of the police with such power as to make them appear ordinary. This is not to argue that the types of resistance present at the Stonewall riots were commonplace during that time, nor to suggest that trans and queer folks do not fight back today; nonetheless one of our aims is to chart the multiple ways that trans and queer folks are subjugated by the police, along with the multiple ways that we have and that we continue to resist in the face of these overwhelming structures.[3]

I start with the Stonewall riot not because it was the first, most important, or last instance of radical refusal of the police state. Indeed, the riots at San Francisco's Compton's Cafeteria in 1966 and at Los Angeles's Cooper's Doughnuts in 1959 remind us that the history of resistance is as long as the history of oppression. However, what is unique about the Stonewall uprising is that, within the United States context, it is made to symbolize the "birth of the gay rights movement." Furthermore, dominant lesbian, gay, bisexual, and transgender (LGBT) political organizations like the Human Rights Campaign (HRC) and the National Gay and Lesbian Task Force (NGLTF) attempt to build an arc of progress starting with the oppression of the Stonewall moment and ending in the current time of "equality" evidenced by campaigns for gay marriage, hate crimes legislation, and gays in the military. *Captive Genders* works to undo this narrative of progress, assimilation, and police cooperation by building an analysis that highlights the historical and contemporary antagonisms between trans/queer folks and the police state.[4]

This collection argues that prison abolition must be one of the centers of trans and queer liberation struggles. Starting with abolition we open questions often disappeared by both mainstream LGBT and anti-prison movements. Among these many silences are the radical trans/queer arguments against the proliferation of hate crimes enhancements. Mainstream LGBT organizations, in collaboration with the state, have been working hard to make us believe that hate crimes enhancements are a necessary and useful way to make trans and queer people safer. Hate crimes enhancements are used to add time to a person's sentence if the offense is deemed to target a group of people. However, hate crimes enhancements ignore the roots of harm, do not act as deterrents, and reproduce the force of the PIC, which produces more, not less harm. Not surprisingly, in October 2009, when President Obama signed the Matthew Shepard and James Byrd, Jr. Hate Crimes Prevention Act into law, extending existing hate crimes enhancements to include "gender and sexuality," there was no mention by the LGBT mainstream of the historical and contemporary ways that the legal system itself works to deaden trans and queer lives. As antidote, this collection works to understand how gender, sexuality, race, ability, class, nationality, and other markers of difference are constricted, often to the point of liquidation, in the name of a normative carceral state.

Among the most volatile points of contact between state violence and one's body is the domain of gender. An understanding of these connections has produced much important activism and research that explores how non-trans women are uniquely harmed through disproportionate prison sentences, sexual assault while in custody, and nonexistent medical care, coupled with other forms of violence. This work was and continues to be a necessary intervention in the ways that prison studies and activism have historically imagined *the prisoner* as always male and have until recently rarely attended to the ways that gendered difference produces carceral differences. Similarly, queer studies and political organizing, along with the growing body of work that might be called trans studies—while attending to the work of gender, sexuality, and more recently to race and nationality—has (with important exceptions) had little to say about the force of imprisonment or about trans/queer prisoners. Productively, we see this as both an absence and an opening for those of us working in trans/queer studies to attend—in a way that centers the experiences of those most directly impacted—to the ways that the prison must emerge as one of the major sites of trans/queer scholarship and political organizing.[5]

In moments of frustration, excitement, isolation, and solidarity, *Captive Genders* grew out of this friction as a rogue text, a necessarily unstable collection of voices, stories, analysis, and plans for action. What these pieces all have in common is that they suggest that gender, ability, and sexuality as written through race, class, and nationality must figure into any and all accounts of incarceration, even when they seem to be nonexistent. Indeed, the oftentimes ghosted ways that gender and heteronormativity function most forcefully are in their presumed absence. In collaboration and sometimes in contestation, this project offers vital ways of understanding not only the specific experience of trans and queer prisoners, but also more broadly the ways that regimes of normative sexuality and gender are organizing structures of the prison industrial complex. To be clear, *Captive Genders* is not offered as a definitive collection. Our hope is that it will work as a space where conversations and connections can multiply with the aim of making abolition flourish.

Gender Lockdown

Gender seems to always escape the confines of the language that we use to capture it. This makes for a difficult place of departure for a book that is

4

about, among other things, gender. For sure, some firmly identify as one or more particular genders while others have a more shifting relation via their racialized bodies, gendered desires, physical presentations, and the words available to comprehend these intersections. Neither a solidly fixed understanding of oneself nor a more fluid idea of gender is necessarily more radically deconstructive than the other. Trans/gender-non-conforming folks are not the answer to the "riddle" of gender, nor are they immune to the assimilationist longing embodied by other marginalized people. To this end, a gendered identity (or any other identity) imagined outside the context of the political offers very little. Here, then, we attempt to always understand gender and sexuality within the space of the political to build beyond generality. Furthermore, one's gender identification and sexual identification are always formed in a series of thick relations to each other. While we acknowledge that gender identity is not co-terminus with sexuality, these connections must be carefully attended to, as they cut through class, race, ability, and nationality, as well as time.[6]

Captive Genders offers no comprehensive theory of gender or sexuality that would be useful as an abstracted description. Nor does it assume that it represents the lived experiences of particular people beyond its authors. We do, however, highlight a number of tendencies that can and sometimes must become abstracted. For example, we know that trans people are disproportionately incarcerated in relation to non-trans people. Yet we also know that some, perhaps many, trans/queer people, as a result of experiencing relentless violence, are in favor of incarceration and believe in its claims of safety. In many ways this book lives among these contradictions as it works to move conversations toward abolition and away from a belief that prisons will ever make us safer.

As a theoretical and embodied practice, gender self-determination is one of the politics that holds this project together. Echoed through the dreams of other liberation movements' understandings of identity and power, gender self-determination at its most basic suggests that we collectively work to create the most space for people to express whatever genders they choose at any given moment. It also understands that these expressions might change and that this change does not delegitimate previous or future identifications. Gender self-determination also acknowledges that gender identification is always formed in relation to other forms of power and thus the words we use to identify others and ourselves are culturally, generationally, and geographically situated. In other words, terms that are more common now, like "transgender," are relatively new to our vocabularies and are not inclusive of all of our embodied experiences. Gender self-determination believes that there are multiple ways to work one's gender and sexuality—and while they might have material differences, they must not be hierarchized in the name of *realness*.[7]

Chain Links

In the recent past, the term *prison industrial complex* has been offered to begin to name the enormity of the prison system. Indeed, "the prison," or the material buildings that comprise prisons and jails are only one component of the PIC. Immigration centers, juvenile justice facilities, county jails, military jails, holding rooms, court rooms, sheriff's offices, psychiatric institutes, along with other spaces build the vastness of the PIC's architecture. Along with these more recognizable spaces, understanding the PIC as a set of relations makes visible the connections among capitalism, globalization, and corporations. From prison labor, privatized prisons, prison guard unions, food suppliers, telephone companies, commissary suppliers, uniform producers, and beyond, the carceral landscape overwhelms. Other than the facilities themselves and the economic and geopolitical connections, the PIC also helps us to think about the practices of surveillance, policing, screening, profiling, and other technologies to partition people and produce "populations" that often occur far beyond the walls of the prison.[8]

This book suggests that anti-trans/queer violence and the reproduction of gender normativity are important ways in which PIC logics proliferate, dangerously unnamed. Gender normativity, understood as a series of cultural, political, legal, and religious assumptions that attempt to divide our bodies into two categories (men/women), is both a product of and a producer of the PIC. In this we mean to suggest that we must pay attention to the ways that the PIC harms trans/gender-non-conforming and queer people and also to how the PIC produces the gender binary and heteronormativity itself. We also acknowledge that trans/queer folks, especially those of color and/or low income, experience overwhelming amounts of personal violence that must be attended to. Here we are not attempting to discredit the severity of this personal violence, but we are suggesting that relying on the PIC as a remedy actually produces more harm and offers little. What, then, might a world look like in which harm is met with healing and support, rather than the displacement and re-violation produced by the PIC?[9]

Outlawed Life

Trans/gender-non-conforming and queer people, along with many others, are born into webs of surveillance. The gendering scan of other children at an early age ("Are you a boy or a girl?") places many in the panopticon long before they enter a prison. For those who do trespass the gender binary or heteronormativity, physical violence, isolation, detention, or parental disappointment become some of the first punishments. As has been well documented, many trans and queer youth are routinely harassed at school and kicked out of home at young ages, while others leave in hopes of escaping the mental and physical violence that they experience at schools and in their houses.

Many trans/queer youth learn how to survive in a hostile world. Often the informal economy becomes the only option for them to make money. Selling drugs, sex work, shoplifting, and scamming are among the few avenues that might ensure they have something to eat and a place to sleep at night. Routinely turned away from shelters because of their gender presentation, abused in residential living situations or foster care, and even harassed in "gay neighborhoods" (as they are assumed to drive down property values or scare off business), they are reminded that they are alone. Habitually picked up for truancy, loitering, or soliciting, many trans/queer people spend their youth shuttling between the anonymity of the streets and the hyper-surveillance of the juvenile justice system. With case managers too overloaded to care, or too transphobic to want to care, they slip through the holes left by others. Picked up—locked up—placed in a home—escape—survive—picked up again. The cycle builds a cage, and the hope for anything else disappears with the crushing reality that their identities form the parameters of possibility.[10]

With few options and aging-out of what little resources there are for "youth," many trans/queer adults are in no better a situation. Employers routinely don't hire "queeny" gay men, trans women who "cannot pass," butches who seem "too hard," or anyone else who is read to be "bad for business." Along with the barriers to employment, most jobs that are open to folks who have been homeless or incarcerated are minimum-wage and thus provide little more than continuing poverty and fleeting stability. Back to where they began—on the streets, hustling to make it, now older—they are often given even longer sentences.

While this cycle of poverty and incarceration speaks to more current experiences, the discursive drives building their motors are nothing new. Inheriting a long history of being made suspect, trans/queer people, via

7

the medicalization of trans identities and homosexuality, have been and continue to be institutionalized, forcibly medicated, sterilized, operated on, shocked, and made into objects of study and experimentation. Similarly, the historical illegality of gender trespassing and of queerness have taught many trans/queer folks that their lives will be intimately bound with the legal system. More recently, the HIV/AIDS pandemic has turned the surveillance technologies inward. One's blood and RNA replication became another site of susceptibility that continues to imprison people through charges of bio-terrorism, under AIDS-phobic laws.

Desiring Abolition

Living through these forms of domination are also moments of devastating resistance where people working together are building joy, tearing down the walls of normative culture, and opening space for a more beautiful, more lively, safer place for all. *Captive Genders* remembers these radical histories and movements as evidence that our legacies are fiercely imaginative and that our collective abilities can, and have, offered freedom even in the most destitute of times.[11]

In the face of the overwhelming violence of the PIC, abolition—and specifically a trans/queer abolition—is one example of this vital defiance. An abolitionist politic does not believe that the prison system is "broken" and in need of reform; indeed, it is, according to its own logic, working quite well. Abolition necessarily moves us away from attempting to "fix" the PIC and helps us imagine an entirely different world—one that is not built upon the historical and contemporary legacies of the racial and gendered brutality that maintain the power of the PIC. What this means is that abolition is not a response to the belief that the PIC is so horrible that reform would not be enough. Although we do believe that the PIC is horrible and that reform is not enough, abolition radically restages our conversations and our ways of living and understanding as to undo our reliance on the PIC and its cultural logics. For us, abolition is not simply a reaction to the PIC but a political commitment that makes the PIC impossible. To this end, the time of abolition is both yet to come and already here. In other words, while we hold on to abolition as a politics for doing anti-PIC work, we also acknowledge there are countless ways that abolition has been and continues to be here now. As a project dedicated to radical deconstruction, abolition must also include at its center a reworking of gender and sexuality that displaces both heterosexuality and gender normativity as measures of worth.[12]

The Stonewall uprising itself must be remembered and celebrated as a moment of a radical trans/queer abolitionist politic that built, in those three nights, the materiality of this vision. As both a dream of the future and a practice of history, we strategize for a world without the multiple ways that our bodies, genders, and sexualities are disciplined. *Captive Genders* is also a telling of a rich history of trans/queer struggle against the PIC, still in the making. This is an invitation to remember these radical legacies of abolition and to continue the struggle to make this dream of the future, lived today.

This piece has benefited from the critical attention of Angela Y. Davis, Toshio Meronek, and Adam Reed. I am also indebted to The Institute for Anarchist Studies who provided support for the completion of this introduction.

NOTES

1. For a conical history of Stonewall, see Martin B. Duberman, *Stonewall* (New York: Plume, 1994).
2. For more on the raid, see "Man Injured During Rainbow Lounge Raid in Fort Worth Speaks Out," *The Dallas Morning News*. Accessed January 8, 2011:

   Also, during the Stonewall uprising, many gays and lesbians disagreed with the rioters. The Mattachine Society of New York put up a sign that read, "We homosexuals pled with our people to please help maintain peaceful and quiet conduct on the streets of the village." Thus, I am not suggesting that during the riots all LGBT people understood the relationship between police repression and queer resistance. However, it seems important to chart how radical resistance gets rewritten under the name of a more conservative political agenda.
3. *Captive Genders* focuses mostly on the United States, Canada, and the United Kingdom. A more transnational reading would offer important insights not always present here.
4. For more on the argument that Stonewall began the "gay rights" movement in the United States, see David Eisenbach, *Gay Power: An American Revolution* (New York: Carroll and Graf, 2006).

   The consumer-driven, anti-political festival of modern Gay Pride celebrations still occurs during the last weekend in June in commemoration of the Stonewall uprising. For more critiques of Gay Pride, see the work of the activist collective Gay Shame.

5.	For a useful reading of gender (as understood by non-trans women) in relation to punishment, see Adrian Howe, *Punish and Critique: Towards a Feminist Analysis of Penality* (London: Routledge, 1994).

It is also important to highlight that women, trans, and queer people (specifically of color) have done much, if not most, of the anti-PIC organizing in the United States.

For more on the Compton's Cafeteria riots, see *Screaming Queens: The Riot at Compton's Cafeteria* [DVD], dir. Victor Silverman and Susan Stryker (San Francisco: Frameline, 2010).

6.	In this introduction, I use "trans" as an umbrella term to signal a wide range of gender non-conformity. I also often use "trans/queer" as a way to mark the connections between gender and sexuality and how they are often conflated via the PIC.

7.	Furthermore, if someone identifies as a "transvestite," "tranny," "queer," or any other identity that is sometimes considered to be derogatory, an ethic of gender self-determination would make space for that identity as equally valid.

8.	See Eve Goldberg and Linda Evans, *The Prison Industrial Complex and the Global Economy* (Montreal: Kersplebedeb, 2003); Angela Y. Davis, *Are Prisons Obsolete?* (New York: Seven Stories Press, 2003); Ruth Wilson Gilmore, *Golden Gulag: Prisons, Surplus, Crisis, and Opposition in Globalizing California* (Berkeley: University of California Press, 2007). Also, for more on the relationship between globalization and imprisonment, see Julia Chinyere Oparah, *Global Lockdown: Race, Gender, and the Prison-Industrial Complex* (New York: Routledge, 2005).

9.	Figuring out responses to anti-trans/queer violence that do not reproduce harm needs much more critical attention. Community accountability models are one example, however, when the person that caused harm is "random" it becomes much more difficult to imagine alternatives.

10.	This is not to suggest that working in the informal economy is less moral than working in more traditional jobs. Indeed, at times it is actually safer and more beneficial to remain in these jobs. I also do not want to suggest that sex workers, in every instance, have no other *choice*. Under capitalism, most have little *choice* in regard to their working conditions. However, I do want to mark the ways that this labor makes one more vulnerable to the PIC.

The case of the New Jersey 4 (NJ4) is another shattering example of the ways that race, class, gender, and sexuality make contact through the crushing force of the PIC. The NJ4 is a group of young, Black, queer/gender-non-conforming people from Newark, NJ, that were hanging out on a summer night in New York's West Village. As they were walking down the street, a man standing on the corner met them with sexual advances. The situation escalated as the NJ4 repeatedly refused his verbal harassment. He began shouting louder, flicked a cigarette toward one of them, and threatened to "fuck them straight." A fight broke out and a number of the NJ4 were physically attacked and the man was wounded but fully recovered. Not surprisingly, all four of the women were found guilty and were subsequently sentenced to between three and a half and eleven years in prison. As gender-non-conforming Black queers, their offense was survival, and they were punished harshly for it.

11. For more on alternatives to imprisonment, see *Instead of Prisons: A Handbook for Abolitionists* (Oakland, Calif.: Critical Resistance, 2005) and *Abolition Now!: Ten Years of Strategy and Struggle against the Prison Industrial Complex* (Oakland, Calif.: AK Press, 2008).

12. My many conversations with Angela Y. Davis continue to help me clarify the point that abolition is not imagined as only in response to the horrors of the PIC.

OUT OF TIME

FROM GAY LIBERATION TO
PRISON ABOLITION

BUILDING AN ABOLITIONIST TRANS AND QUEER MOVEMENT WITH EVERYTHING WE'VE GOT

Morgan Bassichis, Alexander Lee, Dean Spade

As we write this, queer and trans people across the United States and in many parts of the world have just celebrated the fortieth anniversary of the Stonewall Rebellion. On that fateful night back in June 1969, sexual and gender outsiders rose up against ongoing brutal police violence in an inspiring act of defiance. These early freedom fighters knew all too well that the NYPD—"New York's finest"—were the frontline threat to queer and trans survival. Stonewall was the culmination of years of domination, resentment, and upheaval in many marginalized communities coming to a new consciousness of the depth of violence committed by the government against poor people, people of color, women, and queer people both within US borders and around the world. The Stonewall Rebellion, the mass demonstrations against the war in Vietnam, and the campaign to free imprisoned Black-liberation activist Assata Shakur were all powerful examples of a groundswell of energy demanding an end to the "business as usual" of US terror during this time.

Could these groundbreaking and often unsung activists have imagined that only forty years later the "official" gay rights agenda would be largely pro-police, pro-prisons, and pro-war—exactly the forces they worked so hard to resist? Just a few decades later, the most visible and well-funded arms of the "LGBT movement" look much more like a corporate strategizing session than a grassroots social justice movement. There are countless examples of this dramatic shift in priorities. What emerged as a fight against racist, anti-poor, and anti-queer police violence now works hand in hand with local and federal law enforcement agencies—district attorneys are asked to speak at trans rallies, cops march in Gay Pride parades. The agendas of prosecutors—those who lock up our family, friends, and lovers—and many queer and trans organizations are becoming increasingly similar, with sentence- and police-enhancing legislation at the top of the priority list. Hate crimes legislation is tacked on to multi-billion dollar "defense" bills to support US military domination in Palestine, Iraq, Afghanistan, and elsewhere. Despite the rhetoric of an "LGBT community," transgender and gender-non-conforming people are repeatedly abandoned and marginalized in the agendas and priorities of our "lead" organizations—most recently in the 2007 gutting of the Employment Non-Discrimination Act of gender identity protections. And as the rate of people (particularly poor queer and trans people of color) without steady jobs, housing, or healthcare continues to rise, and health and social services continue to be cut, those dubbed the leaders of the "LGBT movement" insist that marriage rights are the way to redress the inequalities in our communities.

For more and more queer and trans people, regardless of marital status, there is no inheritance, no health benefits from employers, no legal immigration status, and no state protection of our relationship to our children. Four decades after queer and trans people took to the streets throwing heels, bottles, bricks, and anything else we had to ward off police, the official word is that, except for being able to get married and fight in the military,[2] we are pretty much free, safe, and equal. And those of us who are not must wait our turn until the "priority" battles are won by the largely white, male, upper-class lawyers and lobbyists who know better than us.[3]

Fortunately, radical queer and trans organizing for deep transformation has also grown alongside this "trickle-down"[4] brand of "equality" politics mentioned above. Although there is no neat line between official gay "equality" politics on the one hand, and radical "justice" politics on the other, it is important to draw out some of the key distinctions in how different parts of our movements today are responding to the main problems that queer and trans people face. This is less about creating false dichotomies between "good" and "bad" approaches, and more about clarifying the actual impact that various strategies have, and recognizing that alternative approaches to the "official" solutions are alive, are politically viable, and are being pursued by activists and organizations around the United States and beyond. In the first column, we identify some of these main challenges; in the second, we summarize what solutions are being offered by the well-resourced[5] segments of our movement; and in the third, we outline some approaches being used by more radical and progressive queer and trans organizing to expand possibilities for broad-based, social-justice solutions to these same problems.

The Current Landscape

BIG PROBLEMS	"OFFICIAL" SOLUTIONS	TRANSFORMATIVE APPROACHES
Queer and trans people, poor people, people of color, and immigrants have minimal access to quality healthcare	Legalize same-sex marriage to allow people with health benefits from their jobs to share with same-sex partners	Strengthen Medicaid and Medicare; win universal healthcare; fight for transgender health benefits; end deadly medical neglect of people in state custody
Queer and trans people experience regular and often fatal violence from partners, family members, community members, employers, law enforcement, and institutional officials	Pass hate crimes legislation to increase prison sentences and strengthen local and federal law enforcement; collect statistics on rates of violence; collaborate with local and federal law enforcement to prosecute hate violence and domestic violence	Build community relationships and infrastructure to support the healing and transformation of people who have been impacted by interpersonal and intergenerational violence; join with movements addressing root causes of queer and trans premature death, including police violence, imprisonment, poverty, immigration policies, and lack of healthcare and housing

BIG PROBLEMS	"OFFICIAL" SOLUTIONS	TRANSFORMATIVE APPROACHES
Queer and trans members of the military experience violence and discrimination	Eliminate bans on participation of gays and lesbians in US military	Join with war resisters, radical veterans, and young people to oppose military intervention, occupation, and war abroad and at home, and demand the reduction/elimination of "defense" budgets
Queer and trans people are targeted by an unfair and punitive immigration system	Legalize same-sex marriage to allow same-sex international couples to apply for legal residency for the non–US citizen spouse	End the use of immigration policy to criminalize people of color, exploit workers, and maintain the deadly wealth gap between the United States and the Global South; support current detainees and end ICE raids, deportations, and police collaboration
Queer and trans families are vulnerable to legal intervention and separation from the state, institutions, and/or non-queer people	Legalize same sex marriage to provide a route to "legalize" families with two parents of the same sex; pass laws banning adoption discrimination on the basis of sexual orientation	Join with struggles of queer/trans and non-queer/trans families of color, imprisoned parents and youth, native families, poor families, military families, and people with disabilities to win community and family self-determination and the right to keep kids, parents, and other family members in their families and communities
Institutions fail to recognize family connections outside of heterosexual marriage in contexts like hospital visitation and inheritance	Legalize same-sex marriage to formally recognize same-sex partners in the eyes of the law	Change policies like hospital visitation to recognize a variety of family structures, not just opposite-sex and same-sex couples; abolish inheritance and demand radical redistribution of wealth and an end to poverty

BIG PROBLEMS	"OFFICIAL" SOLUTIONS	TRANSFORMATIVE APPROACHES
Queer and trans people are disproportionately policed, arrested, and imprisoned, and face high rates of violence in state custody from officials as well as other imprisoned or detained people	Advocate for "cultural competency" training for law enforcement and the construction of queer and trans-specific and "gender-responsive" facilities; create written policies that say that queer and trans people are equal to other people in state custody; stay largely silent on the high rates of imprisonment in queer and trans communities, communities of color, and poor communities	Build ongoing, accountable relationships with and advocate for queer and trans people who are locked up to support their daily well-being, healing, leadership, and survival; build community networks of care to support people coming out of prison and jail; collaborate with other movements to address root causes of queer and trans imprisonment; work to abolish prisons, establish community support for people with disabilities and eliminate medical and psychiatric institutionalization, and provide permanent housing rather than shelter beds for all people without homes

I. How Did We Get Here?

The streams of conservative as well as more progressive and radical queer and trans politics developed over time and in the context of a rapidly changing political, economic, and social landscape. Although we can't offer a full history of how these different streams developed and how the more conservative one gained national dominance, we think it is important to trace the historical context in which these shifts occurred. *To chart a different course for our movements, we need to understand the road we've traveled.* In particular, we believe that there are two major features of the second half of the twentieth century that shaped the context in which the queer and trans movement developed: (1) the active resistance and challenge by radical movement to state violence, and subsequent systematic backlash,[7] and (2) the massive turmoil and transformation of the global economy.[8] Activists and scholars use a range of terms to describe this era in which power, wealth, and oppression were transformed to respond to these two significant "crises"—including neoliberalism, the "New World Order," empire, globalization, free market democracy, or late capitalism.

Each term describes a different aspect or "take" on the current historical moment that we are living in.

It is important to be clear that *none of the strategies of the "New World Order" are new.* They might work faster, use new technologies, and recruit the help of new groups, but they are not new. Oppressive dynamics in the United States are as old as the colonization of this land and the founding of a country based on slavery and genocide. However, they have taken intensified, tricky forms in the past few decades—particularly because our governments keep telling us those institutions and practices have been "abolished." There were no "good old days" in the United States—just times in which our movements and our communities were stronger or weaker, and times when we used different cracks in the system as opportunities for resistance. All in all, we might characterize the past many decades as a time in which policies and ideas were promoted by powerful nations and institutions (such as the World Trade Organization and the International Monetary Fund) to destroy the minimal safety nets set up for vulnerable people, dismantle the gains made by social movements, and redistribute wealth, resources, and life changes upward—away from the poor and toward the elite.[9]

Below are some of the key tactics that the United States and others have used in this most recent chapter of our history:

• Pull Yourself Up by Your Bootstraps, Again

The US government and its ally nations and institutions in the Global North helped pass laws and policies that made it harder for workers to organize into unions; destroyed welfare programs and created the image of people on welfare as immoral and fraudulent; and created international economic policies and trade agreements that reduced safety nets, worker rights, and environmental protections, particularly for nations in the Global South. Together, these efforts have dismantled laws and social programs meant to protect people from poverty, violence, sickness, and other harms of capitalism.

> **EXAMPLE:** In the early 1990s, the North American Free Trade Agreement (NAFTA) was implemented by the United States under Democratic President Clinton to make it easier for corporations to do business across borders between the United States, Mexico, and Canada. Unfortunately, by allowing corporations to outsource their labor much more cheaply, the agreement also led to the loss

of hundreds of thousands of US jobs and wage depression even in "job receiving" countries.[10] Additionally, human rights advocates have documented widespread violations of workers rights since NAFTA, including "favoritism toward employer-controlled unions; firings for workers' organizing efforts; denial of collective bargaining rights; forced pregnancy testing; mistreatment of migrant workers; life-threatening health and safety conditions"; and other violations of the right to freedom of association, freedom from discrimination, and the right to a minimum wage.[11] Loss of jobs in the United States reduced the bargaining power of workers, now more desperate for wages then ever, and both wages and benefits declined, with many workers now forced to work as "temps" or part-time with no benefits or job security.

EXAMPLE: In 1996, President Clinton signed into law the Personal Responsibility and Work Opportunity Reconciliation Act, which effectively dismantled what existed of a welfare state—creating a range of restrictive and targeting measures that required work, limited aid, and increased penalties for welfare recipients. The federal government abdicated its responsibility to provide minimal safety nets for poor and working-class people, using the rhetoric of "personal responsibility" and "work" to justify the exploitation and pain caused by capitalism and racism. Sexist, racist images of poor people as immoral, fraudulent drug addicts fueled these policy changes. Since then, different cities have adopted local measures to gut economic safety nets for poor, homeless, and working-class people. In San Francisco, Mayor Newsom's notorious 2002 "Care Not Cash" program slashed welfare benefits for homeless people, insisting that benefits given to the homeless were being spent on "drugs and alcohol."[12]

• Scapegoating

The decrease in manufacturing jobs and the gutting of social safety nets for the poor and working class created a growing class of people who were marginally employed and housed, and forced into criminalized economies such as sex work and the drug trade. This class of people was blamed for the poverty and inequity they faced—labeled drug dealers, welfare queens, criminals, and hoodlums—and were used to justify harmful policies that expanded violence and harm. At the same time, criminal penalties for behaviors associated with poverty, like drug use, sleeping outside, graffiti, and sex work have increased in many parts the United States, and resources for policing these kinds of "crimes" has also increased.

> **EXAMPLE:** In the 1990s, states across the United States began to sign into law so-called "Three Strikes" measures that mandated standard, long (often life) sentences for people convicted of three felonies, many including non-violent offenses. California's law has resulted in sentences of twenty-five years or more for people convicted of things like shoplifting. The popularity of Three Strikes laws have been fueled by a growing cultural obsession with criminality and punishment that relies on images of violent and dangerous "career criminals" while functioning to imprison enormous numbers of low-income people and people of color whose behaviors are the direct results of economic insecurity.

> **EXAMPLE:** Under President Clinton's 1996 welfare reforms, anyone convicted of a drug-related crime is automatically banned for life from receiving cash assistance and food stamps. Some states have since opted out of this ban, but for people living in fifteen states, this draconian measure presents nearly insurmountable barriers to becoming self-sufficient. Unable to receive cash assistance and subject to job discrimination because of their criminal histories, many people with drug-related convictions go back into the drug trade as the only way to earn enough to pay the rent and put food on the table. The lifetime welfare ban has been shown to particularly harm women and their children.[13]

• Fear-Mongering

The government and corporate media used racist, xenophobic, and misogynist fear-mongering to distract us from increasing economic disparity and a growing underclass in the United States and abroad. The War on Drugs in the 1980s and the Bush Administration's War on Terror, both of which are ongoing, created internal and external enemies ("criminals" and "terrorists") to blame for and distract from the ravages of racism, capitalism, patriarchy, and imperialism. In exchange, these enemies (and anyone who looked like them) could be targeted with violence and murder. During this time, the use of prisons, policing, detention, and surveillance skyrocketed as the government declared formal war against all those who it marks as "criminals" or "terrorists."

EXAMPLE: In the 1980s, the US government declared a "War on Drugs" and drastically increased mandatory sentences for violating drug prohibition laws. It also created new prohibitions for accessing public housing, public benefits, and higher education for people convicted of drug crimes. The result was the imprisonment of over one million people a year, the permanent marginalization and disenfranchisement for people convicted, and a new set of military and foreign policy intervention justifications for the United States to take brutal action in Latin America.

EXAMPLE: Following the September 11, 2001 attacks on the World Trade Center in New York, politicians manipulated the American public's fear and uncertainty to push through a range of new laws and policies justified by a declared "War on Terror." New legislation like the PATRIOT Act, the Immigrant Registration Act, and the Real ID Act, as well as new administrative policies and practices, increased the surveillance state, reduced even the most basic rights and living standards of immigrants, and turned local police, schoolteachers, hospital workers, and others into immigration enforcement officers.

• The Myth That Violence and Discrimination Are Just About "Bad" Individuals

Discrimination laws and hate crimes laws encourage us to understand oppression as something that happens when individuals use bias to deny someone a job because of race or sex or some other characteristic, or beat up or kill someone because of such a characteristic. This way of thinking, sometimes called the "perpetrator perspective,"[14] makes people think about racism, sexism, homophobia, transphobia, and ableism in terms of individual behaviors and bad intentions rather than wide-scale structural oppression that often operates without some obvious individual actor aimed at denying an individual person an opportunity. The violence of imprisoning millions of poor people and people of color, for example, can't be adequately explained by finding one nasty racist individual, but instead requires looking at a whole web of institutions, policies, and practices that make it "normal" and "necessary" to warehouse, displace, discard, and annihilate poor people and people of color. Thinking about violence and oppression as the work of "a few bad apples" undermines our ability to analyze our conditions *systemically* and *intergenerationally*, and to therefore organize for systemic change.

This narrow way of thinking about oppression is repeated in law, policy, the media, and nonprofits.

> **EXAMPLE:** Megan's Laws are statutes that require people convicted of sexual offenses to register and that require this information be available to the public. These laws have been passed in jurisdictions around the country in the last two decades, prompted by and generating public outrage about child sexual abuse (CSA). Studies estimate that 1 in 3 people raised as girls and 1 in 6 people raised as boys were sexually abused as children, as a result of intergenerational trauma, community- and state-sanctioned abusive norms, and alienation. Rather than resourcing comprehensive programs to support the healing of survivors and transformation of people who have been sexually abusive, or interrupt the family and community norms that contribute to the widespread abuse of children, Megan's Laws have ensured that people convicted of a range of sexual offenses face violence, the inability to find work or a place to live, and severely reduced chances of recovery and healing. Despite the limited or nonexistent deterrent effect of such laws, they remain the dominant "official" approach to the systemic problems of CSA.[15]

> **EXAMPLE:** As we write this, the Matthew Shepard Local Law Enforcement Enhancement Act has recently passed in the US Senate, and if signed into law would give $10 million to state and local law enforcement agencies, expand federal law enforcement power focused on hate crimes, and add the death penalty as a possible punishment for those convicted. This bill is heralded as a victory for transgender people because it will make gender identity an included category in Federal Hate Crimes law. Like Megan's Law, this law and the advocacy surrounding it (including advocacy by large LGBT nonprofit organizations) focus attention on individuals who kill people because of their identities. These laws frame the problem of violence in our communities as one of individual "hateful" people, when in reality, trans people face short life-spans because of the enormous systemic violence in welfare systems, shelters, prisons, jails, foster care, juvenile punishment systems, and immigration, and the inability to access basic survival resources. These laws do nothing to prevent our deaths, they just use our deaths to expand a system that endangers our lives and places a chokehold on our communities.[16]

• **Undermining Transformative Organizing**

The second half of the twentieth century saw a major upsurge in radical and revolutionary organizing in oppressed communities in the United States and around the world. This powerful organizing posed a significant threat to the legitimacy of US power and capitalist empire more broadly, and therefore needed to be contained. These movements were undermined by two main strategies: First, the radical movements of the 1960s and '70s were criminalized, with the US government using tactics of imprisonment, torture, sabotage, and assassination to target and destroy groups like the Black Panthers, American Indian Movement, and Young Lords, among others. Second, the growth of the nonprofit sector has seen social movements professionalizing, chasing philanthropic dollars, separating into "issue areas," and moving toward social services and legal reform projects rather than radical projects aimed at the underlying causes of poverty and injustice.[17] These developments left significant sections of the radical left traumatized and decimated, wiping out a generation of revolutionaries and shifting the terms of resistance from revolution and transformation to inclusion and reform, prioritizing state- and foundation-sanctioned legal reforms and social services over mass organizing and direct action.

> **EXAMPLE:** The FBI's Counter-Intelligence Program (COINTEL-PRO) is a notorious example of the US government's use of infiltration, surveillance, and violence to overtly target dissent and resistance. COINTELPRO was exposed when internal government documents were revealed that detailed the outrageous work undertaken by the federal government to dismantle resistance groups in the 1960s and '70s. Although the program was dissolved under that name, the tactics continued and can be seen today in current controversies about wiretapping and torture as well as in the USA PATRIOT Act. Overt action to eliminate resistance and dissent here is as old as the European colonization of North America.[18]

> **EXAMPLE:** In the wake of decades of radical organizing by people in women's prisons and activists on the outside decrying systemic medical neglect, sexual violence, and the destruction of family bonds, California legislators in 2006 proposed a so-called "gender responsive corrections" bill that would allow people in women's prisons to live with their children and receive increased social services. To make this plan

work, the bill called for millions of dollars in new prison construction. The message of "improving the lives of women prisoners" and creating more "humane" prisons—rhetoric that is consistently used by those in power to distract us from the fundamentally violent conditions of a capitalist police state—appealed to liberal, well-intentioned feminist researchers, advocates, and legislators. Anti-prison organizations such as Oakland-based Justice Now and others working in solidarity with the resounding sentiment of people in women's prisons, pointed out that this strategy was actually just a back door to creating 4,500 new prison beds for women in California, yet again expanding opportunities to criminalize poor women and transgender people in one of the nation's most imprisoning states.[19]

• The Hero Mindset

The United States loves its heroes and its narratives—Horatio Alger, rags-to-riches, "pull yourself up by your bootstraps," streets "paved with gold," the rugged frontiersman, the benevolent philanthropist, and Obama as savior, among others. These narratives hide the uneven concentration of wealth, resources, and opportunity among different groups of people—the ways in which not *everybody* can just do anything if they put their minds to it and work hard enough. In the second half of the twentieth century, this individualistic and celebrity-obsessed culture had a deep impact on social movements and how we write narratives. Stories of mass struggle became stories of individuals overcoming great odds. The rise of the nonprofit as a key vehicle for social change bolstered this trend, giving incentives to charismatic leaders (often executive directors, often people with privilege) to frame struggles in ways that prioritize symbolic victories (big court cases, sensationalistic media coverage) and ignore the daily work of building a base and a movement for the long haul. This trend also compromises the accountability of leaders and organizations to their constituencies, and devalues activism in the trenches.

EXAMPLE: Rosa Parks is one of the most well-known symbols of resistance during the African American Civil Rights movement in the 1950s and 1960s. She is remembered primarily for "sparking" the Montgomery Bus Boycott and as the "mother of the civil rights movement."[20] In popular mythology, Ms. Parks was an ordinary woman who simply decided one day that she would not give up her seat to a white person in a "lonely act of defiance."[21] In reality, Ms. Parks was

an experienced civil rights activist who received political education
and civil disobedience training at the well-known leftist Highlander
Folk School, which still exists today. Ms. Parks's refusal to give up her
seat was far from a "lonely act," but was rather just one in a series of
civil disobediences by civil rights leaders to target segregation in public services. The Civil Rights Movement of the period was a product
of the labor and brilliance of countless New-World African enslaved
people, African American people, and their allies working since before the founding of the United States, not simply attributable to any
one person. The portrayal of mass struggles as individual acts hides a
deeper understanding of oppression and the need for broad resistance.

EXAMPLE: Oprah's well-publicized giveaways[22]—as well as a range
of television shows that feature "big wins" such as makeovers, new
houses, and new cars—have helped to create the image of social change
in our society as individual acts of "charity" rather than concerted efforts by mass groups of people to change relationships of power. These
portrayals affirm the false idea that we live in a meritocracy in which
any one individual's perseverance and hard work are the only keys
needed to wealth and success. Such portrayals hide realities like the
racial wealth divide and other conditions that produce and maintain
inequality on a group level, ensuring that most people will not rise
above or fall below their place in the economy, regardless of their individual actions. In reality, real social change that alters the relationships
of power throughout history have actually come about when large
groups of people have worked together toward a common goal.

Together, the tactics that we describe above function as a strategy
of *counter-revolution*—an attempt to squash the collective health and political will of oppressed people, and to buy off people with privilege in
order to support the status quo. This is a profoundly traumatic process
that deepened centuries of pain, loss, and harm experienced by people of
color, immigrants, queer and trans people, women, and others marked as
"disposable." For many of us, this included losing our lives and our loved
ones to the devastating government-sanctioned HIV/AIDS pandemic and
ongoing attacks from family, neighbors, and government officials.

Perhaps one of the most painful features of this period has been the
separating of oppressed communities and movements from one another.
Even though our communities are all overlapping and our struggles for

liberation are fundamentally linked, the "divide and conquer" strategy of the "New World Order" has taught us to think of our identities and struggles as separate and competing. In particular, it was useful to maintaining harmful systems and conditions to create a false divide between purportedly separate ("white") gay issues and ("straight") people of color, immigrant, and working-class issues to prevent deep partnerships across multiple lines of difference for social transformation. In this context, the most visible and well-funded arms of LGBT organizing got caught up in fighting for small-scale reforms and battles to be recognized as "equal" and "visible" under the law and in the media without building the sustained power and self-determination of oppressed communities. Instead of trying to change the system, the official LGBT agenda fought to just be welcomed into it, in exchange for helping to keep other oppressed people at the bottom.

But thankfully that's not the end of the story. As we describe below, this period also nurtured powerful strands of radical queer and trans politics organizing at the intersections of oppressions and struggles and in the legacy of the revolutionary freedom fighters of an earlier generation.

II. Reclaiming a Radical Legacy

Despite the powerful and destructive impacts that the renewed forces of neoliberal globalization and the "New World Order" have had on our communities and our social movements, there are and always have been radical politics and movements to challenge the exploitation that the United States is founded upon. These politics have been developed in communities of color and in poor and working-class, immigrant, queer, disability, and feminist communities in both "colonized" and "colonizing" nations, from the Black Panther Party in Oakland to the Zapatistas in Chiapas to the Audre Lorde Project in New York. As the story of Stonewall teaches us, our movements didn't start out in the courtroom; they started out in the streets! Informing both the strategies of our movements as well as our everyday decisions about how we live our lives and form our relationships, these radical politics offer queer communities and movements a way out of the murderous politics that are masked as invitations to "inclusion" and "equality" within fundamentally exclusive, unequal systems. Sometimes these spaces for transformation are easier to spot than others—but you can find them everywhere, from church halls to lecture halls, from the lessons of our grandmothers to the lessons we learn surviving in the world, from the post-revolutionary Cuba to post-Katrina New Orleans.

These radical lineages have nurtured and guided transformative branches of queer and trans organizing working at the intersections of identities and struggles for collective liberation. These branches have redefined what count as queer and trans issues, losses, victories, and strategies—putting struggles against policing, imprisonment, borders, globalization, violence, and economic exploitation at the center of struggles for gender and sexual self-determination. Exploding the false division between struggles for (implicitly white and middle-class) sexual and gender justice and (implicitly straight) racial and economic justice, there is a groundswell of radical queer and trans organizing that's changing all the rules—you just have to know where to find it. In the chart below, we draw out a few specific strands of these diverse radical lineages that have paved the way for this work. In the first column, we highlight a value that has emerged from these radical lineages. In the second column, we lift up specific organizations striving to embody these values today.[23]

Deepening the Path of Those Who Came Before

RADICAL LINEAGE	CONTEMPORARY DESCENDANT
Liberation is a collective process! The conventional nonprofit hierarchical structure is actually a very recent phenomenon, and one that is modeled off corporations. Radical organizations, particularly feminist and women of color-led organizations, have often prioritized working collectively—where group awareness, consensus, and wholeness is valued over majority rule and individual leadership. Collectivism at its best takes up the concerns of the few as the concerns of the whole. For example, when one member of a group or community cannot attend an event or meeting because the building is not wheelchair accessible, it becomes a moment for all to examine and challenge ableism in our culture—instead of just dismissing it as a "problem" that affects only people who use wheelchairs.	The **Sylvia Rivera Law Project** (SRLP), among many other organizations, has shown just how powerful working collectively can be—with their staff and volunteers, majority people of color, majority trans and gender-nonconforming governing collective, SRLP is showing the world that how we do our work is a vital part of the work, and that doing things collectively helps us to create the world we want to see as we're building it.

RADICAL LINEAGE	CONTEMPORARY DESCENDANT
"Trickle up" change! We know that when those in power say they will "come back" for those at the bottom of the social and economic hierarchy, it will never happen. Marginalization is increased when a part of a marginalized group makes it over the line into the mainstream, leaving others behind and reaffirming the status quo. We've all seen painful examples of this in LGBT politics time after time—from the abandonment of transgender folks in the Employment Non-Discrimination Act (ENDA) to the idea that gay marriage is the first step toward universal healthcare. Instead, we know that freedom and justice for the most oppressed people means freedom and justice for everyone, and that we have to start at the bottom. The changes required to improve the daily material and spiritual lives of low-income queer and transgender people of color would by default include large-scale transformation of our entire economic, education, healthcare, and legal systems. When you put those with the fewest resources and those facing multiple systems of oppression at the center of analysis and organizing, everybody benefits.	**Queers for Economic Justice** in New York City and the **Transgender, Gender Variant, and Intersex Justice Project** in San Francisco are two great examples of "trickle up" change—by focusing on queers on welfare, in the shelter system, and in prison systems, these groups demand social and economic justice for those with the fewest resources and the smallest investment in maintaining the system as it is.
Be careful of all those welcome mats! Learning from history and other social-justice movements is a key principle. Other movements and other moments have been drained of their original power and purpose and appropriated for purposes opposing their principles, either by governments working to dilute and derail transformation or by corporations looking to turn civil unrest into a fashion statement (or both). Looking back critically at where other movements have done right and gone	**Critical Resistance** is a great example of this commitment. In the group's focus on prison abolition (instead of reform), its members examine their strategies and potential proposals through the question "Will we regret this in ten years?" This question is about taking a long-term view and assessing a potential opportunity (such as any given proposal to "improve" or "reform" prisons or sentencing laws) against their commitment to abolishing—not expanding or even maintaining—the prison industrial

RADICAL LINEAGE	CONTEMPORARY DESCENDANT
wrong helps us stay creative and accountable to our communities and our politics.	complex. The message here is that even though it might feel nice to get an invitation to the party, we would be wise to ask about the occasion.
For us, by us! The leadership, wisdom, and labor of those most affected by an issue should be centralized from the start. This allows those with the most to gain from social justice to direct what that justice will look like and gives allies the chance to directly support their leadership.	**FIERCE!** in New York City is a great example of this principle: By building the power of queer and trans youth of color to run campaigns, organize one another, and challenge gentrification and police violence, FIERCE! has become a powerful force that young people of color see themselves in. At FIERCE!, it is the young people directly facing the intersections of ageism, racism, xenophobia, homophobia, and transphobia who identify what the problems, priorities, and strategies should be rather than people whose expertise on these issues derives from advanced degrees or other criteria. The role of people not directly affected by the issues is to support the youth in manifesting their visions, not to control the political possibilities that they are inventing.
Let's practice what we preach! Also known as "praxis," this ideal strives for the alignment of what we do, why we're doing it, and how we do it—not just in our formal work, but also in our daily lives. This goes beyond the campaign goals or strategies of our organizations, and includes how they are organized, how we treat one another, and how we treat ourselves. If we believe that people of color have the most to gain from the end of racism, then we should support and encourage people of color's leadership in fights to end white supremacy, and for a fair economy and an end to the wealth gap. People in our organizations should get paid equally regardless	An inspiring example of praxis can be found in the work of **Southerners on New Ground** (SONG), based in Atlanta, Ga. SONG strives to integrate healing, spirit, and creativity in their work organizing across race, class, gender, and sexuality to embody new (and old!) forms of community, reflective of our commitments to liberation. SONG and other groups show that oppression is traumatic, and trauma needs to be addressed, acknowledged, and held both by individuals and groups of people. If trauma is ignored or swept under the rug, it just comes back as resentment, chaos, and divisiveness. We are all whole, complex human beings that

RADICAL LINEAGE	CONTEMPORARY DESCENDANT
of advanced degrees, and our working conditions and benefits should be generous. If we support a world in which we have time and resources to take care of ourselves, as well as our friends, families, and neighbors, we might not want to work sixty hours a week.	have survived a great deal of violence to get where we are today. Our work must support our full humanity and reflect the world we want to live in.
Real safety means collective transformation! Oppressed communities have always had ways to deal with violence and harm without relying on police, prisons, immigration, or kicking someone out—knowing that relying on those forces would put them in greater danger. Oppressed people have often known that these forces were the main sources of violence that they faced—the central agent of rape, abuse, murder, and exploitation. The criminal punishment system has tried to convince us that we do not know how to solve our own problems and that locking people up and putting more cops on our streets are the only ways we can stay safe or heal from trauma. Unfortunately we often lack other options. Many organizations and groups of people have been working to interrupt the intergenerational practices of intimate violence, sexual violence, hate violence, and police violence without relying on the institutions that target, warehouse, kill, and shame us.	Groups like **Creative Interventions** and **generationFIVE** in Oakland, Calif., **Communities Against Rape and Abuse** in Seattle, Wash., and the Audre Lorde Project's **Safe OUTside the System** (SOS) Collective, have been creating exciting ways to support the healing and transformation of people who have survived and caused harm, as well as the conditions that pass violence down from one generation to another. Because violence touches every queer and trans person directly or indirectly, creating ways to respond to violence that are transformative and healing (instead of oppressive, shaming, or traumatizing) is a tremendous opportunity to reclaim our radical legacy. We can no longer allow for our deaths to be the justification for so many other people's deaths through policing, imprisonment, and detention. Locking people up, having more cops in the streets, or throwing more people out will never heal the wounds of abuse or trauma.

Resisting the Traps, Ending Trans Imprisonment

Even in the context of growing imprisonment rates and deteriorating safety nets, the past decade has brought with it an upsurge in organizing and activism to challenge the imprisonment and policing of transgender and gender-non-conforming communities.[32] Through high-profile lawsuits, human rights and media documentation, conferences and trainings, grassroots organizing, and coalitional efforts, more individuals and organizations are aware of the dynamics of trans imprisonment than ever. This work has both fallen prey to the tricky traps of the "New World Order" that we described above and also generated courageous new ways of doing the work of transformation and resistance that are in line with the radical values that we also trace. What was once either completely erased or significantly marginalized on the agendas of both the LGBT and anti-prison/prisoner rights movements is now gaining more and more visibility and activity. We think of this as a tremendous opportunity to choose which legacies and practices we want for this work moving forward. This is not about playing the blame game and pointing fingers at which work is radical and which is oppressive, but rather about building on all of our collective successes, losses, and contradictions to do work that will transform society (and all of us) as we know it.

Below are a few helpful lessons that have been guided by the values above and generated at the powerful intersections of prison abolition and gender justice:[33]

1. We refuse to create "deserving" vs. "undeserving" victims.[34]
Although we understand that transgender and gender-non-conforming people in prisons, jails, and detention centers experience egregious and often specific forms of violence—including sexual assault, rape, medical neglect and discrimination, and humiliation based on transphobic norms—we recognize that all people impacted by the prison industrial complex are facing severe violence. Instead of saying that transgender people are the "most" oppressed in prisons, we can talk about the different forms of violence that people impacted by the prison industrial complex face, and how those forms of violence help maintain the status quo common sense that the "real bad people"—the "rapists," "murderers," "child molesters," in some cases now the "bigots"—deserve to be locked up. Seeking to understand the specific arrangements that cause certain communities to face particular types of violence at the hands of police and in detention can allow us to develop solidarity around shared *and* different experiences with these forces and build effective resistance that gets to the roots of these problems. Building arguments about trans people as "innocent victims" while other prisoners are cast as dangerous and deserving of detention only undermines the power of a shared resistance strategy that sees imprisonment as a violent, dangerous tactic for everybody it touches.

We know that the push for hate crimes laws as the solution to anti-queer and -trans violence will never actually address the fundamental reasons why we are vulnerable to violence in the first place or why homophobia and transphobia are encouraged in our cultures. Individualizing solutions like hate crimes laws create a false binary of "perpetrator" and "victim" or "bad" and "good" people without addressing the underlying systemic problem, and often strengthen that problem. In place of this common sense, we understand that racism, state violence, and capitalism are the root causes of violence in our culture, not individual "bigots" or even prison guards. *We must end the cycle of oppressed people being pitted against one another.*

2. We support strategies that weaken oppressive institutions, not strengthen them.

We can respond to the crises that our communities are facing right now while refusing long-term compromises that will strengthen the very institutions that are hurting us. As more and more awareness is being raised about the terrible violence that transgender and gender-non-conforming people face in prisons, jails, and detention centers, some prisoner rights and queer and trans researchers and advocates are suggesting that building trans-specific prisons or jails is the only way that imprisoned transgender and gender-non-conforming people will be safe in the short-term. Particularly in light of the dangerous popularity of "gender responsiveness" among legislators and advocates alike, we reject all notions that we must expand the prison industrial complex to respond to immediate conditions of violence. Funneling more money into prison building of any kind strengthens the prison industrial complex's death hold on our communities. We know that if they build it, they will fill it, and getting trans people out of prison is the only real way to address the safety issues that trans prisoners face. *We want strategies that will reduce and ultimately eliminate the number of people and dollars going into prisons, while attending to the immediate healing and redress of individual imprisoned people.*

3. We must transform exploitative dynamics in our work.

A lot of oppressed people are hyper-sexualized in dominant culture as a way to create them as a threat, a fetish, or a caricature—transgender women, black men, Asian and Pacific Islander women, to name a few. Despite often good intentions to raise awareness about the treatment of transgender and gender-non-conforming people in prisons, we recognize

that much of the "public education" work around these issues often relies on sexualization, voyeurism, sensationalism, and fetishization to get
its point across. In general there is a focus on graphic descriptions of
people's bodies (specifically their genitals), sexual violence, and the humiliation they have faced. Imprisoned people (who are usually represented as black) and transgender people (who are usually represented
as transgender women of color in this context) have long been the target of voyeuristic representation—from porn movies that glorify rape
in prison to fetishizing "human rights" research distributed to majority white, middle-class audiences. As transgender people who often have
our bodies on display for non-transgender people who feel empowered
to question, display, and discuss us, we know that this is a dangerous
trend that seriously undercuts the integrity of our work and the types
of relationships that can be formed. Unless we address these exploitative
power dynamics in our work, even our most "well-intentioned" strategies
and movements will reproduce the prison industrial complex's norms of
transphobic, misogynist, and racist sexualized violence. *Research, media,
cultural work, and activism on this issue needs to be accountable to and directed by low-income transgender people and transgender people of color and
our organizations.*

4. We see ending trans imprisonment as part of the larger struggle for transformation.

The violence that transgender people—significantly low-income transgender people of color—face in prisons, jails, and detention centers and
the cycles of poverty and criminalization that leads so many of us to imprisonment is a key place to work for broad-based social and political
transformation. There is no way that transgender people can ever be "safe"
in prisons as long as prisons exist and, as scholar Fred Moten has written, as long as we live in a society that could even *have* prisons. Building
a trans and queer abolitionist movement means building power among
people facing multiple systems of oppression in order to imagine a world
beyond mass devastation, violence, and inequity that occurs within and
between communities. We must resist the trap of being compartmental-
ized into "issues" and "priorities" and sacrificing a broader political vision
and movement to react to the crisis of the here and now. This is the logic
that allows many white and middle-class gay and lesbian folks to think
that marriage is *the* most important and pressing LGBT issue, without
being invested in the real goal of ending racism and capitalism. *Struggling*

against trans imprisonment is one of many key places to radicalize queer and trans politics, expand anti-prison politics, and join in a larger movement for racial, economic, gender, and social justice to end all forms of militarization, criminalization, and warfare.

III. So You Think We're Impossible?

This stuff is heavy, we realize. Our communities and our movements are up against tremendous odds and have inherited a great deal of trauma that we are still struggling to deal with. A common and reasonable response to these conditions is getting overwhelmed, feeling defeated, losing hope. In this kind of emotional and political climate, when activists call for deep change like prison abolition (or, gasp, an LGBT agenda *centered around* prison abolition), our demands get called "impossible" or "idealistic" or even "divisive." As trans people, we've been hearing this for ages. After all, according to our legal system, the media, science, and many of our families and religions, we shouldn't exist! Our ways of living and expressing ourselves break such fundamental rules that systems crash at our feet, close their doors to us, and attempt to wipe us out. And yet we exist, continuing to build and sustain new ways of looking at gender, bodies, family, desire, resistance, and happiness that nourish us and challenge expectations.

In an age when thousands of people are murdered annually in the name of "democracy," millions of people are locked up to "protect public safety," and LGBT organizations march hand in hand with cops in Pride parades, being impossible may just be the best thing we've got going for ourselves: *Impossibility may very well be our only possibility.*

What would it mean to *embrace*, rather than *shy away from*, the impossibility of our ways of living as well as our political visions? What would it mean to desire a future that we can't even imagine but that we are told couldn't ever exist? We see the abolition of policing, prisons, jails, and detention not strictly as a narrow answer to "imprisonment" and the abuses that occur within prisons, but also as a challenge to the rule of poverty, violence, racism, alienation, and disconnection that we face every day. Abolition is not just about closing the doors to violent institutions, but also about building up and recovering institutions and practices and relationships that nurture wholeness, self-determination, and transformation. Abolition is not some distant future but something we create in every moment when we say no to the traps of empire and yes to the nourishing possibilities dreamed of and practiced by our ancestors and friends. Every time we insist on accessible and affirming healthcare, safe and quality education, meaningful and secure employment, loving and healing relationships, and being our full and whole selves, we are doing abolition. Abolition is about breaking down things that oppress and building up things that nourish. Abolition is the practice of transformation in the here and now and the ever after.

Maybe wrestling with such a significant demand is the wake-up call that an increasingly sleepy LGBT movement needs. The true potential of queer and trans politics cannot be found in attempting to reinforce our tenuous right to exist by undermining someone else's. If it is not clear already, we are all in this together. To claim our legacy of beautiful impossibility is to begin practicing ways of being with one another and making movement that sustain all life on this planet, without exception. It is to begin speaking what we have not yet had the words to wish for.

NOTES

1. We would like to thank the friends, comrades, and organizations whose work, love, and thinking have paved the path to this paper and our collective movements for liberation, including: Anna Agathangelou, Audre Lorde Project, Community United Against Violence (CUAV), Communities Against Rape and Abuse (CARA), Critical Resistance, Eric Stanley, FIERCE!, INCITE! Women of Color Against Violence, Justice Now, Lala Yantes, Mari Spira, Miss Major, Mordecai Cohen Ettinger, Nat Smith, Southerners on New Ground (SONG), Sylvia Rivera Law Project (SRLP), Transforming Justice Coalition, Transgender, Gender Variant, Intersex Justice Project (TGIJP), and Vanessa Huang.

2. In the wake of the 2011 repeal of Don't Ask Don't Tell, queer and trans people who oppose the horrible violence committed by the US military all over the world have been disappointed not only by pro-military rhetoric of the campaign to allow gays and lesbians to serve, but also by the new debates that have emerged since then about ROTC on college campuses. Many universities that have excluded the military from campuses are now considering bringing it back to campus, and some activists are arguing that the military should be kept off campus because trans people are still excluded from service. The terms of this debate painfully embraces US militarism, and forgets that long-term campaigns to exclude the US military from college campuses and to disrupt military recruitment campaigns and strategies are based in not only the horrible violence of the military toward service members but also the motivating colonial and imperial purposes of US militarism.

3. This has been painfully illustrated by a range of LGBT foundation and individual funders who, in the months leading up to the struggle over California's

same-sex marriage ban, Proposition 8, declared that marriage equality needed to be the central funding priority and discontinued vital funding for anti-violence, HIV/AIDS, and arts organizations, among others.

4. This is a reference to the "trickle-down" economic policies associated with the Reagan Administration, which promoted tax cuts for the rich under the guise of creating jobs for middle-class and working-class people. The left has rightfully argued that justice, wealth, and safety do not "trickle down," but need to be redistributed first to the people at the bottom of the economic and political ladder. Trickle down policies primarily operate as another opportunity to distribute wealth and security upward.

5. By this we mean the advocacy work and agenda-setting done by wealthy (budgets over $1 million) LGBT-rights organizations such as the Human Rights Campaign and the National Lesbian and Gay Task Force.

6. See the Sylvia Rivera Law Project's *It's War in Here: A Report on the Treatment of Transgender and Gender Non-Conforming People in New York State Prisons* (available online at www.srlp.org) and *Gendered Punishment: Strategies to Protect Transgender, Gender Variant and Intersex People in America's Prisons* (available from TGI Justice Project, info@tgijp.org) for a deeper examination of the cycles of poverty, criminalization, imprisonment, and law-enforcement violence in transgender and gender-non-conforming communities.

7. This was a period of heightened activity by radical and revolutionary national and international movements resisting white supremacy, patriarchy, colonization, and capitalism—embodied by organizations such as the American Indian Movement, the Black Liberation Army, the Young Lords, the Black Panther Party for Self-Defense, the Brown Berets, Earth First!, the Gay Liberation Front, and the Weather Underground in the United States, and anti-colonial organizations in Guinea-Bissau, Jamaica, Vietnam, Puerto Rico, Zimbabwe, and elsewhere. Mass movements throughout the world succeeded in winning major victories against imperialism and white supremacy, and exposing the genocide that lay barely underneath American narratives of democracy, exceptionalism, and liberty.

8. See Ruth Wilson Gilmore, "Globalisation and US Prison Growth: From Military Keynesianism to Post-Keynesian Militarism," *Race and Class,* Vol. 40, No. 2–3, 1998/99.

9. For a compelling analysis of neoliberalism and its impacts on social movements, see Lisa Duggan's *The Twilight of Equality: Neoliberalism, Cultural Politics, and the Attack on Democracy,* published by Beacon Press in 2004.

10. Public Citizen, NAFTA and Workers' Rights and Jobs, 2008, at http://www.citizen.org/trade/nafta/jobs.

11. Human Rights Watch, "NAFTA Labor Accord Ineffective," April 15, 2001, at http://hrw.org/english/docs/2001/04/16/global179.htm. Corporations specifically named in complaints by workers include General Electric, Honeywell, Sony, General Motors, McDonald's, Sprint, and the Washington State apple industry.

12. Sapphire, "A Homeless Man's Alternative to 'Care Not Cash,'" *Poor Magazine*, July 1, 2003, at http://www.poormagazine.org/index.cfm?L1=news&category=50&stor=1241.

13. The Sentencing Project, "Life Sentences: Denying Welfare Benefit to Women Convicted of Drug Offenses," at http://www.sentencingprogrject.org/Admin/Documents/publications/women_smy_lifesentences.pdf.

14. Alan David Freeman, "Legitimizing Racial Discrimination Through Antidiscrimination Law: A Critical Review of Supreme Court Doctrine," 62 MINN. L. REV. 1049, 1052 (1978).

15. Visit generationFIVE at http://www.generationfive.org and Stop It Now! at http://www.stopitnow.org online for more research documenting and tools for ending child sexual abuse.

16. For a critique of hate crimes legislation, see Carolina Cordero Dyer, "The Passage of Hate Crimes Legislation–No Cause to Celebrate," INCITE! Women of Color Against Violence, March 2001 at http://www.incite-national.org/news/_march01/editorial.html. Also see INCITE!-Denver and Denver on Fire's response to the verdict in the 2009 Angie Zapata case at http://www.leftturn.org/?q=node/1310.

17. For an in-depth analysis of the growth and impacts of "nonprofit industrial complex," see INCITE! Women of Color Against Violence's groundbreaking anthology *The Revolution Will Not Be Funded: Beyond the Non-Profit Industrial Complex,* published by South End Press in 2007.

18. For a deeper examination of the FBI's attack on radical movements, see Ward Churchill and Jim Vander Wall's *The COINTELPRO Papers: Documents from the FBI's Secret War Against Domestic Dissent,* published by South End Press in 1990. Also see the Freedom Archive's 2006 documentary *Legacy of Torture: The War Against the Black Liberation Movement* about the important case of the San Francisco 8. Information available online at http://www.freedomarchives.org/BPP/torture.html.

19. See Justice Now co-founder Cassandra Shaylor's essay "Neither Kind Nor Gentle: The Perils of 'Gender Responsive Justice'" in *The Violence of Incarceration,* edited by Phil Scraton and Jude McCulloch, published by Routledge in 2008.

20. Academy of Achievement: A Museum of Living History, "Rosa Parks," October, 25, 2005 at http://www.achievement.org/autodoc/page/par0pro-1.

21. Academy of Achievement: A Museum of Living History, "Rosa Parks," October, 31, 2005 at http://www.achievement.org/autodoc/page/par0bio-1.

22. CNNMoney.com, "Oprah Car Winners Hit with Hefty Tax," September, 22, 2004 at http://money.cnn.com/2004/09/22/news/newsmakers/oprah_car_tax/index.htm.

23. We recognize that we mention only relatively well-funded organizations and mostly organizations in the San Francisco Bay Area and New York City, two strongholds of radical organizing and also places where a significant amount of resources are concentrated. There are hundreds of other organizations around the country and the world that we do not mention and do not know about. *What organizations or spaces do you see embodying radical values?*

24. The Sylvia Rivera Law Project at http://www.srlp.org.

25. Queers for Economic Justice at http://www.q4ej.org.

26. Transgender, Gender Variant, and Intersex Justice Project at http://www.tgijp.org.

27. Critical Resistance at http://www.criticalresistance.org.

28. FIERCE! at http://www.fiercenyc.org.

29. Southerners on New Ground at http://www.southernersonnewground.org .

30. See Creative Interventions at http://www.creative-interventions.org, generationFIVE at http://www.generationfive.org, Communities Against Rape and Abuse at http://www.cara-seattle.org, and Audre Lorde Project's Safe OUTside the System Collective at http://www.alp.org.

31. For examples of LGBTQ-specific organizations creating community-based responses to violence, see the Audre Lorde Project's Safe Outside the System Collective in Brooklyn (www.alp.org), the Northwest Network of BTLG Survivors of Abuse in Seattle, and Community United Against Violence (CUAV) in San Francisco (www.cuav.org).

32. Particularly significant was the Transforming Justice gathering in San Francisco in October 2007, which brought together over two hundred LGBTQ and allied formerly imprisoned people, activists, and attorneys to develop a shared analysis about the cycles of trans poverty, criminalization, and imprisonment and a shared strategy moving forward. Transforming Justice, which has now transitioned to a national coalition, was a culmination of tireless and often invisible work on the part of imprisoned and formerly imprisoned people and their allies over the past many years. For more, see www.transformingjustice.org.

33. See the Transforming Justice Coalition's statement "How We Do Our Work" for a more detailed account of day-to-day organizing ethics, which can be requested from the TGI Justice Project at http://www.tgijp.org.

34. Both of the lessons here were significantly and powerfully articulated and popularized by Critical Resistance and Justice Now, both primarily based in Oakland, CA.

"STREET POWER" AND THE CLAIMING OF PUBLIC SPACE:

San Francisco's "Vanguard" and Pre-Stonewall Queer Radicalism

Jennifer Worley

Between 1965 and 1970, in San Francisco's Tenderloin district, a group of gay male and transgender female youth[1]—most of them sex workers living and working on the streets of this inner-city red-light district—formed a social and political organization called Vanguard. This group has been virtually forgotten by history,[2] but the records that remain reveal an extremely active and organized group whose position as street-based sex workers produced a profound and deeply radical movement in resistance not only to the unequal treatment of sexual minorities before the law, but also to economic forces and state-sponsored violence that served to marginalize and oppress gay and transgender youth. Vanguard's foregrounding of the issues facing gay and transgender youth in the 1960s produced radical insights into the connections between economic class, police violence, incarceration, and homophobia.

Vanguard was first organized in 1965 under the auspices of Glide Memorial Church, a radical congregation of the United Methodist Church. Glide was experimenting with methods of ministering to and addressing the needs of an urban congregation, and it had identified homosexuals as a group that was suffering enormous oppression, particularly in the Tenderloin, the city's primary gay/trans neighborhood, where Glide was located.[3] As a result, by the mid-1960s, the church was working closely with local homophile organizations such as Daughters of Billitis and the Mattachine Society, and had helped establish a ministers' group called the Council for Religion and the Homosexual.

At the same time, the Church was working to convince the federal Office of Economic Opportunity to designate the Tenderloin as a recognized poverty area so that the neighborhood and the programs that Glide was creating would qualify for federal funds from the Johnson administration's War On Poverty programs.[4] This strategic decision to tap into federal anti-poverty programs, paired with the Church's simultaneous work with the homophile movement had a profound result: It led Glide to create a space in the homophile movement for the voices of an extremely marginalized population—young, gay, and transsexual sex workers living and working on the streets. One of these voices was that of Joel Roberts, an early organizer of Vanguard, who, in an oral history given in 1989, explains the connections he saw between sex work, youth, queerness, and radicalism:

> Many years ago, when I first came to San Francisco, part of my life was hustling and being a prostitute. It was a quick way to make money, and I didn't have a lot of credentials and ways of making money. And I was organizing before there was anything called "gay lib" in the streets of San Francisco, in the Tenderloin on Market Street. We'd hang out and I was organizing something that later became called Vanguard. So somehow, having some education and yet being a hustler, the mix was pretty volatile for me.... I remember storming into Glide Methodist Church one day.... I was yelling and screaming. I was really angry. I was being confronted more than ever before with the oppression of being an American. Not just being gay, but being poor. Being on the street and being a kid. All those things, all three things.... Glide Methodist Church...had hired a Texas black pastor named Cecil Williams...and I stormed in and said there's kids on the fucking street selling their ass. There's kids sleeping eight in a hotel

room at night and you people talk about social change…. I was really angry that gay kids were being left out of social change…. And Cecil Williams came out saying, "Young man, anybody that can swear like you I want to talk to."[5]

. Shortly after this incident, in 1965, the church recruited a young divinity student named Ed Hansen from Claremont School of Theology for a yearlong internship doing street outreach for the church. During his intern year, Hansen worked in the red-light district of the Tenderloin, which was home to many gay and transsexual hustlers. The youth he encountered struggled with drug addiction, poverty, mental illness, street violence, and malnutrition, and Hansen came to believe that the best way to help these youth was simply to interact caringly with them to give them an alternate model of adulthood since their other encounters with adults were limited to parental rejection, sex work, arrest, or police harassment. In 1965, Hansen began inviting the young hustlers and drag queens that he met on the streets to open houses at Glide.[6] The youths gradually formed a steady group and began holding regular meetings at the church. Over the course of about five years, the group held dances, drag balls, and coffeehouses; they published a newsletter, produced or attempted to produce one or more films, and organized direct-action protests. In the early 1970s, Vanguard and a group of young lesbians called the Street Orphans merged to form the San Francisco Gay Liberation Front, which was active throughout the '70s.[7]

While Vanguard, with its ties to Glide and the interfaith Council for Religion and the Homosexual, was the first organized (and eventually incorporated) gay and transgender youth group in the city, the ministers who began organizing queer youth in this period were not starting from scratch; they were building upon the efforts of adult gay men, particularly owners of gay bars and restaurants, who had already begun to address the needs of gay and transgender youth less formally. Chuck Lewis, the street outreach assistant to Rev. Don Stuart of the San Francisco Night Ministry during this time, recalls his boss encountering one such institution created to support gay and transgender youth:

[I]n 1964…Don Stuart…went to a [gay] bar called the Gilded Cage, just to drop in and see what was happening. He went, sat down at the bar, and the bartender said, "Who are you?" and Don said, "Oh, I'm Don Stuart. I'm the night minister here in SF. We're a crisis counseling agency just getting started."…. And so he said, "All right, what do you want to drink?"…. So the next night Don went back in again and the same bartender who happened to be the owner came up to him and said, "I called the council of churches today, and they said you're OK, so tonight the drink's on me. What'll you have?"…. He said, "By the way, I want you to know, Father, we have a room in the back we call Pearl's and that's the place where we have after hours starting around midnight that any young kids off the street can go. There's no alcohol served. It's just a gathering place where they can have soft drinks or whatever they want and get together." Don said, "Well, sounds like a good place for me to drop into." So later on that night, after midnight, he dropped in and surprisingly at least six kids immediately lined up to talk to him.[8]

So even before the organized efforts of ministers, the gay men's bar community was recognizing the needs of young hustlers and providing a safe space between the wholly public world of the street and the wholly private world of the heterosexual home—a kind of inverted mirror of the bourgeois heterosexual home from which they had fled or been expelled, a queer home that provided safety without closeting.[9]

Such informal practices for taking care of homeless queer youth illustrate that spaces for queer and trans youth in the Tenderloin pre-existed Vanguard; however, Vanguard was unique in that its mission included not just support and services but also political action through community organizing. Indeed, Ed Hansen recalls that Mark Forrester, an adult homophile activist with whom he worked closely to form Vanguard, explicitly intended to use the principles of community organizing established in Saul Alinsky's *Reveille for Radicals* as a model for Vanguard's practices.[10] Alinsky's influence is visible in the group's writings and radical activism against police harassment brutality as well other forms of institutionalized forms of homophobia and transphobia.

One of the key problems that Vanguard members faced was police periodically harassing, arresting, and brutalizing drag queens, gays, and sex workers simply for being on the public street. Police harassment of gays and trans people was so persistent in the Tenderloin that the sign for one gay bar read, "The Chuckers, Famous for Its Unusual Entertainment, Now Presents POLICE HARASSMENT! Every Fri. & Sat. from 8PM to 6AM"[11] Ed Hansen, Vanguard's liaison to Glide Memorial, recalls that this harassment extended even to the supposedly private spaces known to be frequented by queer youth, recalling his own first encounter with what he discovered to be the routine police harassment of gay and trans youth:

> [In] October of 1965, when I went for the first time wearing my clerical collar to this hotel—I think it may have been the Bachelor Hotel… on the south side, [on] about Fifth or Sixth…and I had been asked to come to a dance and engage in conversation with some of the young guys who were living there who had never encountered a minister like me—so gay-friendly. And while I was there the police showed up, just kind of looking into the situation, and then left. Then they came back a few hours later and I was still there. This time they got together about five or six guys, lined them up and interrogated them and checked their IDs, and I asked the police what was wrong, what was going on. And they couldn't give any good answer…it seemed to me to be police harassment. They wound up taking in one of the guys because he had some outstanding traffic tickets or something. But why did the police come to a hotel in the middle of the night with such scrutiny? That was just not as it should be.[12]

The threat of incarceration and police harassment was exacerbated by the economic marginalization that left gay and transgender street youth with few options for survival but street prostitution. References to the necessity of prostitution appear even on the poetry page of Vanguard's eponymous magazine, punctuating the lyric poems about unrequited love and other themes typical of teenage poetry. On its "Night Songs" page, the magazine's first issue contains a poem called "The Hustler," in which a young gay hustler touchingly explores the tension between his desire for love from other men, and the economic necessity that he commodify that desire in acts of prostitution:

> I'll go to bed for twenty,
> All night for just ten more.
> Now don't get the idea
> That I am just a whore.
> For if I didn't sell my love,
> Where else would it go?
> I have no one to give it to;
> No one who'd care to know.[13]

"The Hustler" marks with melancholy a particular intersection of homophobia and economic marginalization often articulated by Vanguard youth in their more overtly political writing on sex work, which often denounced the businessmen who refused to hire drag queens and effeminate boys in their offices and stores during the day but who benefited from the presence of cheap, easily available hustlers on the streets at night, and who would then turn around once again in the morning to complain about the "filth" on the streets where they were trying to operate legitimate businesses. We see this argument made quite forcefully in a Vanguard flyer:

> We protest being called "queer," "pillhead," and being placed in the position of being outlaws and parasites when we are offered no alternative to this existence.... We demand justice and immediate corrections of the fact that most of the money made in the area is made by the exploitation of youth by so-called normal adults who make a fast buck off situations everyone calls degenerate, perverted and sick.[14]

Here we see that Vanguard, unlike the homophile movement from which it sprung, framed their position as sexual outsiders in terms of class struggle and economic justice. The group's centralization of the sex worker as the typical Vanguard youth produced a strong sense of identity among group members not only as homosexual and transsexual, but also as economically marginalized by their sexuality. This outlook helped to produce a radical class analysis of public space, of sex work, and of queerness itself that is reflected in Vanguard's demonstrations and publications.

Transgender street sex-workers were particularly vulnerable to encounters with the police while they worked because drag itself was treated as a criminal offense. This is made clear in another poem from Vanguard's "Night Songs" section, "The Fairytale Ballad of Katy the Queen" by Miss Shari Kenyon:

> She's a Queen, oh Mary
> and you know it.
> She's a Queen, my luv
> and she shows it.
> She thinks she looks and acts so fair
> But she's only a fake
> and we know it!

She can swing her hips
like a lady
and her violet eyes are
the right shady.
Her blouse and her pants
are so tight,
And she breaks her wrist
just right
BUT, her real name's
Calvin, not Katy.

So here's what happened
to Katy the Queen
She came on too loud on
the Market St. scene;
She blew her mind, and
the Vice's too
'Cause Katy in drag is not
too cool
Now she keeps the Fuzz happy
And the Gay Tank clean.

This brief poem begins as a tribute to and catty critique of a neighborhood queen, concluding on a warning note in which the threat of
incarceration functions as a cautionary tale of sorts for other transgender
street youth: as punishment for her excessive presentation (for "[coming]
on too loud"), Katy is jailed in the "gay tank," slang for the separate area
of the San Francisco County Jail used to house gay men and transsexuals
(now called the "vulnerable male" section). Even more disturbing is the
passage "she keeps the Fuzz happy, and the gay tank clean," implying that
incarcerated transgender women were subject to slavery, including sexual
slavery, at police hands. The poem's flip tone and its nursery-rhyme meter
reveal a matter-of-factness on the part of the author, presumably herself
transgendered, about the violence to which young transwomen were subjected, including sexual servitude to police while incarcerated.

This frankness about police brutality against transsexual women is
echoed in the testimony of Joel Roberts, who worked as a street hustler
in the 1960s. Roberts reports, "My very first recollection coming to San
Francisco was seeing a young drag queen get his ribs broken by a cop and

the cop leaves him there, and I said how come he didn't arrest you and he said, don't worry about me honey, this happens all the time."[15]

The first organized political action by Vanguard was not, initially, a response to police brutality, but instead a response to discrimination by businesses against transsexuals and sex workers—but the results revealed to Vanguard members the symbiotic relationship between discrimination and police violence. In the mid-1960s, Compton's Cafeteria was an all-night diner popular with the Tenderloin's young transsexual and male prostitutes because the night manager was an older gay man who sympathized with queer street youth and allowed them to hang out at the café.[16] When this night manager died, though, the diner hired a replacement who promptly began using private security guards to harass and remove the young drag queens and hustlers if they stayed too long or spent too little money. The youths were upset by this sudden hostile treatment in one of the few public spaces where they had been welcome, and began to discuss the issue at Vanguard meetings. The group decided to take action and organized a two-hour picket of Compton's on July 18, 1966. In a letter home, Vanguard advisor Ed Hansen describes this initial protest:

> Last Monday night and also Wed. night the Tenderloin (TL) kids of the organization called Vanguard picketed Compton's restraunt [sic] on the corner of Taylor and Turk in the middle of the TL. We had between 30 and 50 pickets there each night from 10PM to midnight. We also got radio and TV coverage of our picket. Anytime you get young people—some of whom are pill-heads, prostitutes, or homosexuals picketing somewhere you are bound to get news coverage. The kids where [sic] protesting the unkind treatment they received from the management of Compton's and also the harassment given them by the Pinkerton guard that Compton's has working there.[17]

There was no immediate result, but the picket seems to have consolidated the youths' sense of collective injury. As illustrated in detail by Victor Silverman and Susan Stryker in their documentary film about the event, a month after this initial protest, when the management called the police to remove some transsexual youth, one cop made the mistake of manhandling an already angry queen. She threw her coffee in his face and a riot broke out. The other queens came to their friend's defense, hitting cops in the face with heavy handbags (which were often deliberately weighted so they could be used as emergency weapons if a trick became violent during a date). The drag queens trashed the restaurant, smashed its plate glass windows and the windows of a police car outside, and set the corner newsstand on fire.[18] Many Vanguard members were involved in the riot, and they organized a second protest the following night when Compton's banned drag queens entirely. The second picket was attended by a wider range of community members and it, too, ended in the restaurant's windows being smashed.[19] The Compton's riot marked the first violent, collective protest against harassment in the transgender/queer community.[20]

In addition to violence by the police in the service of businesses that discriminated against transgender women, Vanguard member Joel Roberts recalls the routine San Francisco Police Department practice of "sweeping" the streets of gay neighborhoods for homosexuals: "Every year or two or so, San Francisco would go around and crack down on homosexuals. And they sent out the paddy wagon, and anybody that looked [like] homosexuals or hang [sic] out in front of places where homosexuals hang out were just arrested. I mean, you talk about police state, it was one of them."[21] In the early autumn of 1966, Vanguard responded to these practices by holding a "street sweep" of their own. Borrowing push brooms from the city and carrying hand-lettered signs, about fifty Vanguard members swept the sidewalks of the Tenderloin. Photographs show boys with short hair and peg-leg jeans and a handful of presumably transgender girls in bouffants, skirts, and cigarette pants pushing brooms and posing with signs reading "Fall Clean Up: This Is a Vanguard Community Project" (see Figures 1 and 2). While it seems like a simple enough protest, this "street sweep" was actually a surprisingly sophisticated semiotic act. First, rather than simply picketing, as they had done initially at Compton's, or rioting, as they had done later, Vanguard used performance to literalize the metaphor of the "street sweep," a term normally used for a police action directed at the very subjects performing the protest: queers and sex workers. Doing so, Vanguard took up the symbolic terms of urban renewal projects in which queer and transgender sex workers figured as nothing more than "trash" to be "swept away," manipulating these symbolic terms in order to perform their resistance to this vision. In photographs of the event, the teens pose with brooms in front of them, carrying signs reading "All trash is before the broom," a slogan explained by Vanguard leader J. P. Marat's statement to the press: "We're considered trash by much of society, and we wanted to show the rest of society that we want to work and can work."[22] By performing the act of sweeping the streets, the youths resisted their designation as "trash" subject to "clean-up" by police sweeps, and undermined the utopian vision of urban renewal projects that used the verb "clean" as a euphemism for the harassment, brutalization, and arrests of sex workers, transgenders, and queers. By performing this strangely domestic activity in the public space of the street, Vanguard reconfigured the street itself as a domestic space. This domestication of the street created a visual representation of Vanguard's social status as figurative outsiders (that is, those who are denied full citizenship) and literal outsiders (those who live outdoors and make streets their home). At the same time, with the act of sweeping, the group performed its stewardship of that home, implicating the rest of the culture as those who "trash" it. This point is highlighted again by the group's press release for the event, which inverts the usual terms of social outrage at urban squalor, angrily declaring, "The drug addicts, pillheads, teenage hustlers, lesbians and homosexuals who make San Francisco's 'MEAT RACK' their home are tired of living in the midst of the filth thrown out on to the sidewalks and into the streets by nearby businessmen."[23] Vanguard's performance, then, contested middle class efforts to "clean up the city" by representing themselves as *agents* of change rather than as targets of the middle-class's programs of change.

This protest illustrates how Vanguard's foregrounding of the queer youth or adolescent challenged some of the terms on which the previous homophile movement had been built. Take, for example, the very cliché often used to appeal to American "live and let live" ideals: that the law should not interfere with what "two consenting adults do in the privacy of their own home." Vanguard's street-sweep illustrates the woeful inadequacy of this cliché as an appeal for the rights of queer and trans youth who might be consenting but are not adults, who in many cases had been expelled from the protections of "the home" and its aegis of privacy, and who, as street-based sex workers, depended for their very survival upon queer modes of accessing public—not private—spaces for specifically sexual purposes.

The street sweepers were photographed and interviewed all the while by print and broadcast journalists. Stories went out on the Associated Press and UPI wire services and on local radio. Vanguard youth were savvy about the role that media could play in promoting their causes, as Roberts recalls:

The police would see you organizing.... Of course we had Channel 7 down there and instead of being the quiet oppressed minority of mentally ill criminals. I mean the liberals thought we were mentally ill and the conservatives thought we were criminals. So we got busted either way. We started getting on television—I very much understood very early in the game the power of media. So we called up the radio and TV stations and say, "Hey, gay kids on Market Street are having a demonstration; you'd better get down there." That was unheard of…. And before you know it…we started getting people from all over the country coming in to photograph us and stuff.[24]

In addition to public protests, Vanguard also addressed the issue of police brutality via a campaign of information in its magazine. Nearly every issue contains an informational advertisement about what to do if questioned, arrested, harassed, or beaten by the police: "Never resist or talk back[.] Get that badge number!!! Give your name and address only[.] If arrested demand a phone call until granted[;] phone for assistance as soon as permitted[.] 776-9669." Many issues contain editorials criticizing the vice squad who patrolled the Tenderloin streets for young gay and transgender hustlers.[25]

In addition to disseminating basic legal information to assist gay and transgender street youth and drawing public attention to the mistreatment of queer youth, Vanguard's unprecedented activities allowed a group that previously had little or no sense of cohesion and collective identity to begin thinking of themselves as a group with a collective identity. While adults had the gay bar, gay and transgender youth had little access to institutions or physical spaces where they could gather, and thus did not think of themselves as a distinct community. Vanguard provided a physical "home" by hosting meetings, coffeehouses, dances, and dinners. Similarly, the group's "more or less" monthly magazine functioned as a sort of literary "home" that circulated, like its readers and writers, on the streets of the Tenderloin. Published between August 1966 and January 1970, *Vanguard* was produced by and for queer street youth and featured hand-drawn covers, poetry, art, articles on politics, an advice column by "Horace Horny," queer-themed cartoons, community news, letters to the editor with bitchy replies, announcements about where to get services like medical care or food, short stories (some of them pornographic), articles reprinted (or literally cut and pasted) from other publications, a "president's page" with a message from the group's leader, and interviews with local activists and others from the street community. Advertisers included gay bars, nonprofit groups such as the Mattachine Society and the Society for Individual Rights, grocery stores, pornographers seeking models and photos, print shops and other local left-leaning newspapers. The magazine claimed a subscription list of 1,000,[26] the publication's staff increased from two in the first issues to eight about a year later, and the magazine's length grew with each issue, indicating an increasing budget and circulation and a growing involvement with the community.

Vanguard magazine began publication about a month before the August 1966 Compton's Cafeteria riot.[27] This is no coincidence, for the magazine seems to have served as an important instrument in creating and shaping the new political consciousness that both gave rise to and coalesced around the riot. For example, *Vanguard* magazine used its pages to denounce discrimination against and harassment of sex workers and transsexuals, publishing announcements such as the one that appeared in a 1967 issue: "Anyone who has been directly victimized or discriminated against by Compton's, the Plush Doggie or any other business please report the incident immediately to one of the editors. We remind you to save all evidence."[28] Such announcements went beyond simply stating that X businesses discriminate, and instead gave readers a framework into which they could place their own experiences. By asking them to reflect upon and rethink seemingly disparate personal and individual experiences as acts of institutional discrimination against a group, calls like this interpellated readers as part of Vanguard's activist project.[29] Indeed, the very placement of the call in a magazine read by hundreds highlighted for each reader the collectivity of his or her own personal experiences, simultaneously identifying these experiences as discrimination and addressing readers as citizens entitled to protest such treatment.

Vanguard's focus on issues pertinent to street youth also led them to take a position against mandates within the homophile movement for normativity, particularly around gender presentation. In the second issue of the group's magazine, for example, the president, J. P. Marat, issued a statement denouncing the common practice in homophile groups of banning drag at political meetings:

> Day after day I hear complaints about the prejudices that the straight society has against the gay society. Let's look at our own prejudices.... We ostracize people because they do this that or the other in bed. We make snide remarks about a drag queen who isn't quite convincing enough.... Then there is the hair fairy. *If we want the majority of society to accept us as we are, we are going to have to start accepting ourselves and*

others like us. There are many organizations for homosexuals all over the country. Most of them have rules like no drag, no hair fairies, etc. etc. This is fine in a legal situation, but why shouldn't we take the chance of getting busted? These people are homosexual just like us.[30]

Marat's statement, particularly his championing of hair fairies as "homosexuals just like us," suggests a new view of cross-dressing as an expression of identity rather than simply a practice.

Marat's mention of hair fairies is particularly important here, for this term was used to describe transwomen who wore their own hair long rather than using wigs, which might be put on or taken off, depending on the safety of the situation. Wearing one's hair long in the pre-hippie era was an act of defiance of gender norms that went beyond drag in that it could not be hidden in daily life. In this sense, the hair fairy belied the view of cross-dressing as mere sexual practice or masquerade, instead pointing toward a view more aligned with today's sense of transsexuality as identity. This new view of transsexuality allowed Vanguard to begin holding the homophile movement responsible to its own rhetoric by pointing out the ways that it enacted the very forms of marginalization that it critiqued in the larger community.

Looking at the history of this little-known group provides a model of what queer activism might look like if it were firmly grounded in the interests, experience, and agency of the most marginalized groups within our community, and it reminds us that these groups have in fact been deeply involved in key struggles, often at the very vanguard, of these movements. Moreover, the federal anti-poverty funding of the group meant that Vanguard, unlike the homophile movement from which it had sprung, had institutional reasons to frame their position as sexual outsiders in terms of class struggle and economic justice, since they needed to make the case to their funding source that the neighborhood was marginalized by poverty and thus a good candidate for federal anti-poverty funds. Finally, the fact that many members of the group were sex workers seems to have produced a strong sense of identity among group members not only as homosexual and transsexual, but also as economically marginalized by their sexuality. This outlook helped to produce a radical class analysis of public space, of sex work, and of queerness itself that is reflected in Vanguard's demonstrations and publications.

NOTES

1. In mid-1960s San Francisco, both male-presenting gay men and male-bodied people presenting as female referred to themselves as "gay." While male-bodied people who presented as female might also refer to themselves and be referred to by others in their community as drag queens, hair fairies, transsexuals, cross-dressers, or transvestites, the term "gay" served as a catch-all for people who might now identify as gay men, drag-queens, transsexual women, or transgendered women. Because transwomen self-identified with the term gay as frequently as did masculine homosexual men, many of the sources I quote or paraphrase from this period, as well as oral histories recorded later but reflecting upon this period, use the terms "gay" or "drag queen" to refer to male-bodied or transitioning people who lived full time as women (even though these people might today identify as transgender or transsexual). While this may be confusing or seem to elide or erase transgender experiences, it marks the identity categories that were available at the time. Nevertheless, when discussing female-presenting members of Vanguard from my own vantage point, I use the words transgender and transsexual for clarity's sake, and as a way of acknowledging the contributions of transgender women to this group and claiming their accomplishments as part of transgender history.

2. For much of the information that follows, I am deeply indebted to Susan Stryker, who generously provided me with the transcript of an oral history she recorded with a Vanguard founder.

3. Ed Hansen, Unpublished interview with Susan Stryker. 15 October 1998, 2.

4. Ed Hansen, Letter to Parents, February 26, 1966; June 19, 1966, GLBT Historical Society of Northern California.

5. Joel Roberts, Personal interview with Daniel Bao, December 18, 1989.

6. Ed Hansen, Letter to Parents, July 25, 1966, GLBT Historical Society of Northern California.

7. Stephan Cohen, *The Gay Liberation Youth Movement in New York* (New York: Routledge, 2008).

8. Chuck Lewis, Personal interview with Jallen Rix, July 22, 2006.

9. A similar situation existed until 1966 at the nearby Compton's Cafeteria, where a gay male night manager allowed young drag queens and hustlers to hang out without spending money. Such arrangements provide an interesting countermodel to the symbolic function of the figure of the child in the heteronormative imaginary, as articulated and critiqued by Lee Edelman in his monograph *No Future*. In contrast to the heteronormative discourse that uses arguments about "protecting the children" and "child as future" to dismantle the rights of queer adults in the present, the gay community in this example recognized and valued these youth not as a metaphor for the gay community's own future, nor as a

nostalgic fantasy of adult men's remembered youth, but as integral members of the gay community's own present, who required nurturance, protection from the police, and space to gather with other youth. Even if part of the youth's value to the community was as sexual commodities (most were hustlers), this seems to have translated into greater safety than did their value as children in the heterosexual home. See, Lee Edelman, *No Future: Queer Theory and the Death Drive* (Durham: Duke U.P., 2004).

10. Hansen, Interview, 7–8.
11. Jallen Rix, *The Last Dance Raid*. [Video] (2010).
12. Hansen, Interview, 11.
13. Anonymous, "The Hustler," *Vanguard*, Vol. 1, No. 1, July 1966, GLBT Historical Society of Northern California.
14. David Carter, *Stonewall* (New York: St. Martin's Press, 2004).
15. Joel Roberts, Personal interview with Daniel Bao, December 18, 1989.
16. The previous account of the creation of an informal safe haven for underage gay youth by the owner of the Gilded Cage suggests that adult gay men operating businesses in the pre-Stonewall era may have routinely, and at their own expense, created spaces where queer youth could gather and socialize safely.
17. Ed Hansen, Letter to Parents, July 25, 1966, GLBT Historical Society of Northern California.
18. Victor Silverman and Susan Stryker, dir. *Screaming Queens: The Riot at Compton's Cafeteria*. [Video] (Frameline, 2005).
19. David Carter, *Stonewall*. (New York: St. Martin's Press, 2004): p. 109.
20. *Screaming Queens: The Riot at Compton's Cafeteria*.
21. Joel Roberts, Personal interview with Daniel Bao, December 18, 1989.
22. Anonymous, "Sweep In," *Vanguard*, Vol. 1, No. 1, July 1966, GLBT Historical Society of Northern California.
23. *Vanguard*, Vol. 1, No. 2, December 1966, GLBT Historical Society of Northern California.
24. Joel Roberts, Personal interview with Daniel Bao, December 18, 1989.
25. Straight Guy, "If You Are Involved in or See Police Brutality," *Vanguard*, Vol. 1, No. 3, November 1966, GLBT Historical Society of Northern California.
26. *Vanguard*, Vol. 1, No. 4, December 1966, GLBT Historical Society of Northern California.
27. *Vanguard*'s first issue announces a national planning conference of homophile organizations to occur between August 19 and 28, indicating that the issues probably came out in July or early August at the latest (*Vanguard*, Vol. 1, No. 1, July 1966: p. 2).
28. *Vanguard*, Vol. 1, No. 4, December 1966, GLBT Historical Society of Northern

California: p. 9.

29.   Thanks to Bill Basquin for this insight.

30.   J. P. Marat, "Prejudice," *Vanguard*, Vol. 1, No. 2, October 1967, GLBT Historical Society of Northern California.

BRUSHES WITH
LILY LAW

Tommi Avicolli Mecca

To be a street queen in Philadelphia in the early '70s was to know the police and the prison system intimately. Even gay men who weren't effeminate or didn't run around in drag understood that they could end up in jail any time they stepped into a gay bar. It was illegal in many states, including Pennsylvania, to serve alcohol to a homosexual.

Police raided gay bars when the owners didn't come through with their payoffs or around election time, so that politicians could prove they were "cleaning up" so-called vice. In big cities today, politicians go after the homeless in the same way whenever they need to win points with their base. Payoffs were how those institutions—which were breaking the law every time they served a drink, even a beer, to a homo—stayed open and relatively safe from police harassment.

I was in my first bar raid when I was 19 or 20. I was carrying my older brother's expired driver's license. My brother and I looked like twins except that he had lighter hair. Both floors of the dark, narrow bar were packed to the gills with white gay men. Women, drag queens, and blacks were usually asked to show multiple pieces of identification or were refused admission outright—as in, "Sorry, no women allowed." I didn't know at the time that a year later I would be picketing that bar with the Gay Activists Alliance because of its sexist, transphobic, and racist policy. That day, I was sporting long hair, which was popular at the time, and standard dress: jeans and a T-shirt. I hadn't started doing drag yet.

I wasn't there long when the music suddenly stopped and the lights came on. Someone yelled, "It's the cops!" I had heard about bar raids. I knew I had to escape. I ducked into the kitchen and told a worker that I was underage. He let me out the back door into an alley. I climbed over a fence to safety.

I watched from across the street as patrons were led into the paddy wagon. I was relieved for myself but pissed off as hell at what the boys in blue were doing to my queer brothers. When you got arrested in a bar raid, your name and address ended up in the local newspaper. Many men had their lives and careers ruined by bar raids, even though the charges were eventually dropped.

Then there were the tearooms—public bathrooms that gay men cruised for sex. A tearoom could be in a department store, a university, a rest stop along a highway, or just about anywhere else that men went to relieve themselves. Long before Republican Senator Larry Craig of Idaho walked into that airport bathroom in Minnesota, gay men were signaling each other in stalls and at sinks.

I visited my first tearoom shortly after coming out at Temple University, where I went to school to avoid the draft. It was at the top of a building that housed several student lounges. An old stone building that had the somber appearance of another era, far removed from the freewheeling early '70s. While tearooms were the antithesis of the spirit of the sexual revolution, which advocated free love out in the open, they served the practical function of giving married and closeted men a place to indulge their hidden desires. Not to mention members of the faculty.

The university generally maintained a hands-off policy, especially with the bathroom on the upper-most floor. Except when a student complained. Even then, the university generally didn't call in the city police; a security guard was posted outside the facility to discourage sexual activity. Other establishments, especially department stores, did notify the local boys in blue (there were no female officers in those days). Highway patrol officers dragged off to jail gay men caught at highway stop bathrooms. Vice squad officers went undercover to entrap men making passes at them, then led them away in handcuffs. It was risky being a gay man. Being a queen was even more dangerous. I had been anything but a butch kid. Growing up in South Philly's Little Italy, I was often ostracized for not being a Guido boy. Or at least an Italian stallion wannabe. I survived the name-calling and the feeling of being an outsider in my own family and neighborhood: I found community in the Gay Liberation Front at Temple.

Many of the gay liberationists I met were into radical drag (also known as genderfuck), a form of political dress that mocked traditional gender roles. Its purposes were to show people how arbitrary gender-specific dress and behavior were and to free up men and women to be themselves. Why did men have to be macho and women weak? Why couldn't women earn the bacon and men stay home and take care of the kids? Before long, I was running around in full flaming radical drag: Long, frizzy "straightened" hair, hot pants, blouses, makeup, and colorful platform shoes. I looked like a cross between Bette Midler and the New York Dolls. I elicited an interesting assortment of responses as I made my way down the street to my favorite hangout, even in the gay male area of town. Queens had their own area, separate from the gay boy bars. It was nicknamed the "drag strip" even though it was shared by female hookers and male hustlers. The center of its universe was Dewey's, a 24-hour diner that at times could have been a transgender community center. Queens hung out there at all hours of the day and night, sitting alone at the counter or in groups at the tables along the sides of the room. From what I heard, queens carved out that bit of space for themselves because they were not welcomed in the gay boy bars or cruising areas.

Those gay boys had no sense of history. If they did, they would have known that for many years, starting in the dark ages of the late '50s, queens marched on Halloween night in a defiant display of pride. They assembled at a certain bar (I don't know the name of it) and strutted through the streets of the center of town, putting on a show for the straights who would gather from as far away as the surrounding suburbs. Police Captain Frank Rizzo (who would become police commissioner and then mayor with a widespread reputation for *spacco il capo*, or splitting heads) put a stop to the Halloween marches in the mid-'60s. "Philly's

Finest" had a tradition of roughing up the queens along the drag strip. The gay boys didn't seem to care about that abuse, nor did they understand that queens in New York had recently rioted and given birth to a movement that would soon end the police raids and the entrapment in tearooms and public sex areas.

I didn't quite fit into the scene along the drag strip. Many of the other queens considered me a freak because I didn't want to pass as a woman, nor did I want a sex change. I regularly lectured them about redistributing the wealth and other Marxist and anarchist ideas. They nodded politely, sometimes even offered comments, but generally stared at me blankly. I was the '70s version of a "nerd." And I wasn't a prostitute. Not that I didn't turn a trick or two when the occasion arose. Many times, guys offered me money to go home with them. I usually refused. I was working at a record store run by hippies who accepted my unconventional looks (they thought I was trying to be David Bowie), and I didn't need to sell my body to pay the rent or buy food. More importantly, I didn't trust the guys who approached me. Any john could be an undercover vice cop.

I was terrified of being arrested and thrown in jail. Not only because my Southern Italian *famiglia* would have to come bail me out, but also because I had heard too many horror stories from the older queens. They told of being beaten and sometimes even raped in prison. They described sexual favors they were forced to perform for some of the officers. They were resigned to the fact that every once in a while (especially around election time), the cops came around and "cleaned up" the neighborhood, and off they went to spend time behind bars.

An old queen once showed me a scar she got from resisting arrest in her younger days. It was a mark of pride, but I could still see the pain in her eyes. She had been a hooker for a long time and all the cops knew her well. That didn't stop them from tossing her in a cell when it suited them. Prostitution wasn't the only thing that the cops had over our heads. They also used a state law that prohibited "impersonating the opposite sex," which meant that if you weren't wearing two articles of clothing of your "appropriate" gender, you could be hauled off to prison. I usually wore my Fruit of the Loom briefs, but no other item that could be considered "male." I could have argued, I guess, that my glitter socks or platform shoes were "unisex," as we called them, and therefore technically not "female." It wouldn't have saved me. Philly cops didn't look favorably on that particular fashion trend. I hated cops.

When I was in high school, I fell madly in love this guy in my class. He and I would do homework at his house. It was a chance to be together. Coming home late sometimes, I'd be stopped by cops who thought, as they put it, that I "looked like someone" who had just committed a crime: Ethnic profiling before it was called that. No doubt the description in the police bulletin said "Italian." I had a "Roman nose," therefore I must be a criminal. To my uncle the cop, I was something even worse. When I worked at the gas station that my father operated with his oldest brother, Uncle Cop always needled me about being effeminate. He loved to do it in front of the old guys who hung out at the station. He'd yell across the driveway while I was washing a car: "When're you gonna start acting like a boy!" It achieved its effect: I was totally humiliated. I tried to ignore him, but he kept at it until he was distracted by something else or until I walked off to the bathroom.

At family gatherings, my uncle bragged about beating up the queens along the drag strip. Fortunately, by the time I was hanging out in that area, he had been transferred to another police precinct.

On the drag strip, I had one very close brush with "Lily Law," or "Alice," as we called the cops. I don't know where "Lily Law" came from, but "Alice," or "Alice Bluegown," was the invention of a very loud and proud queen named Alice who used it to signal the other queens when they needed to stop what they were doing. One night on the "merry-go-round," a gay cruising area, I was in a dark alley about to go down on someone when I heard, "Alice!" I took off. Sure enough, a cop car was circling the block.

I wasn't so lucky that summer night on the drag strip. I was talking to a john. I wasn't really going to do anything with him. I liked the fact that he kept telling me how pretty I was, but had no intention of going off with him. A cop car pulled up to the curb. The john fled. He didn't need to worry; the police would never have arrested him. "Get in," the police officer said. He was standard-issue white Anglo. My heart started pumping harder. I knew I had to stay calm. I got in the car, sitting as close to the door as I could, in case I had to make an escape. Of course that would only make me look guiltier.

"Let me see your ID," he said. I handed it to him

"Avicolli? You related to…?

"Yeah, he's my uncle," I said.

"Does he know?"

"No."

He didn't say anything for the longest time. He handed the card back to me. I wanted to beg him to not say anything to my uncle, but I was too scared to talk. I was willing to do anything to avoid being booked. He seemed to be considering something. A blowjob would be a fair exchange for my freedom. He wasn't that bad looking.

"You know this is a dangerous neighborhood," he said.

I was barely breathing, trying to be as still and silent as possible.

"I should take you in." He paused. "But your uncle's a good guy. He don't deserve this."

He was obviously conflicted: duty versus loyalty to a fellow officer. I remained frozen. I figured it best to keep quiet.

"Get outta here," he said, "and don't let me see you out there no more."

I was out of that car before he could reconsider. As I walked back to Dewey's, some of the girls asked me what happened. I just shook my head and kept going. I went straight past the restaurant and toward the bus stop. When the bus pulled up, I got on and sat in the back, still trembling.

Uncle Cop had saved my queer ass.

LOOKING BACK:

The Bathhouse Raids in Toronto, 1981

Nadia Guidotto

A night at the baths: February 5, 1981

Naked faggots rounded up by police armed with sledgehammers and
crowbars
The largest mass arrest since the War Measures Act, they say
Smashing glass, drywall, and well-kept secrets
We stand on guard for thee.

Line 'em up against the shower room walls
Then strike holes in the marble in case they've stashed their drugs inside
Bend over and spread those cheeks ("don't tell us you haven't done that
before").

Of 104 rooms, 3 were left standing
Obliterated, massacred, taught a lesson
"Because that wall belonged to a bunch of fuckin' fruits"[2]
Because that wall between us and them
Normal and perverted, moral and criminal, man and sissy
Had to be penetrated on the Big Boys' terms
Maybe with a bit of excessive "rowdyism"[3]
But we chalk it up to the inevitable:
Boys will be boys.

Post-raid retaliation
The sissies and others-also-fucked-by-police fill the streets
They spill into their public spaces
Not respecting borders
Headline reads: Gay Rage.

I wrote this poem after listening to over twelve hours of interviews conducted by Nancy Nicol with twenty-two men and women who were either present at the now-infamous bathhouse raids of 1981 or who were indirectly involved through their post-raid activist engagements. Though it seems so long ago, so far removed from myself and from what I know to be queer life in the new millennium, something drew me to studying this topic. Indeed, I was born the year of the mass raids in Toronto, and now it seems fitting to probe the archives thirty years later. At first glance, the raids appear to have been a humiliating, horrific, and terrifying event in Canadian queer history. But far from painting a picture of victimization and brutality at the hands of police, I hope that this project will also highlight the tremendous rallying point that this event created for queers in Canada. Post-raid, the demonstrations that filled Yonge Street in downtown Toronto, not to mention the growth and increased visibility of new activist organizations, all testify to the fact that queers and their allies were not going to take the assault lying down. Instead, the police inadvertently created the context within which a more united—though not homogeneous—queer community could take shape, live more openly, support each other, and form important coalitions with other groups who felt similar alienation and discrimination from police and Canadian society at large.

Raids on queer bathhouses occurred in Canada at various points leading up to the mass raid in Toronto (such as the Montreal raid in 1977, for example) and have continued as recently as 2004 when the Warehouse was raided in Hamilton. While I have found studies of these other raids instructive, in the interest of space, I will focus my attention on the 1981 raids chiefly because of the scale of the assault and the impact that it had on queer organizing. Also, I am confident that aspects of the analyses will be applicable today, especially since, as I have mentioned, the raids have not ended. In other words, understanding what came before can shed light on what has been—and on what continues to be—the dominant attitude toward "fringe" sexualities and spaces today.

The Raids

The bathhouse raids in 1981 cannot be understood if we focus only on police brutality or on a romanticized notion of a homogeneous resistance effort. Instead, a multi-directional analysis of power is needed to account for (a) the historical circumstances that led to the raids in the first place, (b) the state violence against a particular targeted group, (c) how that violence motivated a counter-reaction, and, finally, (d) the divisions that existed within the resistance movement. Of course there are probably countless other axes of power that I will have left unaddressed. Thirty years after the 1981 raids, I might touch on issues that, at the time, may not have been addressed. Likewise, thirty years from now, more issues will be raised. I welcome the revisions and invite critiques given that I am working from limited archived material. I view these limitations as opportunities for dialogue, multiple interpretations, and a more dynamic history.

I. Historical Climate

Listening to the interviews from the Oral History Project, I could not help but notice how the phrase "the tenor of the time" kept surfacing in several of the narratives. What exactly was the "tenor"? What was the general mood in society? What were the views on homosexuality, and what was going on politically? Scanning some of the newspapers from both the mainstream and *The Body Politic* revealed that the tenor was particularly charged. As Tanya Gulliver notes in *Xtra!* the raids happened against a backdrop of struggle and tension in the late '70s and early '80s. Gay and lesbian people were not covered under federal nor provincial human rights legislation, and police regularly conducted sweeps, arresting gay men in bathhouses and parks.[4]

On August 1, 1977, Emanual Jacques, a 12-year-old shoeshine boy, was murdered and found on the roof of a Yonge Street body-rub parlor. This generated huge media attention, much of which was virulently homophobic, as the suspects in the case were allegedly homosexuals. Such media attention served to fuel homophobic links between queer sexuality and criminality. On October 22 of that year, there was a large raid on the Truxx gay bar in Montreal, sparking a mass protest the following day. Anita Bryant, the "glamour queen of orange juice,"[5] headed a campaign sponsored by the religious right in the United States to snuff out the rights of homosexuals. Greeted by protests, Bryant spoke at the People's Church in North York on January 15, 1978. On December 9, 1978, the Barracks steambath was raided by Toronto police. Twenty-three men were charged as found-ins and five men were charged as keepers of a common bawdy house.[6] The Ontario election was just called and the Conservatives were trying to get a majority. John Sewell, a gay-positive mayor, and openly gay aldermanic candidate George Hislop had both just lost the election, which inspired an anti-gay backlash.[7] These, among other events across the nation and south of the border, created a politically turbulent climate.

Some felt that the raids were an extension of this anti-gay sentiment. Since the Conservatives wanted a majority, some have speculated that a push to "clean up"[8] the downtown would have been good publicity for the party. Gary Kinsman, in hindsight, has suggested, "Toronto is a city of growing racial, ethnic—and now—sexual minorities. The provincial and municipal establishment foresaw the need for a fairly militarized police force…to decrease the public visibility of these minorities and to keep them contained."[9]

Such pressures to "contain" these groups might have led to the authorization of the mass raid. Such minority groups were seen as unsavory, as racist and homophobic prejudices infused with the collective psyche. These people were considered less worthy than the rest of the population. They presented a threat to the prevailing order and needed to be contained or "cleaned up."

II. Police Brutality

Consider the following testimonials shared by men who were present at the raids:

> I was in a room with someone when I heard a noise. I got up to open the door but it burst open and a guy in plain clothes pushed in and shoved me up against the wall, my face pushed hard. My nose was lacerated and bloodied. The cop kept punching me in the lower back and pulling my hair and saying, "You're disgusting, faggot. Look at

this dirty place." I was choked, and something was jabbed into my neck. Before they took us out of the room, they used a pen to gouge the room number into the backs of our hands. I was naked.... Someone said, "Too bad the place doesn't catch fire...." Somebody else said, "Too bad the showers aren't hooked up to gas."[10]

There were huge holes in the wall.... Why? Because that wall belonged to a bunch of fuckin' fruits. And that's what they were calling us, among other things. The verbal abuse, the damage, the unbelievable noise—that went on for two hours before anyone was processed to be released. They wanted to make sure that everyone inside saw what they were doing and what we could expect if we ever had the nerve to open a place like this again.[11]

More than anything, men described the noise they heard as glass shattered and walls fell all around them. They remember the insults and being ordered around and called names like "queer," "faggot," and "cock-sucker."[12] They remember the sounds of lockers being smashed open with crowbars, even after the keys were offered.[13] They remember being lined up in the snow, freezing cold, wearing only a towel. They were processed and their identities were collected to count, criminalize, and out them to employers who might fire them. They remember being shoved against the walls in the shower rooms, then herded into paddy wagons.[14] To manage the population, they need to track all the deviants. Take their names down, mark their hands to make sure everyone is accounted for. You also need them to be docile. Sledgehammers, crowbars, and words of denigration can help with this task. Mariana Valverde and Miomir Cirak point out that "the fundamental role of police—a role that they by no means monopolize—is *the maintenance of order and the guaranteeing of security*."[15] The raids were not just about crimes—since bawdyhouse provisions have been enforced sporadically if at all—they were about regulation. But it was not regulation evenly applied to the whole population; the queers in particular were targeted.[16] Deborah Brock and Valerie Scott also suggest that "bawdy house laws were originally developed for the regulation of prostitution, and later became extended to the regulation of gay men and sexual policing of gay male spaces."[17] The men in blue were there to intimidate, humiliate, and control gay male space and sexuality. They were there to enforce a particular order, one that is intrinsically heterosexual,[18] one in which "proper" men are ultra-masculine, punch holes in walls, smash glass, and pick on the "little kids."[19] As one sympathetic writer in the *Toronto Star* summarized, "They want a tidy world enriched with their notions of good citizenship, motherhood, and Sunday School."[20] Men do not fuck other men. Indeed, when one found-in was told by police after seeing his wedding band, "You'll wish you had stayed at home with your wife tonight, you fucking queer,"[21] the homophobic motivations of police were clear.

Gay men were disposable—or at least the police suggested they were when they beat the men up and pined for showers hooked up to gas. The men were also criminalized. George Smith argued in 1990 that "the social organization of the Toronto bath raids, for example, was put together in the ideological practices of the police, which were conceptually coordinated at the local level by the idea of gay men as criminals, and the gay community as a criminal minority in the city."[22] This theory is confirmed when we glance at newspaper editorials from the period. M. Feldman likened homosexuals to "social terrorists" who were "intent on establishing totalitarian rule in our country."[23] Another editorial warned, "Either we let the homosexuals have their own way and make this a wide-open city or we support our police in their endeavors to keep it a decent, law-abiding city and not the pawn of organized crime."[24] As criminals, queers became an easy target, the perfect scapegoat for all social ills.

Criminality is not the only perceived feature of gay male sexuality; it is also dirty, and one cannot come in contact with it without sullying oneself. One police officer demanded that a man bend over because he was "just checking for shit,"[25] while another officer described the Barracks as smelling of "excreta."[26] Indeed, descriptions of the Barracks were frequently littered with references to dirt, while the patrons and their sexual proclivities were also described as "filthy dirty."[27] The bathhouse became the homosexual body and vice versa. It was no coincidence that the code name of the police project that included the raids was "Operation Soap."[28]

Related to the discourse of dirt were the frequent associations of homosexuality to sickness and disease. Like the previous raids on clubs in Montreal, many men at the 1981 raids in Toronto were ordered to have a VD test[29] under Section 4 of the Venereal Diseases Prevention Act. The editorials are also instructive on this matter, as citizens equated homosexuality with "cancer, venereal disease and leprosy,"[30] or suggested that "the homosexual problem" is one that "requires treatment" for it to be "curable."[31]

What was difficult for non-queers to understand was that bathhouses "go far beyond the fact of orgasm."[32] Gay men went there to use facilities, relax, meet other men, and, most importantly, to "learn to recognize and affirm each other as members of a group in a way that is denied in the closeted, heterosexually dominated outside world."[33] Or, perhaps, this fact *was* recognized and that is why they were targeted. Perhaps queers were becoming too organized, too politically active, and were making too many demands for protection in a society that was not yet ready to accede. Thus, the police used bawdy house laws, which functioned as "an insidious weapon for interfering with the social spaces where gay men gathered."[34] However, as we shall see, "attacks on the collective life of the community...made a genuine collective response possible."[35]

III. Resistance

Less than twenty-four hours [after the raids], at midnight on February 6, a hastily organized demonstration of 3,000 lesbians and gay men took over one of the main downtown intersections and swept down Yonge Street...and on to the 52nd Division Police Station, where the arrested men had been booked the night before. The crowd rolled over a barricade of police cars, kicking in headlights as it passed.[36]

After the raids and the initial demonstration took place, an astute writer from the *Globe and Mail* wrote of the preceding events: "The violence produced its reactive violence."[37] While state authorities tried to contain queer sexualities and maintain a particular order, this system invariably produced its own weaknesses and vulnerabilities. As Kinsman points out, "These police campaigns were not successful. The attempt to create a 'moral panic' around the 1981 bath raids failed because of the widespread resistance by thousands of gays and our supporters."[38] By mobilizing those who had been arrested and subjected to violence, gay men and their supporters were able to turn their frustration and rage into a counter-attack. But perhaps more importantly, they created a venue to vent to their frustration[39]—not only from the raids but also from their history of sexual repression. Peter Bochove, who had witnessed the raids firsthand, recalled that the police "meant to terrify," but all he felt was "fury."[40] The demonstration after the raids provided a safe space to vent this anger, but it was unique in the way that, while members of the gay community may have been acquainted in more enclosed spaces such as bathhouses and bars, the demonstration was a mass, public coming-together of people who felt similar rage. As one demonstration participant recalled, "you could feel the pulsing of all these people around you."[41] Having been arrested the day before, the demonstration made him feel like he was not alone—which is quite different from the isolation and shame that had until now been the experience of many queers who were forced into the closet. By contrast, the mass mobilization made people feel like "everyone was with [them]."[42]

Apart from this catharsis experienced by gay men, another of the frequently cited "bright sides" of the raids was the tremendous amount of coalitional politics that emerged. While gays and lesbians, for example, did not necessarily engage in resistance practices for the same reasons or see eye to eye on a variety of issues leading up to or following the raids, this event was particularly "galvanizing"[43] because, in a very short time, thousands of men and women came together to fight a common enemy—in fact, "nothing...ha[d] strengthened the gay and lesbian community more."[44] While lesbians, for example, were not at the raids, they were not unaware of how the state could intrude on their bodies. Pamela Godfrey, who attended the demonstration on February 6, noted that lesbians were involved because when they saw "that the state could intervene in that way...most people saw that as a direct attack on our right 'to be'.... If this can happen then certainly other aspects of our lives can be similarly attacked."[45] In an important way, the assault on gay male bodies, sexualities, and spaces became a feminist issue because lesbians and non-lesbian women were acutely aware of the state's regulation of their bodies and their sexualities.

Yet gay men and lesbians were not the only ones marching on February 6. The overt act of sexual repression and violence brought different groups together in the resistance effort, as immigrants and racialized minority groups saw connections to their own oppression at the hands of police. For instance, Lemona Johnson, a black woman whose husband was killed by police,[46] spoke at the post-raid rally because she shared the gay community's experience of violence and anger toward police. In Kinsman's book *The Regulation of Desire*, the author notes how "support came from feminists, unions, civil liberties and religious groups, and progressive members of city council."[47] While there were some sources that were particularly insidious,[48] many mainstream newspapers contained voices in favor of the gay community as well.

IV. Internal Divisions

Such coalitions, of course, should not obscure the fact that there were internal divisions. Some lesbians felt that gay men were not equally as supportive of their issues. Or some wondered why the same outcry did not occur when the Barracks, a "raunchier" S/M club, was raided earlier.

The Barracks catered to clients who were interested in sadomasochism and other types of "fringe" sexualities.[49] As such, it has been speculated that many queers wanted to distance themselves from this reputation. By contrast, during the 1981 raids, more people felt as though they had an investment. It could have been the size of the raids, but also there might have been the added factor—to paraphrase Tim McCaskell—that even if people were not necessarily at the raided bathhouses in 1981, they knew that they *could* have been there.[50] Related to this, Duncan McLaren, one of the found-ins during the 1981 raids, commented that it was "hard to imagine for most middle-class people, which is basically what the crowd was...such hatred" at the hands of police.[51] What this seems to suggest, if this is indeed a fair assessment of the class composition of the patrons in the 1981 raids, is that people who previously may have enjoyed protection under the state were suddenly experiencing a huge violation at the hands of the state. Also, apart from the discussions of coalitions between queers and racial minorities, I did not come across much information on how queers of color were impacted by the raids in particular. Such areas definitely warrant further investigation.

Concluding Remarks

So where does this leave us now? It is undeniable that attitudes toward sexualities and other previously "taboo" practices and identities are changing; however, we still need to put pressure on governments and each other to open their/our minds to alternative modes of expression and being. Sadomasochism is one area that I have already mentioned, but prostitution also continues to be misunderstood and regulated in violent and oppressive ways. Racism still exists, along with sexism, classism, bi-phobia, transphobia, and other imbalanced relations of power. While on the surface these may seem like separate battles from the ones born of the bathhouse raids, a deeper look reveals how homophobia and police brutality intersect with a variety of oppressions. More crucially, beyond merely being aware of the connections, the post-raid demonstrations show how these linkages can help build coalitions between people.

While critics today lament the turn in queer politics from liberation toward rights, from a radical sexual politics to a more neoliberal agenda, we might look back to the raids as an example—albeit with its own internal deficiencies—of the potential of grassroots organizing. We also learn from their mistakes and strive for a more transformative basis for theory and praxis.

71

NOTES

1. Duncan McLaren, *Oral History: The Bath Raids (Toronto, 1981)* [Video], prod. Nancy Nicol (Toronto: Intervention Video, 2002).

2. Quote from Peter Bochove—present at the Richmond Street Health Emporium at time of raid—*Oral History: The Bath Raids (Toronto, 1981)*.

3. The "rowdyism" described in relation to the bathhouse raids comes from a Canadian case involving a professional dominatrix who ran a dungeon for commercial purposes (*R. v. Bedford* [2000], O. J. No. 887). The police ransacked Terry Jean Bedford's home—which was also the site used for the dungeon—seized her equipment, roughed up her employees, and hurled insults at them. The trial judge as well as the judge at the court of appeals dismissed the behavior of the male officers as "rowdyism"—in other words, normal and acceptable expressions of some presumably innate masculine aggression.

4. Tanya Gulliver, "Harnessed Anger," *Xtra!*, Feb. 2, 2006: p. 3.

5. Pamela Godfrey, *Oral History: The Bath Raids (Toronto, 1981)*.

6. This paragraph cited from "Victories and Defeats: A Gay and Lesbian Chronology 1964–1982," *Flaunting It! A Decade of Gay Journalism from* The Body Politic, eds. Ed Jackson and Stan Persky (Vancouver: New Star Books, and Toronto: Pink Triangle Press, 1982): p. 232–235.

7. "Bawdy House Laws: The State's Key to the Bedroom Door," *The Body Politic*, April 1981: p. 13.

8. Gary Kinsman, *The Regulation of Desire: Homo and Hetero Sexualities*, 2nd ed. (Montreal: Black Rose Press, 1996): p. 341.

9. Ibid.

10. Cashier at the Richmond Street Health Emporium quoted in "Rage," *The Body Politic*, March 1981: p. 11.

11. Peter Bochove, *Oral History: The Bath Raids (Toronto, 1981)*.

12. George Hislop, *Oral History: The Bath Raids (Toronto, 1981)*.

13. Peter Bochove in *Stand Together* [Video], prod. Nancy Nicol (Toronto: V Tape, 2002).

14. Nicholas Pron, "3,000 Go on Rampage in Metro Riot," *Toronto Star*, Feb. 7, 1981: p. A1.

15. Miomir Cirak and Mariana Valverde, "Governing Bodies, Creating Gay Spaces: Policing and Security Issues in 'Gay' Downtown Toronto," *British Journal of Criminology*, Issue 43, 2003: p. 104, original emphasis.

16. An article in *The Globe and Mail* suggested that, at this point, there had been "no such raids on heterosexual bawdy houses in Metro Toronto." See "Heavy Hand of the Law," *The Globe and Mail*, Feb. 9, 1981: p. 6.

17. Deborah Brock and Valerie Scott, "Whores, Queers, and Bawdy Houses," unpublished article: p. 1.

18. Kinsman writes, "The way in which people live is often bound up with certain gender and sexual 'truths'…for example, that only heterosexuality is natural and normal and that women and men have separate and distinct natural roles. Any challenge to this order is perceived as a threat." p. 33.

19. Margaret Atwood spoke at a community meeting, commenting on how it makes her sick when "big kids" in the schoolyard beat up on "little kids," referring of course to the police treatment of the patrons of the bathhouses. See the documentary *Track Two* [Video], prod. Gord Keith, et al. (Toronto: Keith, Lemmon, Sutherland Communications Corp., 1983).

20. Larry Solway, "Whose Side Are You on in Bath Raids," *Toronto Star*, Feb. 15, 1981: p. B8.

21. Gerald Hannon, et. al. "Who Is the Next? Me?" *The Body Politic*, April 1981: p. 10.

22. George W. Smith, "Political Activist as Ethnographer," *Social Problems*, Vol. 37, Issue 4, Nov. 1990: p. 632.

23. M. Feldman, "Social Terrorists," *Toronto Star*, Feb. 18, 1981: p. A9.

24. Herbert P. Wood, "Police Were 'Doing Their Duty'," *Toronto Star*, Feb. 13, 1981: p. A7.

25. Gerald Hannon, et. al.: p. 10.

26. Gerald Hannon, "Making Gay Sex Dirty," *The Body Politic*, May 1981: p. 9.

27. Hannon, p. 8.

28. *Stand Together* [Video], prod. Nancy Nicol (Toronto: V Tape, 2002).

29. Ian Mulgrew, "VD Tests to Be Ordered for Men Charged in Raids on Steambaths," *Globe and Mail*, Feb. 12, 1981: p. 5.

30. Ronald C. Inch, "No Connection to Nazi Attack," *Toronto Star*, Feb. 13, 1981: p. A7.

31. W. Pritchard, "Not Problem of 'Human Rights'," *Toronto Star*, Feb. 18, 1981: p. A9.

32. Tim McCaskell, "The Bath Raids and Gay Politics," *Social Movements/Social Change: The Politics and Practice of Organizing*, eds. Frank Cunningham, et al. (Toronto: Between the Lines, 1988): p. 171.

33. Ibid.

34. "Victories and Defeats," p. 225.

35. Ibid.

36. McCaskell, p. 170.

37. "Heavy Hand of the Law," *The Globe and Mail*, Feb. 9, 1981: p. 6.

38. Kinsman, p. 341.

39. John Burt in *Track Two*.

40. Peter Bochove, "RAGE! Toronto Queers: 25 Years Later," Metro Central YMCA Auditorium (Toronto: February 9, 2006).

41. Brian Mossop, *Oral History: The Bath Raids (Toronto, 1981)*.

42. Ibid.

43. Harold B. Desmarais, *Oral History: The Bath Raids (Toronto, 1981)*.

44. "Victories and Defeats," p. 225.

45. Godfrey, *Oral History: The Bath Raids (Toronto, 1981)*.

46. On August 26, 1979, Jamaican immigrant Albert Johnson was shot to death by the police in his downtown Toronto home. Police were called to the Johnson home after receiving a phone call that Johnson was "ranting and raving about police persecution." Johnson resisted arrest, was struck with a billy club, and was subsequently shot when he tried to defend himself with a lawn edger. The police believed it was an axe. Shortly after the ordeal, his widow, Lemona Johnson, became an important activist in Toronto's black community, particularly in matters concerning police brutality. In 1988, she won a $177,000 lawsuit against the Metro Toronto Police. See Kirk Makin, "Widow Gets Settlement from Police in Shooting," *The Globe and Mail*, Feb. 13, 1988: p. A1.

47. Kinsman, p. 342.

48. Andy Fabo, *Oral History: The Bath Raids (Toronto, 1981)*.

49. As an interesting side note, Foucault used to visit the Barracks in the seventies and question Fabo about police raids. Fabo notes in hindsight that he was probably interested in exploring the raids as a "vehicle of control." Ibid.

50. Ibid.

51. Ibid.

PRISON BEYOND
THE PRISON

CRIMINALIZATION OF
THE EVERYDAY

ROUNDING UP THE HOMOSEXUALS:

The Impact of Juvenile Court on Queer and Trans/Gender-Non-Conforming Youth

Wesley Ware

"Tell her the world is beautiful. It's different now." Those are the words that were passed through me from a formerly incarcerated 17-year-old queer youth to his 16-year-old trans friend still confined in a youth prison in Louisiana. His friend, a young transwoman, was still incarcerated in a "secure care" facility—a "boys" prison for kids.

Working with queer and trans/gender-non-conforming youth in the Deep South, I hear stories of state and personal violence from a wide range of people. There was the 16-year-old, black self-identified "stud" in detention after her mom referred her to family court for bringing girls to the house. Then there was the incarcerated white 16-year-old trans youth from a rural town of 642, whose access to transgender healthcare resided in the hands of one juvenile judge. I was told of a black trans-feminine youth in New Orleans who was threatened with contempt for wearing feminine clothing to her court hearing. There was also the 12-year-old boy, perceived to be gay by his mother, who was brought into judge's chambers without his attorney and questioned about being gay before he was sentenced for contempt after being found "ungovernable." There was the public defender who refused to represent his gay client because the lawyer believed him to be "sick" and in need of the "services" offered by prison. And there was the black lesbian arrested over and over again for any crime where witnesses described the perpetrator as an African American "boyish-looking" girl. Nowhere is the literal regulation and policing of gender and sexuality, particularly of low-income queer and trans youth of color, so apparent than in juvenile courts and in the juvenile justice system in the South.

Understanding how the juvenile justice system operates and impacts queer and trans/gender-non-conforming youth requires a critical look at the history of youth rights and the inception of juvenile court. During the Industrial Revolution (1800–1840s), poor youth worked in factories, received no public education and were often arrested for the crime of poverty.[1] These youth, some as young as 7 years old, were incarcerated with adults and placed in prisons until they were 21.[2] Inspired by the belief that young people who committed crimes could be rehabilitated and shocked by the horrific treatment of white children in adult prisons, the juvenile justice system was developed. This new system was based on *parens patriae*, the idea that the role of the system was to place youth in the state's custody when their parents were unable to care for them. Later, in 1899, the first juvenile court was established, designed to "cure" children and provide treatments for them rather than sentences. Still rooted in a Puritan ideology, white young women were often sent to institutions "to protect them from sexual immorality."[3]

Black children, however, who were viewed as incapable of rehabilitation, continued to be sent to adult prisons or were sent to racially segregated institutions. In Louisiana, black youth were sent to work the fields at Angola State Penitentiary, a former slave plantation, until 1948 when the State Industrial School for Colored Youth opened.[4] The facilities were not desegregated until the United States District Court ordered desegregation of juvenile facilities in 1969.[5] More recently, the goal of juvenile justice reform has been to keep youth in their homes and in their communities whenever possible while providing appropriate treatment services to youth and their families.

However, with the juvenile justice system's intent to provide "treatment" to young people, many queer/trans youth inherit the ideology that they are "wrong" or in need of "curing," as evidenced by their stories. As sexual and gender transgressions have been deemed both illegal and pathological, queer and trans youth, who are some of the most vulnerable to "treatments," are not only subjected to incarceration but also to harassment by staff, conversion therapy, and physical violence.[6] Moreover, with the juvenile justice system often housed under the direct authority of state correctional systems and composed of youth referred directly from state police departments, it should not be surprising that young people locked up in the state juvenile system, 80 percent of whom are black in Louisiana,[7] are often actually destroyed by the very system that was created to intervene.

Worse than just providing damaging outcomes for youth once they are incarcerated, this rehabilitative system funnels queer and trans/gender-non-conforming youth into the front doors of the system. Non-accepting parents and guardians can refer their children to family court for arbitrary and subjective behaviors, such as being "ungovernable."[8] Police can bring youth in for status offenses, offenses for which adults cannot be charged, which often become contributing factors to the criminalization of youth. Charges can range from truancy to curfew violations to running away from home. Like in the adult criminal justice system, queer and trans youth can be profiled by the police and brought in for survival crimes like prostitution or theft. Youth may be referred for self-defense arising from conflict with hostile family members or public displays of affection in schools that selectively enforce policies only against queer and trans youth.

Although youths' rights were greatly expanded in 1967 when the Supreme Court decided that the juvenile system was not operating according to its original intent,[9] youth continue to struggle in the courts with fewer protections than adults. Defense lawyers for youth, who are sometimes the only advocates young people have in court, have at times confused their role, advocating for what they believe to be the "best interest" of the youth rather than defending their client's "expressed interest." Juvenile court judges with little accountability have similarly expanded their role with the intent to provide services, through incarceration, to every youth that comes through their courtrooms. In this effort to rehabilitate "deviant" children and without the right to a jury trial for delinquent offenses, the issue of guilt versus innocence can fall to the wayside. Further aggravated by the public's fear of youth sexuality and our desire to control young people and their bodies, juvenile court presents a unique opportunity to destroy the lives of queer and trans/gender-non-conforming youth. The agenda of juvenile court then, for queer and trans youth at least, often becomes to "rehabilitate" youth into fitting heteronormative and gender-typical molds. Guised under the "best interest of the child," the goal often becomes to "protect" the child—or perhaps society—from gender-variant or non-heterosexual behavior.

While not as explicit as the sumptuary laws (laws requiring people to wear at least three items of gender-appropriate clothing) or sodomy laws of the past that led to the Compton's Riots and Stonewall Rebellion, the policing of sexuality and state regulation of gender has continued to exist in practice—perhaps nowhere more than in juvenile courts. In many ways, the system still mirrors the adult criminal justice system, whose roots can be traced to slavery, the commodification of bodies as free labor, institutionalized racism, and state regulation of low-income people of color, immigrants, and anyone deemed otherwise "deviant" or a threat to the political norm. Combined with the Puritan beliefs that helped spark the creation of juvenile courts, it becomes clear that, borrowing the words of Audre Lorde, queer and trans youth of color "were never meant to survive."

In fact, one youth in a Louisiana youth prison responded to the number of queer and trans youth incarcerated by stating, "I'm afraid they're rounding up the homosexuals."

Once locked up, queer and trans youth experience the same horrors that their adult counterparts in the system do, but magnified by a system designed to control, regulate, and pathologize their very existence. In Louisiana's youth prisons, queer and trans youth have been subjected to "sexual-identity confusion counseling," accused of using "gender identity issues" to detract from their rehabilitation, and disciplined for expressing any gender-non-conforming behaviors or actions. Youth are put on lockdown for having hair that is too long or wearing state-issued clothing that is too tight. They are instructed how to walk, talk, and act in their dorms and are prohibited from communicating with other queer youth lest they become too "flamboyant" and cause a disturbance. They are excessively punished for consensual same-sex behavior and spend much of their time in protective custody or in isolation cells. In meetings with representatives from the Juvenile Justice Project of Louisiana, directors of youth jails have referred to non-heterosexual identities as "symptoms" and have conflated youth adjudicated for sex offenses with youth who are queer. In addition, when advocates asked what the biggest problem was at a youth prison in Baker, Louisiana, guards replied, "the lesbians."

Even more troubling, unlike the adult criminal justice system where individuals either "ride out their time" or work toward "good time" or parole, youths' privileges in prison and eventual release dates are often determined by their successful completion of their rehabilitative programming, including relationships with peers and staff. Thus, youth who are seen as "deviant" or "mentally ill," or who otherwise do not conform to the rules set forth by the prison, often spend longer amounts of time incarcerated and are denied their opportunity for early release. For queer and trans/gender-non-conforming youth, this means longer prison terms. In fact, in the last four years of advocacy on behalf of queer and trans youth in prison in Louisiana at the Juvenile Justice Project of Louisiana, not one openly queer or trans youth has been recommended for an early release by the Office of Juvenile Justice.

While protections afforded to youth in the juvenile justice system like a greater right to confidentiality are extremely important for youth, they can also be another strike against queer and trans youth seeking to access resources or support networks while inside. Like queer and trans adults in the criminal justice system who have difficulty receiving information that "promotes homosexuality," youth are unable to access affirming information during a particularly formative time in their lives, which can already be plagued with confusion and questioning. The right to confidentiality for youth in prison can result in their being prohibited from communicating with pen pals or seeking services from community organizations. Other rights are afforded to adults but not to minors, such as accessing legal counsel to challenge the conditions of their confinement. Youth under 18 must rely on their guardians to assist with filing a civil complaint, despite the fact that many queer and trans youth have had difficulty with their families prior to their incarceration—and that those family members may have contributed to their entering into the system in the first place. This barrier also holds true for transgender youth who are minors and seeking healthcare or hormones. These youth may need the approval from a guardian or judge in order to access these services—or approval from a guardian in order to file a civil complaint to request them.

Meanwhile, as state institutions are placing queer and trans/gender-non-conforming youth behind bars and effectively silencing their voices, prominent gay activists are fighting for inclusion in the very systems that criminalize youth of color (such as increased sentencing for hate crimes) under the banner of "we're just like everybody else." A far stray from the radicalism of the early gay rights movement, mainstream "gay issues" have become focused on the right to marry and "don't ask, don't tell" policies in the military, despite the fact that queer youth of color have consistently ranked these at the bottom of their list of priorities of issues that impact their lives.[10] Likewise, the public "face of gay" as white, middle-class men has become a further detriment to queer and trans youth in prison, particularly in the South where queer youth of color are often not "out," and individuals, like in all areas of the country, have difficulty discussing the two issues at the center: race and sexuality.[11] As a result of the invisibility of so many incarcerated queer and trans youth, especially youth of color, juvenile justice stakeholders in the South often mistake queer and trans youth to be white, vulnerable youth usually charged with a sex offense, if they acknowledge them at all. As a result, they assume that any concern for these youth to be coming from white advocates who believe that queer and trans youth have been funneled into a system made for "poor black children;" in other words, into a system that is "OK for some children, but not for others." We must be clear about why we do this work—it is not because *some* children belong locked away at night and others do not—it is because *no* child should be behind bars.

Further, the data tells us that queer and trans youth in detention are equally distributed across race and ethnicity, and comprise 15 percent of youth in detention centers. So far, the data has been consistent among youth in different regions in the United States, including the rural South.[12] Since queer and trans youth are overrepresented in nearly all popular feeders into the juvenile justice system—homelessness, difficulty in school, substance abuse, and difficulty with mental health[13]—the same societal ills, which disproportionately affect youth of color—it should not be surprising that they may be overrepresented in youth prisons and jails as well.

Since incarcerated youth have so few opportunities to speak out, it is critically important for individuals and organizations doing this work to keep a political analysis of the failings of the system at the forefront of the work—particularly the inherent racial disparities in the system—while highlighting the voices of those youth who are most affected and providing vehicles through which they can share their stories.

Despite the targeting and subsequent silencing of queer and trans/gender-non-conforming youth in youth prisons and jails across Louisiana, young people have developed creative acts of resistance and mechanisms for self-preservation and survival. By failing to recognize the ways that young people demonstrate their own agency and affirm each other, we risk perpetuating the idea of vulnerable youth with little agency; victims rather than survivors and active resisters of a brutal system.

Perhaps the most resilient of all youth in prison in Louisiana, incarcerated queer and trans youth have documented their grievances, over and over again, keeping impeccable paper trails of abuse and discrimination for their lawyers and advocates. When confronted by the guards who waged wars against them, one self-identified gay youth let it be known, "You messin' with the wrong punk."

Although prohibited from even speaking publicly with other queer youth in prison, queer and trans youth have formed community across three youth prisons in the state, whispered through fences, and passed messages through sympathetic staff. They have made matching bracelets and necklaces for one another, gotten each other's initials tattooed on their bodies, and written letters to each other's mothers. They have supported each other by alerting advocates when one of them was on lockdown or in trouble and unable to call.

Trans-feminine youth have gone to lockdown instead of cutting their hair and used their bed sheets to design curtains for their cells once they got there. They have smuggled in Kool-Aid to dye their hair, secretly shaved their legs, colored their fingernails with markers, and used crayons for eye shadow. When a lawyer asked her trans-masculine client to dress more "feminine" for court, knowing that the judge was increasingly hostile toward gender-non-conforming youth, her client drew the line at the skirt, fearlessly and proudly demanding that she receive her sentence in baggy pants instead.

Queer and trans/gender-non-conforming youth have made us question the very purpose of the juvenile justice system and holding them behind bars in jails and prisons made for kids. By listening to their voices it becomes apparent that until we dismantle state systems designed to criminalize and police young people and variant expressions of gender and sexuality, none of us will be free. And to my younger client recently released from a youth prison, yes, the world is more beautiful now. Welcome home.

NOTES

1.   M. Larrabee-Garza, *Youth and the US Justice System* (W. Haywood Burns Institute, 2009).

2.   Ibid.

3.   Ibid.

4.   P. Adams, "The History of Louisiana's Juvenile Justice System: Juvenile Justice Policy from 1968 to Present," University of Louisiana at Lafayette, September 21, 2010. http://www.burkfoster.com/juvenile.html.

5.   Office of Juvenile Justice. "History of Juvenile Justice in Louisiana," September 21, 2010. http://www.ojj.la.gov.

6.   W. Ware, "Locked Up and Out: Lesbian, Gay, Bisexual, and Transgender Youth in Louisiana's Juvenile Justice System," Juvenile Justice Project of Louisiana, 2010.

7.   Office of Juvenile Justice. "Demographic Profiles of the Secure Youth Population," September 1, 2010. http://www.ojj.la.gov.

8.   The Louisiana Children's Code Article 728(5) defines "ungovernable" as "the child's habitual disregard of the lawful and reasonable demands of his caretakers and that the child is beyond their control."

9.   *In Re Gault*, 387 US 1, 87 S.Ct. 1428, 18 L.Ed.2d 527 (1967).

10.   FIERCE! "Coming Out, Stepping Up: Organizing to Build the Power of LGBTQ Youth," 2010, p. 11.

11.   E. Bridges, "The Impact of Homophobia and Racism on GLBTQ Youth of Color," Advocates for Youth, 2007.

12.   Angela Irvine, "'We've Had Three of Them': Addressing the Invisibility of Lesbian, Gay, Bisexual, and Gender Non-Conforming Youth in the Juvenile Justice System," *Columbia Journal of Gender and Law*, Vol. 19, 2010 (forthcoming).

13.   K. Majd, J. Marksamer, and C. Reyes, "Hidden Injustice: Lesbian, Gay, Bisexual, and Transgender Youth in Juvenile Courts," The Equity Project, 2009.

HOTEL HELL:

With Continual References to the Insurrection

Ralowe Trinitrotoluene Ampu

In 1997 I had to move out of my girlfriend's studio in Daly City. She'd tempted me away from suburbia with the gift of San Francisco, the gift of not being in Ventura, the gift of gay San Francisco—something that I barely understood then, couldn't imagine, but desired. I was 21 years old, had never lived on my own, and had never successfully held a job for more than three months: I found residence hotels. A lot of residence hotels in San Francisco extort you for shelter charging per hour or night; mine is operated more like a housing project. No hourly rentals here. There's a substantially long waiting list.

The first residence hotel, or SRO (which stands for "Single Resident Occupancy"), that I lived in was the National Hotel. Wait—no, that's not true. I spent two horrible nights at Jefferson Hotel in a room with little unseen scampering creatures prior to that. I must have thought of the National because it's so near Civic Center Station. I was there until '98. I still wish that someone had advised me to wear sandals in the shower, to not walk from the shower barefoot on the carpet of the National Hotel. Practical knowledge. I did figure out was what life might be like no longer in Ventura. For my life finally beginning in San Francisco it was a simple equation. Had desire become wallpaper yet? You had to work to feed yourself and pay rent in San Francisco, where you got to be gay. To explore my desire and sexuality meant to work. I was always going to be OK as long as I remained willing to wash dishes, as I desired to be gay in San Francisco. Was this what my girlfriend wanted? I would never see her again.

So, since I've been in San Francisco, I've only ever really lived in residence hotels. Currently I'm in the Mission District at the Altamont Hotel. It's the best living situation I've ever had. The walls of my room are red. It's Pride Month 2010. The horror of this time of year hasn't gotten to me yet. As I type, my keyboard sits on top of a skinny cast iron vase stand, making a "T" on top of a full sketchbook laid flat so that the lower half nearest me serves as a mousepad—otherwise the mouse sits on the accounting keys to allow space for my palms to rest when typing. The key to my plan was to find a stool, one that folded up to give my 11-by-14 square feet enough space when not in use; I wound up paying for it when plans to shoplift from a prominent, international home-products retailer fell through.

I wonder how the red goes over with the gays in the chat room. I wonder if they notice the aluminum-surface-mounted hydraulic door-closer visible behind me from this angle. I wonder what they think of my hair. It's 9:04PM, Thursday. It's been a very productive day. I've cleaned the algae out of my water bottles, done laundry, took copies of bedbug letters to various bureaucracies. The beat loops, sweeping through my room as I write this, made from a warped record that was mis-sleeved, I thought I would be sampling Irakere's *El Coco*. Later I will write lyrics to it about colonized desire, in bed, after I've vacuumed and filed. I promise. My room looks south. I stand and then sit back to type, as I said, unlike summers in the past, going back to 2005 when I moved into the Altamont, I am not stressed out by the ceaseless Pride Month procession of LGBTs mobbing for the Castro, flowing off the 16th Street Station fresh from SFO with their luggage to go be gay. OK, I don't actually know what terminal they landed in. If I am implicated in the rolling gay luggage and they are no longer stressing me out, does this mean that I have accepted my role as a gentrifier? I watch the cams I've docked. I wonder if the open-mic-night howls of malcontent yuppies in the transit plaza will unduly stress me out. Will I have to dress and leave? Will I not care? I have been kicked from the chat room for not typing anything in the last hour. It's June 10, 9:21PM The sky has finally darkened. The thing just happened for me where you listen to a loop over and over and over and finally you notice something you didn't notice before.

I creep into bed. My thoughts inconspicuously creeping to consider the Creeper. Or the Creep. I'm curious, as I move around my own neighborhood, quiet as crept, scaling back my contact with points of gentrification draw, always on the perimeter, self-excluded, and vigilant. Mission Housing has newly installed wall-mounted bulb-style surveillance cameras on all three floors of the building, one at all four corners of each floor's hallway, looping to the kitchen and back, with a fifth watching the elevator: hence, one above the door to my room. I wonder how many of the rolling-luggage owners on the south side of 16th would consider my fellow neighbors creepy. And of course I consider my own creepiness. All my big ideas. How far is it from creepy to quirky? Remember when people liked quirky? People in my building are in favor of the new surveillance cameras.

I want to quickly think about the science fiction of surveillance in my hotel. Several of us have noted the absence from the lobby guard's booth of the impressive bank of monitors relaying the many surveillance feeds that are allegedly guarding us from ourselves. I've seen a variety of filmmakers exploit the remote cameras for dramatic effect, usually welded on the side of the helmet of the heroic stomping space trooper archetype. It's a marvelous story-telling device, often proving the irrelevance of subjectivity when the contraption fails, cutting out, the signal sharing the same fate of the person it's transmitting from. Though often fatally unreliable to the characters in some usages of the device, it sometimes does manage to capture the grisly final moments. The command center witnessing these live feeds are often prompted to respond, or at the very least are aware that they should have responded sooner, too late. Isn't that the point of the camera—you know, intervention? The cameras in our hotel appear to exist for another purpose. They exist for surveillance alone. To where do they transmit? Do they only record? Could desk clerks be found negligent if they witnessed a criminal activity but failed to intervene?

While I lay in bed trying to identify the Creeper, the obsessive, my thoughts turn to another obsessed figure. Would the dream of the Root Queen be radical to my neighbors? "Files paperwork," a friend explained to me. "Pulls roots." The simple equation that my room is written in code at its root, its bureaucratic mastery detrimental to out-leverage building management from the root, becoming an obsessive rootworker to secure this good fortune of housing in this unlivable city and survive. The beat is looping. Writing about bedbugs, paperwork, paper trail. Letters, correspondences, CCs, notices of violation. Oh, about two weeks ago I noticed a bedbug in my room, the first one since my room became red about five months ago. The new building manager, Gloucester, wrote me back. I'm going to leave the beat looping while I go to Modern Times Bookstore. I often think of creeping the alleys parallel to Valencia, making my way to the store in any way least likely to send off my tendency to lapse into a profound disembodiment from the lie of the left establishment, of San Francisco. Me and my body's role in this. My original gay desire or desire for gayness gives way to the Root Queen's desire to outlast these imperial forces of displacement. I'm fighting so many things, I feel like I'd lose my ability to reason without the stability of my room.

Common perceptions of SROs are that they breed prostitution and drug dealing. Degenerate criminal creeps living in low-rent creepy degeneracy. Luggage rolls past stings, multi-vehicle convergences of badges holding their belts up, twitching at the dispatcher buzzing in and out, as mustachioed and fitted-brimmed detectives shake down insanely dangerous urban parolee creep suspects. DTs dress with inflated bulletproof bravado, looking like severely overgrown suburban middle-school students cutting sixth period. With new athletic shoes, state-issued. Who creates this hysteria? In the civic planning, variables of high-density living lurk a hysterical class war. This hysteria informed the activism that culminated in concessions between SRO-rights advocates and landlords. This concession is called the Uniform Visitor Policy (UVP). This shit went down way before my time but sets enormous limits on my life and everyone else living in SROs. The UVP is legislation enforceable by the cops or the city rent board that says that any person visiting someone in a SRO must present a valid photo ID for admittance. The UVP says that hotel operators may allow tenants no more than eight overnight guests per month (the Altamont graciously allots us two more!). The UVP is basically some cock-blocking bullshit. When I moved in here, people would offer the advice to get around this by using the first of the month to stretch the ten to twenty. Saddest of all, the UVP allows hotel operators to impose a guest curfew. I can't bring people over after 10PM unless they've signed in before. Fucking perfect. What is the point of living in gay San Francisco if I can't bring home trade at night?

I spent five years in North Beach located at the Liguria Hotel on Columbus and Green. The longest relationship I've ever had lasted a year when I lived there. This hotel never enforced the UVP; I want to think that perhaps it may not have even been aware of its existence. Many vital community facilities in residence hotels also have limited hours of access. As in prisons and jails, the understanding is that these containment measures ensure the safety of a community as a whole. All the sex in our year-long relationship took place in my house because it was necessary to remain discreet. Of course these scenarios are not exclusive to the special social stigma that queer and trans people endure. It was clear that my house also functioned as a place of respite. I often wonder what our relationship would have looked like if it were impossible to create a space to share intimacy without rationing time by such a policy?

"Can I read it?"

"No, you can't read it."

"I thought we were friends?"

"No, we're not friends!"

You can't blame someone for not having the same dreams as you.

I want to sing an epic fable of resistance, an elegiac procedural of containment, about the body possibilities of blackness on planet Earth, or at least in San Francisco. It begins on the other block, across Mission at the Redstone Building, in the San Francisco branch office for the Industrial Workers of the World (IWW), where I occasionally slept after our squat in Pacific Heights got busted. I walk back to this fancy neighborhood to remember our angry abolitionist dreaming at 2161 Sutter, now a new condo. Wind and I squatted at this address in a building no longer here, the Mansion. With nearly thirty squatters near the end, the Mansion lasted six months but will burn forever in the soul of the Root Queen. A life-long anti-authoritarian romance acquired a pragmatic immediacy. I saw things that I could actually do in the world. Wind devised a plan to "get off the grid" through networks of mutual aid called the Autonomous Collective.

The Mansion had been part of this, as well as an arrangement we had with a weekly food distribution project through a 501(c)3 called Mission Agenda, down the hall from the IWW. This was supervised by Cluny, and he gave the Autonomous Collective a portion of the food for this. I lived in the squat at a time when I believed that I could challenge power and win. I still believe this. But the introduction of Cluny to the fable of the Root Queen also introduces blackness, introduces Gloucester and S'ym, as well, people I will return to in a moment. Gender and sexuality aren't far behind, nor class. I will always experience the six months in the Mansion as a queer dream because what else could have burned such audacity into existence? What could such a moment of "off the grid" be, other than daring and vibrant difference? My personal desire to dare in this defiant way is also classed in entitlement. This daring dream would affect my relationships to Cluny, S'ym, and Gloucester, question the possibilities of the black body in San Francisco.

Cluny and I went together to the Food Bank to load palettes with donations. Going through dented cans of soup, Cluny would laugh at my insistence on including more vegetable stuff. The Mansion ended around when Mission Agenda went into limbo, and I started fighting with Wind over the recliner in the IWW office for another six months. However, the Code of Federal Regulations says that the Department of Housing and Urban Development may dispense funds for a portion of the lease agreement through the San Francisco Housing Authority to provide shelter to formerly homeless persons at SRO hotels in 24 C.F.R. part 882. A friend got me on the waiting list at the Altamont Hotel, and Cluny worked the front desk guard cage thing. (Cluny himself lived at the Mission Hotel on South Van Ness.) A friend of Cluny's interviewed me—like one of those interviews where the person nods and checks things off, and tells you about bringing you a souvenir on her trip back from Cuba.

The mystery of how it was that Cluny most likely came to be employed at the Altamont wasn't revealed until a little bit later. Cluny had worked at Mission Agenda (MA), and Peter J. explained to me that MA had emerged from the same 1970s anti-displacement organizing that the 501(c)3 that owned our buildings had: Mission Housing Development Corporation (MHDC). MA continued to prioritize fighting poverty while MHDC became a landlord. MHDC has 501(c)3 status but runs its properties through Caritas Management Corporation, a for-profit company. People from Caritas are on the board at MHDC. WTF. Around when I moved into the Altamont, there was a neoliberal internal coup at MHDC that shook out the more activist-minded, who regrouped at Dolores Street Community Services. Thirty years after the fight began, the gentrification of the Mission is nearly complete. My fable shows this class war playing out in the certain roles that individuals take on. I must also take time to clarify the demographics of the Mission District of San Francisco as historically Latino and gentrified white, although mine is incidentally, specifically a fable of blackness.

Future San Francisco Mayor Gavin Newsom was the muse of our sarcastic asides when I moved in; I'd linger near Cluny's guard cage while waiting for the elevator. At the time of my participation with Mission Agenda, I was also doing stuff with Gay Shame—flamboyant clashes with the then-District Supervisor had been our specialty. Most infamous was a direct action in which Gay Shame called out the hypocrisy of the city's LGBT Center. Another horrifying nonprofit-run edifice existing for no other purpose than to be the mundane expenditure of community resources, the Center allowed ruling-class Gavin Newsom to throw them a fundraiser. Gavin Newsom up to this point was most well-known for introducing Care Not Cash, local legislation that would effectively reduce welfare checks from $350 to $59 a month. The Center called the cops on our action; there was a line of police waiting in front, and as soon as Gavin and his wife Kimberly Guilfoyle were safely escorted inside, the cops attacked us, pushing people into traffic and smashing one person's tooth out with a baton. The Center's personnel, including Executive Director Thom Lynch, just watched the cops attack us. Much like the cameras in my building, their own eyes perhaps recording the footage to be transmitted to some military industrial nerve center elsewhere to be carefully analyzed and processed.

Once Gavin became mayor, time wore on and Care Not Cash was gradually implemented. While Gay Shame struggled to prevent the gentrification happening on Polk Street, Gavin became a gay civil-rights champion and Mission Housing turned over and became much worse, just as S'ym became manager of the Altamont and Apollo. A vague hopelessness pervaded the city. S'ym was a tyrant. I can't remember the first fucked up thing S'ym did; maybe it had something to do with him flipping out over me wearing a housecoat to get my mail, but by far the worst of it was how Cluny responded when I crossed S'ym. In 2007, Gavin Newsom was re-elected for a second term, the media grew concerned that the city's black per-capita had dropped to 7 percent, and I told S'ym that I thought I had bedbugs in my room. Then things got really bad, and I had no choice but to start pulling roots, filing paperwork. Cluny started to call me Gavin Newsom.

Did he feel I was ungrateful for his vouch that got me housed? Cluny would complain that I smelled. Cluny wrote me up for inappropriate attire when I did laundry in short shorts. Cluny would turn off fava beans I had cooking in the kitchen. Under the guise of Southern courtesy, Cluny made it a point to strictly abide the UVP's less charming photo ID requirements to repeatedly misgender my guests when addressing them. I mean this is fucking San Francisco. He's lived here at least as long as me. All he had to do was to write their information down and shut the fuck up.

An anti-authoritarian since birth, I was magnetically drawn to the guard cage, Cluny's back turned, pencil scribbling copiously. Did I make out or think I made out the names of my neighbors? Why was this happening? There was another detail to all this logging: the class dilemma of me witnessing Cluny's difficulty with it. If only he were writing anything other than a fucking young adult rat novel in that funky guard cage. I use "funky" with regard to the guard cage's layout. There was special attention paid to how the square shape of it canted off-center 20 degrees to the floor plan of the lobby. Its cant is parallel to the window's line, as the window-door-window triptych arches away from the street. The fence, contributing one wall of the cage, continues this cant, cutting the lobby in half at all but one point: the gate that the guard must buzz. Since living here, ADA requirements have forced management to make the gate open and close on its own, completing the sensation of a cell block. I'm sick of guests complimenting the design of this gate. The funky cant of the guard cage and gate are examples of certain notions in postmodernist architecture of form exceeding function, and I recall the architecture of the LGBT Center. Also, a cafe/laundromat that I washed dishes at. These environments express the neoliberal meanness of style over substance that I will forever associate with San Francisco. I imagine the historical moment when the Altamont's remodel was complete and it was outfitted with all these cheap deconstructivist flourishes, what this style signified. Cluny's placement in this cage might constitute a come-up, and he prides himself on the pain it takes to maintain this station. As if style could transform a prison, the violence of capitalism, the role of a warden. The log's pages were dense, unbroken, obsessive, to-the-margins. At one point, it became evident that nothing was possible in our relationship. This is that moment, Cluny reacts, slams the log shut, shouts, huddles over it, guarding it. I asked if I could read the lobby guard log.

I tried telling Cluny that some component of abolition actually includes opting out of the status quo. It's dicey to insist that total abolition begins and ends with squatting and squatters. Fewer people get hurt, so these liberating dreams rest in better hands than those of a 501(c)3, which can merely dissolve once the struggle is no longer fiscally convenient for their corporate structure. Happens all the time in San Francisco; it's a simple equation. For Cluny, the Root Queen's polymorphous dreaming of a body disentangled from institutional violence through shows of defiance becomes comparable to Gavin. Gavin's PR succeeds, as he owns queer struggle through his marriage moment (running parallel to his gang injunction moment, his homeless-shelter closing moment, and his ICE raids moment).

Cluny's language reminds me of the homophobia that Gay Shame has encountered in the activist community, as he responds to my hotel organizing as a transgression from blackness. MHDC places power figures at racial incongruence to the Mission's historically oppressed demographic, similar to how city bus lines rely on the terror of blackness to prevent backdoor fare evasion. The strategic bodies of MHDC's functionaries all fall out at the Root Queen's will and capacity to self-jeopardize and invoke bureaucracies. This is a pun: I could have Gloucester's job. Why are our dreams so different? The phantasmagoria of these six months at the Mansion are waiting for me in some form at the other end of whatever I am doing here in this room, between the rooms of my neighbors.

History is imprisoned, the facts tracing the placement of bodies in these buildings depoliticized. The current state of relief from the perpetual terror and upheaval I lived in at my home didn't arrive until S'ym was replaced by Gloucester and Cluny took sick leave. What injustices exist when my Southern Californian essay-writing body is able to perform as witness to the systemic disintegration of the Altamont's political context? Cluny recently passed away in Louisiana. I'm reminded of all the conversations I could never cattleprod my father into having. My parents are both black. Pride should be officially over, so I look out the window to check. Yesterday was my mother's birthday; she's 74 years old. My father is 86. They have never seen any room I've lived in since I moved out in '96. I use a pen cap to clip Gloucester's reply to my bedbug letter to my copy of the *Complete Works*, sitting open on a music stand as I prepare to type a response. What does this room mean, what is room for the polymorphous Root Queen? What does the victory of survival cost? It felt as though Cluny conflated blackness with capitulation. Thinking back to when it felt as if Cluny and I had never shared any moment of political solidarity.

Another way in which oppression can be measured is in bedbugs. Headlines expose this crisis of containment, which extends to contain poverty and its bearers as cases of delusional parasitosis on a social scale.

Conspiracy of loneliness or a necessary feature of capitalism, my neighbors are directed to take actions to prevent bedbugs from moving unit to unit on clothing. At a friend's house I notice a bedbug crawl from my sleeve onto their couch. They throw the couch out and contend with a hefty bill for a specially scent-trained detection beagle. I once dozed off on the huge sectional sofas in the lobby of Dolores Street Community Services, orphaned from a suburban memory; now they have all been removed. I have been encouraged many times to discard a plush easy chair I found on the street and keep in my room and have kept in my room from the time I've moved in. Bedbug experts have never discovered any traces in the chair, although I have fallen asleep in it many times. In the future, as it is in prison, all public communal fixtures for the poor will be aluminum.

What are the limits of the prison industrial complex? The extent to which vigilance and ingenuity can resolve to wage against maddening containment and death. This sentence is an affect of entitlement inspired by having dared. Those six months in The Mansion. The singular cultural sequence that brought me to this wherever I am now. The enigma stresses around my room, hegemonic strains on this paradox of cyclical withholding. Revolving between self-enforced banishment and/or rebuked curiosity wandering the shifting and increasingly unfamiliar streets. It's August 2nd. Pride has officially worn off, the sky darkens earlier, my body is again a dispossessed condensing of an embarrassing colonial narrative at frictional dissonance to the class-conflated gay market identity of a citizenry within a specific white civil society on the streets. I'm urged to withdraw, I recoil in terror; cyclical patterns of behavior. This is San Francisco, my idiom merges with hegemony, I enact the familiar colonial narrative of disappearance. Although echoing forced removals, my intentions are again to consolidate my schemes within the sense of my room, my head, this essay. What does the Root Queen have to say? It is now 10:52PM, I have returned from an idea I had while sitting on a bench in the cold mist of Dolores Park, I am back in my room from having gone to see the former squat, the former Mansion, a site of reckoning as concerns the consciousness of land struggles that defines the Root Queen. Is the problem that I don't feel the violence completely crushing the life out of me, haven't endured it for years? I haven't lived enough of the unlivable to understand how to articulate the path to the ideas that emerge within that six-month moment of quasi-liberation in the squat? Resisting the containment of hegemony? The grand structural scheme around our lives that squeezes to the point of death for the sake of profit? Sure anyone can fall off the grid, mostly under less desirable circumstances. As the Root Queen arms paperwork to fight through the contingency of this particular special circumstance, the seemingly contradictory enigmatic engagement with bureaucracy, it is always with the spirit that she is moving toward the memory of those six months, toward something that sincerely bears the shape of total abolition.

The wages are life and death. This essay is about my room in this hotel, the reason I organize around it and also intimately reveals the reason I organize at all. My room is where I am standing right now writing this, and what lives with me is the story of how I got to the room, the reason I am here. If there is any empathy to be felt for my neighbors it must be through the extent to which I can feel that their situations parallel, reflect, mirror mine. Also I can never fully know my neighbor's lives. The contingent of community created through hotel organizing provides a context as we work against the violence of landlording, always moving toward the criminal visioning of the squat. The Root Queen resides this dream in resistance to death.

In November of 2008, Wednesday died. When I first met Wednesday in the elevator I read them as a white woman and adjusted my behavior accordingly. I didn't know how to negotiate the gulf created by legacies of white supremacy, withdrawal, and creating space or creating silence felt like the most judicious manner to deal with the embarrassment of slavery that marks my presentation, the internalized logic of captivity. How I generally deal with white civil society in San Francisco, my presentation as male. I suppose we enacted a gendered drama, heavily racialized by the larger traditional narrative of the Atlantic slave trade, super-imposed upon and gentrifying this historically Latino neighborhood. She was younger than me, perhaps some anxiety was the reasoned premonition of the inevitable displacement that my presence in this hotel set the precedent for. The harshness of these ideas remained unchallenged in silence until I discovered a bedbug in my room. This bed bug was different than the one that Gloucester mentions in his letter to me five paragraphs back. I couldn't catch the one I told Gloucester about, the most recent one. It crawled back down my wall to who knows where. No, this was the one I did catch and carted around with several others to various agencies in a repurposed sterile 80 ML unused urine sample bottle.

I would catch these bugs, show them to management, they would inspect my room and not detect an infestation, and they would decide to not treat my room for bedbugs. At this point there were five bedbugs in the urine sample bottle. It was the final straw, and I began circulating a petition for getting the entire fucking building treated for bedbugs. Wednesday really liked this idea. The spark of a friendship occurred. Suddenly we realized that we had a lot in common. Wednesday really wanted companionship. She was terribly isolated. I discovered that she knew a friend of mine, Durt, and had been involved in Radical Women. She expressed an interest in attending a Gay Shame meeting. There were serious barriers that prevented her from connecting with the world. Having not known her well enough, I can only speculate about the psychological ones, but I can speak directly to the institutional ones. As soon as she helped circulate the petition, Cluny harassed her. One incident concerned the Uniform Visitor Policy. She was asserting the right that allows a visitor to enter the building after the curfew if they are identified to the desk beforehand. She and Cluny got into an argument about it in the lobby, over the phone, and then Cluny left the desk to go knock on Wednesday's door to continue the argument. I don't know the full details of the interaction but the specifics only serve to obscure the essential absurdity one must endure to stay connected with the world outside of this hotel. Wednesday went through so much shit. It was the same shit I went through.

The Root Queen took Gloucester's ass to the Human Rights Commission (I'd asked for Vecna but he chickened out), brought in a pile of three years of cyclical correspondence, brought Peter J., brought Mariana from St. Peters and Jorge from the Mission SRO Collaborative. Gloucester afterwards treated my room, installed baseboards, repaired a hole near the radiator, did my dry-cleaning, replaced my printer broken in 2007 during the first bed bug treatment, and repainted my room red with three gallons of paint that Puck and I purloined from a major building materials emporium. Wednesday was issued a notice to prepare her room for bed bug treatment or be evicted. Wednesday struggled to do this, but her boyfriend/primary support person was being harassed by Cluny. Although she felt welcome when I invited her into my room, she had a lot of anxiety about me entering hers, plus I didn't want to impose upon her relationship with her boyfriend. All my resources were useless to her. Suddenly she died, from a mixture of prescription drugs and alcohol.

I want to mourn Wednesday, but I don't know how.

Unless mourning looks like anger. But what kind of anger destroys the PIC and what kind of anger builds it stronger? I wrote this essay thinking about how prison abolition is articulated in public direct action cultures. My exposure to the cointelbromance of The Insurrection, an ideology formed mostly by 20-something white kids through bad translations of French theory that believe in total negation, has been sadly more extensive than I would have liked, not just through Station 40 (an anarchist space), which I've used as a semi-public living room a few doors down from the lockdown of the Altamont. The Insurrection's abolitionist imagination omits residence hotels, institutionalization, and the capacities of different bodies.

If The Insurrection's vision of abolition doesn't include community building then what is all that rage really about? Following the initial 100-plus Oscar Grant arrests, I asked why anyone hadn't beforehand contacted the National Lawyer's Guild (NLG) to provide legal support to all the random people who joined the march from Fruitvale to downtown. I was told that if the NLG was really on their shit, they wouldn't have needed to be contacted. This recalls a practice in The Insurrection of attacking consensual political discourse as ineffectual and irrelevant: it is the unspoken premise that the essential kernel of Insurrectionary impulse exists natively within every person, waiting for one "moment" of conflict to draw it out, like how super powers are often activated by stress in comic books. The Root Queen's anger swells on this contagious destruction of discourse in a way, which will always carry how helpless I felt with Wednesday's death.

I first began to notice this crypto-nihilist organizing style shortly after CR10, when I got arrested for holding a black flag, running beside a huge banner reading "POLICE OUT OF GREECE! US OUT OF THE WORLD! [punctuation mine]" when we stormed a mall right during the December holiday shopping season. When the initial plan to occupy the abandoned New College building on Valencia in solidarity with the 2008 Greek riots, those gathered decided to just keep going. A week-long riot erupted in Greece following the police shooting murder of 15-year-old Alexandros Grigoropoulos. Nobody seemed interested in having a discussion about this organizing model afterwards. Peter J. and I were of the few people that tried to keep track of the subsequent court dates of the random people who joined our crazy march from the Mission to downtown San Francisco.

This is not an indictment of The Insurrection in particular, but this experience insists on a commitment to the bodies, which participate in the space created in any direct action. What differentiates this vacuum of accountability from other anti-street culture technology, such as public design features that prevent one from sitting or lying down? How must direct actions examine themselves as forces of displacement? These schemes against street culture are continued psychologically through codes like the UVP into my and my neighbors' rooms. The enigmatic strains around my room, debilitated my ability to form reason, incapacitated by breathless anger.

The Insurrection resembles the hegemony I currently endure. What Insurrection wouldn't include those in my hotel? The Insurrection insists on casualties, must they remain the same types of casualties of the status quo? Can there be any other roles for our bodies than casualties? Cluny once said if you don't like living in a place with rules, move out. Move to where? The last time I was at Station 40 I took a copy of *Fire to the Prisons*. You could burn the prisons yet everywhere our bodies are still regulated in deeper institutional ways than we can comfortably admit. Who actually wants to do the work to create an abolitionist world?

I want to end with this anger as a call to action. I want to leave this essay with the Root Queen's irascible resolve against all institutions, to fight. To sustained fighting, waged from my room, the next largest unit of social transformation under my control. Finally.

REGULATORY SITES:

Management, Confinement and HIV/AIDS

Michelle C. Potts

On the night of July 12, 2007, as Victoria Arellano lay in her cell resting after a day spent vomiting, a guard approached her bed, moved her head with his boot and said, "'Hey you, what's wrong with you?'"[1] The other detainees angry with how Victoria had been continuously neglected for weeks, surrounded the guard and began to chant, "ICE, ICE, ICE!"[2] Soon after, a nurse arrived to examine Victoria and stated that there was nothing they could do for her. The only recommendation was that she take Tylenol and water.[3] It's been reported that following this incident as many as eighty detainees refused to get in line for head count and began to shout "Hospital! Hospital! Hospital!"[4] The nurse finally agreed to take Victoria to the infirmary, but two hours later Victoria was back in her cell. Victoria told her cellmate and closest friend Walter Ayala that she had

not been to the infirmary, but instead had been taken to the inmate processing area downstairs.[5] Victoria said she sat there for two hours, being
ridiculed and laughed at before she was finally brought back to her cell.[6]

It wasn't until the following day, July 13, that she was finally taken
to Little Company of Mary Hospital.[7] Walter Ayala described the facility's
continual indifference to her health:

> We made requests to the infirmary asking for help because she was
> so sick. She wasn't eating, she had constant diarrhea, and she was
> vomiting blood. The nurse who responded was totally inhumane. She
> said, "Oh, is that the same person you complained to us about before?
> The doctor hasn't approved any medication. Just give her Tylenol and
> water, and it'll go away." This happened each time we made a request
> for six days.[8]

When finally taken to the hospital, Victoria was given amoxicillin,
an antibiotic, which according to doctors is "not used to treat AIDS-
related infections,"[9] and then sent back to her cell. Up until that point,
inmates had been the only ones taking care of Victoria. They dampened
their own towels in an attempt to reduce her fever, as well as cleaned
up her vomit and helped her to the bathroom. Olga Arellano, Victoria's
mother, reported that Ayala phoned her and said that Victoria was not
eating and was urinating blood, but that the officials were unwilling to
give her medical attention. Ayala told Olga, "Get outside help, but try not
to worry. We'll take care of your daughter."[10]

Victoria returned from the hospital feeling better, but soon after was
again in extreme pain due to intense vomiting and diarrhea. On July 16,
Victoria was taken to the hospital for the last time.[11] ICE finally contacted
her mother who then rushed to the hospital to be with her daughter. On
July 20, 2007, after almost a week of being hospitalized, Victoria died of
pneumonia and meningitis.[12] Olga reported that "Victoria was breathing through a respirator and her foot was chained to the bed while two
guards stood outside her hospital room."[13] She said that she pleaded with
the guard to remove the chain from her daughter's foot. When he finally
agreed, Victoria died minutes later.[14]

Deliberate Denial

Victoria Arellano was a 23-year-old, undocumented transgendered woman who was arrested in Los Angeles on April 9, 2007 for driving under the

influence and without a license.[15] On May 22, 2007, Victoria arrived at the San Pedro Processing Center[16] where, within eight weeks, she would die. Before being detained, Victoria worked in West Hollywood at a supermarket in addition to volunteering at a drug and alcohol treatment facility.[17] It was reported that she was extremely well liked at work and that she even received the "Community Hero" award for the work she did with recovering addicts.

Victoria was HIV-positive and prior to being detained was in good health—before switching to the antibiotic Daposone, Victoria had been taking Bactrim, which helped prevent pulmonary infections from developing into pneumonia. But, during her two months of detainment, she was repeatedly denied Daposone, exposing her to a multitude of HIV/AIDS-related infections.[18] Commenting on the severity of the situation, Steven Archer, the Arellano family lawyer, said,

> They never gave her any of the proper medications for her AIDS diagnosis. They did give her a prescription for a urinary tract infection, but even then, they filled her prescription with the wrong strength, and they never diagnosed the meningitis, even though she had been complaining about headaches, sweats, and generalized pain for weeks. That is what killed her in the end. It was so advanced that it involved her brain, her liver, her lungs, her heart, and a couple of other organs. She died in terrible pain.[19]

Victoria Arellano's official cause of death was AIDS-related infections. But really the cause of death was San Pedro's refusal to give her the medicine, which was sustaining her life. The death of Victoria Arellano at the hands of the state serves as a testament to the ways that transgendered immigrants have a particularly violent relationship with the prison industrial complex.[20] Victoria Arellano's story, and the countless others that we may never hear, points to the need to think about the intersections of gender violence with immigration detention.[21] Her death is but one example illustrating the ways that historically racialized and sexualized groups are subjected to ever increasing criminalization and violence by the state. Ultimately, the death of Victoria expounds the structural violence inherent in and essential to US confinement practices.

Soon after Victoria's death, Human Rights Watch released a report on the lack of medical treatment given to HIV-positive detainees in US detention facilities.[22] The report makes clear that ICE does not meet the required medical standard of care within its detention facilities. This report draws attention to the ways that detention centers are not delivering anti-retroviral regimes, are not monitoring detainees' medical conditions, and are not prescribing medication to those in need. However, only mentioned once in this report are the ways that gay and transgendered detainees are more vulnerable to violence and discrimination when placed in confinement.

Likewise, the numerous articles written on Victoria's death, with the exception of very few, make little to no reference to transgendered people's experiences with incarceration or detention. The horrific treatment of Victoria was attributed solely to the detention facility's failure to provide for the health of its detainees; with no mention of the ways that the dehumanizing treatment was also very much compounded by the fact that she was a transgendered woman, in addition to being HIV-positive. Victoria Arellano, as a transgender detainee, underscores the immediate need for an analysis that is at once critical of prisons and detention centers but also of the ways that the state is managing and policing gender and sexuality inside *and* outside of these institutions.[23]

Medical records showed that at one point during Victoria's time in detention her "T-cell count was 53 and viral load was more than 555,000."[24] How is it possible that she was not prescribed medicine immediately—or at the very least admitted to the hospital to be tested for life-threatening infections? The alienation that Victoria endured operates through the intersecting forms of violence that transgender prisoners face when in confinement, highlighting the ways in which the state is managing queer bodies living with HIV/AIDS. In my attempt to think about what made Victoria's death possible, I am also calling into question the current ways that HIV/AIDS is treated and imagined within the prison. When the signification of HIV/AIDS is compounded with the signification of the prison, one is able to conceptualize the ways that knowledge is produced and sustained.[25]

Walking Bioweapons[26]

A bioterrorism attack is the deliberate release of viruses, bacteria, or other germs (agents) used to cause illness or death in people, animals, or plants.... Terrorists may use biological agents because they can be extremely difficult to detect and do not cause illness for several hours to several days. Some bioterrorism agents, like the smallpox virus, can be spread from person to person and some, like anthrax, cannot.

—US-based Centers for Disease Control and Prevention

"Are you HIV-positive?" asked Bill Gallagher in a live interview with Daniel Allen. Allen responded "yes," and within a week Macomb County prosecutor Eric Smith was seeking the additional charge of "possession or uses of a harmful device," better known as bioterrorism. The ACLU has reported that this is the first documented case in which a terrorism law is being applied to a person with HIV who is also being prosecuted for a felony. Judge Linda Davis sided with Smith's charge of bioterrorism stating that, "Allen knew he was HIV-positive, and he bit the guy…that on its own shows intent."[27] The case of Daniel Allen, much like the case of Victoria Arellano's death, is a reminder of the ways that HIV/AIDS continues to be attached to trans/queer bodies and imagined as a threat to Western society.[28] The trans/queer body with HIV/AIDS is used as a site of regulation and management, imbricating sexuality, gender, and race in ways that make legible who, as well as which acts, falls outside the lines of normative citizenry.[29] In charging Allen with intent to spread HIV through a bite, Fernandis and his attorney constructed Allen's body as a monstrous weapon.

Before being asked to confess his serostatus on television, Allen, who is a 45-year-old self-identified gay man, was already facing two felony charges for aggravated assault and assault with intent to maim. It all began October 18, 2009 in Clinton Township, Michigan, when a neighborhood fight broke out between Winfred Fernandis, Jr. and Daniel Allen. Though it is debated what exactly happened that day, Fernandis alleges that it all began when neighborhood kids kicked a football into Allen's yard. Supposedly Allen kicked the ball away from the kids, and Fernandis, who was watching, decided to confront him. Fernandis reports that it was at this point that Allen scratched him and bit through his lip "while also growling."[30] Fernandis was then hospitalized and required stitches for his lip. Allen however, reported that he never bit Fernandis and that it was actually Fernandis, his wife, and his father who attacked him. The *Michigan Messenger* reported that during a November 2 hearing, Allen and his attorney James Galen, Jr. "presented 37 photographs of injuries, including bite marks to Allen's body."[31] Allen and Galen contend that Fernandis and his family had been harassing Allen for the previous two years with racial slurs as well as incidents of spitting on him. Allen believes the harassment to be because of his sexuality and maintains that the attack on October 18 was a "hate crime."[32]

Due to Allen's felony charges, the case has since been passed on to Circuit Court where Judge Peter Maceroni on June 3, 2010, dismissed the bioterrorism charge due to insufficient evidence. However, Allen still faces two ten-year felony charges for assault with intent to maim and assault to do great bodily harm less than murder.[33] Allen has said that the dismissal of the bioterrorism charge will clear up some of the fears and misunderstandings about HIV.[34] Whether that is true or not, it is clear that post-September 11 rhetoric and the current "war on terror" has made it so that historically racialized groups are now subjected to ever increasing criminalization. It was, after all, the result of a 2007 Michigan Court of Appeals ruling that made it possible for Fernandis and his attorney to charge Allen with bioterrorism. This ruling came out of the case *People v. Antoine Deshaw Odom*. Odom was a HIV-positive prisoner who, on December 12, 2004, allegedly spat blood in the face of a corrections officer during a physical altercation. It wasn't until 2007 that the Michigan Court of Appeals released its ruling stating that "HIV infected blood is a 'harmful biological substance,' as defined by Michigan statute, because it is a substance produced by a human organism that contains a virus that can spread or cause disease in humans."[35]

Michigan's history of criminalizing HIV began, however, well before *People v. Antoine Deshaw Odom*. In 1990, a federal law passed mandating all states to certify that each had a law in place to criminally prosecute people with HIV. By 2000, all fifty states had certified. In 1998, Michigan passed a law making it a felony for any person who knows that he or she is HIV-positive to have sex without first disclosing their HIV status.[36] The HIV disclosure statute and now the bioterrorism law have nothing to do with prevention of HIV, but instead have everything to do with regulation and the stigmatization of HIV and the bodies that live with it.

Much of what this paper seeks to trace is the violence, and at times even ridiculousness, of how HIV/AIDS continues to be treated, imagined, and spoken about in the United States' current social reality. Daniel Allen having been charged with bioterrorism is at once indicative of the state's intent of criminalizing HIV by any means necessary, as well as illustrative of just how little has changed since the '80s and '90s in terms of the ways that HIV is spoken about. I think about the cases of Victoria Arellano and Daniel Allen not as two completely different situations but instead as continuums of one another, both highlighting what is made possible when one falls outside of "responsible" citizenry. The criminalization of HIV is not about prevention, reduction, or "risk," but is instead about the policing of sex, gender, and sexuality. The state appears to believe that the way to deal with HIV is to criminalize it, further stigmatize it, and perpetuate the conflation of HIV/AIDS and queerness. Although it's understandable why Allen would have thought that the dismissal of the bioterrorism charge would help to correct some of the problematic misconceptions of HIV, it seems that the HIV-segregated prisons of Alabama and South Carolina serve as reminders that when it comes to the state, HIV-positive bodies are still weapons, ready and willing to infect at any moment.

Blood

How might we think about the ways that the fiction of blood, like that of the "infected" queer body, have come to be ways of knowing, which in turn enable the violence of the state to become naturalized and even unsurprising? The HIV-segregated prisons in Alabama and South Carolina, much like the bioterrorism charge against Daniel Allen, are made possible not simply by misconceptions concerning how HIV can be contracted and spread; such discursive and material violences are made possible because of much longer histories of violence. Similar to the way that Daniel Allen as a racialized black, gay man could be compared to a monster, blood also has imaginaries floating around it, justifying the placement of prisoners in solitary confinement for twenty-three hours a day as a method of containing and managing bodies that are deemed infectious.

The recently published ACLU report on the segregation of HIV-positive prisoners in Alabama and South Carolina highlighted many of the human rights abuses implicit in housing HIV-positive inmates in separate units. The report states that upon arrival at the prison, each prisoner must undergo a mandatory HIV test and if found positive is ordered into immediate isolation. Once placed in solitary confinement, they are there for anywhere between a week and several months until they are moved to a bed in one of the HIV units. Prisoners in these states are prohibited from access to many in-prison jobs and programs, and South Carolina is the only state that prohibits all access to work-release programs for its HIV-positive prisoners.[37]

In both Alabama and South Carolina, prisoners are prohibited from working in the kitchens, dining halls, and canteens. A poll conducted on Alabama prisoners found that the majority did not feel comfortable being served in the dining halls by HIV-positive inmates. However, misconceptions about HIV transmission are not limited to only those incarcerated. A recent survey by Kaiser Family Foundation showed that fifty-one percent of adults reported that they would feel uncomfortable having their food prepared by someone who was HIV-positive.[38] Prison administrations felt that prohibiting HIV-positive inmates from food service was justified because, after all, prisoners in the general population would not tolerate "openly gay" prisoners handling their food.[39] Thus, Alabama prisons do not allow for any inmates who identify or who are identified as "openly gay" to work in the kitchen, be they HIV-positive or not. The Alabama prison system makes clear that to prevent the spread of a virus is to prevent the spread of queerness. The conflation between disease and sexuality is a remnant of a time when HIV was referred to as the Gay Related Immune Disorder (GRID) and the moment when blood banks became sites of queer contaminated blood rather than sites of gift-giving citizenry.[40] HIV-segregated prisons become the meeting place for sexuality, disease, and deviancy to come together and make the law's violent management of bodies seem like a favor to the nation.

The special units that house HIV-positive prisoners are telling us that blood is something to be feared and kept segregated. AIDS and its historical conflation with queerness has impacted the ways that people imagine particular bodies and has in effect become, as Catherine Waldby and Robert Mitchell write, "a dangerous mediator between clean and infected sectors of populations."[41] Even in light of some pretty heavy criticism, neither Alabama nor South Carolina plans on desegregating their prisons. They claim that segregation prevents HIV transmission between inmates as well as allows for the inmates to have access to special medical needs. Yet Emily Bass, in the 2000 article "Separate but Equal?," reports that no medical care is given to prisoners during time spent in solitary confinement; in addition, prisoners report that they could wait up to six months to receive antiretroviral medication and that instead of being given medication that prevents infection, they are given ibuprofen.[42] Victoria Arellano was given Tylenol in detention, prisoners in the South are given ibuprofen, and very few are being given their antiretrovirals.

Confinement: Solitary and Otherwise

Colin Dayan in her text "Legal Slaves and Civil Bodies" is likewise interested in the implications of blood. Dayan traces the "corruption of blood" in English common law to that of chattel slavery and the modern state prison. Central to her work is the role of the metaphoricity of blood as tied to biological destiny. Dayan elucidates the ways that owning property and capital are essential to ideas of personhood. With this in mind, Dayan thinks about blood and its role in legitimizing particular continuums of torture from chattel slavery to solitary confinement in the supermax prison. Thus, both the law and the metaphor hold the power to render material the conceptual. By tracing the genealogies of words such as blood, infection, and corruption, Dayan illustrates colonial legal history's emphasis on the language of blood and the power it held in denying one's inheritance to property as well as one's right to freedom.

The power of blood points to the genealogies of the prison industrial complex and the role that race plays in the construction of "criminality" and "deviancy." In thinking about what the metaphor of clean versus infected blood made possible, Dayan writes, "Inmates are not warehoused because of their crimes, but for their 'nature,' which makes them 'institutional risks.'"[43] Dayan helps show how we arrived at the supermax prison and solitary confinement as an apparatus of the prison. Dayan likens solitary confinement to a device of death in which subjectivity becomes the privilege of the ones in power. The violence of isolation materializes in both the metaphoric and literal death of HIV-positive people locked in solitary and denied their medication.

This past year, Maria Benita Santamaria, a transgender prisoner, spoke to many of Dayan's concerns in relation to solitary confinement. Santamaria spent six months in solitary confinement in a Virginia jail.[44] Santamaria, who was arrested for drug trafficking, was placed in solitary confinement because jail officials believed that she would be raped by the other male inmates if not placed in protective custody. She told officials that she would risk being hurt in general population rather than stay in isolation. Prior to being arrested, she was taking hormones, but after being detained, she was immediately taken off them. Once in protective custody, Santamaria reported that the jail guards routinely referred to her as "it."[45]

There are no cameras in protective custody, no communication or contact with anyone aside from the officers. Assault and harassment by correctional officers is the reality of solitary confinement. Physical, emotional, and sexual abuse have all been reported by transgender prisoners in and outside of solitary confinement. Isolation also means not being allowed to participate in work-release programs or other skill-based programs, in addition to being denied access to hormones, as was the case with Santamaria, who had been taking hormones for at least two years before being incarcerated.[46]

Placing transgender prisoners in forced isolation limits individuals from finding their place or community in prison and serves only to produce more violence.[47] Solitary confinement like that of HIV-segregated prisons is a tactic of the state to manage and surveil bodies. The different stories about confinement found in this paper speak to the fictions of

HIV and queerness. The death of Victoria Arellano is an obvious example of the violence of the state, but twenty-three hours a day in solitary confinement should be just as central to our analysis. Indeed, the forced idleness of the body and mind is just another violent form of management and regulation.

Imagining More

A month after Victoria Arellano's death, thirty-nine people from her pod, including all identified gay and transgender detainees were transferred to a privately contracted ICE facility and then again transferred to a county jail.[48] They were immediately placed in solitary confinement and many waited weeks to receive their HIV medications. ICE refused to say why they transferred these detainees. Martinez, another cellmate of Victoria's reported that the detainees who had spoken to reporters about Victoria's death and treatment were not allowed access to telephones for two weeks. By October 19, most of the detainees had been transferred back to the San Pedro Processing Center, but that night ICE unexpectedly began to evacuate the entire detention center. By morning, over 400 detainees were transferred to other facilities.[49] ICE detention has not gotten any better since Victoria's death. Earlier this year, ICE publicly admitted to 107 deaths that have occurred in their detention centers since 2003.[50]

We live in a time when some life is not presupposed, and the stories woven throughout this chapter attest to this and to the pasts that haunt them. I began and I will end with the story of Victoria Arellano. In many ways, it is a story that has become spectacularized and one that has gotten many talking in immigrant rights and activist communities. I think it wise to never let her story or the stories of others rest. Her death speaks to the ways that the state can dictate the conditions of possibility for one's life as well as one's death, elucidating the inherent violence of the prison industrial complex. But it also speaks to the possibilities of forming unlikely communities inside of detention and to the possibilities of demanding life when the law has already deemed you dead.

I want to remember Victoria Arellano and her story. I want to remember eighty detainees demanding her right to live. And I realize that in many ways it seems that the case of Victoria Arellano only attests to death, to the ever-increasing violence against transgender detainees and to those with HIV/AIDS. But then I think about eighty men chanting "Hospital! Hospital! Hospital!" and I think that there is substance and even life to be found in these men taking care of Victoria as she died. I don't want to romanticize her death or the ones who were there for those final eight weeks, but I do want to take seriously the solidarity and the care with which they treated her and extend those forms of resistances to the larger project of prison abolition.

NOTES

1. Ben Ehrenreich, "Death on Terminal Island," *Los Angeles Magazine*, Sept. 2008. http://lamag.com/featuredarticle.aspx?id=9366.

    Throughout this chapter I quote from various news stories that have been written on the death of Victoria Arellano. All have been taken from online publications. For the most part they are all similar in the ways that they tell the story as well as in the sources they cite. It has been difficult deciding not only what information is most important from these articles, but also deciding how I personally wish to re-tell Victoria's story.

2. ICE stands for US Immigration and Customs Enforcement. Their official Web site states, "ICE formed in 2003 as part of the federal government's response to the 9/11 attacks, ICE's mission is to protect the security of the American people and homeland by vigilantly enforcing the nation's immigration and customs laws." More information on ICE and its programs is available at http://www.ice.gov/index.htm.

3. Sandra Hernandez, "Denied Medication, AIDS Patient Dies in Custody," *Los Angeles Daily Journal*, Aug. 9, 2007. I am quoting from an online transcript of the *Los Angeles Daily Journal* article from culturekitchen.com. http://www.culturekitchen.com/shreya_mandal/forum/denied_medication_aids_patient_dies_in_.

4. Ehrenreich, "Death on Terminal Island."

5. Ibid.

6. Ibid.

7. Hernandez, "Denied Medication, AIDS Patient Dies in Custody."

8. Leslie Feinberg, "Death of Trans Immigrant in Detention Forges United Protests," *The Workers World*, Sept. 8, 2007. http://www.workers.org/2007/us/trans-0913/index.html.

9. Hernandez, "Denied Medication, AIDS Patient Dies in Custody."

10. The Associated Press of Mexico City, "HIV-Positive Migrants Accuse US of Neglect," *USA Today*, Aug. 4, 2008. http://www.usatoday.com/news/world/2008-08-04-AIDS-mexico_N.html.

11. Ehrenreich, "Death on Terminal Island."

12. Ibid.

13 Luciente Zamora, "Victoria Arellano: Shackled and Denied Life-Saving Medi-

cine," *Revolution*, No. 103, Oct. 7, 2007. http://www.rwor.org/a/103/victoria-arellano-en.html.

14. The Associated Press of Mexico City, "HIV-Positive Migrants Accuse US of Neglect."

15. Ehrenreich, "Death on Terminal Island."

16. There are three different types of ICE facilities. A Service Processing Center such as the one where Victoria was detained is an ICE-run detention facility. There are also Contract Detention Facilities, which are detention facilities operated by independent contractors. Intergovernmental Service Agreement facilities are facilities in which ICE has an agreement with the given State, territory, or political subdivision to run confinement and detention services. More information is available at http://www.ice.gov/doclib/PBNDS/pdf/definitions.pdf.

17. Feinberg, "Death of Trans Immigrant in Detention Forges United Protests."

18. Ibid.

19. The Associated Press of Mexico City, "HIV-Positive Migrants Accuse US of Neglect."

20. See Angela Y. Davis, *Are Prisons Obsolete?* (New York: Seven Stories Press, 2003) for a more detailed account of what is currently understood as the prison industrial complex. Davis writes, "The notion of a prison industrial complex insists on understandings of the punishment process that take into account economic and political structures and ideologies, rather than focusing myopically on individual criminal conduct and efforts to 'curb crime'" (85).

21. See David Manuel Hernandez, "Pursuant to Deportation: Latinos and Immigrant Detention," for more on the criminalization and surveillance of Latinos in the United States. He makes important connections between post-September 11 security discourse and subsequent anti-immigrant sentiment.

22. Human Rights Watch, "Chronic Indifference: HIV/AIDS Services for Immigrants Detained by the United States," Vol. 19, No. 5, Dec. 2007: G. http://www.hrw.org/en/node/10575/section/6.

23. See the Sylvia Rivera Law Project, "It's War in Here: A Report on the Treatment of Transgendered and Intersex People in New York State Prisons" (2007). This report deals specifically with transgendered confinement. Although the report does not specifically focus on detention centers, its specificity as to why such a disproportionate number of trans people are currently incarcerated is important when thinking about which subjects are left out of conversations concerning the prison industrial complex. The report can be accessed at http://srlp.org/resources/pubs/warinhere.

24. Ehrenreich, "Death on Terminal Island." As Ehrenreich notes in his piece, Victoria's white-cell count was incredibly low. Generally a healthy person has a

white blood-cell count of about 2,000. Full-blown AIDS usually has a white-cell count of anywhere between zero and 250.

25. See Paula A. Treichler, *How to Have Theory in an Epidemic* (Durham, N.C.: Duke University Press, 1999) for more on the signification of AIDS. Treichler's argument thinks about the AIDS epidemic as an "epidemic of signification," which I take to mean that AIDS is a linguistic construct with multiple meanings and metaphors attached to it. In particular, Treichler is interested in the ways that AIDS became constructed as a "gay disease" and the consequences that this continues to bear on scientific research as well as on discourses surrounding sexuality.

26. Hannah Clay Wareham, "HIV: Assault with a Deadly Weapon?" *Bay Windows*, Nov. 22, 2009. http://www.aegis.org/news/bayw/2009/BY091105.html. With regard to the 2007 Michigan Court of Appeals, Wareham writes, "The decision classified HIV-positive Michigan residents as walking bioweapons."

27. Jameson Cook, "HIV-Positive Biter Faces 3 Felonies," *The Macomb Daily*, Nov. 3, 2009. http://www.macombdaily.com/articles/2009/11/03/news/srv0000006746974.txt.

28. See Treichler, *How to Have Theory in an Epidemic*. See also Joe Rollins, *AIDS and the Sexuality of Law: Ironic Jurisprudence* (New York: Palgrave Macmillan, 2004).

29. For more on the racialized construction of the monster post–September 11, see Jasbir Puar and Amit Rai, "Monster, Terrorist, Fag: The War on Terrorism and the Production of Docile Patriots," *Social Text* 72, Vol. 20, No. 3, Fall 2002.

30. Ibid.

31. Todd A. Heywood, "State Lawmakers Question Terrorism Charges for HIV-positive Man," *The Michigan Messenger*. Nov. 10, 2009. http://michiganmessenger.com/29816/state-lawmakers-question-terrorism-charges-for-hiv-positive-man.

32. Cook, "HIV-Positive biter faces 3 felonies."

33. Jameson Cook, "Judge Dismisses Bio-terrorism Charge Against HIV-positive Man," *The Macomb Daily*, June 3, 2010. http://www.macombdaily.com/articles/2010/06/03/news/doc4c07dc5416c93197632281.txt.

34. Ibid.

35. State of Michigan Court of Appeals, 3. http://coa.courts.mi.gov/documents/opinions/final/coa/20070809_c267867_80_144o.267867.opn.coa.pdf.

36. Todd A. Heywood, "Michigan's HIV Disclosure Law: Overly Broad and Open to Abuse," *RH Reality Check*, May 9, 2009. http://www.rhrealitycheck.org/blog/2009/05/01/michigans-hiv-disclosure-law-overly-broad-and-open-abuse.

37. ACLU and Human Rights Watch, "Sentenced to Stigma: Segregation of HIV-

Positive Prisoners in Alabama and South Carolina," April 2010. http://www.aclu.org/prisoners-rights/sentenced-stigma-segregation-hiv-positive-prisoners-alabama-and-south-carolina.

38. See Kaiser Family Foundation, "2009 Survey of Americans on HIV/AIDS: Summary of Findings on the Domestic Epidemic." http://kff.org/kaiserpolls/upload/7889.pdf.

39. ACLU and Human Rights Watch, "Sentenced to Stigma: Segregation of HIV-Positive Prisoners in Alabama and South Carolina" (33).

40. See Catherine Waldby and Robert Mitchell, "Blood Banks, Risk, and Autologous Donation" in *Tissue Economies: Blood, Organs and Cell Lines in Late Capitalism* for more on blood banks.

41. Ibid., 41.

42. Emily Bass, "Separate but Equal? Weighing the Pros and Cons of Quarantine," *HIV Plus*, No. 6, January 2000. http://aidsinfonyc.org/hivplus/issue6/report/segre.html.

43. Colin Dayan, "Legal Slaves and Civil Bodies," *Nepantla: Views from the South*, Vol. 2, No. 1, 2001: 22.

44. Freeman Klopott, "Va. Transgendered Inmate Removed from Lockdown," *The Washington Examiner*. Jan. 3, 2010. http://www.washington-examiner.com/local/crime/Va_-transgendered-inmate-removed-from-lock-down-8705670-80436387.html.

45. Ibid.

46. Important to keep in mind are the ways that the prison segregates according to the gender binary. The prison as a form of gendered punishment enforces normative expression of gender and seeks to punish any person who does not align with or live within the normative confines of gender self-expression. Depriving trans prisoners of hormones and medication is very much a part of incarceration. For a more detailed account on this, see Alexander L. Lee, "Nowhere to Go but Out: The Collision Between Transgender and Gender-Variant Prisoners and the Gender Binary in America's Prisons," 2003.

47. For more on the violence against trans prisoners and the importance of community and solidarity, see Gabriel Arkles, "Safety and Solidarity Across Gender Lines: Rethinking Segregation of Transgender People in Detention," *Temple Political and Civil Rights Law Review*, Vol. 18, No. 515, 2009.

48. Ehrenreich, "Death on Terminal Island."

49. Ibid.

50. Nina Bernstein, "Officials Hid Truth of Immigrant Deaths in Jail," *The New York Times*, Jan. 9, 2010. http://www.nytimes.com/2010/01/10/us/10detain.html?_r=1&ref=nyregion.

AWFUL ACTS AND
THE TROUBLE
WITH NORMAL

Erica R. Meiners

In my Canadian hometown, where the store in my dad's neighborhood, Iron Mountain, still sells WD-40 next to the tampons, Clifford Olson "snatched up girls like you," my principal Mr. Gayle told my best friend Carla and me. "He will capture you and then…"

Olson permeated the spring and summer of 1981. School assemblies lectured us on how to recognize the Car of the Stranger. The ice rink, parks, and other public spaces were closed, and the yellow-striped Royal Canadian Mountain Police were everywhere.

One afternoon that summer, Carla and I were illicitly at Mount Crescent Elementary School on the tire swing, and she told me that her uncle— she did not use the words molested or rape or even sex. In fact, I don't even remember what she said. I just remember that day, the dizzy circles on the tire swing, and awkwardly now, that I thought she was bragging.

Caught in "the biggest manhunt in the country," Olson was picked up in late summer 1981, and I later watched Carla's uncle buy her a shot for her birthday.

Hunts for sex offenders and serial killers are a soundtrack to my life.

Registries

Prior to the US Supreme Court's 2003 six-to-three decision in *Lawrence and Garner v. State of Texas*, ruling anti-sodomy laws unconstitutional, sodomy, or simply the intent, was a crime in many states. While penalties varied, a conviction on a sodomy-related charge carried an average maximum prison term of ten years. For example, legal scholar Robert Jacobsen[1] documents that over a three-year period in Los Angeles in the early 1960s, 493 men were arrested for consensual sodomy, with 257 convicted, and 104 imprisoned.[2] While forms of harassment, surveillance, and corresponding data collection by police and other state agencies were not made available to the public, keeping records of "sex offenders"— a malleable category that included "known homosexuals"—flourished throughout urban centers in the United States during the 1940s. Research by historians William Eskridge[3] and Margot Canaday[4] also documents that police collected and centralized information on other charges levied against men perceived to be engaging in non–gender-normative or same-sex sexual practices and activities, including "lewd conduct," "lewd vagrancy," and "outraging public decency," and targeted "fairies, inverts, and cross dressers."

In 1947, as historian William Eskridge documents in *Dishonorable Passions*, the California legislature "unanimously passed a law to require convicted sex offenders to register with the police in their home jurisdictions," and Chief Justice Warren (the author of the Brown desegregation decisions) requested that this law be extended to include those convicted of "lewd vagrancy" to force more homosexuals to register.[5] In 1950, the FBI was collecting from the states information, including fingerprints, for those charged with sodomy, oral copulation, lewd vagrancy (and serious crimes against minors) to create a "national bank of sex offenders and known homosexuals."[6] The category of sex offender was never applied uniformly. For example, "in the 1930s, when only 6 percent of its adult male population was non-white, 20 percent of New York City's sex offenders were black."[7]

As cumbersome, private documents internal to police forces, these practices diminished as the century progressed. Police harassment was less necessary if formal civil penalties, employment, and housing all regulated gender and sexual practices, and by 1953, Eisenhower had barred all gays and lesbians from holding federal employment.[8] Canaday writes that this state regulation was gendered (and racialized), as tracking female bodies (except for those perceived to be engaged in sex work) held less interest for the state: "Male perverts mattered so much more to the state because male citizens did" and apartheid already regulated non-white bodies through prohibitions on citizenship, mobility, employment, and education.[9]

Yet state regulation and harassment by punitive agencies fostered resistances. In tandem with civil rights and gay and lesbian liberation movements, as the homosexual began a tentative move away from "sex offender." By the 1980s, the category of sexual offender and the corresponding structures of surveillance and documentation identified a new target in child predators. Judith Levine[10] and Phillip Jenkins[11] suggest that the phenomenal expansion of sex offender registries (SOR) in the United States to track those convicted of child-related sex offenses was due to multiple factors: the explosion and fetishization of "stranger danger" and child abductions in mass media, escalating and racialized fears of public urban spaces, and the growing anxieties of adults about that achingly empty signifier, "the child."

In the mid-'90s, weighed down with the precious ennui afforded only by universities and cheap marijuana, I lived, worked, and hung out in bars near the "low track" on the downtown East Side of Vancouver.

Like the spring snow melt, female sex workers disappeared.

These women never made the evening news or the front page of the paper, but their photos, usually from high school, were stapled to telephone poles around the downtown East Side.

Sixty-three had disappeared by 2004. Many were indigenous, not from the city, and poor.

Tanya Holyk, 23, last seen October 1996
Olivia Williams, 22, last seen December 1996
Stephanie Lane, 20, last seen March 1997

Despite candle vigils and marches, the police's tepid non-response throughout the 1990s indicated that these were disposable women who did not merit the full protection, let alone the basic interest, of police. If these women got hurt, they were partially culpable. They were not innocent, and they were probably never children. And how do you know they were missing? These kinds of girls just run away.

Safe Spaces

In Illinois, the 1986 Habitual Child Sex Offender Registration Law established the first public registry for those convicted of child sexual offenses. In the subsequent twenty years, registration requirements have been expanded to include a broader range of offenses, including essentially all sex offenses and other crimes against children. Over the years, SORs also increased the information available to the public (the Illinois State Public Sex offender Web site was up by 1999) and amplified the restrictions attached to registration. In 1996, in direct response to the abduction and murder of twelve-year-old Polly Klaas in 1992 and seven-year-old Megan Kanka in 1994 by two men with prior convictions for violent sexual crimes, the federal government passed Megan's Law, establishing a public national sex-offender registry.

SORs require those convicted of a range of offenses, from public indecency and lewdness to aggravated child sexual assault, to register every ninety days for at least ten years. SORs also restrict employment, housing, and mobility, particularly in public spaces where children congregate. The restrictions are specific and local and vary across states and even between cities. As of 2010, registered sex offenders in Illinois were prohibited from living within "500 feet of a school, playground, or any facility providing programs or services exclusively directed toward people under age 18." In Iowa, convicted sex offenders cannot reside within 2,000 feet of schools or places where children congregate, thus effectively prohibiting anyone on the SOR from living in an urban center. SOR restrictions, like most laws, tend to be selectively enforced. For example, a project that I am affiliated with in Chicago has provided temporary housing for a few registered sex offenders for a number of years. The school nearby is more than 500 feet away when measured by the street but under 500 feet when measured "as the crow flies." As the neighborhood gentrifies (and whitens up), the shelter's proximity to a school has been explicitly questioned, though I suspect that none of the new homeowners would ever enroll their children in this school.

Through these mobility and public-space restrictions, SORs construct meanings about what kinds of public space are dangerous for children, where children are most at risk or vulnerable, and by default, what kinds of spaces are safe or risk-free. With the Bureau of Justice documenting that 70 percent of all reported sexual assaults against children are committed in a residence, usually the victim's, this emphasis on "public spaces," namely parks and schools, is clearly misplaced.

SORs and the construction of sex offenses are flexibly deployed in other ways. Journalist Jordan Flaherty highlighted that in 2010, sex workers in New Orleans, Louisiana (often transwomen and/or women of color) were charged under a state-wide law that makes it a crime against nature to engage in "unnatural copulation" (committing "crimes against nature" or acts of oral or anal sex[12]). Conviction requires registration as a SO and to have "sex offender" stamped on their driver's license. The deployment of these laws in New Orleans has little to do with public safety; rather these laws are used to harass sex workers and to "protect" the interests of local businesses and homeowners.

While strangers do hurt children, SORs create a culture in which the perceptions of violence and harm to children and youth occur outside of the child's life. The Bureau of Justice clearly identifies that "acquaintances," and then family members, are the highest risk category for sexually assaulting children, and for children under 18, strangers are consistently the *least likely*—generally significantly less than 10 percent—to be perpetrators of sexual violence.[13] Given that these are reported incidents to law enforcement, and that the sanctions for children (or anyone economically or otherwise dependent) against identifying family or friends as the perpetrators of violence are high, these numbers are conservative.

The real fear for women and children are not strangers, but the men they know.

In 1999, I moved to Chicago, still a full three years before Robert Pickton would be charged with the murders of twenty-seven women, almost all sex workers, from the downtown East Side.

I hauled myself to the neighborhood "block club meeting" (where the debates are usually about who has the most garbage on their lawn), because my landlord is renovating my apartment and I mistakenly think that this group can be effective.

The people in the room, mainly women, mostly mothers, murmured indignantly as a homemade flyer with the title "Child Molester" is distributed in the cool church basement. The discussion, righteous, is about what to do.

Picket his building? Get him to move out!
Leaflet and poster the entire neighborhood?
Absolutely warn the school.

As I looked around the room, I wanted to ask, Which one of you lives in the apartment where I hear a woman scream almost every night? Are you the one I saw being dragged from your car by your hair, in broad daylight, and we knocked on your door and were told it was "nothing?"

What does it mean that we are so willing to notice certain kinds of violence, to picket and organize, but the other, equally devastating and even more intimate harm, is so carefully protected?

Beyond the Good, the Bad, and the Innocent

While problematizing SORs, I do not minimize the persistent, pervasive violence against women, girls, queers, and trans-folk—those viewed as three-fifths human, those without correct documentation, and others on the margins. Rather, the state has always valued the lives and "innocence" of specific children and women more highly, and this is reflected at every level of our systems, from child welfare policies to drug laws, in word and in application.

From reproductive rights for white women that were dependent upon the sterilization of women of color and the premise of their sexual unfitness and immorality, to miscegenation laws that protected the constructed category of whiteness through the criminalization of "inter-racial" marriage and sexual acts, to the lynching of black men to preserve the safety and the racial purity of white women, the sexual innocence of select white women is enshrined in policies and written into the very conception of the nation-state itself as many, from Ida B. Wells[14] to Andie Smith,[15] continue to document. The United States has typically passed laws that protect *their interests* in women's bodies and sexualities; interests explicitly shaped by white supremacy, investments in hetero-gender-normativity, class, and ability.

Just as drug-free zones around schools do not reduce youth drug usage but instead criminalize entire communities as the Justice Policy Institute has identified[16]; and as zero tolerance policies in schools, "tough on crime" laws, and the "war on terror" don't make us any safer, expanding SORs does not reduce persistent, often state-sanctioned violence against women, girls, and others. These laws and policies disproportionately impact poor people and others already under surveillance and targeted by the state.

In a nation without an adequate or affordable childcare system, no universal healthcare, expensive to prohibitive costs for higher education, and a minimum wage that is not a living wage, there are no *registries* for the officials and employers who routinely implement policies that actively damage all people, including or even *particularly* children.

SORs are expanding. Civil commitment laws, passed in a dozen states by 2006 and upheld by the Supreme Court in a 2005 decision, aim to geographically detain and segregate certain categories of sex offenders, *indefinitely*, after release.[17] Escalating housing and employment prohibitions make life difficult for those convicted of sex offenses and, most centrally, do nothing to make our communities safer or better. And, in a nation of compulsory heteronormativity and cissexism, what is *normal* sexual and gender development?

The relative silence from anti-prison activists, feminists, and queers regarding carceral expansion is troubling. Historically, assimilation, or the "price of the ticket" to borrow from James Baldwin,[18] is often promised at the cost of participating in the demonization of those of lesser value. Yet colluding with this framework does nothing to make our lives safer. We need people to ask questions and to dialogue. What are the factors that support and naturalize the expansion of the SOR? Which children (and adults) benefit from the construction of the child as vulnerable and in need of protection and surveillance? How do SORs protect those with the most power and privileges? How do we, especially those most impacted and harmed, humanize the lives of those convicted, or not, of sexual offenses? How might public dialogues about these questions shift ideas about *health* and *safety* in homes and communities, and even perhaps, shift conceptions about *childhood, sexuality, family and gender*?

This analysis is not new. Organizations and individuals are working to make changes, including generationFIVE, that is dedicated to ending violence against children in five generations without state intervention and Critical Resistance that works towards ending the nation's prison industrial complex and for prison abolition. These organizations, and many other small, local, and unfunded collaboratives, work in communities to create alternatives without stigmatizing populations and without using and legitimating punitive systems. This is much easier to write about than to practice.

Martin, the part-time building maintenance worker, can't find anywhere to live. Landlords won't take him, he doesn't have enough money, or there is a nearby school or park. Stammering with anxiety, he blurts his crisis, continuously, to those nearby.

Martin is no friend of mine. I rarely make eye contact aside from a breezy and too loud "hello." I justify my exclusion with the rationale that I have known too many women in my life that have survived violence from men. When he has his housing crisis I think that someone else will assist him, and of course, in our posse of deviants (queers, nuns, on-again-off-again sex workers) someone else listens. Undereducated, poor, and with a personal history of violence, I know that my exclusion of Martin is illogical, and possibly harmful, yet of all the things to unlearn in my life, somehow this is not a priority.

NOTES

In honor of a life of fierceness and brilliance—Carla Salvail 1969–2005 An earlier version of this piece was originally published in AREA Chicago (2007).

1. Robert Jacobson, "'Megan's Laws': Reinforcing Old Patterns of Anti-Gay Police Harassment," *Georgetown Law Journal*, Vol. 87, No. 7, 1999: p. 2431–2473.

2. Ibid., p. 2433.

3. William Eskridge, *Dishonorable Passions: Sodomy Laws in America, 1861–2003* (New York: Viking, 2003).

4. Margot Canaday, *The Straight State: Sexuality and Citizenship in Twentieth Century America* (Princeton, N.J.: Princeton University Press, 2009).

5. Eskridge, p. 82.

6. Ibid.

7. Ibid., p. 81.

8. John D'Emilio and Estelle Freedman, *Intimate Matters: A History of Sexuality in America* (Chicago: University of Chicago Press, 1998): p. 293.

9. Canaday, p. 13.

10. Judith Levine, *Harmful to Minors: The Perils of Protecting Children from Sex* (Minneapolis: University of Minnesota Press, 2002).

11. Phillip Jenkins, *Moral Panic: Changing Conceptions of the Child Molester* (New Haven: Yale University Press, 1998).

12. Jordan Flaherty, "Her Crime? Sex Work in New Orleans," *Colorlines*, Jan. 13, 2010. http://www.colorlines.com/archives/2010/01.

13. Howard N. Snyder, "Sexual Assault of Young Children as Reported to Law Enforcement: Victim, Incident, and Offender Characteristics." *Bureau of Justice*

Statistics, July 2000.

14. Ida B. Wells-Barnett, *On Lynchings* (Amherst, N.Y.: Humanity Books, 2002).

15. Andrea Smith, *Conquest: Sexual Violence and American Indian Genocide* (Boston: South End Press, 2005).

16. Greene, K. Pranis, and J. Ziedenberg, *Disparity by Design: How Drug-Free Zone Laws Impact Racial Disparity—and Fail to Protect Youth* (Washington, D.C.: Justice Policy Institute, 2006).

17. A. Feuer, "Pataki Uses State Law to Hold Sex Offenders After Prison." *The New York Times*, Oct. 4, 2005: p. B4.

18. James Baldwin, *The Price of the Ticket: Collected Nonfiction, 1948–1985* (New York: Martin's Press, 1985).

HOW TO MAKE PRISONS DISAPPEAR:

Queer Immigrants, the Shackles of Love, and the Invisibility of the Prison Industrial Complex

Yasmin Nair

Before I knew it, I was handcuffed and taken away like a criminal. I was put in a van with two men in yellow jumpsuits and chains and searched like a criminal, in a way that I have only seen on television and in the movies.
—Shirley Tan

Shirley Tan was describing her experience of being woken up early one morning in her Pacifica, California, home by Immigration and Customs Enforcement (ICE) agents for violating a court order for her deportation.[1] She was speaking to a special congressional hearing United States Senate Committee on the Judiciary about the need for the Uniting American Families Act (UAFA), legislation meant to secure the right of lesbians and gays to sponsor their partners for immigration.[2]

By any standards, Tan's testimony was a unique moment in the history of the Senate. Facing a row of Senators, including Committee chairman Patrick Leahy, and surrounded by portraits of former presidents, Tan, a lesbian and an undocumented immigrant, appeared in a court-like setting with her twin sons and very butch-looking partner, Jay Mercado.[3]

Tan's account of what she felt was clearly a violation and disruption of her life was strategically meant to drive home the point that she, an exceptional and all-American immigrant, had done everything necessary to deserve citizenship and nothing to deserve the treatment meted out to her—except for the slight wrinkle of her legal status. According to her, the ankle bracelet that the state made her wear worsened her experience. So ashamed was she of the bracelet, she told the Senators, that she went out of her way to hide it from her children.

As Tan delivered her testimony, a different case was unfolding in Chicago. Rigo Padilla was fitted with an ankle bracelet and served an order of deportation in early 2009, but, unlike Tan's story, his received comparatively little sympathy until the late fall of 2009 when he was finally able to corral public support for his case.

Padilla was brought to the United States in 1994, at the age of six, by his undocumented Mexican parents. In January 2009, he was stopped on a traffic violation and was also charged with driving under the influence of alcohol. He had no driver's license and his only form of identification was from the Mexican consulate; he was taken to Chicago's Cook County Jail. Once there, he met with a public defender who asked him about his immigration status (a question that had no bearing on the DUI case and that the defender had no right to ask). After finding out that Padilla was undocumented, the defender left. Minutes later, Immigration and Customs Enforcement (ICE) agents entered the room and took him to a federal prison. All of this happened despite the fact that Chicago claims to be a "sanctuary city" where city employees are legally barred from enforcing federal laws.

Padilla was informed that his best chance was to seek voluntary departure. It took him weeks to find an attorney to represent him. He even wrote an open letter to Illinois Senator Dick Durbin, asking for clemency until the Dream Act might come into effect (the Act would grant relief to the undocumented children of immigrants).[4] But the fact that he had been apprehended under a DUI appeared to have turned people off the case. A friend of Padilla told me that Durbin's office made a categorical statement to this effect: "We only work with the good immigrants, the ones who don't break laws."

Served with an order to leave the country in December, Padilla and his friends set about drumming up public support for him. Finally, at the last minute and after a long and sustained media campaign, with the help of thousands of individuals and many activist groups, including Gender JUST (of which I am a member), Padilla gained a one-year deferment of his deportation. If deported, he would have had to return to a country he had not visited since his departure and be separated from his parents and siblings. If he had resisted deportation, he would have been arrested and detained, possibly indefinitely, or flown out of the country.

In contrast, Tan brought her citizen partner (Mercado is originally from the Philippines but a naturalized citizen) and her two sons, native-born US citizens, to the hearing. They were even featured in a *People* magazine two-page spread, which included photos of the family in their comfortable Pacifica home (Mercado works in the information technology industry, and the family is well off). Padilla, worried about his undocumented parents, did not and does not discuss them. In an interview, he politely declined to tell me anything about them, concerned that the slightest detail might provide ICE with clues as to their whereabouts. While the coverage about Tan emphasized the possible pain of separation from her family, little was said about the pain that Padilla's family might feel at seeing him taken away from them. Tan, despite her undocumented status, garnered enough attention that Senator Diane Feinstein sponsored a private bill in her name. Illinois US State Representative Jan Schakowsky also introduced a private bill for Padilla, but this came much later, in the fall of 2009.[5]

How do we account for two such diametrically opposed accounts and experiences of undocumented immigrants? How is it that Padilla, who is not queer, was treated with disdain, at least initially (and he still elicits the ire of many), while Tan, an out lesbian with a significantly butch and consequently gender-non-conforming partner was able to fly to Washington, D.C. and address a bevy of senators? If we are to follow the established logic of the heteronormative state, it is Tan who should have been vilified as a lesbian *and* undocumented immigrant. Why did she instead get the kind of special treatment accorded to her?

The exceptional treatment accorded to Shirley Tan is symptomatic of the ways in which the issue of LGBT immigration separates some gay and lesbian identities (and to a much lesser extent trans people), the kind that are recognizable as synonymous with class and privilege, from immigrant identities. In addition, this separation renders prison invisible. Tan's shock at being lumped with inmates in yellow jumpsuits reflects the ways in which the realities of prison have been dematerialized for gay and lesbian immigrants like her. That dematerialization is furthered by the discourse around LGBT immigration, which only emphasizes what the UAFA already did up front, and the bonds of "love," and erases the reality that gays and lesbians are also workers.[6]

At the time of this writing, immigration activists of all stripes are calling for much-needed reform to the current immigration system. But increasingly these calls for reform are being made within affective calls to reward the bonds of immigrant families instead of emphasizing the truth that most Americans seem unwilling to confront: that the crisis in immigration will not go away as long as we enable the severe exploitation of immigrants that enables America's neoliberal—and severely worsening—economy. The excessive priority given to Shirley Tan and her family signals a neoliberal state that strategically deploys sexual identities and the affective discourses around them as tools with which to build up new categories of exclusion while erasing the realities of the exploitation of labor that enables the status quo.

Padilla's experiences are more typical of what happens to undocumented immigrants caught by ICE. Not only are ankle bracelets par for the course, but most undocumented immigrants are raided in their workplaces or homes and hunted down brutally and "disappeared." Until 2007, undocumented parents and children were incarcerated at the infamous Texas Hutto Center, where children were threatened with separation from their families as a disciplinary measure. Tan, in contrast, was able to return to her suburban home and family. Padilla's arrest was predetermined by a history of the state's surveillance and instant deportation of undocumented people; his DUI arrest formally made him a "bad" immigrant, but his personal history as a young Mexican had already marked him as such.[7]

Many undocumented people, for instance, become such by simply living here on expired visas, and, for that reason, what many describe as a "broken system" is in fact an advantage for those who need to remain under the radar. At the same time, the lack of access to benefits like healthcare and the real dangers of being exposed while traveling or working make the life of an undocumented person fraught with peril on a daily basis. The undocumented "alien" is always a prospect for arrest, by sheer dint of the multiple webs of laws and surveillance mechanisms that exist primarily to make the presence of the undocumented visible. But all this can be significantly alleviated by circumstances of class and access, making the experiences of undocumented immigrants vastly different depending on factors like education and job history. In effect, the two ankle bracelets stood in for different things. By Tan's account, the bracelet was a horrifying aberration, a wrinkle in her self-described "almost perfect" existence. In Padilla's case, the bracelet was an inevitability, not something that he expected but something that no one would question.

Tan's Story, or, How We Got Here

Tan first came to the United States from the Philippines in the mid-1980s on a vacation designed as a graduation present from her father, who accompanied her. Once here, she met and fell in love with Jay Mercado and returned when her six-month tourist visa expired. Upon returning to the Philippines, she found out that the man who had murdered her sister and mother ten years ago had been released; her fear of him compelled her to go to Jay, to a place "where [she] knew [she] would be safe." In 1995, she hired an attorney to apply for asylum and legalize her stay in the US Then, she claims, "When my application was denied, my attorney appealed the decision. I did not know it, but my appeal had also been denied. All the while Jay and I went about building our lives together."

Tan emphasized the harmony of their lives and how they fit into every (stereotypical) image of the all-American family: "Our family has always been like every American family and I am so proud of Jay and the twins." The American-ness of the family was further highlighted by its religiosity: "The boys attended Catholic school through sixth grade and are now in Cabrillo Elementary School.... I am a Eucharistic minister at Good Shepherd Church, where Jay and I both sing in the Sunday Mass choir." According to Tan, they were such exemplary parents that, even as lesbians, they never felt stigmatized, saying that, "We have never felt discriminated against in our community" and "our friends, mostly heterosexual couples, call us the model family. And even said we are their role models. We try to mirror the best family values and attribute the fact that our children are so well adjusted to the love, security, and consistency that we as parents have been able to provide."

Coming to the point of her presentation, she described her arrest in these terms: "Our lives, I can say without any doubt, were almost perfect until the morning of January 28, 2009. That morning at 6:30AM, Immigration and Customs Enforcement officials showed up at my door. The agents showed me a piece of paper, which was a 2002 deportation letter, which I informed them I had never seen."

Tan went on to describe how ICE agents took her away "like a criminal." She continued with her account of her concern for her family: "All the while, my family was first and foremost the center of everything on my mind. How would Jay work and take care of the kids if I was not there? Who would continue to take care of Jay's ailing mother—the mother I have come to love—if I was not there? Who would continue to take care of my family if I was not there? In an instant, my family—my American family—was being ripped away from me."

As Tan told her story, she received constant support and affirmation from Senator Leahy. At one point, when Tan's son showed visible signs of anguish, the senator stopped the proceedings to ask if the child needed to go into another room, saying, "I have a grandson the same age," and "Young man, I want you to know your mother is a very brave woman." Tan went on plead to the UAFA with these words, "We have a home together. Jay has a great job. We have a pension, mortgage, friends, and a community. We have everything together and it would be impossible to [re-]establish elsewhere. We have followed the law, respected the judicial system, and simply want to keep our family together."

Tan's emphasis on the American-ness of her family was obviously strategic, even if she was also sincere in her emotions. A plea for clemency to an inherently conservative immigration process that values an adherence to American values cannot deconstruct the very foundation upon which that process rests. But it's also inarguable that the lengths she went to paint herself as not a criminal also threw into relief the figure of the "illegal alien," a figure that is the flashpoint of so much contentious debate. Or, as Rachel Tiven, executive director of IE put it to *People* magazine with no subtlety, "*They* are exactly the kinds of immigrants you want in this country" [emphasis mine].

Tan's version of her story also made it appear that her status as an undocumented person did not define her existence but that, instead, her brush with ICE was simply a minor blip in an otherwise "almost perfect life," in which she moved about in complete freedom, blissfully unaware of her status. In fact, despite her assertion of having "respected the judicial system," it's unlikely that the lawyer she hired did not tell her that her application had been rejected. Given her access to legal expertise and her partner's career in Information Technology, a field filled with highly educated foreign nationals and immigrants, she had to be aware of the rudiments required for an extended stay in the United States. It's also unlikely that she would not have inquired into getting a green card, or wondered what documentation she was to use from there on—especially since without such, she would not have been able to travel outside the country, or even within it under some circumstances. It is not unusual for people to ignore the letters of deportation and simply not show up for their departure.

My point here is not to expose Tan as a liar. The current immigration system is set up to exploit and terrorize the undocumented who are here in such large numbers because the US economy is sustained on and encourages the development of a pool of exploitable and cheap labor. The system is set up so that people like Tan and others are compelled to lie and obfuscate their origins in order to survive. In this context, defining some immigrants as more or less honest than others does nothing to address the fact that it is the state, with its willingness to dehumanize and exploit those it deems expendable, that commits atrocities beyond mere lies.

I'm pointing to the fact that even under senatorial scrutiny, the verifiable truth of her account was less important than the construction of a supposedly authentic narrative about her honesty and uprightness as a citizen—unmarred except for the fact that she was not a citizen. That authenticity involved purging the possibility of prison or any evidence of wrongdoing, of not having "respected" the judicial system. It also involved explicating her lesbianism within contained terms (by clarifying that most of their friends were heterosexual couples) and demonstrating her adherence to the kind of gender roles that could legitimize her family. Where ordinarily her partner's butch self-presentation might have proved a liability, in this case they were able to use it as an advantage. Mercado emerged as the manly figure who protected Tan, supported her financially, and provided food and shelter for the family. At the same time, like the stereotypical male, Mercado was declared unable to perform basic household chores while also working—this, despite the fact that she was clearly socialized as female.[8]

Tan's version of what happened to her hides the brutal reality of undocumented life, transmogrifying it into an ethereal suburban paradise shattered only by the unexpected visit from ICE. But for millions of day laborers and factory workers, and countless trans/queer sex workers, life is a constant climate of fear and surveillance, with exploitative jobs for which employers can underpay, threatening to turn them over to ICE if they complain about wages or mistreatment.

Tan's testimony is quite typical of the discourse around LGBT immigration, which has, in recent years, been distilled down to just one issue: that of lovelorn US citizens or permanent residents needing to be with their foreign partners. In addressing the need for the Uniting American Families Act, proponents describe the situation of bi-national couples in excessively melodramatic terms, going so far as to describe US citizens and permanent residents who might leave the country to be with their partners as "exiles," as if a romantic partnership were akin to the trials of Pablo Neruda. The shackles of love replace the reality of the very real shackles that await many thousands of undocumented aliens, queer and otherwise, who are swept up and disappeared from their neighborhoods and then detained in often inhumane conditions before being deported. But, as Tiven emphasizes, gays and lesbians like Tan are not to be confused with the criminals in yellow jumpsuits.

Sexuality and the State

But what then of the relationship of queers to the state? The history of queer immigration to the United States has been a fraught one. The current emphasis on UAFA provides the illusion that the entrance of queers/LGBTs into the United States has been determined entirely by their status *as* queers/LGBTs, but in fact queer immigration has always been interlinked with the history of immigrant labor and has always been affected by the gendering of that labor.

Until 1990, gays and lesbians were barred from entry as immigrants.[9] That might seem shockingly recent until we remember that *Bowers v. Hardwick* was only repealed in 2003. Over the years, especially beginning in the mid-1990s, the "gay rights movement" has become a perfect replica of the neoliberal state. Marriage, Don't Ask Don't Tell, and hate crimes legislation have taken over the agenda. None of these are anything but rank conservative issues, and the last in particular simply adds to the number of those detained by the legal system. Despite the obvious conservatism of these issues and the fact that far greater issues—like poverty and the lack of healthcare—affect millions of gays and straights, the average American assumes that "gay rights" are automatically left/progressive issues.

Through the gay marriage movement, gays and lesbians are now mostly conceived of in terms of their relationships and, within that context, it is only natural that UAFA should be seen as *the* immigration issue for gays and lesbians. Given the history of illegality of the queer body in the United States, and how clearly that has been a construct and until how recently, we might imagine that queers of all people would be suspicious of any attempt to collude with the state. Yet, as the push for UAFA shows, many gays and lesbians have bought wholesale into the idea that the state can and should affirm their identities, and they have sought to engage the process of normalization as much as possible.[10]

The dilemma now facing advocates for queer immigrants is, How do we make queer visible? And what does that visibility look like? In cases of appeals for asylum on the grounds for sexual orientation, for instance, lawyers are compelled to prove the sheer brutality and repression of home cultures. This strategy comes with its costs. It is certainly true that queer life in some countries is subject to violent repression, but the one-sided portrayal of "other" cultures as sexually repressive helps to efface the reality of queer life in the United States, where both normative and non-normative homosexuality are continually policed and brutalized. In addition, asylum seekers are often held up to cultural stereotypes, with asylum officers refusing admission on the grounds that applicants don't "look" or "act" gay/lesbian enough.

In this context, where queer immigrants must fit into fictional narratives that seek a pre-determined authenticity, family and love become the only modes by which queers can assert themselves *as* queer. They are to be either connected to families or hounded by them. In addition, the fact that immigration reform efforts are still bound by the idea of "family reunification," despite every indication that addressing labor issues would be more worthwhile. Queer immigrants in particular are harmed by an emphasis on family reunification because their families of origin may, in many cases, prove dangerous to them; many queers, including non-immigrants, leave their birth homes in their teens for these very reasons.

Gender, Sexuality, and Labor

Gender and reproduction have been interlinked with labor in US immigration law, which has, historically, been concerned with the literal and metaphorical reproduction of the state. This emphasis on reproduction is linked to the principle of "family reunification," which dictates that immigration law should be designed to enable families to stay together. However, this is applied only when convenient. When Mexicans and other Latin Americans reproduce, they are accused of having "anchor babies," a term that implies that families use their native-born children to gain permanent residence in this country. Immigration has also been intensely racialized and that racialization has been about surveilling and controlling the reproduction of non-white foreigners. For instance, the 1857 Page Act effectively banned Chinese women from immigrating, on the grounds of prostitution, but the ban was meant to prevent Chinese men from forming families here. The anti-immigrant fervor of recent years has brought about a backlash against "chain migration" and calls for revoking natural birth citizenship from the children of "illegal aliens." The paranoia about "anchor babies" adds to this backlash. All of this is, of course, clearly a class-inflected paranoia—nobody has anything to say about well-paid professionals who have babies in the US

UAFA, which is being endorsed as a part of "family reunification," replicates the problematic construction of the gendered family by insisting that same-sex partners of US citizens and permanent residents demonstrate their financial dependence. By law, the sponsoring partner must be able to demonstrate that he or she can support the other and provide 125 percent of the income required for a single-family unit. In addition, they are legally bound to agree to support their partners for a period of ten years; the notion of "interdependence" mapped out by UAFA is, in fact, dependence. UAFA reproduces the ultimate class fantasy of the immigrant, as made visibly evident through Tan: a suburban home, a place in the church, two suburban soccer-playing kids, and a dominant partner to take on the financial burdens of the household.

In fact, family reunification, far from being solely about bringing families together, disguises the realities of gendered labor that are a part of immigration and that can and do exist, even in lesbian relationships, and it avoids the stigma faced by millions of families who are deemed unworthy of rights. Families like Padilla's are constructed as labor units by immigration but ignored as families when convenient. The neoliberal reality of a world devastated by economic "free" trade acts like NAFTA is that entire families are compelled to move across borders to seek better lives because their own economies have been laid to waste and cannot sustain them. In the process, some families are held up as more ideal than others. Those that can adhere to the heteronormative ideal of a sole breadwinner assuming responsibility for the entire family have their filial emotions validated. Those that must remain invisible because they don't present themselves as ideal (for example, undocumented adolescents whose labor cannot yet be exploited, at least legally) are considered less than human, and their filial relationships and emotions are erased. In the strategic deployment of family reunification, Tan was hailed as the ideal citizen-to-be, but there was little public concern about Padilla's parents losing their son to deportation. One family's tragic loss is seen as another's punishment for being illegal in the first place.[12]

Caught in the Vectors

Traveling back home to Chicago in the Spring of 2009, Juan (out of concern for his parents, he does not want his full name used), an out queer student, dozed off on the Greyhound bus and slept through it stopping. He woke up to find ICE agents making their way toward him, the only Latino on the bus. They demanded to see his papers. Juan, brought here as a child by his parents, does not have an American passport and records indicated his undocumented status. He was apprehended and placed in detention for weeks while his parents, working-class Chicagoans, scraped together the $8,000 required to get him out of jail. At the time of this writing, Juan is awaiting an indefinitely postponed series of trials. When I asked him how his queerness might have affected his experience, he described what happened when he was allowed to make a phone call. Overcome with emotion, he began to cry on the phone. "I'm not afraid to be emotional," explained Juan, attributing this to his queerness. When he turned around after the call, he saw ICE agents laughing at him and mimicking him.

Prerna Lal is a Fijian immigrant who came here with her parents and two sisters when her father came to the United States for graduate studies. Their original plan was for everyone in the family to gain citizenship through her grandmother, but through a complicated series of setbacks and delays, Lal ended up being the only person in her family to remain undocumented, a situation that she has written about publicly quite often (she's a co-founder of the DREAM activist network). Her life has also been marked by significant amounts of physical and emotional abuse, and she was put to work in the family business while still a student at San Francisco State University.

Lal came out as queer in high school, and her father sent her to a counselor because he refused to believe that she was "normal." During a counseling session, Lal revealed that her father beat her, and her revelation resulted in child protective services showing up at her high school and home, prepared to take her away and arrest her father. At the time, her father, in between his school years and in the process of getting his green card, was undocumented. Lal, afraid that the family breadwinner would be deported, eventually retracted her story of abuse.

Both Juan and Lal's stories reveal that queer immigrants come from backgrounds infinitely more complex and different than the "almost perfect" suburban ideal held up by Tan. As Lal put it to me in a telephone interview, her family's travails and her own undocumented status were in large part due to their lack of cultural capital. Although her father was here as a student, their class status as working-class Fijian immigrants precluded their access to the kinds of legal and cultural expertise required to maneuver through the complicated and labyrinthine processes required for citizenship. Within her family, her status as a lesbian put her in physical and emotional danger on two fronts: an abusive parent who clearly saw her as abnormal, and child protective services that could recognize the physical danger to her but could do nothing about her invisible status as the undocumented child of an undocumented man.

The stories of Juan and Lal reveal the contradictions in which immigrants find themselves. When I asked Juan what he considered suitable solutions for people like him, he was quick to say that UAFA would help queer immigrants. But when I asked him how that was supposed to help uncoupled queers, he confessed that he hadn't considered that marriage/coupledom was not the ideal solution. Lal publicly supports UAFA and gay marriage, even joining the board of Immigration Equality in 2010, which is bewildering given the extent to which the legislation and the marriage movement reinforce exactly the kinds of gendered and sexualized dependencies and family formations that made her vulnerable in the first place. The fact that people like Lal and Juan echo support for measures that contradict the realities of their existence only proves the power of the discursive frameworks within which such immigrants must operate.

Conclusion

To consider a case where queerness intersected with immigration and where neither framework provided any safety, we could look at the life and horrific death of Victoria Arellano. Arellano was a 23-year-old, transgender Mexican immigrant who died of complications from AIDS while in the custody of the Department of Immigration and Customs Enforcement in a San Pedro, California, facility. Arellano had been in this country since the age of six and had been caught entering the United States for the second time in May 2007.

While in detention, she was denied medication and medical attention despite her diagnosis of HIV. After a particularly brutal relapse resulting from not having access to proper medications (her fellow inmates took turns tending to her and walking her to the bathroom), Arellano was only prescribed amoxicillin, a standard drug prescribed for common bacterial infections. She was eventually taken to a San Pedro hospital but was returned to the prison the next day. When her condition worsened, she was taken out again and placed in the intensive care unit of Little Company of Mary Hospital in San Pedro. There, she was handcuffed to her bed while immigration agents watched the door. She died there on July 20, 2007.

Arellano's story is a common one, and hers happens to be one of the few that garnered some media attention. While the mainstream gay community focuses on UAFA, it ignores cases like Arellano's. But what happened to her is far more typical for transgender and queer immigrants than what happened to Shirley Tan. Her gender identity and her undocumented status caused her death by willful negligence within a system designed to brutalize a non-conforming body, one that could not be interpolated into normative discourses about perfect assimilationist families.[13]

How do we remedy matters so that the issues facing people like Padilla, Juan, and Arellano are brought to the forefront? The strategy engaged by so-called progressive and left immigration-rights activists so far has been to render immigrants' stories in palatable terms by discussing the pathos and vulnerability of their lives. This strategy has failed miserably except in individual cases. Victories like Padilla's constitute short-term wins for individuals, but they do nothing to cease the systemic problems with the system. Padilla's success and the intense campaign around it galvanized an already vibrant undocumented-youth movement, and various groups of students have been engaging in acts of civil disobedience across the country in order to gain support for the DREAM Act (Development, Relief, and Education for Alien Minors). This federal legislation is designed to provide a path to citizenship for anyone brought here as an undocumented minor under the age of 16. But while the DREAM Activists, as they call themselves, provide poignant reasons why the legislation should pass, their rhetoric echoes the same problematic kinds of exclusion as used by Shirley Tan and the supporters of UAFA.[14] Over and over, these youth describe themselves as exceptional immigrants, pointing to their academic achievements and exemplary citizenship. One of the chief ironies of the DREAM Act is that it requires such students to rhetorically turn against their own parents. One of the requirements of the DREAM Act is that qualified students either attend college or join the military for two years. Given that so many of the youth who would benefit from the DREAM Act are of color and from families for which college might be a hardship, it's likely that a great number of them will be compelled to join the army and become fodder for one of the endless and meaningless wars being waged by the United States. In this way, they will join the ranks of the millions of youth of color who have been coerced into war.

In order to create real change, we have to center the violence at the heart of these experiences, to speak and write of them *as* experiences with the brutal power of the state, not as narratives about good versus bad immigrants. If we are to undo the prison industrial complex and interrogate its relationship to racialized immigration, gender, and sexuality, we need to first make manifest the violence that marks immigration from the start: the violence at the border, the sexualized brutality, the psychic and epistemological violence at the heart of the family that compels children and women in particular to remain silent, the violence of gender normativity, and the crushing force that dehumanizes and kills immigrant detainees. We need to recover the discourse on violence instead of relying on the notion of love in order to rematerialize the specter of the prison. Paradoxically, this is what it will take to make it vanish forever.

The current discourse on queer immigration presents an idealized and bourgeois version of transgender and queer immigrants, a discourse that makes the reality of the prison industrial complex completely invisible. If we are to seek an end to the nightmare of the PIC and the disaster that is "immigration reform" in this country, we need to reintegrate an analysis of the violence of the PIC back into the discourse on immigration and queers. We need to abolish the walls of prison and the discourse of normative attachment, a discourse that only succeeds in making prison disappear under the fog of love.

NOTES

1. At the same time, the mainstream gay and lesbian community only pays attention to queer immigrants in terms of their relationships (as in its concern for UAFA) in the midst of the push for gay marriage, or in terms that can pathologize them, as in the issue of asylum on the grounds of sexual orientation. Gay organizations like Immigration Equality are quick to support UAFA but have nothing to say about, for instance, the issue of no-match letters, except when necessary to gain entry into immigration rights circles.

    The marriage issue brings with it narratives about legitimacy and illegitimacy. The gay and lesbian mainstream wants a bourgeois identity, to march onward in its attempts to gain respectability. Within this relentless search, the only clarity comes within the demarcation of the good and bad immigrant, the documented and the undocumented. Mainstream gay activists seek to legitimize the bourgeois gay subject as one that will not contest the state or unsettle its hierarchies. This is a deeply conservative and neoliberal agenda that neither changes the structure nor makes it more equitable. Instead, it simply wants to expand the category of the bourgeois heteronormative subject to include women like Tan. http://www.youtube.com/watch?v=9cTojNqjnP4.

2.   Gay and lesbian activists for UAFA are pushing for the law on the grounds that it would grant same-sex couples the same rights as married straight couples, claiming that the legislation is especially needed since they cannot marry under federal law.

3.   Mercado's appearance as a butch woman would be a significant, even if unacknowledged, factor in the press coverage and the pair's attempts to drum up sympathy for their cause (visibly aided by Immigration Equality).

4.   http://www.dreamactivist.org/rigoberto-padilla-fights-deportation-open-letter/.

5.   A private bill is often inserted as a section of a larger piece of legislation and used to further the case of an individual. These rarely pass.

6.   In the case of Tan and Mercado, the latter's job placed her in a field that is already dematerialized to the extent that the IT industry still functions as a virtual job sphere, despite the fact that it increasingly requires millions of overworked and underpaid temp workers to sustain it.

7.   A further complication in the Tan-Mercado case, which cannot be ignored, is that they were from the Philippines. The United States' relationship with the Philippines has always been one between colonizer and colonized and, as is typical of such relationships, has been a gendered one. The Philippines have historically been cast as a feminine Other in relation to the United States, as the sexual and sensual willing handmaiden to the strong, masculine imperial force of the US The fact that the Philippines' biggest export is its labor in the form of domestic workers and nurses, whose remittances form an important part of the country's economy, estimated at nearly 17 billion in 2009, further lends to this historical feminization. The gendering of the Tan-Mercado relationship, of an outwardly butch and femme lesbian couple, played into this gendering.

In contrast, Mexico, in the imagination and political reality of the United States, has always been marked as nothing more than a cheap source of expendable migrant labor. Metaphorically, Mexico has been cast as the houseboy of the United States, while the Philippines are cast as its eternal concubine. In more recent iterations of her statement, Tan has begun to state that ICE agents gained entry into her home by pretending to be looking for a "Mexican girl." This detail was absent from her earlier versions of her story, including the videotaped testimony in front of US senators and has only recently begun to surface. It does appear in a written form of her testimony on the Web site of the United States Senate Committee on the Judiciary—but even this is, as far as I can tell, a relatively recent addition; the statement was not on the Web site for much of 2009. In the context of the family's increasing efforts to appear as "good," this new detail appears to be a way to distance Tan from the "bad" Mexican immigrants.

8. The *People* article also reported that they had even considered the possibility of Mercado transitioning as male so that they could get married as a heterosexual couple—presumably with the hope that it would be easier for Mercado to sponsor Tan as a spouse.

9. See "Eithne Luibhéid and Bridget Anderson–Gendering Borders: An Exchange," *Re-Public: Re-imagining Democracy.* http://www.re-public.gr/en/?p=471.

10. See also Karma Chavez's "Border (In)Securities: Normative and Differential Belonging in LGBTQ and Immigrant Rights Discourse," *Communication and Critical/Cultural Studies*, Vol. 7, No. 2, 2010: p. 136–155. See also Eithne Luibhéid, *Entry Denied: Controlling Sexuality at the Border* (Minneapolis: University of Minnesota Press, 2002).

11. The Social Security Administration sends "no-match" letters when the names or Social Security numbers on an employer's W-2 do not match SSA's records. Ostensibly a measure to track fraudulent SSNs, the system is in fact so unreliable that the Department of Homeland Security rescinded its "no-match" rule in late 2009. For instance, this system cannot detect human errors such as misspellings of names. Furthermore, although the SSA clearly states that the letter cannot be used as proof that an employee intentionally provided misinformation, unscrupulous employers can use it to fire or intimidate workers who complain about workplace conditions. http://www.nilc.org/immsemplymnt/ssa-nm_toolkit/index.htm.

12. Also left out of the picture, via the lesbian domesticity of the Tan-Mercado family, is the more threatening and potential spectacle of a same-sex male couple. It is clear that the gendered relationship between Tan and Mercado also facilitated their acceptance—and it is highly unlikely that the sight of two gay men, invoking the more threatening vision of gay sex, would have been as reassuring to the senators or to the general public. In other words, the reassurance provided by Tan and Mercado is a fragile one and does nothing to erase the fact that homosexuality and the state are still considered incompatible.

13. Immigrants and especially queer immigrants with HIV/AIDS face multiple threats to their safety and health. The United States instituted a bar against travelers and immigrants with HIV in 1987, and that had a dangerous effect on both the spread of the epidemic and the health of the immigrant population. The ban was lifted in 2009, but there is little information about how that the government is going out of its way to now reach out to HIV-positive immigrants and encourage them to come forward for testing and treatment. Furthermore, with states like Arizona enacting virulent anti-immigrant measures that will, along with other measures, cut off social and health services to the undocumented

(and position every brown-skinned person as an "illegal" who needs to prove his or her status), it's unlikely that HIV rates among immigrants will go down significantly. That burden will be left to social service agencies. Without proper counseling or outreach, immigrants with HIV are likely to go undiagnosed until the late stages of the disease, and then they are likely to go underground. They are likely to be among the most exploited workers in the economy, given their fear of exposure to or by employers. They face the greatest risk to their health, given that most states deny healthcare to the undocumented. Even when states, like Illinois, do provide treatment without asking questions about documentation, most HIV-positive immigrants are not aware of these services given the stigma of their communities and the fear of being outed to ICE.

14. Interestingly, several of the DREAM Activists are openly queer. They include Mohammad Abdollahi and Prerna Lal, co-founders of the DREAM Web site.

IDENTITIES UNDER SIEGE:

Violence Against Transpersons of Color

Lori A. Saffin

Within the war we are all waging with the forces of death, subtle and otherwise, conscious or not—I am not only a casualty, I am also a warrior.
　　—Audre Lorde[1]

As news reports and statistical data have shown, one of the more egregious realities that many transpersons encounter is that of violence. From the schoolyard to street harassment to brutal murders, transgender people are the targets of many of the most vicious and blatant forms of violence. The National Coalition of Anti-Violence Programs reports that in 2009 transgender victims represented 17 percent of the violence enacted against LGBT persons nationally.[2] However, transgender persons do not occupy one homogenous category of identity, but instead occupy multiple subjectivities across race, class, nationality, and ability. For example, transgender women were disproportionately targeted for hate-motivated violence, representing roughly 65 percent of the reported violence against transpersons in 2009, and of the twenty-two anti-LGBTQ murders reported, people of color accounted for 79 percent of these murders, and 50 percent of those murdered were transgender women.[3]

Most current discussions of transgender issues separate out transphobia, heterosexism, and misogyny from racism, ethnocentrism, and Eurocentrism.[4] In examining transgender identities in isolation, a white, middle-class transgendered subject is assumed. By analyzing anti-transgender violence as separate from race and class, the lived experiences and specificity of transpersons of color are ignored. Moreover, examination of violence against transpersons in isolation is myopic because it fails to connect anti-transgender violence to other systems of oppression, such as poverty and racism.

The interconnection of racism, classism, and transphobia propels many transpersons of color into positions that put them at an increased risk for violence. Due to rejection from the lesbian and gay community, as well as the structural realities of racism, many transpersons of color who are victims of violence have limited support systems in place and thus, for survival purposes, often have to consider performing dangerous work. For example, many turn to sex work out of economic necessity, or work long hours in minimum-wage jobs because they have been forced to quit school or leave home, resulting in a lack of social, economic, and emotional resources. By foregrounding violence enacted against transpersons of color while also demonstrating that this violence is not individual or random, but part of a much larger structure of racism, classism, and trans/homo-phobia, a more complex, multilayered way of understanding identity and the interlocking systems of oppression and violence can be mapped.

Barbara Perry argues that hate crimes are assaults against the community to which an individual appears to belong and are significantly oriented toward creating a spectacle of subordination, as well as physical harm.[5] Hate crimes, Perry argues, are intended to send a message to the communities who bear witness, as well as to the immediate victims, to get back "in their place."[6] Even though the bulk of hate crimes are not committed by hate groups, acts of transphobic or racist violence are nonetheless attempts to turn beliefs in transgender "deviance" or white supremacy into concrete realities.[7] One of these concrete realities was the brutal death of Jessica Mercado. Jessica was a 24-year-old, Latina transwoman who lived in New Haven, Connecticut. In May 2003, firefighters and police found Jessica's body riddled with stab wounds, draped over a mattress, and set ablaze.[8] Fire investigators determined that the mattress was purposefully set on fire and police suspected that the killers ignited it, hoping to cover all evidence of the crime.[9] Police classified the death as a homicide because under current law, Connecticut does not have hate crime penalties for attacks based on *gender* identity.[10] In September 2004, four sentences appeared in the local New Haven paper in an article entitled "Arrest Made in Transvestite Murder." Michael Streater plead guilty to murder and arson and was sentenced to thirty years in prison.[11]

The New Haven queer community held no marches or candlelight vigils following Mercado's murder. Not one person took to the street in protest. The *Hartford Advocate* interviewed multiple members of the LGB community to understand why queers were not expressing a public outcry. Several suggested that it was Jessica's occupation as a prostitute that prevented many from caring about her brutal death. Some gay community members claimed that her role as a sex worker pointed to a motive—the rage of an unsuspecting client, surprised to learn that she was anatomically male.[12]

However, this silence from the queer community is not an anomaly. Like Jessica, several other anti-transgender deaths from hate-motivated violence reveal glaring similarities. For example, Shelby Tracey Tom was a 40-year-old Asian transsexual and sex worker who was murdered in North Vancouver twenty-two days after Jessica. Her body was discovered in a shopping cart behind a Laundromat.[13] Although the police waited several days to announce Tracey's death, there was still no newspaper or media record of her murder and no public outrage or grief from the LGB community.[14] Another transgender victim, Donathyn J. Rodgers, a 19-year-old African American transwoman and sex worker from Cleveland, Ohio, was shot multiple times and killed in November 2005.[15] Although she was active in the Lesbian-Gay Community Service Center of Greater Cleveland, the center published no memoriam or information about her death, and her case remains unsolved. Similarly, Selena Álvarez-Hernández was a Latina transwoman who worked in a meatpacking plant in Omaha, Nebraska, and was found stabbed several times and unconscious on the lawn of a house in Council Bluffs, Iowa, in 2003.[16] She was pronounced dead a short time after being found, and there is little to no information available on possible suspects. Additionally, Christina Smith was a 20-year-old African American transwoman who had been evacuated from New Orleans following the aftermath of Hurricane Katrina.[17] She relocated to Houston, Texas, and was found shot in the head on the patio of her apartment in October 2005. Her murder remains unsolved.

These brutal murders were not isolated incidences: From 2003 to 2009, there has been an average of eighteen reported LGBTQ-identified persons killed each year, and transgender persons have disproportionately been the target of the most brutal and vicious forms of hate-motivated violence.[18] Most recently, Caprice Curry, a 31-year-old black transgender woman was assaulted and stabbed to death in January 2009 in San Francisco's Tenderloin District. Kelly Watson and Terri Benally, both Navajo transwomen, were fatally assaulted in Albuquerque, New Mexico, in June 2009. Tyli'a Mack, a black transgender woman, was attacked and stabbed to death while walking into a Washington, D.C. drop-in center in broad daylight in August 2009. Dee Green, a black transgender woman, was found unconscious, stabbed in the heart, and left dead on the street in Baltimore in October 2009.

These cases, among many others, are clearly not aberrations, and as the National Transgender Advocacy Coalition asserts, murders and violence against transgendered individuals across the country averages to more than one per month.[19] However, this statistic most likely does not capture the true number of crimes enacted against transgender persons due to the distrust and fear of revictimization within a largely transphobic criminal justice system.[20] Certainly the heinousness and brutality surrounding all of these murders would merit a public outcry and point to the level of queer hatred exuded not just by particular individuals, but also embedded within larger social systems. It is the structural connectedness of racism, classism, and heterosexism that produces a disproportionate number of transpersons of color as hate crime victims and also contributes to the silence and apathy surrounding mobilization efforts.

The countless reported and unreported victims of hate-motivated violence point to several structural intersections. Most of the victims of gender-based violence are people of color. Black and Latino/a individuals account for 85 percent of the known victims of gender-based violence.[21] This suggests that the intersection of race and gender-non-conformity is crucial to increasing a person's vulnerability to fatal assault. Richard Juang argues that anti-transgender discrimination and violence are often accompanied by racial and ethnic discrimination, and conversely, that situations interpreted as instances of racial and ethnic injustice often also involve a policing of gender and sexual boundaries.[22]

Moreover, most of the hate crime victims of anti-transgender violence are poor. They have been forced out of school, out of homes, and out of jobs, resulting in the interconnection of poverty and gender-non-conformity in many of these fatalities. Victims are disproportionately from economically disadvantaged communities and are forced to rely on low-paying jobs (such as that of Álvarez-Hernández who worked in a meatpacking plant), or because of other mitigating factors, such as Christina Smith's forced uprooting and temporary homelessness after Hurricane Katrina.

The lack of money and resources forces many victims, like Jessica Mercado, Donathyn Rodgers, and Shelby Tracey Tom, to trade temporary sex work for food and shelter, increasing their vulnerability to assault from a client and police. Most of these victims of gender-based violence are ignored by the media and oftentimes also ignored by the mainstream lesbian and gay communities. According to a recent GenderPAC report on violence against queers, only eleven victims generated sustained media coverage, and then only when an arrest and public trial was involved.[23] The thirty-two non-trial murders averaged only a single 500-word article, and 24 percent of victims received no coverage at all.[24]

Most of the victims of gender-based violence suffered multiple stab or bullet wounds, or a combination of strangling, stabbing, and beating. In a number of cases, victims appeared to have been shot, stabbed, or bludgeoned, even after death. The extreme violence used by assailants suggests that the attacks were motivated by intense rage and that the purpose of these attacks was not simply to terminate life, but to punish and torture for gender-non-conformity. Furthermore, most of the murders of transpersons of color are often unsolved and unrecognized not just by the nation and mainstream presses, but also by the communities in which these individuals resided.

Queer Racism

Many transpersons of color cannot seek refuge in the larger LGBT community because of racism.[25] Racism in the queer community is nothing new, as numerous historical examples illustrate pervasive racism, from the white-run gay bars and clubs of 1950s, where gays and lesbians of color were not welcome, to the multiple forms of identification still needed from queers of color to get into bars. Even the celebration of Stonewall as the "birth" of the gay and lesbian movement often denies the existence of queers of color as historical participants shaping LGBT politics and policies.[26] Charles Nero contends that the exclusion of black gays from full participation in queer culture is widespread.[27] Similarly, Brian Freeman, a member of the performance art group Pomo Afro Homo, remarks in the 1997 documentary *The Castro* that black gay men are unwanted, unseen, and invisible within San Francisco's "gay mecca."[28] More recently, the Human Rights Commission issued a report in 2005 on *SF Badlands*, a club within the Castro district, stating that the bar's employees had engaged in racist business practices, including referring to African American patrons as "non-Badlands customers" and often requiring African Americans to produce extra forms of ID at the door.[29] Accounts such as these are all too familiar to queers of color, and many LGBT persons of color feel excluded, exploited, and patronized by the dominant white gay organizations. Furthermore, the lack of presence, visibility, participation, and leadership of people of color within the LGBT community points to structural racism embedded in queer communities and organizations.

Since the Civil Rights Movement of the 1960s, ideological and legal discourses have taken a "colorblind" approach to conceptualizing race. Violent racism becomes a phenomenon of history's past, and now the United States has entered a post-racial moment.[30] With social systems premised on liberalism, multiculturalism (tokenism), and universal subjectivity, racism has been deemed by many as no longer an issue. However, when most queer organizations are run by whites, national political agendas, such as gay marriage, are fronted by white gay men, and the visibility and voices of queers of color are rarely a central focus, it is difficult to deny the marginalized positioning of LGBT persons of color.[31] As Dean Spade contends,

> The most well-publicized and well-funded LGB organizations have notoriously marginalized low-income people and people of Color, and framed political agendas that have reflected concern for economic opportunity and family recognition for well-resourced and disproportionately white LGB populations. Low income people, people of Color, and gender-transgressive people have been notoriously underrepresented from leadership and decision-making power in this movement.[32]

When racism is relegated to the periphery of a white-dominated gay agenda, politics, and community, finding safety and empowerment in this space is typically bleak for most queers of color.

Racism within the LGBT community, together with possible ostracism from one's own ethnic community, puts transpersons of color in a very precarious position as outsiders among the margins, forced to differentiate between identities that both communities deem as conflicting. This becomes particularly damaging as binaries become reinscribed, where the queer body equals a white body, and the brown or black body equals a heterosexual body. Rigidly constructing and reinforcing the boundaries of identity erase the lived realities of transgendered persons of color. As a result, when brown or black queer folks, like Jessica Mercado, Shelby Tracey Tom, Christina Smith, Selena Álvarez-Hernández, or Donathyn Rodgers are violently killed, their bodies are marked as "unknown" or "unidentified," and it is the silence from both the LGBT community and racial communities that mark their deaths. Yet, the murder of any queer person of color sends a message loud and clear to both the LGBT community *and* to racial communities: structural violence remains a lived reality.

Homophobic Sentiments Within Communities of Color

Communities of color are no more homophobic or transphobic than whites; however, accusations of homo- or transphobia are generalized to an entire community, despite the pervasiveness of homophobia cross-culturally. Queer persons of color, like whites, are still frequently rejected from their families or communities because of homo- or transphobia. Keith Boykin contends that "unfortunately in the Black community at large, homophobia and heterosexism reach all demographic groups...and are frequently seen not as prejudices but survival skills for the Black race or the Black individual."[33] Sometimes, queers of color are associated with the decline of the community whereby queerness is seen as an outgrowth of white racism or as a by-product of the breakdown of the family.

Queerness is also viewed as a threat to the continued existence of the heterosexual family and community, consequently justifying homophobia and forcing many queers of color to separate their racial identities from their (homo)sexuality. Joseph Beam demonstrates this struggle with identity as well as his frustrations with homophobia purported by the black community in stating,

> I know anger. My body contains as much anger as water.... I am angry because of the treatment I am afforded as a Black man. That fiery anger is stoked additionally with the fuels of contempt and despisal shown to me by my community because I am gay. I cannot go home

as who I am. When I speak of home, I mean not only the familial
constellation from which I grew, but the entire Black community....
I am most often rendered invisible, perceived as a threat to the family,
or I am tolerated if I am silent and inconspicuous. I cannot go home
as who I am and that hurts me deeply... I dare myself to dream of a
time when I will pass a group of brothers on the corner, and the words
"fuckin' faggot" will not move the air around my ears.[34]

Stephan Lee Dais shares similar frustrations with homophobia in the
black community. He argues that

two of the most difficult aspects of being Black and gay are the lack of
acceptance and affirmation shown to me by my community. I want to
serve my community as a man, a gay man, and a member of the Black
community. By dismissing Black gays, the Black community denies a
considerable portion of its identity. The Black community that needs
me, won't let me serve it; unless, I hide my identity, my values, my
beliefs, and my self.[35]

Although Beam and Dais both discuss accounts of homophobia
from the late 1980s, homophobia within the black community persists.
In their article "Talking About It: Homophobia in the Black Community," Barbara Smith and Jewelle Gomez suggest that "one of the challenges we face in trying to raise the issues of lesbian and gay identity
within the Black community is to try to get our people to the place where
they see that they can indeed oppress someone after having spent a life
seeing themselves as being oppressed."[36] Moreover, Kelly Brown Douglas
connects current discourses of homophobia within the black community to the influences of conservative shifts in politics and religion at
the beginning of the twenty-first century.[37] Even Democratic Presidential
candidate Barack Obama told worshippers at Atlanta's Ebenezer Baptist
Church, where Martin Luther King, Jr. once preached, that, "If we are
honest with ourselves, we'll acknowledge that our own community has
not always been true to King's vision of a beloved community. We have
scorned our gay brothers and sisters instead of embracing them."[38] The
assertions made by these various authors suggest that ostracism from
friends, family, and community can have very damaging affects. Consequently, many queers of color are forced into the closet in order to be
accepted within the larger racial or ethnic community.

148

Expressing homophobic sentiments within political mobilization efforts also has extremely dangerous consequences. In addition to many queer people of color being outcast from their families or rejected by the larger community, queerness is considered a threat to the unity of a racialized political group. Black political leaders, such as Amiri Baraka, Eldridge Cleaver, and Haki Madhubuti view "homosexuality negatively and fear that it will become pervasive within the Black community.[39] Keith Boykin details a number of political leaders who have used homophobia to rally members of racial or ethnic communities into action.[40] However, by politically challenging and organizing only around racism, many communities of color re-inscribe relations of domination because they rely on heterosexist and patriarchal agendas. Homophobia, then, becomes a scapegoat for the survival of a race in a white-dominated and white supremacist society.

The above discussion on homophobia in communities of color centers particularly on the black community. However, homophobia is rampant across racial and ethnic lines. Nayan Shah discusses his feelings of queer invisibility within his own South Asian community stating that "homosexual relationships are labeled a white disease whereby the politics of race are used to condemn lesbians and gay men. They perceive queer identities as a threat to the cultural integrity of South Asian immigrants. The rhetoric is lethal, and well understood."[41] Similarly, Surina Khan relays her own experiences with homophobia, resulting in Khan cutting ties with her Pakistani community, including her family.[42] Although the experiences of queers of color attempting to navigate within immigrant communities and black communities have obvious differences, what remains painfully similar is the frequent rejection by family and community members. Furthermore, across racial and ethnic lines, queers of color encounter the pressure to bifurcate their identities, often forced to choose between primarily identifying with their race or with their sexuality.

Economic Inequality

Economically, raced-based inequalities result in a disproportionate number of people of color living in poverty. According to the 2008 US Census Press Release, the poverty rate for people of color was drastically higher than—and in fact, almost triple that of—whites. Blacks had a poverty rate of 33 percent, Asians 20 percent, "Hispanics" 31 percent, and American Indians 23 percent, compared to whites, whose poverty rate was estimated at about 12 percent.[43] These numbers indubitably demonstrate that gross economic disparities exist for people of color. Although studies suggest that poverty has decreased among blacks and "Hispanics" in recent years, issues of food, housing, and employment hardships have remained.[44] These economic inequalities have forced many people of color into low-paying, dangerous jobs that subject them to economic, physical, and emotional vulnerability.

Racialized economic inequity is important to consider when looking at the hate-motivated violence affecting communities of color. Wealth affords access to institutions of power, including educational systems, the media, community resources, and political systems. Economics shapes whose story is told, how a community can afford to respond, what legal action is taken, and the ways in which the media can be used to publicize issues of hate or violence within local communities. When families cannot afford food or adequate healthcare and are competing for the limited resources available to them, challenging violence or legislating protection may not be a first priority for community action: survival is. Because of the effects of racist economic inequities from a white-dominated capitalist system, many people of color are denied access to these larger systems of power, perpetuating silence surrounding hate crimes within poor communities of color.

However, access to resources becomes compounded when examining people of color who are queer. Without community or familial support, many queers of color are pushed into even more economic vulnerability, with no family to fall back on in times of crisis or community to provide emotional support. Coupling racial economic inequity with homophobic attitudes leaves many queers of color in insecure, isolating conditions. The perceived gender transgression by many transpersons of color can cause serious consequences, ranging from daily abuse or harassment at home to being banished from their families and communities. As a result, many transpersons often end up homeless. Adult homeless shelters are inaccessible because of the fact that most facilities are sex-segregated and will either turn down a transgender person outright or refuse to house them according to their lived gender identity.

Similarly, harassment and violence against transpersons is rampant in schools, and many drop out or are kicked out before finishing. This leads to less opportunity in a job market that already severely discriminates against transpersons.[45] Many transgender persons are fearful of applying to jobs because paperwork or other documents might reveal their old name or birth sex. They also might be fired for transitioning on the job or when a transperson's gender identity comes to the attention of a supervisor.[46] These fears, coupled with transphobia in employment, leave many transpersons with few opportunities to live economically secure lives.

Discrimination against transpersons also permeates access to government benefits, such as welfare, Medicaid, and Social Security. Those transpersons who do seek social services to assist them out of homelessness, poverty, or drug addiction, or aid in accessing services or resources will oftentimes have difficulty finding advocates to assist them.[47] The resulting lack of access to social services and resources leaves a disproportionate number of transgender persons in severe poverty and dependent on criminalized work such as sex work or the drug economy to survive.

Sex Work: Working on the Margins

As in the cases of Jessica Mercado, Shelby Tracey Tom, and Donathyn Rodgers, economic *need* and limited avenues of support propels many transgender persons of color into sex work. With few sources of social support compounded by economic inequality, sex work becomes, perhaps, the *only* means for survival. This not only puts queers of color at high risk for violence, such as exploitation, rape, robbery, and physical threats, but also endangers their health from increased exposure to HIV and STIs. Economic and class position influences a sex worker's ability to screen out undesirable clients and to refuse dangerous services. Sex workers with little class privilege working in low-status positions are generally afforded the least respect and are considered the most "deserving" of abuse by clients, the police, and the public.[48] Queers of color—specifically transgender women—who are poor and who work as sex workers are under constant surveillance from police and frequently subject to ongoing harassment and violence.

Viviane Namaste interviews several transgender and transsexual sex workers to explore some of the additional healthcare and social service concerns required for this specific population that is often rendered invisible.[49] One of her first assertions is that many transgender persons obtained their hormones on the streets through an underground market. Some transgender individuals obtained multiple prescriptions and then sold the hormones to interested persons. Many transpersons in her study found it extremely difficult to find a doctor who was willing to prescribe hormones. This creates a situation in which transgender persons buy their hormones on the street even though they would like to secure them through a doctor and have their health monitored. Research in the field of HIV/AIDS education has suggested that in the context of American inner-city trans communities, transgender persons may share needles with their lovers and friends in order to inject their hormones. This practice puts transpersons at an increased risk of contracting HIV as well as other health complications.

Namaste recounts stories of police harassment, intimidation, and verbal abuse against transpersons. She maintains that

> verbal abuse consisted of uniformed police officers yelling "faggot" and "queers" at sex trade workers in areas known for TS/TG prostitution. In addition to such insults, police officers would harass the prostitutes in a variety of ways. Participants reported that police officers would stand right next to them on the street corner where they were working, thus preventing any client from approaching. Officers would also follow prostitutes down the street in their cars, keeping pace with them as they walked. Some officers would also take Polaroid photographs of prostitutes, telling them that they would keep their picture on file.[50]

The interactions between the police officers and transgender prostitutes offer additional evidence of police harassment. Transgender sex workers who had been assaulted said that the police officers they sought on the street often refused to take a report of the incidents. Sex workers were also told that violence against prostitutes was not important enough to file a report. In additional to scorn, ridicule, and harassment, police officers may intimidate transgender sex workers with whom they come in contact, resulting in many transgender persons not reporting incidents of violence. Moreover, many transgender persons of color decide not to turn to other social services out of fear of harassment. In this manner, various social institutions intersect to further marginalize transgender individuals from services greatly needed.[51]

In the United States, almost all forms of sex work are currently illegal, but prostitution remains widely practiced throughout the country. Expensive attempts to control commercial sex through prohibition have been extremely inefficient in curbing the practice. And, as we can see from the queer community's apathetic response to Jessica's murder and the absence of *any* response to Tracey and Donathyn's murders, the demonization of sex work effects the mobilization efforts following a hate crime and blames the victim for the violence perpetrated against them. By claiming that sex work is simply "immoral," social systems that force many queers of color into sex work for mere survival and that maintain inequalities based on race, class, gender, and sexuality are erased. Similarly, the criminalization of sex work forces many queers of color to remain silent about violence committed against them for fear of legal indictment. LGBT persons of color often feel isolated and vulnerable because of the ongoing violent relationship between their communities and police departments due to racism, community policing in poor areas, and anti-gay violence at the hands of law enforcement. Criminalization thus leaves sex workers more vulnerable and subject to greater exploitation, violence, and harm.

Jessica Mercado, Shelby Tracey Tom, Christina Smith, Selena Álvarez-Hernández, and Donathyn Rodgers are just a few examples among the countless transgender victims of color that are frequently unnamed, unknown, or their murders unsolved. Gender transgression and material and economic conditions enable a disproportionate amount of violence to occur against transpersons of color. Racism within the LGBT community, homophobia within communities of color, and racialized economic inequality, force transgender persons of color into extremely vulnerable and volatile positions, lacking access to resources, social services, and oftentimes pushed into streets, where homelessness, sex work, and drugs become the only means for survival.

Hate Crimes Laws = Emancipation for Whom?

In theory, hate crimes legislation has been created to protect the rights of individuals who have been victimized by hate-motivated violence. However, this legislation also enforces extremely narrow, binary views of identity. Because of the interconnectedness of racism, classism, and heterosexism, hate crimes against queers of color are not individual acts of violence but larger structural inequities that disproportionately target specific *groups* of people. Hate crimes do not just affect the individual who is attacked, but also generate a message of violence that spreads community-wide. When transpersons of color are murdered, the effects of these crimes do not just spread within the racial or ethnic population or the queer community, but through both, including the various ways in which these communities intersect.[52]

The legal system enacts its own form of violence against LGBT persons of color, and this has direct implications on how hate crimes are tried and which cases are publicized. Andrew Sharpe highlights how one of the major theoretical problems in transgender legal reform is determining the exact moment at which legal recognition, and legal rights, will be afforded to a transgender person who has adopted a new gender role.[53] In almost all jurisdictions, Sharpe points out, both statute and case law determine the only possible point of change to be genital surgery. As a result, transgender persons who cannot afford, do not wish to undergo, or do not have access to genital surgery will never be recognized as their chosen identity. Likewise, the legislative separation of gender identity from sexual identity limits the individuals who can be included under these umbrellas, and enacts another form of violence.

It is the structural interconnection of racism, classism, forced gender conformity, and heterosexism that allows violence to continue against transpersons of color and also contributes to the apathy exuded by communities of color and the lesbian and gay community. Although the last decade has witnessed an increase in discursive material produced about gender and sexuality, the ways in which queerness and transgender identities intersect with race, political economy, and the law are often ignored. When transpersons are subject to violence, how communities respond to violence and how hate crimes are exposed is predicated on the economic status, race, and gender of the victim.

Hate crimes have become an important focus in contemporary US lesbian and gay politics. National LGBT organizations, such as the Human Rights Campaign (HRC), the National Gay and Lesbian Task Force (NGLTF), and the Lambda Legal Defense and Education Fund, have successfully lobbied for the inclusion and protection of sexual orientation and gender identity under the Local Law Enforcement Hate Crime Prevention Act, also known as the Matthew Shepard Act, and have asserted the need for increased research, reporting methods, and social services for victims of hate crimes. This law—which gives the federal Justice Department the ability to aid state and local jurisdictions with investigations and prosecutions of violent criminals motivated by bias—was recently ratified under the Obama Administration in October 2009.[54] Together with local LGBT groups, HRC, NGLTF, and Lambda Legal have urged the mainstream press to more frequently cover hate crimes, thereby increasing public awareness of violence against gays and lesbians, garnering support and sympathy from the heterosexual majority while also opening up avenues for prosecuting violent crimes committed against LGBT individuals.[55]

One way that this hate crimes organizing is limited is that it seeks inclusion and equality within existing social structures. While arguing for the basic legal protection for queer persons against hate-motivated violence is necessary and crucial to attaining rudimentary civil rights, rights-based discourses are often procedural rather than substantive.[56] However, adjudication of "equality" and the upholding of basic constitutional rights and protections are dependent on the legal system—the same legal system that has historically ignored, condemned, and failed to protect LGBT persons. "Equality," then, is enacted at the discretion of white heterosexual males who preside over the legal system. Moreover, because the legal system relies on precedent, the historical erasure and deprecation of queer persons is significant because the courts continue to rely on and enforce previously flawed interpretations of the law.[57] In doing so, heterosexism and homophobia are built into the structures of the law, and the legal system only permits reforms to those laws.

Hate crimes activism maintained by national LGBT organizations also renders acts of violence as individual acts of prejudice instead of macroscopically connecting anti-queer violence to other structural inequalities. Hate crimes are usually only named as such when extreme acts of violence are enacted by a perpetrator who specifically targets individuals because they represent a particular identity category. In contrast, the ordinariness of subtler, more covert experiences of homophobia and heterosexism that remain outside of legal adjudication are ignored. By failing to connect hate-motivated violence to larger social structures, the articulations made by HRC, NGLTF, and Lambda Legal render hate crimes as individual acts of explicit violence that reflect an anomaly. When only the most egregious forms of violence are legally recognized, the ways in which homophobia and transphobia play out as everyday, covert forms of spirit murder are erased.

Rights-based discourses construct hate crimes as irrational, aberrational, individual acts of violence perpetrated by homophobic people: they do not connect anti-queer hate crimes to larger structures of heterosexism. While seeking equality and legal protection from violence is an essential component to civil rights, it remains inadequate because it ignores the ways in which structural violence is perpetrated against queers. Arguing for the inclusion of sexual orientation and gender identity in state hate crimes laws will ultimately end in limited social *reform* because "equality" within the existing social system only accounts for and remedies the most blatant forms of injustice. The remedies, then, proposed by the National Gay and Lesbian Task Force, the Human Rights Campaign, and Lambda Legal simply hope to target and punish the individual perpetrators of homophobic and transphobic violence, failing to link the individual acts of violence to larger a system of heteronormativity. Hate crimes legislation and protection maintained by these national LGBT organizations in the end settles for access into a heterosexist system, thereby marginalizing the connection between individual hate crimes, historical legal precedent, and institutional violence. As a result, these groups espouse conservative, myopic political strategies and reject the opportunity for a more revolutionary and transformative politic that centers on broader conceptions of social justice.

By not taking into consideration the ways in which the criminal justice system regulates, pursues, controls, and punishes the poor and communities of color, LGBT hate crimes initiatives reproduce harm and do not end it. Calling for an increased role of the criminal justice system in enforcing hate crimes legislation is insular in that it assumes a white, gay, wealthy subject while also soliciting victims of hate-motivated violence to report into a penal system without regard for the fact that people of color and the poor are disproportionately punished. By ignoring racism and economic inequality in their arguments for hate crimes statutes, national gay rights organizations assume an assimilationist stance that reinforces the status quo at the expense of communities of color and the poor.

Political Failings—Sustaining the Prison Industrial Complex

Hate crimes legislation proposed by national LGBT organizations like the Human Rights Campaign, the National Gay and Lesbian Task Force, and the Lambda Legal Defense and Education Fund is fundamentally flawed. Hate-motivated violence is an important issue, but one that must be examined through the lens of "oppressive violence" and contextualized within intersecting systems subordination, including racism, classism, sexism, and heterosexism. As Cathy Cohen writes, "We must…start our political work from the recognition that multiple systems of oppression are in operation and that these systems use institutionalized categories and identities to regulate and socialize."[58] When national LGBT organizations place anti-gay violence at the center of analysis without regard for how their legislation is dependent on a punitive criminal justice system; the marginalization of communities of color and the poor; static, uncomplicated, and myopic versions of identity; and assimilation into existing systems of domination, they are refusing to acknowledge their own complicity in maintaining systemic oppression.

When national LGBT groups rely on political projects that further hate crimes legislation, they are feeding the prison industrial complex. Hate crimes legislation is punitive in that it is only enacted after someone is harmed or murdered. This does not tackle the structural roots of transphobia or homophobia but simply puts people who are found guilty of committing these crimes behind bars. As numerous studies have shown, prison systems are ineffectual at "reforming" criminals, deterring or decreasing crime, and reconciling the victims of crime.[59] Therefore, hate crimes legislation does not benefit anyone. Passing hate crimes legislation to protect queer folks after they have been harmed is only feeding a racist, classist, and transphobic/homophobic industry that disproportionately targets and punishes those with the fewest resources. Moreover, relying on a punitive system to hold an individual accountable for their crime promotes more oppressive violence: Individuals are simply locked up, not actively educated about or engaged in repairing the harm they have created; they are further divided from their families and support networks, perpetuating more damage, isolation, and devastation within their communities; and the system upholds the legacy of racism and classism that is and has been so prevalent throughout all aspects of the criminal justice system. Acknowledging, targeting, and punishing perpetrators of antitransgender violence is necessary but must also be placed within a larger context of the growing prison industrial complex.

Given the lack of access to support and resources due to transphobia, classism, and racism, as well as the disproportionately high rates of violence directed toward transpersons, making connections between broader systems of oppression and hate-motivated violence is imperative. A broader, systemic approach to problems of violence and oppression could involve cross-community coalitions opposing police brutality; local commitments to resist the processes of gentrification that criminalize homelessness and drive out poor, immigrant families; coalition work between sex deviants who frequently face criminal justice consequences, such as sex workers and people who engage in public sex, and those who face such consequences less often.[60] Addressing the unequal distribution of wealth and structures of inequality, including racism, alongside of transphobic and homophobic violence would challenge the uncritical reproduction of marginalization and open up sites of resistance and activism that all queers could collaborate in, benefit from, and support.

NOTES

1. Audre Lorde, "The Transformation of Silence into Language and Action," in *Sister Outsider: Essays and Speeches by Audre Lorde* (Trumansburg, N.Y.: Crossing Press, 1984): p. 41.

2. National Coalition of Anti-Violence Programs, "Hate Violence Against the Lesbian, Gay, Bisexual, Transgender, and Queer Communities in the United States in 2009." http://www.avp.org/documents/NCAVP2009HateViolenceReportforWeb.pdf.

3. Ibid.

4. Richard Juang, "Transgendering and the Politics of Recognition," *The Transgender Studies Reader* (New York: Routledge, 2006): p. 707.

5. Barbara Perry, *In the Name of Hate: Understanding Hate Crimes* (New York: Routledge, 2001).

6. Ibid., p. 38.

7. Juang, "Transgendering and the Politics of Recognition," p. 713.

8. Jessica Mercado, "Remembering Our Dead." http://www.rememberingourdead.org/JessicaMercado (accessed June 6, 2008).

9. Chris Harris, "We're Here, We're Queer, Who Cares?" *The Hartford Advocate*, August 28, 2003.

10. LLEGO (National Latina/o Lesbian, Gay Bisexual, and Transgender Organization), "LLEGO Urges Full Investigation into Possible Hate Crime in Murder of Transgender Latina," *Seattle Gay News*, May 23, 2003.

11. GPAC, "50 Under 30: Masculinity and the War on America's Youth: A Human Rights Report." http://iambecauseweare.files.wordpress.com/2007/05/50u30.pdf.

12. Harris, "We're Here, We're Queer, Who Cares?"

13. Shelby Tracey Tom, "Remembering Our Dead." http://www.rememberingourdead.org/ShelbyTraceyTom (accessed June 6, 2008).

14. Jeremy Hainsworth, "Trans Prostitute Killed," *Xtra! West*, June 12, 2003.

15. Donathyn J. Rodgers, "Remembering Our Dead." http://www.rememberingourdead.org/DonathynJRodgers, (accessed June 6, 2008).

16. Selena Alvarez Hernandez, "Remembering Our Dead." http://www.rememberingourdead.org/SelenaAlvarezHernandez (accessed June 6, 2008).

17. Christina Smith, "Remembering Our Dead," http://www.rememberingourdead.org/ChristinaSmith (accessed June 6, 2008).

18. According to the NCAVP, the number of reported anti-LGBTQ murders is as follows: 2003: 18; 2004: 13; 2005: 11; 2006: 10; 2007: 21; 2008: 29; 2009: 22. http://www.avp.org/documents/NCAVP2009HateViolenceReportforWeb.pdf.

19. National Transgender Advocacy Coalition, http://www.ntac.org/ (accessed June 6, 2008).

20. According to the most recent reports by the NCAVP, survivors and victims of hate-motivated violence report to the police approximately 25 percent of the time. Complaint refusals, survivor arrest, and police responses that may range

from indifferent to abusive are often deterrents from reporting hate-motivated violence to police. http://www.avp.org/documents/NCAVP2009HateViolenceReportforWeb.pdf.

21. Gender Public Advocacy Coalition, "Masculinity and the War on America's Youth." http://files.meetup.com/80123/5030.pdf.

22. Richard Juang, "Transgendering and the Politics of Recognition," p. 706.

23. GenderPAC classifies "sustained media coverage" as three or more articles in Top-100–ranked newspapers. Gender Public Advocacy Coalition, "Masculinity and the War on America's Youth." http://files.meetup.com/80123/5030.pdf.

24. Ibid.

25. I am referencing a generalized LGBT community here, including trans communities, which are often led and organized by white transgendered persons.

26. The Stonewall Inn was historically a white, working-class bar. As Thomas Lanigan-Schmidt recounts, "[We were] the sons and daughters of postal workers, welfare mothers, cab drivers, mechanics and nurse aids…. We all ended up together at the Stonewall." Quoted in Molly McGarry and Fred Wasserman's *Becoming Visible: An Illustrated History of Lesbian and Gay Life in Twentieth-Century America* (New York: New York Public Library and Penguin Studio, 1998): p. 4–5. The authors also support the claim that queers of color were often turned away from Stonewall. Jeremiah Newton states, "The Stonewall was not without very serious problems. If you were black, Puerto-Rican or even Chinese, it was next to impossible to get in. To be a woman or a drag queen was as bad. That peephole would open and close like the shutter of a lens and that was that" (5). More recent accounts involving the "celebration" of the Stonewall Inn and the Stonewall Riots erase the presence of working-class gays and lesbians, drag queens, and queers of color, viewing it instead as that "a mainstream gay riot that brought the community together" (19).

27. Charles Nero, "Why Are the Gay Ghettoes White?" *Black Queer Studies: A Critical Anthology*, eds. E. Patrick Johnson and Mae G. Henderson, (Durham: Duke University Press, 2005): p. 228–245.

28. Peter L. Stein, dir. *Neighborhoods: The Hidden Cities of San Francisco—The Castro* [Video] (Wolfe Video, 1997).

29. Cristi Hegranes, "Badlands Confidential," *SF Weekly*, June 29, 2005. http://www.sfweekly.com/2005-06-29/news/badlands-confidential/.

30. Howard Winant, "Racism Today," *The New Politics of Race: Globalism, Difference, Justice* (Minneapolis and London: University of Minnesota Press, 2004).

31. Keith Boykin, "Gay Racism in the Castro," *In Sexuality*. http://www.keithboykin. com/arch/2005/05/04/gay_racism_in_t, (accessed June 6, 2008); Keith Boykin, "Gay Racism," *One More River to Cross: Black and Gay in America* (New

York: First Anchor Books, 1996); Jasmyne Cannick, "White Gay Groups Silent on Black Gay Hate Crime Too." http://jasmynecannick.typepad.com/jasmynecannickcom/2006/10/white_gays_grou.html.

32. Dean Spade, "Compliance Is Gendered: Struggling for Gender Self-Determination in a Hostile Economy," *Transgender Rights* (Minneapolis: University of Minnesota Press, 2006): p. 218.

33. Keith Boykin, "Black Homophobia," *One More River to Cross: Black and Gay in America* (New York: First Anchor Books, 1996): p. 167.

34. Joseph Beam, "Brother to Brother: Words from the Heart," *In the Life: A Black Gay Anthology* (Boston: Alyson Publications, 1986): p. 230–39.

35. Stephan Lee Dais, "Don't Turn Your Back on Me," *In the Life: A Black Gay Anthology* (Boston: Alyson Publications, 1986): p. 60–62.

36. Jewelle Gomez and Barbara Smith, "Talking About It: Homophobia in the Black Community," *Feminist Review*, No. 34, 1990: p. 48.

37. Kelly Brown Douglas, "Breaking the Chains: Homophobia in the Black Community," *The Other Side*, September 2000. See also Dwight A. McBride, "Can the Queen Speak?: Sexuality, Racial Essentialism, and the Problem of Authority," *Why I Hate Abercrombie and Fitch: Essays on Race and Sexuality* (New York: New York University Press, 2005): p. 203–226.

38. Matthew Harwood, "Obama Takes on Black Community's Homophobia," *The Guardian*, Jan. 25, 2008.

39. Boykin, "Black Homophobia."

40. Ibid.

41. Nayan Shah, "Sexuality, Identity and the Uses of History," *Social Perspectives in Lesbian and Gay Studies* (New York: Routledge, 1998): p. 484.

42. Surina A. Khan, "The All-American Queer Pakistani Girl," *Women's Lives: Multicultural Perspectives* (New York: McGraw-Hill, 2006).

43. Urban Institute and Kaiser Commission on Medicaid and the Uninsured estimates based on the Census Bureau's March 2008 and 2009 Current Population Survey (CPS: Annual Social and Economic Supplements), "Poverty Rate by Race/Ethnicity: 2007–2008." http://www.statehealthfacts.org/comparebar.jsp?ind=14&cat=1. See also US Census Press Release, "Income, Poverty, and Health Insurance Coverage in the United States: 2003." http://www.census.gov/PressRelease/www/release/archives/income_wealth/002484.html for similar findings.

44. Kenneth Finegold and Laura Wherry, "Race, Ethnicity, and Economic Well-Being," *Urban Institute Research Report*, March 18, 2004.

45. Dean Spade, "Compliance is Gendered," p. 219.

46. Ibid., p. 219–228.

47. Ibid., p. 228.

48. Wendy Chapkis, "Locating Difference," *Live Sex Acts: Women Performing Erotic Labor* (New York: Routledge, 1997).

49. Viviane K. Namaste, *Invisible Lives* (Chicago: University of Chicago Press, 2000): p. 147.

50. Ibid., p. 170.

51. Ibid.

52. Darren Lenard Hutchinson, "Ignoring the Sexualization of Race: Heteronormativity, Critical Race Theory, and Anti-Racist Politics," *Buffalo Law Review*, No. 47, Winter 1999: p. 1–116.

53. Andre Sharpe, "From Functionality to Aesthetics: The Architecture of Transgender Jurisprudence," *The Transgender Studies Reader* (New York: Routledge, 2006): p. 621.

54. Human Rights Campaign, "The Local Law Enforcement Hate Crimes Prevention Act." http://www.hrc.org/laws_and_elections/5660.htm. The LLEHCPA provides the Justice Department with the ability to prosecute violent crimes in which a perpetrator has selected the victim because of the person's actual or perceived race, color, religion, national origin, gender, sexual orientation, gender identity, or disability. The LLEHCPA also makes grants available to state and local communities to combat violent crimes committed by juveniles, to train law enforcement officers, or to assist in state and local investigations and prosecutions of bias-motivated crimes.

55. For a discussion on the importance of hate crime politics and activism, see AnnJanette Rosga, "Policing the State," *Georgetown Journal of Gender and Law*, Inaugural Issue, Summer 1999: p.153.

56. See Kimberlé Crenshaw, et al., "Introduction," *Critical Race Theory: The Key Writings That Formed the Movement* (New York: The New Press, 1995): p. xxiii; Alan Freeman, "Legitimizing Racial Discrimination Through Antidiscrimination Law: A Critical Review of Supreme Court Doctrine," *Critical Race Theory: The Key Writings That Formed the Movement* (New York: The New Press, 1995): p. 29–45.

57. Precedents, in order to make the law efficient, reliable, and less subjective, hold courts to previous decisions made in similar cases because the past cases are assumed to be reasonable. See Howard Abadinsky, *Law and Justice: An Introduction to the American Legal System* (Chicago: Burnham, Inc., 1995): p. 38.

58. Cathy J. Cohen, "Punks, Bulldaggers, and Welfare Queens: The Radical Potential of Queer Politics?" *Gay and Lesbian Quarterly*, No. 3, 1997: p. 458.

59. See Angela Y. Davis, "The Prison Industrial Complex," *Colorlines*, Fall 1998; Eric Schlosser, "The Prison Industrial Complex," *Atlantic Monthly*, December 1998;

Joel Dyer, *The Perpetual Prisoner Machine—How America Profits from Crime* (Boulder, Co.: Westview Press, 2000); Critical Resistance, "Not So Common Language." http://www.criticalresistance.org/article.php?id=49.

60. Dean Spade and Craig Willse, "Confronting the Limits of Gay + Hate Crimes Activism," p. 50–51.

WALLED LIVES

CONSOLIDATING DIFFERENCE,
DISAPPEARING POSSIBILITIES

KRYSTAL IS KRISTOPHER AND VICE VERSA

Kristopher Shelley "Krystal"

My name is Kris Shelley and I have been incarcerated for nine years. I am what you call a gender-non-conforming lesbian. I started my time at juvenile hall when I was three months into being 17 years old. They were confused with where to place me because I looked like a boy. The girls would never say anything negative, but the boys would snicker, laugh, and point at me because I had to wear the girl's uniform color. This never really bothered me unless they stood up to the plate and attacked me. When they did I would beat them up with all the hatred they used on me. I felt like I had to show them who was boss.

I had to move on to another juvenile hall, and that's where the trouble started. The head coordinator started picking on me before she even knew me. She didn't want me to live with anybody (no roommates) because I looked so different. After some time there I finished high school and graduated with more than enough credits and a 3.6 GPA. So I became a tutor in elementary education. This young girl I tutored loved me as a human being, mentor, and friend. She saw me as no different than anyone else, which made me love her for not judging me or trying to fit me into a category. She was 9 years old and in juvy for being disrespectful to her mother, but for some reason she respected me and would listen to me.

I started going to court for my case, and the judge said to me, "You look more like the mastermind and more aggressive than your co-defendant." My co-defendant was Asian, his dad was a minister, and we were the same age but I was black, lesbian, and from a broken home. My minister and his wife came to court for me, along with my boss (from school jobs) with her daughter, and even my teacher. All just to try to set me free! Having no prior record and being tried as an adult, I received twelve years. Of those twelve years I would have to serve ten years and two months. My co-defendant received three years. Our case got separated into two different cases due to the fact that my co-defendant blamed possession of the gun on me, though the gun was not loaded. So for a frame, I got ten years and a "good luck" from Judge Knupp at the Norwalk (aka "No Walk") courthouse.

At 17 years old, off to the county jail I went—all alone. So alone I sat thinking, praying, and singing in 211 of Twin Towers County Jail. Still 17, off to prison I went. On the receiving yard (A-yard), I felt I was only able to walk because I looked like a grown, big black mutt, ready for whatever. I acted as though I wasn't afraid of anything and no one messed with me.

The week I turned 18, off to Stockton Prison I went. At first everyone seemed cool, until I met this one sergeant that wanted me to shave my face every day, because of my strong male appearance. Every time I saw her, I dreaded life in that place. She made me lock in until I shaved, or she would send me back from work and threaten me with a 115 (a disciplinary charge document). All because I was being me and I was going to stay being me, no matter how she felt. This is a medical condition I have for life and I felt that she was going to have to deal with it and move on. (Medical services gave me a chrono to not have to shave and groom, as my wants and styles may vary.) Then the correctional officers wanted to force me to wear a bearded mask while working in the kitchen. Every single day brought more and more harassment.

When I came to Valley State Prison for Women I was praying for a new beginning, but that just couldn't happen. Not in this system. On my fourth day I was coming back from chow with a lady I had been calling mom since Stockton, and her woman started flipping out and called me over. I went toward her with no problem, but the cops took her inside and trapped me in between the buildings. Suddenly I was blocked by officers I hadn't realized were right there. So I started trying to walk, but they said I was refusing to lock in. As I was walking through the front door, I turned to see three cans of pepper spray and eighteen correctional officers set to attack me. They saw me as aggressive and so they used extra force. As I went to jail (Administrative Segregation, or Ad-Seg), I sat thinking about how this could be my third strike for something I didn't even do. I sat for two months in solitary before I was found guilty, only for them to come back two days later to say I was not guilty, apologizing to me several times, to my face. After that I was terrified of Sergeant Earn and all the other staff too.

Last but not least, when I got out of Ad-Seg, the cop in my unit tried to say that I assaulted him with my room door. The cops, the sergeants, cooking staff, and free world staff would make side comments about my appearance, which made me angry and want to fight them. Very few of the men did not bother me. Only years later did they finally leave me alone. When they messed with me, I had something to say right back to them. Then all of a sudden I grew up and learned how to become quiet and humble and not bite into their words. That's when they finally left me alone and stopped pulling me out of line at chow or out to the yard for no reason. Then they saw that fighting was not in my character for real. I've heard all kinds of comments, like: "Man, you grow a better goatee than me," "Man, I can't get any facial hair—can you hook me up?" "You look like a man, but can you fight like one?" and "Are you transgender or do you have both parts?" and so on and so on....

As far as people asking, I don't mind at all. I would prefer to be asked first than to be discussed without any facts. I believe God made me this way. I can handle it with God, and as I've gotten older in life, it's gotten easier to explain my hormonal issues that were discovered when I was about nine. My male hormones were as high as almost two grown men, which made me the way I am even now. Even though my hormone levels are where they are supposed to be, I still have polycystic ovary syndrome. I have cysts and tumors on my ovaries, making my levels increase all over again, which makes my male features stronger.

But guess what? I wouldn't give my life up for any other one. This struggle has made me who I am today. And may my path that is less traveled make it easier for those who will follow.

THE ONLY FREEDOM I CAN SEE:

Imprisoned Queer Writing and the Politics of the Unimaginable

Stephen Dillon

If we feel calm, what must we forget to inhabit such a restful feeling?
—Jasbir Puar[2]

In one of his first letters to me, "C," a fifty-year-old queer (non-norma-tively gendered) Latino prisoner incarcerated in south Texas for more than twenty years, wrote the following: "The only trip I've had was on a bus called Blue Bird when I was transferred from my hometown to where I am right now. If you have a little time tell me how it feels...when you are on a plane way up there in the air."[3] This passage, and C's larger body of writing, narrates the ways that the US prison regime works with race, gender, space, and mobility to structure regimes of knowledge—not only how we understand the forces that bring us into being, but also, quite literally, what we are able to know. As a young, poor farmer growing up in the shadow of the local prison, C understands his arrest and imprisonment within the institutional vocabulary of the prison. C describes being "transferred" from his hometown to "where I am right now." One is normally transferred from one prison to another, one unit to another, from the debilitating loneliness of the isolation unit to the unknown terror of the general population. But for C, the prison's vocabulary ("transfer") best describes the experience of being forcibly relocated from one space of unfreedom to another, from outside to inside, ostensibly free to immobilized and detained. C understands the free world as intimately connected to and constituted by the prison, and further, that the free world is anything but free; rather, it is an extension of the *unfreedom* central to the mundane operations of the prison. C was not captured, detained, or forcibly confined; he was processed and moved from one space to another; he was simply and profoundly *transferred*. C's writing points to the ways the logics of the US prison regime have structured his understanding of the social and cultural world, and also alludes to how the prison structures *what we can know*. His question about the feeling of flight captures the ways that carceral state violence underwrites various epistemological gaps, fissures, and impossibilities.

And so at C's request, I've tried to explain what it is like to fly. My nervousness before the takeoff, my headaches from the pressure change that linger throughout the next day, my daydreams of falling through the sky, and my sense of relief once the plane lands. He often asks me to explain something that is a mundane occurrence to me, something I wouldn't think twice about, but something that is unimaginable to him: swimming at dawn next to the Chicago skyline, dancing with friends, the life of a student, the ocean at night. As I write letters to him, I have to remind myself to explain every detail, every assumption—everything that whiteness, capital, and heteropatriarchy have rendered normal for me and impossible for him. In our correspondence, our vocabularies continually fail us: the intricacies and effects of state violence, of subjection and subjectivity, of knowing and unknowing, constantly render our ability to convey our worlds to each other a failure. Even as I describe flying, he tells me he can't imagine it. As I tell him about my day-to-day, he says that he can't understand it: The absence of violence and terror, the ease with which my body moves through the world, the joys and pleasures that are so normal for me that I forget they are there. In turn, his everyday is indescribable. There are some experiences he could never make legible, and even if he could vocalize the unspeakable, the unimaginable, there are some things that are simply incomprehensible for those of us on the outside of the prison. His writing leaves so much unsaid, a tactic for avoiding the terror of memory and the surveillance by guards of anything he writes. He assumes that by reading between the lines and completing his unfinished thoughts, I will understand what must be done if a friend is attacked or what happens when a guard comes at night.

The reasons that he is there in a 9-by-12 foot cage for twenty-three hours a day and that I am here in the "free world" writing to him are not the result of random coincidence, personal choice, or isolated luck. Rather, I am here and he is there because of the (institutionalized) disparate distribution of wealth and poverty; health and illness; freedom and subjection; mobility and captivity; and life and death that is intimately informed by our skin, gender, class, queerness, and so much more. White supremacy, heteropatriarchy, and neoliberal capitalism have made the co-erced disintegration of his mind and body acceptable, mundane, unseen, and unknown. He has been rendered expendable, surplus, worthy of being immobilized, worthy of being held captive. According to Anna Agathangelou, M. Daniel Bassichis, and Tamara Spira, the last forty years of collusion between white supremacy, heteropatriarchy, neoliberalism, and the prison industrial complex have produced "those who can and must be killed, warehoused, and watched, and those whose civic duty requires their complicity in the killing."[4] He has been rendered killable, and I complicit and entangled in his living-death and potential future biological death under the prison's production of illness and disease, bodily disintegration, physical and psychological terror, and the directive to "shoot to kill."

The only time C left his small town in Texas was through coercion, the product of histories that have been forcefully forgotten and mechanisms of life and death larger than he or I can grasp. Deeply embedded within the explanations of my everyday to C are the epistemological and ethical crises with which our correspondence is riddled: How does one correspond with people who are socially and civically disappeared, people whose right to exist has been eliminated, people subjected to bodily and psychic disintegration? What mechanisms structure the failures of our correspondence? What technologies produce the terror and subjection that intimately collude with freedom, life, and possibility? What options emerge from within the US prison regime's production of so many impossibilities (spatial, temporal, affective, bodily, etc.)? In this chapter, I use my correspondence with two imprisoned queer people whom I call

"R" and "C" (for reasons of privacy and safety), to analyze the role that heteronormativity and heteropatriarchy play in animating neoliberalism, white supremacy, and the US prison regime.[5]

Free Markets and Captive Bodies

In the last forty years, neoliberalism has become a pervasive mechanism for organizing institutional and discursive life in the United States and around the world. As an ideology and epistemology, it is embedded in our values, thoughts, and desires; it is a technology that structures collective common sense. Neoliberalism manages cultural, political, and economic life to prioritize and maximize the mobility and proliferation of capital at all costs.[6] Neoliberalism attempts to "free" the market and private enterprise from constraints implemented by the state. This is accomplished by dismantling unions; public funding of social services (welfare, education, infrastructure, and so on); environmental, labor, health, and safety regulations; price controls; and any barriers to "free trade." The neoliberal project is to disembed capital from any and all constraints.[7] In addition, any state-owned institutions that control key industries like transportation, energy, education, healthcare, food, water, and prisons, are privatized in the name of efficiency, deregulation, and freedom.

Discourses of personal responsibility, choice, and individuality are central to the ideological and institutional shifts that have taken place under neoliberalism. Under neoliberal regimes of freedom, one's subjection to "the state-sanctioned or extralegal production" of premature death through homelessness, abject poverty, illness, over-work, addiction, or incarceration is the result of an isolated, individual choice.[8] This logic is used against those hardest hit by environmental devastation, imperialism, forced famine, privatization of services and deregulation of governments, the restructuring of paid and unpaid work, the dismantling of welfare apparatuses, increased policing and surveillance, and the hyper-immobilization of black and brown bodies in an ever-expanding regime of incarceration and detention.[9] Simply, those most susceptible to production of premature death are blamed for their vulnerability to regimes of power far beyond their control: the drowned, the starved, the impoverished, the bombed, the occupied.

In *A Brief History of Neoliberalism*, David Harvey argues that neoliberalism is "a political project to re-establish the conditions of capital accumulation and to restore the power of economic elites."[10] For Harvey, neoliberalism is fundamentally about the restoration of class power to a handful of powerful corporations and individuals. Yet, Harvey disregards the ways that white supremacy and heteropatriarchy are central to neoliberalism's distribution of profit, power, and death. Harvey fails to account for the ways that, as neoliberalism funnels capital upward, one's access to a variety of life chances are diminished in ways that are profoundly racialized and gendered. Neoliberalism does not just produce terror, to paraphrase Henry Giroux, or "downsize democracy" in the words of Lisa Duggan; it also produces and proliferates possibilities for some lives to grow and prosper.[11] Neoliberalism is not just a project of capital; it is also a project of white supremacy and heteropatriarchy. It proliferates capital at the same time that it proliferates whiteness and heteronormativity.

The neoliberal turn has been part of a broader strategy of state and corporate counterinsurgency mobilized in the wake of revolutionary decolonization movements threatening capitalism, heteropatriarchy, and white supremacy.[12] In the 1970s, the United States, a "normatively aggressive, crisis-driven state," facing political insurrection and debilitating economic crises, did what it had always done: systematically identify, coercively control, and violently eliminate foreign and domestic "enemies."[13] The US prison regime emerged to discipline portions of the working poor considered "surplus" or incorrigible to new precarious, low-wage, service work; to neutralize and contain potentially rebellious populations; and to reaffirm the authority of racially gendered state and corporate power.[14] In the late 1970s and early 1980s, criminalization became the weapon of choice in dealing with the globalization of capital and the resistance it engendered.[15]

These new regimes of accumulation, discipline, and immobilization build on much older regimes of racist and patriarchal terror and exploitation in order to fabricate populations vulnerable to criminalization (black, brown, indigenous, poor, queer, and trans people); to militarize and legally empower police and criminal justice apparatuses; and to produce a popular and public discourse that organizes a "grammar of social necessity and ideological consent" around the emergence and expansion of the prison industrial complex.[16] When one factors in the ways that heteronormativity structures the visibility of certain bodies (and particular tactics of survival) to the police and technologies of discipline and containment, LGBTIQ poor people and people of color become one of the populations hardest hit by white supremacy and neoliberalism's funneling of millions of human beings into the US prison regime.

Living Neoliberal Terror

In forty meticulously handwritten pages of poetry, prose, and memoir that have taken her nearly two years to write and send to me from a cell in rural Texas, R has told me about freedom, oppression, terror, joy, boredom, fear, loneliness, and captivity. R is a 48-year-old white non-normatively gendered person ("gay," "nelly," "drag queen," "sister") who has spent close to the last thirty years of her life in prison. Twelve of those years were in administrative segregation ("the hole"), a roughly 45 square foot cell where one is forced to remain alone for twenty-three hours a day. She is HIV and HCV positive, has no family and no friends (she has "acquaintances" in prison). Her soonest release date is in 2011; her furthest is in 2018. The only other person she communicates with is a nun who writes to her once a year.

In her first letters, she wrote about her life in non-linear, fragmented pieces threaded together by the fuzziness of memory, prefaced by a disclaimer, "Note: Not everything that *happened to me, or did not happen* to me is covered. But in the following, what is covered is the truth" [my emphasis].[17] R's qualification recognizes the contingency of the knowledge that she will relay through her letters—that the truth of her life is haunted by (and riddled with) absences, gaps, and silences that are rendered all the more glaring by positivistic demands on knowledge and the ways that white supremacy, queerphobia, capitalism, and the law collude to render prisoners pathological liars, manipulators, biologically and socially sick, unreliable, and disposable. How do we understand her narrative that rests between the *happened* and the *did not happen?* Where is the line between the fictive and the factual and the imaginary and the real? For R, truth resides somewhere in the space between *the happened* and *the did not happen,* or as Kamala Visweswaran writes, "Memory, as we know, is not to be relied upon; memory always indexes a loss," and truth, as R highlights, resides somewhere within this loss, in the space between *the happened* and *the did not happen.*[18] Her poetry is engulfed in loss, not only the physical and psychic loss she has experienced, but also the loss necessary in the attempt to describe that which is so often unspeakable and unnamable. R's theorization of truth describes an epistemology that is attuned to that which is present in its conspicuous absence, or in Avery Gordon's words, R describes "a method attentive to what is elusive, fantastic, contingent, and often barely there."[19]

R tells of her life up to her incarceration in a poem titled, "And Life Goes On." She begins by asking,

Why can't I get my life in harmony?
And be like any other person?
For I know life can't be this cruel, cause even animals have it better
that live in a zoo.
I mean life looks so gloomy for a person like me.
But what did I do to make it this way?

She then goes on to trace the interpersonal and institutional mechanisms—not mentioned in her question—that ensnared her in the US prison regime at the precise moment when hundreds of thousands of people (soon to be millions) were swept up by regimes of immobilization as neoliberalism emptied cities of capital and jobs. I want to briefly summarize R's poetic life narrative.[20]

R was born into the foster system ("I had no family of my own") and passed from family to family ("none would call me there [sic] own"). For the first ten years of her life, she lived off "grease from a frying pan" and "beer from the night before." "I don't remember much before I was six, but I know at this age I only weighed thirty-six [pounds]." When she was finally placed with a family she hoped would be "home," she was "adopted only in name" and was "nothing but a slave…to work on a farm and to be beat for anything that went wrong." At thirteen, her foster father raped her for the first time. "He took me," and like so many children subjected to sexual violence and extreme poverty, she began using drugs, running away, and stealing. At sixteen, she escaped the foster system for good and began traveling around the South, surviving by stealing. In 1978 she was arrested for burglary, and while in jail she was beaten within an inch of her life by seventeen prisoners and raped by six—"but in reality" her life was saved "to face more of the same." When she was released, she traveled from Louisiana to Texas, "still running and trying to survive," and was arrested for burglary again and sentenced to a year and a half of prison and "was raped once again and beat down a couple of times, but still I try to fight, not just to keep the wolves off, but to survive."

The whole poem fills one page of prison-issued paper, a life summarized in thirty lines. The gaps of white space between each of R's stanzas, textual silences that encompass years, speak loudly and constitute more intangible (unseen) forms of knowing. There is so much she can't say, can't write down, or simply can't remember. The final stanza of the poem reads, "I got released from prison in 81/but as luck would have it/Two and Half months later/I was in penitentiary for burglary again."[21]

In December 2005, after spending almost half her life in prison, R was released on parole. She writes of this experience:

> While I was in the free-world I had 5 marks against me, which were: 1. I had a prison record; 2. I was a S.I.S.P. parole; 3. I am a homosexual; 4. I have HIV. And HCV.; 5. I have a major depression disorder. All of the above hurt me in some way when I was looking for a job or a place to live. And if these didn't hurt me, then parole rules that the parole board placed on me would. And they did stop me from getting a home and a job… parole is set-up for failure here in Texas.[22]

R's concept of five marks—the ways her body and her conditional freedom were metaphorically and literally marked with her incarceration, queerness, depression, and HIV- and HCV-positive status theorizes heteronormativity as foundational to the diffusion of disciplinary power beyond the formal walls of the prison. R experienced queerphobic verbal assault from both the staff and residents at the halfway house she was placed in. She could not get adequate medical care for her depression and illness. She was denied financial support from Planned Parenthood (by the parole board), which would have given her six months of rent, and she struggled to get a job due to her status as an ex-convict and visibly queer person. For R, the prison regime's collusion with heteronormativity and other disciplinary mechanisms made living in the free world virtually indistinguishable from the subjection of incarceration. Like C's articulation of being "transferred" from his hometown to prison, R theorizes gender and sexuality as central to prison's dispersal of disciplinary power into the free world. The regulation and violence that queer bodies are subjected to on the outside of the prison colluded with the parole system to render R's ability to survive outside of the prison virtually impossible. After finding the free world uninhabitable, R eventually "gave up" and crossed state lines because "I wanted to get picked up and sent back to prison." She writes in a poem,

If I have to remain in prison
I will never get released
So please allow me to stay in prison
So I can die in my rightful place…So how can you force me
To live in the free world now?
Where I have no chance

to survive in any way
Cause parole is set up for failure
If you have no family on your side
So the only freedom I can see
Is death in a prison cell.[23]

R's poetry echoes Michel Foucault's concept of "circular elimination," where the cycle of violence and incarceration experienced by so many people on the edges of heteronormativity, white supremacy, and neoliberal capitalism functions as "a machine for elimination...a kidney that consumes, destroys, breaks up and then rejects, and that consumes in order to eliminate what it has already eliminated."[24] R's poetic life narrative demonstrates the ways that poverty, sexual violence, the criminalization of crimes of survival, and the dismantling of social support networks under neoliberal restructuring intertwine to over-determine the presence of poor non-normatively gendered people in the US prison regime.

R's poetry and writing also highlight the forms of extra-legal violence that imprisoned queer people are subjected to in the form of physical and sexual assault at the hands of other inmates and guards. Protecting oneself against this violence can lead to extended sentences, so that one's attempts to survive the inconceivable horrors of captivity are met with an intensification of one's subjection to state violence. R was originally sentenced to twelve years for burglary but was then charged with multiple counts of "possession of a deadly weapon" and "attempted murder" while she was incarcerated. R writes,

At one time if you were gay in this man made hell you were in trouble. Cause the guards did not care about you. Then the white people you were doing time with hated us that were gay and white. For they claimed we made the white race weak. So they were out to get us.... But then again this is the way all gay people were treated. Not just white gays.... And when gay people were getting beat down, raped, hogged, jacked, killed, used and abused, the guards would turn their head...there was always a group of us that would fight back...and we kept weapons, and had records of keeping them, and using them. And most of the time this was the only protection we had.... I kept weapons on me 24 hours day...in my bunk when I was asleep...even in Ad. Seg [administrative segregation]...I kept weapons to protect myself and at times to protect my sisters.[25]

R's writing makes visible the heteronormative logic central to white supremacy. She writes,

> To me, the guards that give me the most problems are the white male ones. And the most inmates I have problems with are the white ones. The reasons that "nelly" prisoners like myself have problems with white guards and prisoners alike is that they feel that gay white males make the white race weak. Now think about that! Are they full of it or what?[26]

R highlights the ways that heteronormativity is not only is central to the prisons' daily operations, but that it is also foundational to white supremacy. White supremacy is never separate from other technologies of power; it is intimately intertwined with capital, heteropatriarchy, and the prison. R is not only punished by the state through her incarceration, but she is also ritually and routinely punished by other inmates (who are not stopped by the prison administration) and state employees for her queerness. Imprisoned queer people experience a particular form of carceral violence and living-death, one produced by heteronormativity and white supremacy.

R's description of her resistance to the institutionalized white supremacist and heterosexist violence articulates a vision of the US prison regime in which acts of (racialized) sexual violence are not exceptional nor spectacular, but rather are routine, mundane, and everyday. This violence is not a deviation, corruption, or pathological disruption from the "normal" functioning of the prison. Instead, this violence is foundational and constitutive of regimes of punishment in the United States. Within the larger economies of neoliberalism, the racially gendered and sexualized violence foundational to the prison regime is intimately connected to larger regimes of exceptional force that render queer and trans bodies (especially queer and trans bodies of color) surplus to neoliberal capitalism.[27] R is the embodiment of this theorization. Poverty, sexual violence, and heteronormativity funneled R into the prison industrial complex, further punished her once she was inside, and drove her back once she was released. R's poetry makes visible the ways that various spaces and technologies of confinement collude to discipline nationally, racially, and sexually aberrant subjects.

Within this theorization, the prison underpins and produces not just state power, but also racialized, gendered, national, and sexual social formations. While it inhabits a realm of everyday common sense and enjoys a popular consensus around its seemingly isolated architecture of domination, the prison produces discursive and ontological forces that emanate beyond its formal walls.[28] Judith Butler's concept of "construction as constitutive constraint" is instructive here. Butler argues that the same regimes of power that produce intelligible and knowable bodies also produce a domain of unthinkable, abject, and unlivable bodies.[29] It is those subjects who are physically and discursively forced to inhabit spaces of exclusion and deferred death who continually haunt and constitute the bodies and lives that are permitted to flourish. The US prison regime's mass incapacitation of bodies of color and queer bodies not only marks and immobilizes those bodies as disposable, but it also produces the discourses needed for other bodies to be "free." Laura Whitehorn, a white lesbian political prisoner captures this relationship when she writes, "Our lack of freedom does affect how free you are. If we can be violated so can you."[30] Many imprisoned queer writers understand that civil society relies on carceral unfreedom to render itself intelligible.[31] In addition, they reconceptualize the supposedly abnormal or exceptional violence central to the prison's existence, as a fundamental organizing logic of life in the United States.[32] The prison is thus not outside of social production, but rather, foundational to it, making subjects on all sides of the prison walls.

R's multiply determined status as a poor, imprisoned queer is productive of a particular vision of the US prison regime and the ways that it animates and haunts civil society. She makes visible the intertwining networks of power that over-determine the presence of queer and transgender people in the US prison regime. Writing from within a liminal space—between life and death; freedom and subjection; known and unknown; *the happened* and the *did not happen*—R speaks directly out of a epistemological formation produced in the crisis and conflict that inevitably accompanies the oppressive logic of white supremacy, heteropatriarchy, neoliberalism, and state violence. R's writing and epistemology returns an image of the free world that makes visible the terror of the everyday that is rendered invisible by normative ways of knowing and seeing, or is so routine as to not merit attention or outrage. R's forced transfer from the foster system to prison, to the free world, to prison, to the parole system, and back to prison, demonstrates the ways that the US prison regime animates and is produced by sexual, psychological, and physical violence, neoliberalism, heteropatriarchy, and white supremacy to render certain subjects—what Angela Davis has called "detritus"—as human surplus.

Queering Abolition, Undoing Homonormativity

When I asked R what she needed from me as a scholar, activist, and friend, she responded,

> The last thing I would want is for someone to feel sorry for me. For what I need most help in is to overcome all the negative in my life and become a more positive person, but not just for myself but for my people within the gay community and in the free-world, and here behind these prison bars.... But Steve, what hurts me the most is this! The lack of knowledge within the gay community in the free-world concerning LGBT people behind bars. It makes me feel like my brothers and sisters in the free-world could care less about us that are behind prison bars, or we must be the *forgotten ones*. And this I don't understand [my emphasis].[33]

What has this forgetting made possible? What subjects arise out of this loss? In *Criminal Intimacy: Prison and the Uneven History of Modern American Sexuality*, Regina Kunzel charts the forced forgetting of imprisoned LGBTQ people by free-world queer activist communities. By looking at mainstream gay and queer left publications, Kunzel notes a transition from a politics of solidarity with imprisoned LGBTQ people in the 1970s ("We are all prisoners," "We are all fugitives," and "Free our sisters! Free ourselves!") to a position of distance and disidentification beginning in the 1980s.[34] Kunzel notes the ways that in the 1970s queer activists connected their experiences of personal and institutionalized racism and homophobia with the struggles of all prisoners: "Because we understand that the system that has created and maintained prisons as method of social control is the same system that oppresses [those of] us on the outside."[35] This liberatory queer politic was not concerned with giving queer prisoners a "helping hand," but rather sought to build "a new kind of community" that could simultaneously challenge the racialized politics of criminality, social control, bodily regulation, and the management of queer desire.

In the 1980s, Kunzel marks a decline in prison pen-pal projects and a shift from a revolutionary politics to a liberal politics bent on social inclusion, rights, and gay marriage. Many queer activists' concerns shifted to "winnable battles," in which queer prisoners were constructed as a "negative element" in the overall debate concerning "gay rights"; gay activists sought to build a movement with "as little fragmentation as possible."[36]

Middle-class gay white men argued that "gay rights" should remain a legislative issue and that "legally sanctioned gay marriage should be a primary concern for all of us."[37] Kunzel charts the ways that the forced forgetting of queer and trans prisoners was central to the coalescing of "new gay norms," "gay respectability," and homonormativity. This disciplining of the queer left was a racialized project that coalesced around shoring up the privileges afforded by whiteness, gender normativity, and capital. It was a movement to proliferate the life-enhancing norms of white supremacy and neoliberalism at the expense of so many lives, in addition to a movement and politics bent on the liberation of all.

The purging of imprisoned queer and trans people from "the community" has, in part, acted as the condition of possibility for the privileges and power afforded to those not ensnared in the nexus of power produced by neoliberalism, heteropatriarchy, white supremacy, and regimes of incarceration. The forgotten, the expunged, and the eradicated are intimately constitutive of what we remember, how we know, and where we are. As some seek safety and security under racially gendered state and corporate power, what quotidian deaths will make such shelter possible? What norms will proliferate? What bodies and lives will be constructed as disposable or even unimaginable by a movement for inclusion? Whose doors will continue to be kicked down? Who will continue to be taken at night, or under the light of day?

Imagining the Impossible

In his description of the differences between death row and administrative segregation (the hole), C captures the possibilities that lie within the immobilizing contradictions of states of captivity:

> Did I feel differently being on death row? Honestly, to me the only difference between death row and Ad.-Seg. [is] that in Ad.-Seg one day when you do all your sentence you will go home and in death row you don't go home, you get killed…but in death row at least you have a small window in your cell and here in Ad.-Seg [there is] not even a window to at least see [the] outside, the blue sky, or the night stars.[38]

In her poetry, R articulates a similar theorization of possibility within the immobilization and incomprehensibility of captivity when she writes, "The only freedom I can see/Is death in a prison cell."[39] This contradictory logic—that freedom comes with death inside one's cell (and not release into the "free" world), that a window on the way to biological death is more desirable than a state of isolated living-death—is precisely the epistemology required to fight against unimaginable and incomprehensible formations of power. R and C's writings point to a political logic (queer visions) that exceeds the boundaries of liberalism. It embodies a way of thinking that is derailed from normative common sense. Coming to terms with C and R's intimate understanding of power's mobilization of biological death and living-death, in addition to their conceptions of freedom, pushes us toward a never-ending insurgency that cannot be satisfied with polity, patience, or reform. Cultural theorist Dennis Childs captures this when he writes, "The enormity of racialized carceral genocide in the United States and its continued accretion into/within our current moment both domestically and globally disallows any model of tidy or triumphalist resistance."[40] We are faced with conditions whereby life itself has become the object of "variable forms of destruction, annihilation, and quiet exterminations."[41] R and C's writings push us toward imagining forms of insurgency and resistance that refuse to settle for bigger cells, softer chains, or normative notions of freedom. They remind us that reform is a pathway to more insidious forms of subjugation and that what disguises itself as humanity, hope, freedom, and possibility may end up destroying us in the end. They push us toward imagining the impossible and reckoning with the unimaginable, as we are faced with the inconceivable, unthinkable, and indescribable. They beg the question, what possibilities open up when we become intimate with the impossibility that lies before us?

NOTES

1. I would like to thank "R" and "C" for sharing their writing and editing drafts of this essay. I'd also like to thank Allison Page, Jennifer Pierce, Regina Kunzel, and Roderick Ferguson for their encouragement and support throughout this project.

2. Jasbir Puar, *Terrorist Assemblages: Homonationalism in Queer Tines* (Durham: Duke University Press, 2007): p. xviii.

3. "C," Personal correspondence, April 18, 2007.

4. Anna Agathangelou, et al. "Intimate Investments: Homonormativity, Global Lockdown, and the Seductions of Empire" *Radical History Review*, No. 100, Winter 2008: p. 134.

5. I use "queer" to describe C and R's sexual and gender non-normativity. They both use queer to describe themselves in addition to many other terms: "gay,"

"nelly," "drag queen," "sister." While some prisoners present in gender-non-normative ways, they may not describe themselves as "trans" or "transgender."

6. Henry A. Giroux, *The Terror of Neoliberalism Authoritarianism and the Eclipse of Democracy* (New York: Paradigm, 2004): p. xiii.

7. David Harvey, *A Brief History of Neoliberalism* (Oxford: Oxford University Press, 2005): p. 11.

8. Ruth Wilson Gilmore, *Golden Gulag: Prisons, Surplus, Crisis, and Opposition in Globalizing California* (Berkeley: University of California Press, 2007): p. 28.

9. Chandra Mohanty, *Feminism Without Borders: Decolonizing Theory, Practicing Solidarity* (London: Duke University Press, 2003): p. 234.

10. Harvey, p. 19.

11. See in general Henry Giroux, *The Terror of Neoliberalism: Authoritarianism and the Eclipse of Democracy* (London: Paradigm, 2004) and Lisa Duggan, *The Twilight of Equality? Neoliberalism, Cultural Politics, and the Attack on Democracy* (Boston: Beacon Press, 2003).

12. Anna Agathangelou, et al. "Intimate Investments: Homonormativity, Global Lockdown, and the Seductions of Empire," p. 137.

13. Ruth Wilson Gilmore, "Globalisation and US Prison Growth: From Military Keynesianism to Post-Keynesian Militarism," *Race & Class*, Vol. 40, No. 2/3, 1998/99: p. 178.

14. Loïc Wacquant, "The Penalisation of Poverty and the Rise of Neoliberalism," *European Journal on Criminal Policy and Research*, No. 9, 2001: p. 405.

15. Julia Sudbury, "Celling Black Bodies: Black Women in the Global Prison Industrial Complex," *Feminist Review*, No. 80, 2005: p. 166.

16. Dylan Rodríguez, "'I Would Wish Death on You…:' Race, Gender, and Immigration in the Globality of the US Prison Regime," *The Scholar and Feminist Online*, Vol. 6, No. 3, Summer 2008: p. 12.

17. "R," Personal correspondence, March 4, 2008: p. 5.

18. Kamala Visweswaran, *Fictions of Feminist Ethnography* (Minneapolis: University of Minnesota Press, 1994): p. 68.

19. Avery Gordon, *Ghostly Matters: Haunting and the Sociological Imagination* (Minneapolis: University of Minnesota Press, 1997): p. 26.

20. While I am cautious about doing so, I share R's life story and experiences at her request. I take seriously critiques of the representational crises involved in writing about violence and terror. For instance in her work on terror, violence, and slavery, Saidiya Hartman writes, "[H]ow does one give expression to these outrages without exacerbating the indifference to suffering that is consequence of the benumbing spectacle or contend with the narcissistic identification that obliterates the other or prurience that too often is the response to such displays?"

So while I do discuss forms of spectacular violence that R has been subjected to, I also try to highlight the ways that terror also exists within the mundane and routine. See: Saidiya Hartman, *Scenes of Subjection: Terror, Slavery, and Self-Making in Nineteenth-Century America* (Oxford: Oxford University Press, 1997): p. 4.

21. "R," Personal correspondence, Feb. 20, 2008.

22. "R," Personal correspondence, March 4, 2008: p. 5–6.

23. "R," Personal correspondence, March 4, 2008: p. 6–7.

24. Quoted in Angela Y. Davis, "Racialized Punishment and Prison Abolition" in *The Angela Davis Reader,* ed. Joy James (Malden: Blackwell Publishers, 1998): p. 98.

25. "R," Personal correspondence, Aug. 18, 2008: p. 1–2.

26. "R," Personal correspondence, July 17, 2008.

27. Anna Agathangelou, et al. "Intimate Investments: Homonormativity, Global Lockdown, and the Seductions of Empire," p. 135.

28. Dylan Rodríguez, *Forced Passages: Imprisoned Radical Intellectuals and the US Prison Regime* (Minneapolis: University of Minnesota Press, 2006): p. 43–44.

29. Judith Butler, *Bodies That Matter: On the Discursive Limits of "Sex"* (New York: Routledge, 1993): p. xi.

30. Linda Evans, Susan Rosenberg, and Laura Whitehorn, "Dykes and Fags Wanna Know: Interview with Lesbian Political Prisoners by the Members of QUISP," in *Imprisoned Intellectuals: America's Political Prisoners Write on Life, Liberation, and Rebellion,* ed. Joy James (Oxford: Rowman and Littlefield Publishers, 2003): p. 270.

31. Dylan Rodríguez, *Forced Passages: Imprisoned Radical Intellectuals and the US Prison Regime.* (Minneapolis: University of Minnesota Press, 2006): p. 170.

32. Ibid., p. 7.

33. "R," Personal correspondence, July 17, 2008.

34. Regina Kunzel, *Criminal Intimacy: Prisons and the Uneven History of Modern Sexuality* (Chicago: University of Chicago Press, 2008): p. 192, 222.

35. Kunzel, p. 193–194.

36. Kunzel, p. 223.

37. Kunzel, p. 223.

38. "C," Personal correspondence, July, 2, 2008.

39. "R," Personal correspondence, March 4, 2008: p. 6–7.

40. Dennis Childs, "'You Ain't Seen Nothing Yet:' *Beloved,* The American Chain Gang, and Middle Passage Remix," *American Quarterly,* Vol. 61, No. 2, June 2009: p. 290.

41. Julian Reid, "Life Struggles: War, Discipline, and Biopolitics in the Thought of Michel Foucault," *Social Text,* Vol. 24, No. 1, Spring 2006: p. 149.

BEING AN INCARCERATED TRANSPERSON:

Shouldn't People Care?

Clifton Goring/Candi Raine Sweet

I was born in New York State and deserted by my family. I was really raised by many group homes and residential treatment centers. I have been homeless and I am still currently poor. While in prison, I have been cut by other prisoners for refusing to perform sexual acts for them, and I have been beaten and sexually assaulted (sodomized with the nightstick) by correctional staff. I see first-hand the very issues that the system needs to change.

No one in the prison system really cares about us trans people, gays, or gender-non-conforming people; they say they do, but when it really comes down to it, the facts will always show that the majority of the prison believes this nasty saying that "only the strong shall survive and only the weak perish"—which is such a cruel saying and, when you think about it, doesn't really make much sense. But not much ever really gets done regarding the violence within the very prison walls.

Rapes, very nasty physical assaults, and beatings take place, by other inmates and by the very same prison personnel who are sworn to protect each and every inmate. Regardless of the degree of such brutality, many of the staff known as "the administration" turn their heads the other way as one of various non-conforming people is being harmed, truly violated, and or in better words—straight up—put through hell by the hands of inmates and staff members.

These very same prison staff do not even get punished for their violating actions. Nothing usually happens to the staff, which really compounds an already unsafe atmosphere and makes it an even less safe place for gay persons, transfolk, or two-spirited persons. If anything, the most that happens to employees is a suspension for a period of time, but that's about it. Like nothing ever took place, like the world stopped as they hurt someone, they don't face charges for their acts—they don't even get fired, but they are simply let back to work, bragging about what they've done and or how they did it, they sometimes even taunt the person harmed with other fellow employees.

Instead of protecting each and every inmate, in accordance with their duty, they discriminate based on the complexion of one's skin, or the way a person looks, or the type of lifestyle one chooses to live, whether it is as a person being bi, gay, trans-based, queer, gender variant, or two-spirited men and women, or femme queens, non-femme queens, or feminine men.

The one thing that we all have in common in this life is our very human being itself; though in our own ways we are very different, we are still people with meaningful personalities, feelings, ways of thinking, ways that we conduct our day-to-day dealings, ways that we interact, ways that we cry, and even viewpoints. But that should not, under any circumstances, mean that we should be viewed in a separate light from the next person and treated differently.

This is a fact: Straight people, or ones who are not of trans nature, do not face the same kind of violence or the same negative aspects of prison life as much as gay persons, queer persons, bisexual people, two-spirited people, femme queens, non-femme queens, femme men, gender variants, gender-non-conforming people, or us transfolks have to face. Why? Well that is very simple. As it stands, I believe that this world isn't really ready to accept us yet—point blank, no sugar coating it or putting it into a better bunch of words, this world, not just this harsh prison system, is not truly ready for us yet. Most of this world deals with or interacts with us because they simply have no choice in the matter, whether they like it or not. And the others are starting to honestly realize that we, too, are people with feelings, that we, too, shouldn't be harmed or violated in any way whatsoever, and that we, too, need support at times in life.

This entire prison system is truly and utterly so corrupted in every sense of the word. Violence toward us occurs but nothing ever happens, rarely if anything, to the ones who attack us. We face long periods of isolation a lot, because of non-acceptance and fear of being harmed, and even fear of death. Because of many issues caused by the prison system, we face a lot of emotional issues, whether they be of self-esteem and/or other elements caused by the core of the prison environment, which in itself is a world of its own. We all have one very strange fear in common, which is the fear of being harmed by the very ones who are there to protect us: the "staff." These guards have no regard for us, and this forces us to constantly worry about our safety, which is truly never a sure thing. Why? Because at times we suffer from way to much stress, paranoia, fear, and isolation. We suffer from the elements of being poor; most of us do not have family, friends, or any type of outside support. Most of us are going through these very painful stages in life, alone, which in its own way compounds the issues we face on the day-to-day basis.

There is so much that the system can and should do to change the way it functions, though it's easier said than done. The ways of Congress play a major part in the system and how it works, yet they turn a blind eye as the most of society believes that everyone in prison is a savage of some kind.

These changes are so very sound, simple enough to correct over the course of a year or so more, yet it may never take place because not much care is really directed toward this cruel system and the way it runs.

The work of the Sylvia Rivera Law Project and other allies seeks to change this very problem, for it is way overdue for us to have a voice, to not be alone, and face such harm and whatnot. The road is long, but the light is so very bright. Change is near, and it is very much needed.

OUT OF COMPLIANCE:

Masculine-Identified People in Women's Prisons

Lori Girshick

Well, I don't care how long I live. Over this I have no control, but I do care about what kind of life I live, and I can control this. I may not live but another five minutes, but it will be five minutes definitely on my terms.
— George Jackson

George Jackson was responding to the racist treatment he endured while incarcerated. There isn't one issue concerning incarcerated individuals that can be viewed separately from how the prison industrial complex attempts to control people and strip them of their dignity and respect as unique human beings. Rae,[2] a transgender male inmate at Central California Women's Facility, said to me regarding the homophobia and transphobia he was faced with,

…you're trying to take my identity from me. You're trying to take my soul from me, you're just trying to take everything from me. You've already taken my freedom, but I had a large part to play in that, so there's not a blame game going on here. But, come on now, you can't, that's all I have left is who I am and they are trying to take that from me.

Individuals whose gender identity is outside the traditional gender binary of masculine and feminine for the bodies they are perceived to have challenge gender expectations. I am using "transgender" as an umbrella term that encompasses several types of gender transgressors. This umbrella term includes transsexuals, cross-dressers, masculine-identified female-bodied people, drag kings and drag queens, androgynous people, ungendered people, two-spirit individuals, intersex people, and others who do not neatly fit into the two boxes of a gender binary. This study[3] involves individuals who were medically assigned as female at birth and who identify as masculine. Most are content to be in their female bodies, while some feel they are men and are interested in transitioning socially and physically to live their lives as men. One prisoner lived as a man for over twenty years before arrest, though without any medical changes to his body.

Since most states where this study was conducted house prisoners according to their genitalia, including California, people identifying as men are living in women's prisons, and individuals identifying as women are housed in men's prisons. Some attention has been paid to transwomen and feminine men incarcerated in men's prison facilities. Their issues and abuse—verbal, emotional, physical, and sexual—is portrayed in the 2006 documentary movie *Cruel and Unusual*.[4] Legal issues surrounding housing, access to hormones and sex reassignment surgery, and safety from sexual assault have been written about in legal journals.[5] Transgender rights and prison rights activists have written reports about the range of concerns of transgender prisoners in documents such as "It's War in Here."[6] This study examines the less-known concerns of masculine-identified people in two women's prisons in California.

Valley State Prison for Women (VSPW) and Central California Women's Facility (CCWF) vie for the recognition as the largest women's prison in the world. Located in Chowchilla, California, in the San Joaquin Valley in Madera County, they are literally across the street from each other. Both were designed for just over 2,000-bed capacity, but each house just under 3,900 people today. CCWF opened in 1990, and VSPW followed in 1995.

There is no official count of how many transgender prisoners there are in the California system. Woodward wrote in 2006 that based on activist estimates, there were probably 200 transgender people (who had or were interested in transitioning) and another thousand who were gender variant and did not fit the gender binary. This takes on heightened significance because prisons are highly gendered spaces in terms of masculinity and femininity, and also in terms of sexuality. Men's prisons are set up to emasculate men, and women's prisons are designed to reinforce dependence and passive roles for women.[7] Both environments mirror a hyper expression of traditional gender roles. While violent control over men in prison breeds violence in return, either through the violence of guards over prisoners or the violence among prisoners through gang violence, sexual assault, or guards allowing prisoners to prey upon each other, this is seen as an inevitable result of concentrated masculinity. That is, the control is designed to be violent, to reinforce the hyper-masculinity of competition, dominance, control, force, suppression of emotion or weakness, and especially heterosexuality, where punks, or "women," are forced into sexual submission.

Female prisoners are expected to be passive, emotional, weak, submissive, and dependent. Since *non-feminine* behavior landed them in prison, incarceration should "restore them to it."[8] They should display subservient behavior, including in heterosexual relations. Due to the constant monitoring of sexual behavior (where *any* touching between prisoners can be defined as sexual) and the fact that more guards are male than female, there is a highly sexualized environment that includes flirting between male guards and prisoners, whether due to dependence on them for access to goods and privileges or in search of attention, kindness, or father figures. This dependence mirrors the traditional relationship outside of prison in which women are supposed to be at the beck and call of men in their lives. Furthermore, Lutze reminds us, this leads to women continuing "to see themselves as a commodity to be used by men."[9] That incarcerated females have defied feminine expectations and morality is shown in a comment by gender-non-conforming Cookie: "They just feel that this is part of my delinquency. You know, they attribute it to my delinquency. They don't attribute it to just me as a person."

The Sample

Twenty-two masculine-identified people at CCWF (16) and VSPW (6) filled out surveys, and fourteen of this group were interviewed in

191

person in a follow-up.[10] Their age range was 22 to 63. The average age was just over 39. Half of those interviewed (11) were in their thirties. The sample was mostly minority: Ten people identified as African American, one as black Cuban, and one as Haitian/Dominican. Four were Hispanic, and one identified as Chicano. Two people were white, not Hispanic. There was one Native American person, one Pacific Islander, and one mixed-race person (Hispanic and African American). These prisoners had very long sentences. Forty-one percent (9) were lifers (one had life without parole, or LWOP). The other sentences ranged from four months to nineteen years, but for these thirteen people, they averaged a nine-year sentence. Their educational attainment was not high: Five had dropped out of high school, two had graduated from high school, and six had attained a General Equivalency Degree (GED). There was one college graduate, one with an Associate's degree, and seven had some college. One person had also graduated from the California Military Academy.

Every person was in the study because they identified as "masculine." However, the words they used to describe their identity differed. Transgender terminology is in much debate and flux. Individuals use terms differently, disagree on meanings, or use multiple terms to describe their identities.[11] In this study, the term *aggressive* was used by fourteen individuals, *masculine* (3), *stud* (4), *butch* (1), *gender-non-conforming* (1), and *transgender male*, *transman*, and *man trapped in a woman's body* (4). Numbers add up to more than twenty-two due to multiple terms used in some cases. The term *aggressive* is commonly used in prisons for the female-assigned masculine person, though this may partly be connected to the *aggressive* attitude and demeanor that these masculine prisoners display or are accused of displaying. But the term is not only used within prison walls. According to the profiles in the documentary film, *The Aggressives*,[12] aggressives are female-bodied persons who have been tomboys, who feel masculine but accept their female bodies, and who see this masculinity as a gender identity. They dress and act in ways consistent with a masculine presentation. Some aggressives are transsexual and want to transition, but not most. Aggressives are generally lesbians.

Ten of the prisoners prefer the pronoun "he." Six listed "she," and six said either he or she, or no pronoun.[13] Eighteen people identified as gay or lesbian, and two listed that they were either bisexual or open. Two people identified as straight; they were both transgender males, meaning they were attracted to women while they identified as men. So, every person in the study was attracted to women either exclusively or to both women and men.

Conflation of Gender Identity and Sexual Orientation

Before moving on to a discussion of what these prisoners experience in their daily lives based on their gender identification, it's important to acknowledge that gender identity is often viewed as the same as sexual orientation to most people—most people in the general public and probably most people in prison, whether prisoner or guard. In my earlier research, transsexuals have told me that the first question their family members ask them when they tell them about their transition is often, "Does this mean you're gay?" This conflation in the prison is seen when staff (common term for guards) make homophobic comments in response to *gender* issues or when, in this study, I asked a gender question and was answered with a sexual orientation reply. For example, "You said your gender identity was butch, can you tell me what that means to you?" Reply from Mike: "I've always been sporty and whatever, [and] when I was growing up I just leaned toward women, you know, that was who I wanted to be with." And, Potatoes, who identifies as a masculine woman, was telling me how she overheard others talking about aggressives, and these prisoners said, "Well, isn't that something you choose? Nobody makes you be homosexual." Kango defined her identity, aggressive, this way: "I've always been a tomboy growing up, so I do boy things and not so feminine like. And I've been gay pretty much all of my life." Rae said, "I didn't know about aggressives until I came here and heard the prison lingo. Out there in the free world there's just gay, so I've learned transmale in here as well in identifying with others. But in the free world, I'm gay and that's what I am."

Since gender identity is a concept that examines how people identify in terms of masculinity and femininity (as defined by the culture), and sexual orientation addresses issues related to attraction and intimacy, these are quite different concepts and look at different aspects of the self. They involve different behaviors, ideas, activities, relationships, and emotions. Gender presentation is not the same thing as who one's sexual partner is. But, in our culture, we conflate these when it comes to those who violate *either* gender norms *or* sexuality norms. While someone who is gay or lesbian is not automatically seen as being transgender but are often seen as transgressing gender boundaries, someone who is transgender *is* often assumed to be gay. Whether it is because homophobic attitudes

193

and expressions are so widespread that these are familiar and easy to use, or because being gay is seen as a gender violation so the language of and about homophobia is easily applied, I'm not sure. Many people who do not accept gay or transgender people view both as unnatural, whether based on religious beliefs or learned prejudices. As long as homophobia is deeply entrenched in our society, transgender individuals will have a difficult time being accepted.

I've Always Been a Tomboy

Probably the most commonly shared aspect of their lives was that, growing up, these individuals were tomboys. *Tomboy* was the specific word I heard used when people described their identities. For example, Kool identified as a masculine female. To her, that means being "kind of hard.... Always very aggressive, tomboy, basketball, baseball, all of that.... It's always been, probably raised more of a tomboy than a girl because I never wore makeup, anything. Never tried to bring out my feminine ways." Joy, an aggressive, "always got called tomboy. So, I always had the lifestyle of being rough, so that's aggressive in my eyes and other people's eyes.... I never wore make-up or anything like that. But I've always had the rough edge about me." Terri, another aggressive, echoes, "Like a little boy, they [prisoners] call us, because we're aggressives because we don't do what the girls do. We don't put on makeup, we're always wrestling around, playing sports. We're more like the little boys. That's how they prefer to call us: *hes*." These identities complicated life, whether outside or inside prison. Buba, an aggressive, reports that people did not know whether she was a girl or a boy. Potatoes had guys "plant themselves in front of me and chest butt me, and say, 'You want to act like a man?' I mean, totally unprovoked!"

Insane identified as masculine and was comfortable with the pronouns he or she. While fine with a female body, Insane was "nowhere near a feminine female." He said, "I like to play softball, well, here we have softball, basketball, something like that. You don't see me up there with the aerobics people, or you know, jump rope or something." Insane compared himself to feminine females who "stand in the mirror combing their hair; me, I'm just like, getting some braids, wash my face, brush my teeth, and get moving. In other words, some of them stay there for hours, while I get ready on a drop of a dime. And that's like my brothers or something, so that's why I put myself in that category." Growing up, Insane fought with his mother over wearing dresses and sitting properly. He sees the masculine influence in how he dresses and the way he carries himself.

194

Potatoes also referred to demeanor: "Well, it's how I carry myself. I don't have a feminine walk. I prefer not to go out with my eyebrows plucked."

Cookie "always wanted to be a boy." He was called tomboy and dyke. In junior high school, girls refused to shower with him in PE class. For years he felt something was wrong with him because he did not feel like he was "supposed to." Growing up there were fights with his grandmother over wearing dresses. Wearing girl's clothes at graduation was awkward. Cookie tried to conform to being more feminine, but it was never comfortable. He tried to not be called names and to fit societal and family expectations. Today, Cookie uses the terms gender-non-conforming, aggressive, and stud, but gender-non-conforming expresses it best.

Richard identifies as a transgender male. "Essentially I was born in the wrong body. I call it the wrong suit. Since I was very, very young I have thought about that I was a boy and why wouldn't anybody recognize it?" Things went along OK until high school. "I dropped out because then you had to wear dresses and all that, and they're real strict about dividing boys and girls, and stuff like that. At the time I quit school I could not vocalize what, why, I just didn't want to go anymore, that is all I could say." Richard started living as a man at age fifteen up until his incarceration at thirty-seven. "Nobody knew that I was female except for my partner."

Respondents also mentioned that being aggressive meant having a hard edge, being perceived as non-deferential, and treating women with respect (for example, not calling a woman a bitch and not hitting a woman). These standards of masculinity are backed up by appearance norms such as shaved heads, big and baggy clothing, less feminine clothing, no makeup, more masculine postures, and being assertive speakers. Their gender presentation is more masculine by societal standards even within the tight parameters of prison clothing options—the issue we turn to next.

Femininity Standards

All people wear clothing and accessories that convey gender messages. If you look in any clothing store, there are different styles, colors, fabrics, clothing cuts, buttons, belts, ruffles, and so forth that indicate whether these clothes are to be worn by women or men. These style ideas are widespread in society and taught to children without their even realizing that they are absorbing and accepting them as natural. People in a women's prison who want to express masculinity will want to express a certain look. This can only be done based on prison-issue clothing and what products are available in the vendor boxes.[14] This and their comfort level wearing certain types of clothing are factors to take into account with how masculine-identified prisoners present. The main clothing issues that surfaced in the interviews were baggy, loose or sagging clothing, the new state-issue blue jersey tops, boxer shorts, and muumuus. Other presentation issues include grooming standards (in particular, facial hair) and tone of voice.

Comments from staff about baggy clothes (baggy as in oversized) and sagging clothes (sagging down low, by the hips or lower) were common. Many prisoners mentioned that they were more comfortable in large or oversized clothes. But this created problems for them. For example, Buba said that she had received harassing comments such as "Put your pants up! You're not a man!" and "Oh, you think you're a man, I'm going to treat you like a man." Lodown, an aggressive, wrote, "[I've had] write-ups for wearing too big clothes and shaving my head." Kool brought up the problem of being identified as a gang member if an inmate wore baggy clothes, when many had either never been in a gang or were no longer gang-affiliated. For Kool, who has been incarcerated for over thirty years, clothing is no incidental item. "The clothes, especially the blouses, and their bras and they underwears, they are not cool with me."

Most of the people I spoke with talked about the state-issued blue jerseys. I noticed that most of the people I met with wore baseball jerseys—white T-shirts with navy three-quarter-length raglan sleeves. But these were the "old" issue Potatoes explained:

> We had what they call a change in the matrix last year. No baseball shirts, and change in the denim jeans. With pockets they fit better. They came out with this new clothing. [The new shirt] has the woman's neckline, which is different than a T-shirt. It's big, and if you have a brand new shirt, it will go up here, but if you wash it five times it opens up and comes all the way down here.

With washings, the necklines stretch out and at times even fall down one shoulder. Insane said, "I'm not OK with those ugly wide-neck shirts. They try to make you look all feminine, I'm not wearing that. We just cut the sleeves, get it sewed up, get something to taper it [the neck] a little bit, make it so we can deal with it." Brown Eyes, an aggressive, feels these are "girly" shirts, and she does not wear them. To some prisoners, these clothing changes are, as Rae commented, "trying to make us more like femmes all the time." Cookie called it "forced feminization." Concerning the loss of the baseball jerseys, elasticized jeans, and the banning of belts, he said, "to me this is about making us wear tighter clothes, which is again going back to what their picture is of rehabilitated females."

Potatoes, like several others, hoarded the baseball shirts. They had them stashed in different places. Eventually, they were told, the baseball shirts will be confiscated. But Potatoes has stated that she will never wear the more feminine shirts. "I said, 'Well, I'll just go to jail.' They said, 'Well, you can't go to jail forever,' and I said, 'Yes, I can.' I would hit a staff and go to jail before I would walk around in a round-collared shirt."

The comfort issue around clothing is especially acute when it comes to underwear. Terri mentioned, "I always wore boxers. I feel more comfortable, and that was one of those issues, why can't we have them? I don't understand why we can't have them here." People in women's prisoners wear panties, not boxer shorts, the under garments of choice for many aggressives and masculine-identified individuals. But, boxer shorts are considered contraband in women's prisons. Some people cut the legs off their thermal pants, and wear them as underwear, but for much of the year it is too hot to wear those. Boxer shorts are not available from vendor boxes (unless you are housed at a men's facility), but prisoners do get them. There are a few ways of getting this contraband item. Prison Industry Authority (PIA) makes inmate clothing, including boxer shorts. Prisoners have found a way to get boxers out of there, though not directly from stealing them since they are searched when they return to their units after work. As Buba reported, "[In] PIA laundry, we wash men's clothes, some people be getting some boxers out of there and they sell them on the main yard." Insane mentioned another way of getting boxer shorts. "You find a hook-up and get you some clothes made, you know. They have PIA fabric and they make boxers for me, so you can get, if they have a pattern. There's some talented people here, that's why they can make you boxers out of a sheet."

Mike does feel constrained from getting black market boxers, since you can get into trouble for having contraband items. "I have a few pairs, but you try not to get caught. I would be removed from my job because I work where they make them, so...." But to CJ, an aggressive, "I know it's contraband, but I cannot do panties." Cookie questions the whole premise of keeping boxer shorts from people who feel more comfortable wearing them. He said,

> Boxers don't make me act more aggressive. Boxers don't make me break more rules, they don't make me want to use more drugs, they don't make me want to do anything but feel more comfortable when walking

around.... Like I said, it's forced feminization, they're going to make us wear these panties. They've determined what women wear and that's it.

In addition, Cookie points out that if boxers were part of the clothing matrix it would stop the theft of boxers and eliminate a black market item.

It would be easy to allow access to boxer shorts for people in women's prisons. They are already made at PIA and they could be part of the clothing matrix. Vendor boxes already have approved vendors that supply men's prisons with boxer shorts; prisoners in women's facilities could order from the same vendor. And there is the example of the New York state Office of Children and Family Services that now stocks bras and panties in boys' juvenile facilities and men's underwear in girls' centers to accommodate transgender youth. A spokesman said, "The policy is all about tolerance and respect,"[15] and on this point all of the people I interviewed would certainly agree.

When female prisoners are transported from one prison or unit to another, or if they go into the hospital, they are made to wear a muumuu. This dress can be humiliating for a masculine-identified person to wear. Potatoes said to me,

> But they bring you over in a muumuu, in a dress, for what purpose? They transport you in a dress. What does that mean? What's wrong with a jumpsuit? It's just wrong to keep us docile, to degrade you, I don't know. Even women that wear them, are upset, I've never asked them why they're upset. The time I wore one I walked to A yard [receiving] to the yard, and I put my bag on the bed and said "what do I have that I can trade," to the room, "what do I have that I can trade for a shirt and a pair of pants?" I had just shopped the day before. I didn't care what they wanted. I was going to walk out of that room with a shirt and a pair of pants, and I did. But, I don't know what I would've done. I would've taken them off somebody, that's what I would've done. If I didn't have the canteen, I would have took them off somebody, I hate to say.

Standards of femininity are enforced to the extent that if a prisoner is outside of gender expectations, they will be out of "compliance." This compliance is to the grooming standards—for example, the idea that women will not have facial hair, mustaches, or beards. So, for example, when Kango was going to medical for a lab test she was stopped and told to "go in compliance" before she would be allowed to have her test! She at first thought the officer thought she had shorts on instead of long pants, but no, he said, "Go shave your face." In fact, Kango does have facial hair, but she also has a chrono from a doctor stating that she can have it and keep it trimmed. She had tried to remove the hair with cream, but it burned her face. Plucking left marks, and shaving made her break out. The dermatologist sided with her that she was better off to just leave the hair on her chin. But, whenever officers demand she shave her face, she has to produce the chrono.

Visa, an aggressive stud, also has facial hair. Staff have said to her, "Get that fucking shit off your face!" But Visa is on A yard where razors aren't allowed. "So, I've got to get mistreated with the verbal abuse" when she cannot fulfill the demands of the grooming standards. Mike mentioned that most prisoners who have facial hair do shave, complying with the expectations of femininity.

According to Brownmiller in her classic work, *Femininity*, "speech is an assertive act... and male and female are schooled in different ways."[16] The voice pitch, pronunciation, tone, vocabulary, females ending a sentence as if asking a question—all aspects of speech are gendered. "Women are not supposed to be authoritative."[17] To be verbally aggressive is to be like men, who are trained to be argumentative and assertive. Females, on the other hand, should reflect their passivity and support roles in their manner of speech. Consequently, tone of voice is a major issue for the aggressives and masculine women I interviewed. Insane spoke for many individuals when he said, "You respect me, I'll respect you. You don't respect me, I don't respect you.... You're not going to take all my dignity from me just trying to talk to me like I'm nobody on the face of the earth." He continued, "They take your disposition as being a threatening manner, or if we have an argument, you talking crazy to me, I talk back crazy to you, you step, I step, you know your hands are in the arguing, the first thing they're gonna do is take you to ad seg."[18]

"Not being submissive to staff," "being an aggressive speaker," and "tone of voice" were just ahead of "clothing" and "appearance regulation" as difficulties these masculine-identified prisoners faced. Kool felt that stereotyping by staff has a lot to do with her problems. She said,

> they do not try to get to know me, they don't want to know me, they take one look at me and feel like I'm this evil mean bitch because I'm dark-skinned. I walk kind of boyish-like, I'm into my own little world,

and I have a right to express my opinion and my voice when I'm angry or when I'm upset. There's a correct way of doing things. And I try to do the correct things.

But, for an aggressive, there is no "correct way that will work." Lodown said he experienced constant harassment. "I've had officers ruff [sic] me up and say 'How much of a man are you?' Then I've had them tell me 'So how big is your dick? I bet mine is bigger.'"

Aggressives and Male Staff as Competitors

Most of the prisoners I spoke with identified male staff as the main source of harassment and problems, not other prisoners, and not many problems with female staff. Male staff were the ones who made the homophobic comments, male staff were the ones who harassed the aggressives by roughing them up, male staff talked about dick size, and male staff were the ones who flirted with the femme prisoners. The aggressives perceived that they were singled out for harsher treatment than the femme inmates.

The problems with "homosecting"—any behavior seen as sexual, whether sitting too close to another prisoner, touching a prisoner, or actually engaging in sexual acts—ranges from homophobic comments to receiving a write-up for behavior against the rules. Not only is the threat of a disciplinary action around homosecting a constant, but to many officers, homosexuality is a moral issue. This gives staff a certain license to bring sexuality into their everyday conversation. To CJ, "my sexuality has nothing to do with why I'm in prison, how I act in prison. In fact, my sexuality is none of your business. It's my own. And it's hard for police here, certain police, to understand that. They feel that you're going to hell, and I'm here to let you know that."

Rae completed the requirements for the religious program Evangelism Explosion. Yet, because he challenged a free world staffer when she was not going to allow a program participant to graduate because she was a lesbian, Rae also was not allowed to graduate. The inmates had put their full energy into the program but when it came to graduation night they were informed they could not attend based on their sexual orientation. CJ said if there's a disagreement between two prisoners certain officers will make an unrelated comment like, "What, they trying to make you a dyke?" Once, when Cookie was sitting close to his girlfriend an officer said, "This is disgusting." Richard has "received retaliation because of my perceived intimate relations with attractive female prisoners. I have received retalia-

tory transfers and disciplinaries because of these relationships and for asserting constitutional rights, and for prison activism." These examples of
homophobia are a small sampling of what the prisoners experience daily.

There is a widespread feeling that staff treat the aggressives more
harshly than the femme prisoners. John feels because of his gender identity as a transman he has "been verbally harassed, mocked, put-down,
made to go to the end of clothing, canteen, and dining room lines. I've
had my cell torn-up and trashed on a regular basis. I've also had male c/o's
aggressively search me or have a female c/o strip search me for no reason."
Similarly, Richard wrote, "On more than one occasion I have received
disciplinary write-ups, cell searches, and punishment (continued denial
of parole suitability) which I believe to be due to my transgender male
identity." Cookie believes the fact he had a bald head worked to his disad-
vantage when an incident was blown out of proportion and he landed in
ad seg for a year. Why does this happen? According to CJ, some male staff
are like this one in particular—"As long as you're not masculine, he don't
have a problem with you. If he see that you're masculine, it's over." As
Visa told me, "I was locked up in the hole and I was coming in from the
yard, so I was cuffed, he grabbed me and smashed my face in the concrete,
for no reason at all…. There's a lot of aggressive women here and a lot of
them get treated real bad." She also believes that staff are quicker to use
batons on aggressives without warning than on other prisoners.

Insane has been singled out of a group and told to "Hit the wall….
Put your hands up, let me see some ID." He feels the officers do not like
his appearance, or how he carries himself. "So being as they don't like it,
they gonna try to mistreat me any way they can." Similarly, Mike has been
singled out as the only aggressive in a group, "Hey, come here!" And as he
says, "You can't really argue." Kool has watched the favoritism of femmes
over aggressives for decades. Many masculine women feel, as Buba said,
staff's attitude is, "Oh, you think you're a man, I'm going to treat you like
a man…. The hard way."

Aggressives who have girlfriends see the difference in how they are
treated compared to their partners. Why is the girlfriend not harassed?
Because "she's a girl," said Buba. Cookie was very sick one time and the
nurse refused to give him an excuse from work. His (now ex-)girlfriend
walked in right after, with no real illness, all smiles and sweetness, and
walked out with a work excuse. "I'm expected to tolerate more pain. I
don't cry, so I couldn't be in pain." "If you want to be a man, be a man,
tough it out" is the attitude Cookie feels aggressives are looked at with. As

Joy told me, "I feel like if I was a femme and I go to the cop shop and do all the smiles—'cause I've watched it, you know—'Oh, sure, you can get in,' or 'Go ahead.'" Another way the femmes are treated differently than the aggressives is through favoritism. Kango said, "They give them things that, like, we're allowed one, let's say laundry soap, we get laundry soap every month, and they give us a bag of laundry soap. So, this officer might give this femme two or three bags of laundry soap."

One reason why staff treat aggressives so harshly is because of their homophobia. They conflate their masculine gender presentation with being gay and this challenges their own sexuality issues or their religious views. The other major perspective is that the aggressives' maleness threatens the masculinity of the male staff. Male staff often flirt with women prisoners; hence, aggressives are seen as competition for the femmes' attention. Moosey Baby, an aggressive stud, states, "The correctional officers get jealous because the aggressives are more aggressive than they are and we (aggressives) get more attention from the female inmates and correctional officers than they (men) do." Rae feels that some male officers are attracted to his girlfriend, "so they have problems with me because they can't get to her."

Sadly, sexual abuse and sexual assaults of women prisoners by male officers in correctional facilities around the country is too common. Documented in the report *All Too Familiar*,[19] some male officers take advantage of the vulnerability of prisoners (both that they are locked up and that they are frequently survivors of incest, rapes, and domestic violence prior to incarceration). It cannot be denied that a sexualized atmosphere exists in prisons, whether as flirting, manipulation, or outright abuse and assaults. Sometimes the flirting behavior between male staff and femme prisoners creates problems for aggressives. Kool talked about this experience,

[One officer] used to flirt with my girlfriend, the one that I've been with since '89. "Hey, you need to be with a real man," and all kinds of stuff, and I used to tell him all the time, "Quit disrespecting me." And he'd laugh. He used to flirt with my girlfriend all the time in front of my face. I can't hit no man, what could I do? I was scared to say anything, because if I say anything, he'll probably put me on another yard in another unit, but I should've because that's what he did anyway when he couldn't get his way with my girlfriend. He went after somebody else who lived in my cell. And still made me feel uncomfortable. That's one example. When he talked, he would grab his private part; [who] he think he be super fly?

Similarly, when a male officer disrespected Insane's girlfriend, the officer said to him, "Oh, what you gonna do? What you gonna do? You're no man."

Transgender Concerns

Masculine female-assigned prisoners do not face the same issues as feminine male-assigned prisoners. In general, there aren't the same fears of sexual or physical assault from other inmates, and the need for protection isn't there. Whether considering homosexuality or gender identity, masculine-identified women have greater concerns regarding officers than other prisoners. Housing segregation would be needed only in highly individualized circumstances in women's prisons. When I asked people in my study if they felt gay or transgender prisoners should be segregated, they almost all said absolutely not.

This is not an idle consideration. Legislation is being considered in California to segregate lesbian, gay, bisexual, transgender (LGBT) prisoners who self-identify at receiving. I would caution the wholesale support of this measure since considerations in men's facilities are different than in women's facilities. Currently in California, prisoners are classified by their genitalia, not their gender identity. This policy means transsexual prisoners who have not had sex reassignment surgery are housed in facilities that may not be the best placement for them. With the lack of understanding of transgender issues and the conflation of gender identity with sexual orientation, prisons have become sites of compounded punishment beyond punishment for the crimes committed. Many prison advocates feel transgender prisoners should be housed based on subjective gender identity and in the place they feel safest.[20] This would be a step in the right direction, but we should be under no illusion that the prison industrial complex can exist without gender violence.

Another reason aggressives oppose segregation is the complete access staff would have to them to harass and abuse them. Prisoners would have fewer protections, not enhanced safety. In fact, for more than a year, inmates in a Virginia women's prison were sent to a "butch wing" based on their "loose-fitting clothing, short hair, or otherwise masculine looks."[21] Straight and gay prisoners were sent to this unit "in a deliberate strategy by a building manager" to break up relationships and punish perceived gay appearance. The inmates were harassed verbally and subjected to comments like "Here come the little boys." The unit was referred to as the "little boys wing," "locker room wing," or "studs wing."[22] This policy was just reversed in June 2009. Civil rights groups claimed it was unconstitutional to segregate people based on their appearance as it violates the equal protection and free speech guarantees of the constitution.

I spoke to prisoners at Valley State who had recently started to meet in a support group for those who are transgender males and masculine women who are harassed because of their appearance. The group offers support, information, and hopes to gather resources to share with group members. One concern is access to hormones to those who would like to continue their transition and enable their bodies and emotions to fit their male gender identity. California Department of Corrections and Rehabilitation policy is that if the incoming prisoner had a prescription for testosterone (or estrogen for male-to-female transsexuals) when they were admitted to prison, that prescription will be continued. For those that want to start hormones after their sentences begins, there is a protocol for them to follow to see a primary care provider for a request for service to be evaluated by a specialist regarding gender identity. Prisoners run into many roadblocks in this access. For example, the primary care provider is sometimes someone who does not understand gender identity issues. Sometimes it can take months or years to be seen and referred, ultimately, to Dr. Lori Kohler, who sees all the patients in California prisons on hormone therapy. Currently, Dr. Kohler sees about sixty patients.[23] At the time of our interview, Richard had just recently received word that he would be evaluated for hormone therapy. Others in the study would also like to start on testosterone.

Discussion

This study was based on a small sample but highlights several issues of concern for masculine-identified people in women's prisons. Masculine-identified prisoners, or aggressives as they commonly identify, face more harassment from male staff than from female staff or other prisoners. This harassment can be verbal, physical, or impact access to goods and services, or land you in jail. Masculine appearance, posturing, and tone of voice seem to challenge the authority or personal sensibilities of male staff. Prisoners and officers are already in a relationship of control and subordination; this gendered component adds to the power dynamic.

In its broadest sense, "transgender" refers to those individuals who do not neatly fit into gender boxes and who cross gender lines in how they look, act, feel, and live. All of the people in this study fit that criteria. But whether they all mean the exact same thing by the transgender terms they use and apply to others, and why some use the pronoun he, while others use she, these are issues that complicate an easy understanding of gender, how people identify, and what these identities mean to them. We need to continue our work to further understand what gender identity terms mean, especially in the context of prison where incarcerated people live and are not free to express their identities.

The conflation of sexual orientation and gender identity complicates the understanding of masculine women and transgender male prisoners. Virtually all of those I interviewed are attracted to women, so to prison staff, they are in homosexual relationships. The transgender males I interviewed identified as straight and thus are in heterosexual relationships. Further research is needed to tease apart what of the negative reactions coming from staff is based on their ideas of gender and how "women" should properly behave versus their attitudes of lesbian attraction and sexuality. Are both of these seen as gender violations (women should look and act as women, *and* women should be partnered with men as a gender role)? Is homophobia both about sexual behavior *and* gender behavior?

Some women in prison are "gay for the stay" (in other words, partner with women in prison but resume their heterosexual identity when they are released), and some are "aggressive for the stay" as well. A few prisoners mentioned to me that some women enter prison, shave their heads, and assume a masculine posturing, pulling off another scam. They gain from this—femmes will take care of aggressives, including commissary items. Further research might examine how individuals take on gender roles for utilitarian reasons and not gender identity reasons.

While not a focus of this study, I heard many stories of various healthcare difficulties. This is a huge problem in general for people in prison—gaining access to and receiving adequate healthcare, as well as basic health information. For those prisoners who want access to hormones, they need prompt access, monitoring of their hormone levels, and continuous access to their medication. Hormones should not be stopped and started sporadically.

Concluding Comments

I began this article talking about respect and control. Masculine-identified people in women's prisons do not feel respected for who they are. Incarceration takes away their freedom, but it should not take away their dignity. However, prison facilities and prison staff are within a societal context that still significantly stigmatizes gay people and transgender individuals. Lack of legal protections, discrimination, and hate crimes are daily problems that LGBT people face. Within prison we find some of these same problems. It isn't reasonable to expect prisons will be enlightened locations of social justice and equality. However, it is important to bring to light some of these harassments and problems aggressives face in prison, which have been fairly invisible up to this time. Reform and abolition movements of all kinds have started incorporating the concerns of LGBT people into their agendas, and prison advocates are at the forefront. This examination of gender is also instructive to the society as a whole. Even outside of prison transgender people are often not free to be their authentic selves due to multiple risks in coming out as transgender. These walls imprisoning gender itself need to be torn down.

REFERENCES

Baus, Janet; Hunt, Dan; & Williams, Reid. (2006). *Cruel and Unusual.* New York: Outcast Films.

Brownmiller, Susan. (1984). *Femininity.* New York: Fawcett Columbine.

Girshick, Lori B. (2008). *Transgender Voices: Beyond Women and Men.* Hanover: University Press of New England.

Human Rights Watch. (1996). *All Too Familiar: Sexual Abuse of Women in US State Prisons.* New York: Human Rights Watch.

Jackson, George. (1994). *Soledad Brother: The Prison Letters of George Jackson.* Chicago: Lawrence Hill Books.

Lee, Alexander. (2004, Summer). "Gendered crime & punishment: Strategies to protect transgender, gender variant & intersex people in America's prisons." *GIC TIP Journal IV,* (3), pp. 1, 4–12.

Lovett, Kenneth. (2008). "Male juvenile lockups ordered to gender-bend clothes regulations." *New York Daily News.* June 18.

Lutze, Faith E. (2003). "Ultramasculine Stereotypes and Violence in the Control of Women Inmates." In *Women in Prison: Gender and Social Control,* edited by Barbara Zaitzow and Jim Thomas, pp.183–203. Boulder: Lynne Rienner.

Peddle, Daniel. (2005). *The Aggressives.* Seventh Art Releasing, distributor.

Peek, Christine. (2004). "Breaking out of the prison hierarchy: Transgender prisoners, rape, and the eighth amendment." *Santa Clara Law Review 44,* 1211–1248.

Potter, Dena. (2009, June 10). "Virginia women's prison segregated lesbians, others." http://www.huffingtonpost.com/2009/06/10/virginia-womens-prison-segregated-lesbians-others. Accessed 7/28/09.

Sylvia Rivera Law Project. (2007). *"It's War in Here": A Report on the Treatment of Transgender and Intersex People in New York State Men's Prisons.* New York: Sylvia Rivera Law Project.

Woodward, Tali. (2006). "Life in hell: In California prisons, an unconventional gen-

der identity can be like an added sentence." http://www.womenandprison.org/
violence/woodward.html. Accessed 7/28/09.

NOTES

1. Jackson, 1994, 101–102 (comment originally written on January 23, 1967).
2. All names used in this paper were chosen by the prisoners.
3. This study could never have been conducted without the collaboration of Justice Now in Oakland, CA and California Coalition for Women Prisoners (CCWP) in San Francisco. The mission of Justice Now is "to end violence against women and stop their imprisonment. We believe that prisons and policing are not making our communities safe and whole but that, in fact, the current system severely damages the people it imprisons and the communities most affected by it. We promote alternatives to policing and prisons and challenge the prison industrial complex in all its forms." They can be contacted at 510-839-7654. "CCWP is a grassroots social justice organization, with members inside and outside prison, that challenges the institutional violence imposed on women, transgender people, and communities of color by the prison industrial complex (PIC). We see the struggle for racial and gender justice as central to dismantling the PIC and we prioritize the leadership of the people, families, and communities most impacted in building this movement." They can be reached at 415-255-7036. Both these agencies are doing amazing work and I am in full gratitude for their feedback, collaboration, and justice work modeling.
4. Baus, Hunt & Williams, 2006.
5. See, for example, Peek, 2004, and Lee, 2004.
6. Sylvia Rivera Law Project, 2007.
7. Lutze, 2003.
8. Lutze, 2003, 187.
9. Lutze, 2003, 195.
10. This study was approved by the Institutional Review Board of the Maricopa County Community College District. I teach at Chandler-Gilbert Community College in Chandler, AZ.
11. Girshick, 2008.
12. Peddle, 2005.
13. In this paper I use the pronoun the individual prefers. If the person said either, I used male pronouns.
14. Prisoners can have boxes sent in from outsiders once a quarter with orders from a pre-approved list of vendors.
15. Lovett, 2008.
16. Brownmiller, 1984, 115.

17. Brownmiller, 1984, 118.
18. Administrative segregation, also called jail.
19. Human Rights Watch, 1996.
20. Peek, 2004.
21. Potter, 2009.
22. Potter, 2009.
23. Personal communication with Dr. Lori Kohler of the UCSF Correctional Medicine Consultation Network.

MY STORY

Paula Rae Witherspoon

I am a Transsexual Woman incarcerated in the Texas Department of Criminal Justice (TDCJ), and this is just part of my story. I was on probation from Williamson County, in Dallas on transfer from Williamson County Adult Probation because my home, my means of support, and my family were all in Dallas. Probation in Texas is designed to ensure that people are sent back to prison by way of the excessive, unrealistic parole stipulations that the courts require probationers to adhere to while on probation. I had over thirty-six such stipulations, several requiring me to pay large monthly fees, expensive counseling, polygraph tests, drug testing, and any other services that the counselor, probation officers, and court deem necessary. Now, when Texas lets you out of prison, they *only* give you $50 and a bus ticket, then let you out. I was *lucky* they allowed me to do my probation in Dallas, where I was *lucky* to have family to help me get back on my feet. Most people released from Texas prisons don't have *anyone* to help them, so most have to commit more crimes just to survive. After all, $50 does not go very far when you don't have a job, food, and a place to live.

My family witnessed me doing my best to look for work, odd jobs, *anything* to make a living. They watched me fill out hundreds of applications, fax resumes, search newspapers, drive to job interviews, go to companies to apply for jobs, and do this every day for over a year. No one wanted to hire this ex-con transsexual woman on probation. All the applications ask about my criminal history, sex, gender, name, and all the other information that employers use to disqualify this electronic engineer technician and college teacher of computer science with over thirty years of experience.

What makes job hunting so hard nowadays is that most applications *must* be submitted over the Internet. Some of my probation stipulations forbid me access to computers with modems, the Internet, or any form of electronic data transfer. The Texas Work Force (TWF) database is *on* the Internet, so I had to get permission from my Probation Officer (PO) to log on and search for jobs. This is how TWF works: First you fill out this *real* long application on the Internet TWF database and a counselor runs it to check for matches of jobs versus skills, then prints out five for you to go check out. While you do that, the computer will send you a notice of other matches, as they come up, by US Mail. The problems with this system should be pretty obvious. By the time you get to the company, their personnel department has already reviewed and screened *thousands* of applications for this job, hired someone, and closed the job out.

Dallas has *two* large gayborhoods and my PO wouldn't allow me to take the jobs that were guaranteed me by friends there because the stores had a *few* (less than 10 percent of the stock) adult items for sale or rent, *mainly* items of GBLT nature. My PO said that if I even had *one* item sold or rented that was an adult item, I could not take the jobs. [I think] a transsexual *cannot* get a job *outside* the gayborhoods if they are open and honest on their job applications, even if they get past the name, sex, and gender questions, because of fears they have about customer *and* employee responses to a transsexual working at their company. So my probation was revoked and I was sent back to prison because I couldn't pay all the court mandated fees, for counseling and such.

I was arrested at the PO's office in *full* female attire and appearance. Taken to Williamson Country Jail for in-processing. A male LT there had me lean against the wall so *he* could "pat search" me as cameras and other officers watched. He squeezed my breasts so hard that tears came to my eyes and my knees buckled. He screamed, "What *gender* are you?" I replied, "Female." He screamed, "This paperwork says you a *male*." I replied, "My gender is female, my sex is male, and my orientation is a *certified* Transsexual Woman." He stepped back, looked me up and down, and said, " I don't know how to handle *this*," and called a female LT over to search me down. She took one look at me and said, "I got this one," patted me down, and took me to the infirmary to be housed.

The next day I went before the Magistrate, still in my dress, as a woman, to have bail denied me and taken back to my one-person cell in the infirmary. Later on, I sent a complaint form in and asked about the jail's policy on the treatment of transsexual prisoners because I felt I was mistreated. A female, Captain Pokoodo, was called to handle my complaint and was *very* understanding and issued orders clearing the way for me to get panties, bras, my HRT medications and depression meds I was taken to TDCJ Byrd Unit by special transport squad car. Williamson County Jail wanted to pass this "hot potato" on to TDCJ as soon as possible, in hopes that I would not file charges and a lawsuit against them.

In the intake of TDCJ at Byrd Unit, transsexual women are STRIPPED OF THEIR IDENTITIES AND DIGNITY. I was put in a caged area where over 200 men witnessed, gawked, and made fun of me. Some made passes, some made lewd comments, and others made known their desire to have sex with me. The officers shouted comments at me like "Yea, now you got to pull your nuts back out and be a man," "Your cellie is going to REALLY be glad to see you," and "Are those REAL tits or silicone?" Then I was forced to strip off my clothes, bra, panties and stand nude in front of them while I changed clothes. This generated a lot of "cat calls," whistles, and more lewd comments. The floor Sgt got so mad he pulled me out, emptied the barber shop out, and ordered the barber to "skin him like and onion and cut those DAMN NAILS." The barber shaved my head and handed me a pair of nail clippers. The LT came in, looked at my pink finger and toe nails, asked what they were painted with and took off furious towards the infirmary. He comes back with some different kinds of pads and told me to wipe them clean. When the polish wouldn't come off, I informed him it would require polish remover to take it off and his face turned so red I thought it would pop, as he stormed off saying "We'll see about that." The Capt came back with a nurse and more pads. When she couldn't take the polish off he said, "You don't

WANT it to come off, do you?" I said, "Not really." The other inmates screamed, "Guess she showed you Captain." Which made him even more furious. He had two guards handcuff me and escort me to the infirmary where a nurse looked at all the medications that came with me from Williamson County Jail, which I paid for, and said "Well I'm not sure I'll let him have these," referring to my hormone medications. The nurse had ALL my medications, except my Prozac depression medication, destroyed and I have been fighting ever since to get allowed to have access to take my HRTs again. TDCJ has a policy #G-51.11 that allows for transsexuals to get them, but we are routinely denied GID and HRT treatments. That's why there is such a high suicide rate among the transsexual women in TDCJ, which is covered up. TDCJ has NO IDEA how many GBLT people they have locked up and they want to keep it that way. Because what isn't documented can't come back to haunt them in a courtroom. Next, two guards take me to a shower and WATCH me take a shower, shave my body (my choice) and get dressed again. All the time making lewd comments to each other about my tattoo. (Two colored roses on my buttocks, red.) Then they handcuff me and escort me to "the punk tank" in AD. SEG. Where I was welcomed by other inmates in "SAFE KEEP-ING." I was put in a cell by myself, but was able to talk to the others out the bars on the front of the cells. But only if you are able to scream louder than they can. My stay at Byrd Unit was another story, all its own, so I'll move on.

One day I was told to pack up, because I was on the chain to my main unit assignment. I was handcuffed to a HUGE man that lead me into the center of a bus crammed tight with about 80 other inmates. In the dark, on the long trip to the layover unit, the guy I was handcuffed to whispered something to the other inmates around us and the next thing I know, I was being forced to have oral sex with the man as the others blocked the view of the guards. My gums started to bleed because I have a bad case of pyria, just as he ejaculated in my mouth. I spit it and the blood on to my sleeve, hoping I don't catch anything. The sun starts to come up, so I'm not forced to have sex with anyone else. Thank God for that bit of mercy. We arrive at this ROBINSON hold over unit and a Sgt sees the blood on my shirt. He asks me in front of EVERYONE that was on the bus, "How did you get that blood on you?" I look around at all their stern warning faces and replied, "My gums bleed." The Sgt looks at me, then them and says "Right." He un-handcuffs me and puts me in a cell by myself for the night. Early in the morning, I'm loaded onto a small van, handcuffed to myself, with four other inmates and two guards, headed towards my assigned unit, ALLRED UNIT. This is an ALL "male" unit that is one of eight units, out of over 160 units, that TDCJ has designated as "SAFE PRSION" units to house inmates needing "SAFE KEEPING" to comply with the Prison Rape Elimination Act of 2003. Or at least give that appearance. Right away, I notice I'm not the only transsexual woman with breasts on this unit, in fact there are over 75 of us, just a rough estimate. NONE of us are allowed treatments for or GID or HRTs. The horror stories on this unit concerning transsexual women and their abuse are stories all their own. Many are rape victims, some are intersex, one of whom gave birth to a "rape baby" and still has milk in her breasts. Could you imagine her horror being assigned and forced to live in the same cell with a sexually aggressive man? I help her write the grievances to get moved to a cell with a transsexual, because her cellmate keeps making sexual advances on her. The administration and staff here are made up of typical Texans that they call "BUBBAs," who are proud Southern Baptist homophobes first and guards second. Since I have lived on many units in TDCJ, both as an "in the closet" homosexual and an "out of the closet" transsexual woman, I've observed this to be the typical employee of TDCJ. Even the homosexual employees don't dare to be "out of the closet" on the units for fear of retaliation from other employees of the inmates guards use to "scare them straight." Transsexuals don't have a voice or any protections outside of prison, much less inside. Just look how transsexual was removed from the ENDA legislation as proof of that and you'll clearly see how even the GBLT community/organizations agreed we should be eliminated from ENDA. If there ever was a minority people that need constitutional protection, it's the transsexual people of the USA. But who will speak and lobby for transsexuals? HRC, GLADD, Lambda Legal, Texas Legislators, US Congress, how about ACLU? Is there ANY-ONE willing to speak up for such a small minority of human beings in the USA? Only the future knows the answers to these questions, but in my experience the transsexual population is hoping, praying, and trusting that President Obama will have the guts to affect REAL changes, like he promised, that will correct the horrors that transsexuals live every day.

EXPOSURE

Cholo

Prison is possessed by hatred and violence. This hatred leads to violence that oftentimes results in death, and death after rape is what transgender people and queers are subjected to in prison. Transgenders and queers in prison are enduring inhumane treatments and their cries are not really being heard during their walk through the valley of the shadow of death, and the few that are hearing their pleas are small in number. They are only able to do things that will make them the target of verbal, physical, or sexual abuse before they are equally treated in the manner that most prison queers and transgender people are treated.

These diabolical acts are brutal forms of self-expression that are normally produced by prison guards and prisoners. These individuals are often, but not always, closeted queers. The harm that the prisoners have to endure is usually performed in front of others. They do this in hopes that these acts will provide the impression that they are not queer and will protect them from attacks by others in prison. These individuals are motivated by fear and these acts are often done in order to survive. Their survival is based on the maltreatment of others, and if we continue down this path, how can we expect to survive when our enemies are destroying us and we are helping them in the process?

The truth of the matter is that we will not survive; we will all perish if we continue to do to ourselves that which the enemy is doing to us, and this will happen sooner than we think if we do not come together. And I use the word *together* because I realized that our strength rests within our unity and that our downfall rests within the opposite.

It has been my love for black or African American transgender people, transsexuals, and the queer community as a whole, coupled with the pain that I often felt when one of them was mistreated within the system, and that inspired me to put work in on the predators. I hope to open your eyes to some of the things that are not greatly spoken about so that some of you may begin to address these behaviors.

NO ONE ENTERS LIKE THEM:

Health, Gender Variance, and the PIC

blake nemec

"Police" is hollered while five cops slam open the door to Kim Love's apartment; two aim their barrels at our faces. "Hands *up*, get your *hands* up, get *back*. Where are the guns? Get *back*."

"OK, OK," I've leapt off the couch where Kim and I had been sitting—talking.

"*What's* going on? Hands up, *hands* up!"

"OK, OK," our tongues echo. Our hands have remained high since they flew up in shock the second the cops entered the apartment.

"Just stay back, *stay* back!" Their guns close in on our bodies.

"Are there any guns? Where are the guns?"

"There's no guns," Kim states.

"What's going on here?" Two of them go to Kim who is still sitting

217

on the couch, naked except underwear, and demand that she stands up. The cops grab her arms and pull her up so that she is standing in the middle of the room while they hold her arms behind her back. They turn her around—they're poking and prodding her, demanding answers and personal information about her body.

"We're just talking. Is there a problem?" we request, shaking. They are loud and demand that we be silent.

"You are in her home—please tell us what is the problem," I say. They pull out handcuffs and start to put Kim in them. Kim does not resist as they continue interrogating her about what we are doing, about guns. They want to know if there are guns. Kim tells them there are no guns.

"What is the problem?" I repeat, somehow only able to question like a cop in my failed attempts to stop the assault.

"We got a call, we need to make sure she is safe, we need to make sure she is not harming herself."

"This isn't right," Kim is saying, and she says it louder as they continue to poke and prod her.

"We do not consent to this," I spit in a mumbled staccato. Kim and I continue to voice our confusion, to voice our shock.

The more that I say "There is not a problem here" and "We do not consent to your presence, searches, or interrogation," the more they scream "*Relax!*" at us.

I become the beat of one cop, and his job is to keep me out of the way: He leads me by the arm to a corner of the room and stands in front of me. It works. I watch them handcuff my friend, question her about what she has been doing to her body, and keep her standing in the middle of her apartment as the other four cops stand over her and I become more conscious of how outnumbered we are. I am more visibly aware that the privacy of her apartment makes the situation more unsafe. I'm going to go off. I'm fighting against my common sense to defend my friend at all costs and stop them from parading her, to stop them treating her like an animal.

"OK, we're *OK*, she's not hurting herself, please leave. Kim where's a pen?" I say. Kim tells me where a pen is but the cops physically and verbally block me from getting it: "Relax, *relax*, stay *back*."

Cops start coming in and out of her apartment like a forensics team.

"Shut the door, please shut the door," I keep restating.

"Ma'am, relax or we'll need to take you in. Ma'am can you step outside for a minute?"

"No—I am not comfortable with that, I am not comfortable leaving her with you—you're hurting her. Why is this happening? She's screaming, do you hear that? She's afraid. You're terrorizing her while asking her if she's hurting herself. You OK, Kim?" I ask.

"They're hurting me, blake, make them stop!" She then tells them she is humiliated by being exposed in front of a group of males.

Kim and I begin to voice tenderness to each other—we are apologizing to each other for what is happening, we are reminding each other that we are there together.

"Ma'am, you need to relax, you need to calm down."

"I'm not relaxed—this is not relaxing, this is not safe—there are five uniformed and armed police holding my friend at gunpoint in her home—she is naked and you have her standing in the middle of the room—handcuffed. It is very stressful—this is a stressful situation. I am very concerned—you're hurting her—she's bleeding!"

"blake, make them stop!" Kim pleads as her wrists begin to bleed from the handcuffs.

"Sir, you need to relax," they tell Kim while her breasts are staged for them all to see."

"This is not right," Kim repeats, "you're humiliating me. I'm an African American woman standing naked in front of five mostly white males—this is not right."

"Please un-cuff her," I plead.

"Ma'am, can you please step outside with us?" they ask me again. They tell me that the handcuffs stay on until the paramedics get there. They tell me to relax and step away. My knowledge of police brutality provokes me to question them, but I know this is also dangerous, and it's hard to know what to do. I fear leaving the apartment to go to the hallway as they want, but not more than I fear them separating us. I go to the door and block it with my body, so I can still see Kim; we are terrified of what could happen next, so we keep talking loud so we can hear ourselves repeat what is happening. Kim keeps telling me how she's feeling afraid and humiliated. They will not take the handcuffs off her. I am getting names and a star number: M. Hodge (the "nice cop" keeping me "relaxed") and Star 655 (the one who was handcuffing and manhandling Kim).

The paramedics come and keep her handcuffed while manhandling her.

"Is it necessary to handcuff her while seeing if her body is hurt?"

"The handcuffs are not a problem for us," they reply.

The door keeps being left open, and they still have Kim standing in the center of the apartment for anyone passing to see.

We continue to plead for them to leave. After an hour, the ten- to twenty-person group finally did leave. They never produced a warrant. Their alarmist and sustained actions came from one call with allegations that were never confirmed by their search.

The question that continues to surface in my reflection of this invasion is, what is a logical response to shock? It once again became clear to me the ease with which one can be charged with resisting arrest or failure to comply with police procedure, as the cop's physical and verbal intimidation tactics spark all our instincts for self-defense: stating we're being hurt, that we don't consent to unwarranted searches, blocking a billy-club, and so on.

Similar to the unwarranted takeover of Kim's apartment, I've witnessed San Francisco cops stopping transgender women on the street under the alleged suspicion of solicitation, when in reality the women were simply walking home. Love and I were diplomatic during an illegal search and interrogation, yet the cops made it clear to both of us that questioning or any implied act of resistance would warrant our arrests.

Violence, Health, and Survival: A Conversation with Kim Love

Like the story I just recounted, the cultural normalcy of violence in all locations of the prison industrial complex is experienced by everyone who has survived incarceration and is witnessed by those who do restorative justice work inside prisons or work with formerly incarcerated people. Gender-variant people who have done time are forced to accept varying amounts of violence as realities of completing their sentence. This takes different forms of active emotional/physical violence as well as "inactive" violence like neglect or denial of necessary medical care. In order to understand the complexities of these systems, we must understand how both active and inactive forms of violence work together.

blake nemec: Could you introduce yourself and talk about your work?

Kim Love: My name is Kim Love. I sit on the TGIJP (Transgender, Gender Variant, Intersex Justice Project) board, which is a committee about transgenders in prison, and I also periodically facilitate harm reduction groups. TGIJP is awesome: They try to help all transgenders in prison. If people need someone to write to because they don't have anyone, we have somebody designated to write people in there. We advocate for them, we get their stories out, and basically that's what we do. We rally up!

bn: In TGIJP, what decisions have you made with your work that are based upon your experiences with prisons?

KL: Everything that I do with TGIJP is a reflection of the treatment of transgenders that are incarcerated in county jails and in prisons, specifically transgenders of color. In 1999, toward the end of '99, I was incarcerated, I went to jail. I took a case for my man, and I figured I would beat it because I wasn't on any paperwork for the case. I was fighting for seven months; during that time a deputy sheriff raped me for a couple of months until I couldn't deal with it any longer and I exposed it. I was treated very, very badly by the female deputies. When they would come to give us our lunch they would look at me and just hold my bag lunch and just stare, and I'm like, "Can I have my lunch?" and they would look, and one would even go so far as to say, "You're a man, he [referring to the deputy sheriff] would never touch you." And I was like, "Girl, give me my bag!" So they ended up having to move me from the new jail to the old jail for my *protection*. They stuck me in the hole…way in the hole, because some of the COs (the deputy sheriffs) were gunning for me. Because I was being harassed a lot.

bn: When you were in, you talked about a couple of different things: you talked about the sexual violence that you experienced, and you also were serving time for your man. Can you expand on what the charges were initially?

KL: It was for burglary, I took a burglary charge for him. He was seen, and we both had on all black, and when the police came, I told them it wasn't him it was me. And he said "Well, dude pointed him out," and we were both wearing all black and our hair was in a ponytail, so I said it was me. And that's how I ended up going to prison. I fought for seven months, and ended up going to prison for three years. I sued Sheriff Hennessey—and I settled out of court with him.

bn: For the rape charges?

KL: Yeah, I sued Sheriff Hennessey and I also sued Deputy Anthony

Hughes, and I settled out of court with him, too. I'm currently on parole and will be off in three months.

bn: So was the healthcare, the food, and the treatment really different in jail versus prison?

KL: Yeah, it is. It's way different. County jails, there's no freedom, especially for transgenders. You go to gym once a week. If they feel like taking you to the gym. As opposed to all the other inmates who get to go at least twice or three times a week. It's segregated like that. In prison, from morning until time to lock up, you can go outside, except during count time. But you have more freedom. And you're more recognized in prison, because you are a commodity in prison. The COs use the transgendered prisoners to keep the violence rate down.

bn: What is CO is an abbreviation for?

KL: Oh—correctional officer, they're basically pimpin'. If you look like a female, they'll put you in a cell. I've *had* them put me in a shock holdin' cell, and I told them I did not want to be there. They told me that's gonna be your husband, and that's where you're going to be and you're going to love him. And I did my time with him.

bn: Sorry, that's horrible.

KL: It's horrible. Without the sexual tension being brought down, the prisoners would probably overturn that place. Because there's more prisoners than there is COs. They use us.

bn: Were you able to file a report of any kind?

KL: For what? CDC [California Department of Corrections] is the hardest thing to fight. We've had so many transgenders that have been *raped* in CDC and had *proof*. One of them even had the towel the CO wiped his semen on. Today I haven't heard of one case that a transgender won against a law officer, against CDC. So, no, I would never attempt to do that, and besides, they have their own games. The officers do, and if I would have tried to bring a lawsuit against CDC, they would have gotten one of the lifers to stick me or hurt me.

bn: How long did it go on?

KL: As long as I was there. For three years.

bn: So, did you know about the lost CDC cases while you were experiencing rape? Was there cultural information that you had heard while you were serving time that it wasn't worth it to report that?

KL: No, because you're locked up. You're in a place where you don't get ice water, you don't get popcorn, certain things that you're accustomed to having that are so small and minute that you don't get. But if you play by their rules, they'll bring you…. In the summertime, it gets a hundred and some degrees in a cell like this. So they'll bring you buckets of ice, and cold sodas, and pizzas, and food from the street, anything to pacify you. You want some bras and panties, your man think you look good in that? Here—some panties and bra. You need some lipstick?

bn: I want to back up a second: So in the jail—SF jail?—there's a transgender section?

KL: There was one when I was there. When I was raped, there was a transgendered section. They had a split level: Down on the lower level there are guys, and half the upper level is the transgenders, and after I got raped, they stopped us from having interaction with the men, period. Even though it was the deputy sheriff that raped me.

bn: Sorry that that happened. And what about in prison, there were not transgender cells?

KL: No. No, you fell in with men.

bn: You talked about, that there were not venues for repercussions against rape in prison. What about other healthcare and taking care of your body?

KL: No, it's deplorable, as any place else. San Quentin has been written up so many times for health violations. They have all of these epidemics breaking out. It's deplorable—it's deplorable. I must say this, they did make sure that I had a sports bra. So they gave me bras, and stuff, but it wasn't for me; they said it was because they could see my nipples through my shirt and I could start a riot. So, go figure.

bn: What about other things, condoms, lube, anything for safe sex?

KL: No, they don't give any of that there. We take those plastic gloves, you can cut the fingers out and use it as a condom.

bn: You get the plastic gloves from the doctor or the nurse or something?

KL: Um, no, you get whatever you need. Your guy or sometimes the guards, just tell them: Look, me and my husband are starting to have relations, I decided to be his wife—I need some gloves.

bn: I'm really interested to know what people's relationships are with nurses, with doctors, who work inside of prisons. If they get the prescriptions that they need.

KL: We call them fag hags. You meet some of the females, doctors/nurses, that love the girls, and they'll bend over backwards to get you what you need. You're lucky if you get one of them. If not, then it's the draw of the dice.

bn: OK, so the fag hag nurses are really good. What was your experience with other nurses or doctors? Do they do regular exams?

KL: No, you have to submit to see the doctors. You have to have money on your books. Whoever doesn't have money on their books, they go last. If you have money on your books, you go first. But then, the prisoners that don't have money, the prison will take that money from your gate money. So each visit is like five dollars, last time I was there.

bn: How long would it be for you to accrue five bucks?

KL: My paycheck, when I worked, at what four cents an hour, so figure it out. It takes a long time.

bn: And if you had the five dollars right there, how long would it take you once you signed up, to see the doctor?

KL: Probably a week. Being a transgender, probably a week or two.

bn: Did you have hormone treatment inside?

KL: Inside I was getting my hormone treatment, yeah.

bn: And how was that?

KL: That was good, they never denied me my hormone treatment. But like I said, I worked the man, I knew how to work the man. I knew what they wanted, the deputies, the COs wanted. I knew what the sergeants and lieutenants wanted. So, it's scratch my back, or I'll scratch yours. And then I'll tell them, look at my CDC file. I don't have a problem with doing my time in the hole. So either meet me half way or you can lock me in the hole and I'll do my time there.

bn: So you always got your scripts filled, for hormones. What about any verbal abuse, or any harassment with the doctors in terms of transgender issues? Any inappropriate questions?

KL: No, more fascinated than anything, some would take it as inappropriate, but I wouldn't because of where I was. Where I was in prison, they don't have many of us with 38 DD's and looking like a woman. They have 'em looking like switchin', poppin', but buffed and all the weight power; liftin' weights. And runnin around "Oh, girl—miss thing." So the questions they asked me I accepted because they only wanted to learn. The doctors would say, "I've never seen that on a man before, and you're not a man, I'm looking at you, you're not a man. Can I touch them please?" Most people would think that would be inappropriate, but I understood. He's never seen that, and he's curious or he's really—what? And my little mind at that time was quick and I would do things like touching my nipples to get them erected so I could catch their eye, because there is no telling what I would need from them.

bn: So your scripts got filled, you knew how to negotiate getting care from the doctors, any other health stuff that you want to talk about? Did you get any HIV or STI testing?

KL: No, I never would. Never. It's the worst thing you can do.

bn: How's that?

KL: They have a ward for once they find out you're 'pos' (HIV-positive). One of the nurses came and she told the deputy. And he got on the loud-speaker and said to all of the general population: "Kim Love, they've got a bed in Ward Lalala for you" (the ward for HIV positive people).

bn: So then you went to the HIV-pos ward?

KL: No, because then that would be admitting I was pos. The procedure should have been to contact the prisoner anonymously, to offer them a bed. It should be anonymous, be separated (the conversation) from general population.

bn: So then what happened?

KL: I played it off.

bn: You stayed in the cell you had, you didn't go to the HIV-pos ward?

KL: Exactly.

bn: Can you talk about other community stuff, about other trans people that you were serving time with, and how those dynamics were?

KL: I was picked by a captain to be with a shot caller that was running the coomey car. My whole focus was to be this man's wife. Being his wife meant I didn't go outside unless he walked me, like a dog. I was his pet an hour a day. We could socialize, but I could not make eye contact with anyone else. Other girls, oh yeah, for a minute. "Baby, can I go talk to my girlfriends?" "You have two minutes." That's how it was.

bn: Can you elaborate?

KL: I was so focused on my husband and my life in there. I couldn't get close to anybody. He would whoop me, he would literally whoop me. He would go to work and somebody would be at my door talking to me, the guards would come over and say he didn't want nobody over here while he's at work, you got to go. And you can only come out to take a shower.

You can sit in the day room if you want for thirty minutes, but he wants you to stay in the cell until he gets home.

bn: Do you want to say anything about what you see would be solutions to any of the problems that you brought up?

KL: Some people say they should let transgenders be guards, that they should let some transgenders get in places where they only have heterosexual people working so that they can make a difference in the quality of life, in the way people do business. People say trans guards, but you know, that would not change it. The prison system is a moneymaker and nothing's gonna change that.

Capitalism Not Healthcare

The existing prison healthcare mechanisms, such as those highlighted by Kim Love, point to institutional interests in fulfilling state and federal *reporting* demands so the prisons can keep their funding. As CHAMP (Community HIV/AIDS Mobilizing Project) observes, capital, not medical forces, guides the actual placement of testing mechanisms. As "prisons and jails were never set up to do healthcare, and by and large, healthcare is being provided by for-profit corporations," all of those imprisoned are viewed as potential coins in the funding well.[1] Under this lens, it's easier to understand the difficulties in confronting the PIC's blind eye or deliberate indifference to violent prison conditions.[2]

HIV/STI tests, regardless of prison public health codes, are typically done at the end of a sentence, not upon intake. This prevents medical accountability by the prison if the jailed are HIV/STI-positive and in need of treatment, because the prison can claim ignorance to medical conditions. Even if incarcerated folks are at the end of their sentence with only six more months or less to serve, it is in the best interest of the prison and the United States' wellness at large if testing and medications are a periodic healthcare *option* for people to consider throughout their sentence.

Parallel to the absence of safe-sex paraphernalia, the same capitalist entities rule against medical access to HIV medication or HIV specialized and knowledgeable care. It is necessary to have specialty HIV medical care for prisoners to avoid distributing counter indicated medications, to monitor the efficacy of the medicines, and to reduce the possibility of transmission.

Risks of Current Infectious Disease Protocols and Legislature

The sexual environment of prison is overwhelmingly non-consensual, lacking in safe-sex paraphernalia, and transphobic. Legislation, like the Stop AIDS in Prison Act 2009 (HR 1429) that mandates testing upon prisoner intake, have not become law. Even as this Act and other similar legislation that includes sexual education, counseling, and sex barrier distribution exist, the clauses that require mandatory testing alongside other intake steps are concerning. Harm reduction counseling, proven to lower sex, drugs, and lifestyle risks, has been eliminated in some US county hospitals that are performing mandatory testing upon intake. The testing sessions are "streamlined," and it's likely that greater ignorance around people's sex or drug harms will accompany the assembly-line testing procedure. Equally precarious, the test result information is then in the hands of the prison intake officer, and in the case of prison testing they would give the state this information.[3]

In prison, streamlined HIV testing alongside "housing segregation" for HIV-positive people could, as Kim Love suggested, expose them to greater harassment and violence. There is social stigma from the general prison population that can visibly note who is "segregated" or living with HIV. Love speaks to some benefits of resisting such public labeling (confidentiality and a form of protection by cisgendered cell-mates) that occurs with housing segregation. An isolated placement can also be a further opportunity for behind the scenes sexual violations from prison staff.

The confidentiality of a prisoner's status can similarly be jeopardized by forcing people to wait in line to receive medication, if HIV medications are in fact being distributed. Laura McNighe and Pascal Emmet consistently observed confidentiality breaches with HIV medical care inside Pennsylvania prisons. Other prisoners have direct visibility of medications in integrated medication lines; segregated medication lines are typically structured around viral conditions and thus create a non-consensual system of visual disclosure for all prisoners living with viral conditions. Guards often distribute medications, even though they have no formal training to do so.

V-Coding Women

As Kim Love's experience shows, it is a prison industrial complex norm to use women's bodies in unsafe ways to pacify male inmates. The prison staff and the PIC create sexually opportune environments (e.g., cage women in the same cells as straight men), coerce women into having unsafe sex with their cell-mates because there are few if any barriers for the sex acts, then validate the sexual roles with toiletries or medical favors (exchange of goods or services).

Forced boarding by a third party for sexual contact, or in prison "V-coding," on the streets would be seen as pimping, as Kim Love called it. The placement of such coercion inside of prison, however, serves to locate pimping as a central part of a transwoman's sentence. Most acts performed by prison staff, violent or not, are unfortunately upheld as the norm of prison culture. The vision of "sexual tension being brought down, to where there's no sexual tension—they would probably overturn that place" screams to Love's understanding of prison staff using her body to pacify her "husband."

While Love's remarkable survival skills speak to a particular angle of resilience, Emmet Pascal witnessed many women attempting to resist or refuse being "V-coded," but guards only turn a blind eye. The refusal of prison guards to acknowledge such violence (deliberate indifference), if not to directly coerce it, places the guards in a pimping position. Legal definitions of pimping consistently include *intentionally inducing another to become a prostitute or soliciting a patron for sex acts with the sex provider.* At what point do prison staff members receive such direct immunity from pandering or procuring customers ("husbands" or men they want to silence) for a sex act?[4]

In an equally abusive placement, gender-variant women are being V-coded close to the end of their sentences. This location works to keep women incarcerated because if they defend themselves against rape or other violence that occurs with their "husband" or cellmate, it is common for them to be charged with assault then placed in the "hole." The assault charge then shreds the previous parole possibility or release date.

Looking Forward

It's vital to continue asking *how many stories like Love's must be amplified before people understand reforming the PIC holds severe limitations?* Love ends by stating, "The prison system is a money maker and nothing's gonna change that." While solidarity work with currently incarcerated people can provide witness to violations like those that Kim Love experienced, or mobilizations to free caged people, we must not stop there.

Financial support for peer-based educational programs that collaborate with hospitals, schools, and other public institutions in effort to provide community-based knowledge and information on sex work, gender-variant groups of people, and people living with viral diseases would be a more sustainable and harm-reducing model, compared to the costly and violent results created by the PIC. Accomplished by peers, the empirical knowledge can address social as well as health and economic concerns that speak for those specific groups of people. Also, political and monetary support for decriminalizing prostitution efforts can cut overtime hours of cops currently directed toward violent policing tactics that are paid for by taxpayers.

These are some economical and educational prison abolition steps we can take to empower our friends, our neighbors, and ourselves. In parallel, groups like Write to Win (a grassroots collective that creates epistolary relationships between incarcerated gender-variant people and the collective members, many of whom are gender-variant) offer emotional and resource solidarity to their pen-pals; it acts as an alternative accountability paradigm in concert with other abolition groups. As a volunteer group, it doesn't fear losing funding or compromising its politics, as is unfortunately seen in many non-profit agencies.[5]

Movement-building that creates innovative models of justice that do not pimp prisoners for the success of capitalism are possible. It is time to view the current US economic hardships as an exit opportunity away from dependency on conservative foundations and government funding vehicles that bar groups from work that threatens pharmaceutical industries or gender/sexuality norms. Transformative justice models that empower lovers, friends, and groups of people to be accountable to one another rather than rely on unjust and unsustainable US systems, can work to abolish the prison industrial complex. We can, and are, creating these in forms that facilitate a domino effect of cultural and economic churnings.

NOTES

1. Laura McNighe. Project Unshackle/CHAMP. http://www.champnetwork.org/unshackle. Personal phone interview, April 14, 2009.
2. Community Health Mobilization Project. This Philadelphia-based organization is a national initiative building a powerful community-based movement bridging HIV/AIDS, human rights, and struggles for social and economic justice—which we call HIV Prevention Justice. http://www.champnetwork.org. Also see, Transgender Health Information Project (TIP). TIP is a comprehensive HIV prevention and health education project designed by and for transgendered, transsexual, and gender-variant people in Philadelphia. http://www.preventionpointphilly.org/services/services-trans.html.

3. HR 1429: Stop AIDS in Prison Act has also been named HR 6063: The Justice Act of 2006, and was designed to reduce the spread of STIs or HIV in prisons. It never became law.

4. "Deliberate indifference" is the conscious or reckless disregard of the consequences of one's acts or omissions. In prisons, and in relation to sexual violence against transgender women, refer to *Farmer v. Brennan*, supra; *Wilson v. Seiter*, 501 US 294, 111 S.Ct. 2321 (1991); *Cottrell v. Caldwell*, supra. A very good discussion by the 11th Circuit of what conduct is and is not deliberately indifferent can be found in *Hill v. DeKalb Youth Detention Center*, 40 F.3d 1176 (11th Cir. 1994).

5. See the Write to Win Collective. http://www.writetowin.wordpress.com.

BUSTIN' OUT:

ORGANIZING RESISTANCE AND
BUILDING ALTERNATIVES

TRANSFORMING CARCERAL LOGICS:

10 Reasons to Dismantle the Prison Industrial Complex Through Queer/Trans Analysis and Action

S. Lamble

It's hard for us to believe what we're hearing these days. Thousands are losing their homes, and gays want a day named after Harvey Milk. The US military is continuing its path of destruction, and gays want to be allowed to fight. Cops are still killing unarmed black men and bashing queers, and gays want more policing. More and more Americans are suffering and dying because they can't get decent health care, and gays want weddings. What happened to us?
—Queer Kids of Queer Parents Against Gay Marriage[1]

This article arose from an ongoing need to make stronger connections between struggles for gender and sexual justice, and the growing crisis of mass incarceration, over-policing, and cultures of control. Too often, these issues are considered in isolation from each other. On the one hand, prisoner justice activists have not always paid sufficient attention to the gender and sexual dimensions of prisons,[2] especially for queer, trans, and gender-non-conforming people.[3] On the other hand, queer and trans organizers have often excluded prisoners from our communities and not prioritized prisoner justice issues within broader movement struggles. Within antiviolence movement politics, some feminist, queer, and trans activists have also been too quick to equate justice with imprisonment—by embracing hate crimes laws, advocating for longer prison sentences for those who commit sexual violence, and calling for increased "community" policing.[4]

But struggles against abuse, assault, poverty, racism, and social control require clearer connections between the violence of gender/sexual oppression and the violence of the prison system. Indeed, many of us who are involved in antiviolence work through rape crisis centers, homeless shelters, and queer/trans safe spaces are also committed to struggles against imprisonment. For some, our anti-prison politics grew out of that antiviolence work. After years of repeatedly responding to the same forms of violence, and after dealing with the ongoing failures and injustices of the criminal system, it has become clear that prisons not only fail to protect our communities from violence, but actually enable, perpetuate, and foster *more* violence.

Engaging in struggles against imprisonment is particularly urgent now, as the so-called "war on terror" intensifies, as attacks on migrants and people of color increase, as violence against women, queers, and trans people show few signs of abating, and as the global prison population expands dramatically. These trends are closely related to changes in the global political economy; as governments continue to slash welfare, education, housing, and health budgets on the one hand, they increase spending on prisons, police, military, and border controls on the other.

Never before has the prison industrial complex[5] been so powerful, particularly in the Global North. While the United States takes the global lead in locking up its people (with 1 in every 100 adults currently behind bars and more than 7.3 million people in prison, on probation, or on parole[6]), other countries, such as Britain, Canada, and Australia are rapidly following suit. England and Wales, for example, has nearly doubled its prison population since 1992 and is currently embarking on a £3.2–4.7 billion ($5–7 billion USD) prison-building spree to create space for more than 10,500 new prisoners by 2014.[7] Canada has recently passed tougher sentencing laws, and prison expansion proposals are looming.[8]

Examining these overall trends, however, does not provide an accurate picture of who is most affected by the growth in the prison industrial complex. Prison expansion disproportionately targets particular groups of people, especially communities of color, poor and working class people, youth, immigrants, women, people with learning disabilities and mental health issues, as well as queer, trans, and gender-non-conforming people, who are increasingly forced into greater cycles of poverty, criminalization, incarceration, and violence.

As the more privileged members of lesbian, gay, bisexual, and trans (LGBT) communities are ushered into new forms of neoliberal citizenship—where buying power, respectability, assimilation, and nationalism are the price of welcome—and as some LGBT groups are developing closer ties with police and military forces through recruitment campaigns, advisory boards, and liaison committees, we need to question who is bearing the costs of so-called "inclusion." If such inclusion means complicity with the violence and racism of the prison industrial complex, we must rethink those strategies. It is more important than ever to reject strategies that allow queer, trans, and feminist politics to be used for war, imprisonment, state violence, and racism. We must put antiviolence, anti-racism, and anti-prison struggles at the center of queer, trans, and feminist organizing efforts.

This article makes the case for a queer/trans politics of prison abolition. When using the term "queer/trans politics," I'm referring less to "queer" and "trans" as umbrella identity terms and more to a political approach that questions, disrupts, and transforms dominant ideas about what is normal. Questioning the normalcy of the prison, a queer/trans politics not only helps identify the role of imprisonment in perpetuating gender, racial, and sexual violence, but also provides tools for developing alternative community responses that better address problems of harm. Drawing from my experiences as a non-imprisoned person engaging in prisoner support and activist work in Canada and Britain, I outline ten reasons why we should dismantle the prison industrial complex using a queer/trans analysis. In making these arguments, I hope to highlight relationships between gender, sexuality, policing, and imprisonment and provide some analytic starting points that might prompt further community organizing around these issues.

This article is written with a diverse audience and multiple purposes in mind—it is for queer and trans communities who have not prioritized prison and policing issues; it is for prison activists who have not considered the gender/sexuality dimensions of the prison industrial complex; it is for folks who recognize that prisons are harmful but are skeptical of abolitionist ideas; it is for communities who are broadly committed to social, economic, and racial justice. Most of all, it is written as a tool for discussion. It is a contribution to ongoing debates about what kind of world we want to live in. For a growing number of people, that world must be one without prisons.

Before setting out the arguments for a queer/trans politics of prison abolition, I want to offer three important caveats:

First, the following arguments are not new, nor is queer and trans prison activism a novel phenomenon. Because prisons, police, immigration officials, and psychiatric institutions have long punished people for transgressing sexual and gender norms, queer and trans people have a long tradition of resistance to institutions of punishment.[9] Building on previous organizing histories as well as contemporary struggles, this article argues for a renewed queer/trans anti-prison politics.

Second, in writing on prison issues, particularly those of us who have not directly spent time behind bars, it is important not to fetishize or sensationalize the experiences of prisoners. Much of the general public's ideas about prison come from corporate media, which not only provides distorted and misleading information, but usually treats prisoners as objects of fascination, fuel for fear-mongering, or targets of pity.[10] To counter the media's sensationalist pull, it is important to critically reflect on how and why we approach prison issues. For some, we may have been imprisoned ourselves or people we love are imprisoned. For others, we may be tacitly driven by fantasies about saving oppressed "others," desires to claim a place of belonging within "radical" political communities, or a commitment to prison reform. However well-intentioned we might be, it is important to critically challenge our motivations and assumptions, particularly those that perpetuate rather than undo patterns of oppression. More importantly, there remains an ongoing need to prioritize the voices, perspectives, and experiences of prisoners, ex-prisoners, and those most directly affected by criminalization and imprisonment.

Third, although I draw from academic research to support my arguments, I want to emphasize that these studies generally confirm what many prisoners already know from their own experiences of the prison system. The danger of using academic research is that it perpetuates the assumption that prisoners' knowledge is less valid or legitimate than institutional knowledge. As such, I want to emphasize that much of my own analysis would be impossible without the knowledge, experiences, and analyses that prisoners have shared with me over the years.[11]

Ten Reasons to Fight the Prison Industrial Complex
Using a Queer/Trans Analysis

1. **Queer, trans, and gender-non-conforming people have been historically subject to oppressive laws, gender policing, and criminal punishment—a legacy that continues today despite ongoing legal reforms.**

Law enforcement officials (including police, courts, immigration officers, prison guards, and other state agents) have a long history of targeting, punishing, and criminalizing sexual dissidents and gender-non-conforming people.[12] While many overtly homophobic and transphobic laws have been recently overturned in Canada, the United States, and Britain, the criminalization and punishment of queer and trans people extends well beyond formal legislation.[13] State officials enable or participate in violence against queer, trans, and gender-non-conforming communities by (a) ignoring everyday violence against queer and trans people; (b) selectively enforcing laws and policies in transphobic and homophobic ways; (c) using discretion to over-police and enact harsher penalties against queer and trans people; and (d) engaging in acts of violence, harassment, sexual assault, and discrimination against queer and trans people.[14] While some police departments are increasingly putting on a "gay-positive" public face, the problem of state violence against queer and trans people nonetheless persists and has been well documented by numerous police- and prison-monitoring groups.[15]

This ongoing legacy of violence should make queer and trans people both cautious of the state's power to criminalize our lives and wary of the state's claim to protect us from harm. Although some people believe that we can train transphobia out of law enforcement agents or eliminate homophobic discrimination by hiring more LGBT prison guards, police, and immigration officials, such perspectives wrongly assume that discrimination is a "flaw" in the system, rather than intrinsic to the system itself. Efforts to make prison and police institutions more "gay-friendly" perpetuate the myth that such systems are in place to protect us. But as the uneven history of criminalization trends in Canada, the United States, and Britain so clearly demonstrate (that is, the way that the system targets some people and not others), the prison industrial complex is less about protecting the public from violence and more about controlling, labeling, disciplining, and in some cases killing particular groups of people—especially those who potentially disrupt the social, economic, and political status quo.[16]

While the state might stop harassing, assaulting, and criminalizing some people within queer and trans communities (namely those upwardly mobile, racially privileged, and property-owning folks), the criminal system will continue to target those within our communities who are deemed economically unproductive, politically threatening, or socially undesirable. As people who have historically been (and continue to be) targeted by this unjust system, queer, trans, and gender-non-conforming communities must move away from efforts to make the prison industrial complex more "LGBT-friendly" and instead fight the underlying logic of the system itself.

2. **Queer, trans, and gender-non-conforming people, particularly those from low-income backgrounds and communities of color, are directly targeted by criminalization, punishment, and imprisonment.**

We do not know exactly how many queer, trans, and gender-non-conforming people are currently incarcerated. This is partly because most governments do not collect information on the sexual and gender identity of prisoners and partly because prisoners are not always safe to disclose their gender or sexual identities. However, we know that queer, trans, and gender-non-conforming people in Canada, the United States, and Britain are frequently over-policed, over-criminalized, and over-represented in the prison system.[17] Levels of harassment, targeting, and arrest are high, particularly for young queer and trans people, those from low-income communities, people with learning disabilities and mental health issues, and people of color. Trans community organizers in the San Francisco Bay Area, for example, report that nearly half of the 20,000 transgender people in the region have been in prison or jail.[18]

Queer, trans, and gender-non-conforming people are funneled into the criminal system for many reasons but primarily due to systemic oppression. Because trans, queer, and gender-variant people experience widespread discrimination, harassment, and violence, we are at greater risk of social and economic marginalization. This translates into higher risks of imprisonment. We know that queer and trans youth, for example, are more likely to be homeless, unemployed, bullied at school, harassed on the street, estranged from family, and targeted by sexual violence—factors that greatly increase the risks of criminalization and imprisonment especially for queer and trans people of color.[19] Trans people in particular, and those who are visibly gender-non-conforming, are routinely harassed by law enforcement and security officials for undertaking basic daily activities like using the toilet, accessing public services, or walking down the street.[20]

Groups like FIERCE! have shown how the "school-to-prison-pipeline" disproportionately affects queer and trans youth.[21] Whether dropping out of school because of severe harassment and discrimination, feeling alienated from education curriculum, experiencing suicidal thoughts, or turning to criminalized coping mechanisms like drug and alcohol use, queer and trans youth often have less chances for success in school.[22] "Zero tolerance" policies, heightened surveillance, and increased police presence in schools further contribute to criminalization and dropout rates, particularly for queer and trans youth of color. "Quality of life" ordinances, such as "anti-social behavior orders" and "safe streets acts," are also routinely used to remove queer and trans youth from public spaces and criminalize their social activities.[23] Coupled with problems at home, many queer and trans youth find themselves homeless and unemployed.[24] Once on the street, queer and trans youth have trouble accessing services and supports to get their basic needs met. Many homeless shelters and social services, for example, are not safe places for trans people (sometimes banning trans people outright), and problems with gender categories on identity documents can restrict welfare access.[25] Without income, housing, family, or community support, survival often means working in criminalized economies like drug and sex trade.

Queer, trans, and gender-non-conforming youth who are bullied, harassed, and assaulted—particularly those who don't fit the stereotype of the passive, innocent, white victim—are blamed and punished when they defend themselves. The recent case of the New Jersey 7, in which seven young African American lesbians were criminalized for defending themselves against sexist and homophobic harassment, provides a case in point.[26] Given that criminalization and imprisonment both arise from, and further exacerbate, experiences of social marginalization and oppression, efforts to address queer and trans homelessness, unemployment, suicide, school dropout rates, harassment, and abuse cannot stop short of prison issues.

3. Prisons reinforce oppressive gender and sexual norms.
Prisons reinforce gender and sexual norms in three key ways: First, sex-segregated prisons restrict people's right to determine and express their

own gender identity and sexuality. Because most prisons divide people according to their perceived genitals rather than their self-expressed gender identity, prisoners who don't identify as "male" or "female" or who are gender-non-conforming are often sent to segregation or forced to share a cell with prisoners of a different gender, often with little regard for their safety. In Britain, even trans people who have obtained a Gender Recognition Certificate (a state document that legally recognizes a person's self-defined gender) have been held in prisons with people of a different gender.[27] By segregating institutions along sex/gender lines, prisons work to make invisible, isolate, and stigmatize those bodies and gender identity expressions that defy imposed gender binaries.[28]

Second, gender segregation in prisons plays a key role in "correctional" efforts to modify prisoner behavior in accordance with gender norms. Historically, women's prisons were designed to transform "fallen" women into better wives, mothers, homemakers, and domestic servants, whereas men's prisons were designed to transform males into disciplined individuals, productive workers, and masculine citizens.[29] These gendered goals persist today, particularly in the division of prison labor. For example, when a new mixed-gender prison was built in Peterborough, England in 2005, all parts of the institution were duplicated to provide separate male and female areas, except for the single kitchen, where women were expected to do all the cooking.[30] The current trend toward so-called "gender responsive" prisons is likewise framed as a measure to address the specific needs of female prisoners, but usually works to discipline, enforce, and regulate gender norms.[31] Moreover, gender-responsive prison reforms are increasingly used to justify building new prisons (without closing existing ones), thereby furthering prison expansion.[32]

Third, sexual violence plays a key role in maintaining order and control within prisons, a tactic that relies on oppressive sexual and gender norms.[33] Sexual violence in prison, including harassment, rape, and assault, is shockingly widespread and often institutionally condoned. According to Stop Prisoner Rape, 1 in 5 males and 1 in 4 females face sexual assault in US prisons.[34] To call attention to the enforcement of gender/sexual norms in prison is not to suggest that prison culture is uniform across or within institutions, or that prisoners are more sexist, homophobic, or transphobic than non-prisoners. Rather, prisons as institutions tend to reinforce, perpetuate, and entrench gender/sex hierarchies and create environments in which sexual violence flourishes.

4. Prisons are harmful, violent, and damaging places, especially for queer, trans, and gender-non-conforming folks.

Prisons are violent institutions. People in prison and detention experience brutal human rights abuses, including physical assault, psychological abuse, rape, harassment, and medical neglect. Aside from these violations, the act of putting people in cages is a form of violence in itself. Such violence leads to extremely high rates of self-harm and suicide, both in prison and following release.[35] These problems are neither exceptional nor occasional; violence is endemic to prisons.

It is important to bear in mind that prison violence stems largely from the institutional structure of incarceration rather than from something supposedly inherent to prisoners themselves. Against the popular myth that prisons are filled with violent and dangerous people, the vast majority of people are held in prison for non-violent crimes, especially drug offenses and crimes of poverty.[36] For the small number of people who pose a genuine risk to themselves or others, prisons often make those risks worse. In other words, prisons are dangerous not because of who is locked inside, but instead prisons both require and foster violence as part of their punitive function. For this reason, reform efforts may reduce, but cannot ultimately eliminate, prison violence.

The high number of deaths in state custody speaks to the devastating consequences of imprisonment. Between 1995 and 2007, the British prison-monitoring group Inquest documented more than 2,500 deaths in police and prison custody.[37] Homicide and suicide rates in Canadian prisons are nearly eight times the rate found in non-institutional settings.[38] In the United States between 2001 and 2006, there were 18,550 adult deaths in state prisons,[39] and between 2003 and 2005, there were an additional 2,002 arrest-related deaths.[40] It is extremely rare for state officials to be held accountable for these deaths. For example, among the deaths that Inquest has documented in Britain, not one police or prison officer to date has been held criminally responsible.[41]

Deaths in custody are symptomatic of the daily violence and harm that prisoners endure. Queer, trans, and gender-non-conforming people are subject to these harms in specific ways:

- *High risk of assault and abuse:* Queer, trans, and gender-non-conforming people are subject to widespread sexual assault, abuse, and other gross human rights violations, not only from other prisoners, but from prison staff as well.[42]

- *Denial of healthcare*: Many prisoners must fight to even see a doctor, let alone get adequate medical care. Trans people in particular are regularly denied basic medical needs, especially surgery and hormones. Many prisons have no guidelines for the care of trans and gender-variant persons, and even where guidelines exist, they are insufficient or not followed.[43] Inadequate policy and practice on HIV/AIDS and Hep C prevention is another major health problem in prison, where transmission rates are exceptionally high.[44] These risks increase dramatically for trans people, who already experience high rates of HIV/AIDS.[45] This combination of high transmission risks, poor healthcare provision, inadequate sexual health policies, and long-term health effects of imprisonment (including shorter life expectancies), mean that prison is a serious health hazard for queer and trans people.

- *Subject to solitary confinement and strip-searching:* Trans and gender-non-conforming prisoners are regularly placed in solitary confinement as a "solution" to the problem of sex-segregated prisons. Even when used for safety purposes, "protective custody" constitutes a form of punishment, as it usually means reduced access to recreational and educational programs, and increased psychological stress as a result of isolation. Trans and gender-non-conforming people are also frequently subject to humiliating, degrading, abusive, and overtly transphobic strip-searches.[46]

- *High risk of self-harm and suicide:* Queer and trans people, especially youth, have higher rates of suicide attempts and self-harm. Such risks increase in prison and are heightened in segregation, particularly when prisoners are isolated from queer and trans supports.[47] These risks are not limited to incarceration but continue after release. A study in Britain for example, found that men who leave prison were eight times more likely to commit suicide than the general population, and women released from prison were thirty-six times more likely to commit suicide.[48]

The prison system is literally killing, damaging, and harming people from our communities. Whether we consider physical death caused by self-harm, medical neglect, and state violence; social death caused by subsequent unemployment, homelessness, and stigmatization; or civil death experienced through political disenfranchisement and exclusion from citizenship rights, the violence of imprisonment is undeniable.

5. Ending violence against queer, trans, and gender-non-conforming people requires a focus on the prison industrial complex.

The pervasiveness of state violence against queer and transgender people is reason enough to fight the prison industrial complex. But it is important to include anti-prison work as part of antiviolence struggles more broadly. Too often mainstream antiviolence work around hate crimes, sexual violence, child, and partner abuse excludes or remains disconnected from struggles against state violence.

Incorporating anti-prison work within broader antiviolence struggles is vital because prisons perpetuate—rather than break—cycles of violence. People are less likely to cause harm to others when they feel part of a community, because social inclusion brings both supports and responsibilities. Yet prisons have the opposite effect: Prisons remove people from their communities, isolate them from social support, and disconnect them from frameworks of accountability. During their sentences, many prisoners become estranged from their families and separated from partners. Many lose their personal possessions and most lose their jobs. Imprisonment also exacerbates mental health issues.[49] As a result, people often come out of prison in a much worse position than when they went in, putting them at increased risk of the situations that landed them in prison in the first place. These effects can be devastating not only for prisoners but also for friends and family members. The British Social Exclusion Unit, for example, found that 65 percent of boys with a convicted parent are subsequently convicted themselves.[50] These cycles of social exclusion, poverty, and imprisonment pave the way for more harm and violence.

The criminal system also reduces community capacity to hold people to account for their actions. Though prison is often framed as a means of serving "justice" and "accountability," this is rarely the case. At most, prisons demand accountability to the state rather than to the people who were actually affected by the original harm. Locking people away does not require that people respond to those they harmed or take responsibility for their actions. By removing from the community people who have committed harm, the state actually prevents communities from holding that person accountable. More importantly, imprisonment does not assist with collective healing processes nor does it work to prevent harms from recurring in future. Effective antiviolence work means developing alternative, community-based processes that prioritize the needs of those who were harmed, address underlying issues that lead to harm, and work to prevent future violence.

245

6. Prisons reinforce dominant relations of power, especially racism, classism, ableism, and colonial oppression.

The modern prison grew out of, and continues to be deeply embedded within, the European colonial project and the legacy of slavery.[51] This history, which includes medical experimentation, forced psychiatric treatment, sterilization, and eugenics, continues to shape the contemporary prison system today. Whether we consider who is most targeted by prisons or the socio-economic power relations that sustain imprisonment, the prison industrial complex remains a fundamentally racist, classist, and ableist institution.[52] The statistics on who is in prison make these realities painfully clear. In Britain, for example, although people of color made up less than 9 percent of the general population, they comprised 27 percent of prisoners in 2008.[53] Blacks in particular are seven times more likely than whites to be stopped and searched by police, and are far more likely to receive a custodial sentence if convicted of a crime.[54] In 2002, there were more African Caribbean entrants to prison (over 11,500) than there were to U.K. universities (around 8,000).[55] In Canada, Aboriginal women make up less than 2 percent of the general population but comprise 32 percent of women held in federal prison and are more likely to be classified as dangerous offenders than non-Aboriginals.[56] In the United States, 1 in every 9 African American men between the ages of 20 and 34 is now behind bars.[57] The vast majority of prisoners come from poor economic backgrounds, and people with mental health issues and learning disabilities are locked up at disproportionate rates.[58]

While corporate media attempt to justify these differential rates with claims that some people are more criminal, the reality is that some people are more *criminalized*. For example, though blacks use drugs at similar (if not lower) rates than whites, they are up to ten times more likely to be admitted to prison for drug offenses than whites.[59] Governments, politicians, and corporate media continually reinvent images of prisoners as violent, pathological, and morally depraved people, but the vast majority are imprisoned for crimes related to poverty, social exclusion, and systemic oppression. Indeed, communities that are most criminalized tend also to be most victimized.[60] For example, in 2003, the Canadian Human Rights Commission found that 80 percent of all federally sentenced women were survivors of physical and/or sexual violence—and for Aboriginal women the rate increased to 90 percent.[61] Drawing attention to these underlying factors is not to deny the harms that people in prison may have committed, but rather to put those acts in their social, economic, political, and colonial contexts. When we recognize "crime" as symptomatic of broader social injustices rather than as individual "bad choices," we are better able to devise strategies that address root causes and actually reduce harm and violence.

Queer and transgender communities are not immune from the oppressive logic of imprisonment. Not only do many of us internalize the racist, classist, ableist, and punitive norms of the prison system, but we also create our own kinds of oppressive cages when we uphold social barriers that exclude, marginalize, and stigmatize people in our communities. For this reason, it is important to prioritize, support, and take action in struggles against institutions such as prison, where such oppression is most rampant.[62] Just as struggles against gender and sexuality-based oppression are distorted and incomplete without race, class, and disability analysis, struggles for social justice are incomplete without attention to the violence of cages.

7. Prisons and policing take vital resources away from much-needed community programs, services, and self-empowerment projects.

The economic costs of imprisonment are staggering. In 2008, for example, it cost an average of £45,000 per year (more than £120 per day) to keep a person in prison in England and Wales.[63] In Canada, the average cost per year to keep a person in a maximum security federal prison is $110,223 (CAD) for men and $150,867 for women. Medium and minimum security costs average $70,000 per year.[64] In the United States, the average operational costs per prisoner in 2005 was $23,876 (USD), and capital costs were estimated at $65,000 per bed.[65]

Contrary to mainstream media claims of lavish prisons, the high costs of prison do not reflect the living conditions that prisoners endure. In Britain, for example, public-sector prisons spend less than £2 per day on food for each prisoner, and official inspectorate reports reveal that prison conditions regularly breach minimum standards of hygiene and safety.[66] Moreover, many prison costs are also absorbed by the prisoners themselves who provide unpaid or cheap labor (£4 per week in England and Wales) to maintain prison operations.[67]

Global expansion in the prison industrial complex, alongside growth in private industries that make profits from imprisonment, means that police and prison spending continue to rise. Over the past ten years, for example, US federal and state governments have increased police department budgets by 77 percent.[68] In 2007, total corrections spending in the United

States topped $49 billion, up from $12 billion in 1978.[69] Prison expenditure in Britain has increased from £2.84 billion in 1995 to £4.33 billion in 2006. The U.K. now spends more per capita on prisons than the US.[70]

Increases in law enforcement budgets are directly related to cuts in welfare, housing, medical care, and community programming. Massive amounts of public money are being channeled into military, policing, and imprisonment regimes, while queer and trans-specific services, such as HIV prevention, drop-in centers, education supports, peer mentoring programs, employment training, and violence-prevention programs are chronically underfunded. Not surprisingly, there is an inverse relationship between the amount of money a country invests in social welfare and the amount of crime it experiences: States with better welfare systems and more equal distribution of wealth tend to have lower incarceration rates.[71] When we consider what might be accomplished if even a fraction of prison and policing budgets were redirected into community-based violence prevention projects, the fiscal injustice of the prison system is even more striking.

8. Prison growth is reaching a global crisis, and LGBTQ people are becoming increasingly complicit in its expansion.
Using prisons, policing, and militarization as a response to social, political, and economic problems is a phenomenon that has grown dramatically in the past thirty years. Though the modern prison is a relatively new invention that only dates back to the 1800s, its most dramatic expansion in the United States, Canada, and Britain has occurred in the past thirty years.

Consider the following:

- Between 1994 and 2004, the number of children sentenced to penal custody in England and Wales increased by 90 percent, despite declining rates of recorded crime by children.[72]
- As of April 2010, there were 12,918 people serving indefinite sentences in Britain, compared to fewer than 3,000 in 1992.[73]
- The racial demographics of the US prison population underwent a complete reversal in a mere four decades, shifting from a population that was 70 percent white at mid-century to 70 percent black and Latino by the 1990s—even though racial patterns of "criminal activity" did not change significantly during that period.[74]

- Between 1970 and 2001, the incarceration rate of women in the United States rose by a staggering 2,800 percent (5,600 women prisoners in 1970 and 161,200 in 2001).[75]
- The number of people in the United States serving life sentences without parole increased by 22 percent between 2003 and 2008 (from 33,633 to 41,095).[76]

Contrary to popular assumptions, prison populations are growing not because more people are committing crime, more people are being caught, or more people are being found guilty. Rather, sentences are getting longer, custodial sentences are given out with increasing frequency, and governments are widening the criminalization net by creating new criminal offenses.[77] Between 2000 to 2007, for example, the US Congress added 454 new offenses to the federal criminal code, which coincided with a 32 percent increase in the number of federal prisoners.[78] While in power from 1997 to 2010, the British Labour government created more than 3,600 new criminal offenses—almost one for every day it was in office.[79]

Although many people assume that prison expansion is a response to increased crime, the main causes of prison expansion have less to do with so-called crime waves and more to do with political and economic policy: the "war on drugs," the criminalization of homelessness and poverty, the lack of community support for people with mental health issues, the increased detention of undocumented workers, the expanding use of secret prisons, and the so-called war on terror.

Unfortunately, many LGBT organizations in Canada, Britain, and the United States—particularly white-dominated and class-privileged ones—are increasingly complicit in the forces of prison expansion: calling for increased penalties under hate crimes laws; participating in police, military, and prison officer recruitment campaigns; endorsing "law and order" politicians, contributing to gentrification of poor, working-class and immigrant neighborhoods; and supporting "quality of life" ordinances that drive queer and trans street youth from public spaces. To give a particularly chilling example, LGBT groups lobbying for the Local Law Enforcement Hate Crime Prevention Act in the United States (also known as the Matthew Shepard and James Byrd, Jr. Hate Crimes Prevention Act), recently found themselves in the unsavory position of supporting legislation that, thanks to a Republican amendment, included the death penalty among its available sanctions.[80] While several LGBT groups released statements opposing the death penalty amendment, few acknowledged that hate crimes laws (which function primarily by applying harsher sentences to crimes deemed as hate-motivated) grow out of, and feed, the same punitive logics that sustain the death penalty. Ironically, most of the arguments used by LGBT groups to oppose the death penalty (for example, its racist application, lack of deterrent effect, and perpetuation of violence) also apply to the criminal justice system more broadly.[81] Although the death penalty amendment was subsequently removed from the final legislation, by advocating for punishment-based hate crimes laws, LGBT groups nonetheless helped to legitimize imprisonment and channel further resources into locking people up—despite a lack of evidence that such measures reduce hate-motivated violence.[82] It is also no coincidence that the act was passed as part the National Defense Authorization Bill, a package of reforms that provides $680 billion to the US military "defense" budget, including $130 billion (USD) for ongoing military operations in Afghanistan and Iraq.[83] Given the devastating effects of the prison industrial complex and its broader connections with militarism and empire, queer and trans people must end their complicity with such projects.[84]

9. Prisons and police do not make queer, trans, and gender-non-conforming communities safer.

The biggest myth of prison industrial complex is that prisons and cops keep us safe. Yet when we examine state track records, prisons have failed to protect communities from violence. Just as criminal justice remedies for domestic violence have not kept women safe from harm, so too have prisons failed to protect queer, trans, and gender-non-conforming people.[85]

Although queer, trans, and gender-variant people are disproportionately subject to harassment, bullying, sexual assault, and violence, many do not feel safe going to the police for help. A recent U.K. study found that 1 in 5 lesbian and gay people had been a victim of homophobic hate crime in the last three years, yet 75 percent did not report it to the police. The incidents ranged from insults on the street to physical and sexual assaults. Of those incidents reported, half resulted in no action being taken, and two thirds of those who reported were offered no advice or support services.[86] Trans people are particularly vulnerable when reporting incidents to police, not only because of ID issues, but also because police routinely assume that trans people are suspects rather than witnesses or victims of crime.[87]

Some argue that the answer to this problem is to encourage people to report violence to police and to advocate for criminal punishment against those who commit such acts of violence. But the introduction of hate crimes laws has not reduced violence against queer, trans, and gender-non-conforming people. In fact, when we examine the overall impact of the criminal system, imprisonment has never worked effectively to protect communities from harm. Here's why:

Re-offending: Prisons have a terrible track record when it comes to re-offending. In Britain, approximately 65 percent of prisoners are re-convicted within two years of being released. For young men aged 18 to 20, reconviction rates tend to hover around 75 percent.[88] Though recidivism rates vary among particular groups and offenses (most people convicted of murder, for example, do not re-offend), Canada and the United States have similarly high re-offense rates overall.[89] A growing body of evidence also suggests that prison expansion tends to increase re-offense rates.[90]

Deterrence: Prisons and punishment are poor mechanisms for deterring crime. Considerable evidence indicates, for example, that harsher sentences do not reduce crime, particularly with respect to youth. In some cases, harsher punishments may actually increase re-offense rates.[91] Indeed, US states with the lowest incarceration rates also have the lowest crime rates.[92] The logic that punishment will deter harm wrongly assumes that violence is the result of individual, rational decisions made in contexts of "free choice." While some violent acts are indeed premeditated (especially white-collar crime), most harms arise from a more complex set of social, political, and economic factors. Because prisons do not address but rather exacerbate these factors, the deterrent effects of imprisonment are limited. As former Senior Home Office researcher Carol Hedderman notes, "Prison will never be an effective crime-control tool because the evidence clearly demonstrates that it actively creates or compounds the factors that contribute to offending."[93]

Rehabilitation: Rehabilitation programs have limited success and in some cases can actually cause more harm than good.[94] This is partly because most rehabilitation programs assume that the main problem lies in the individual rather than in broader social, economic, and political circumstances. Moreover, prison-based rehabilitation programs operate within coercive and disciplinary contexts and rarely coincide with adequate economic and social supports following release. By contrast, voluntary harm-reduction programs that take place within supportive community settings are generally more successful—and much less expensive.[95]

The systematic failure of imprisonment is not only noted by anti-prison activists, but also widely recognized among criminologists, legal professionals, and even government officials. As the Daubney Commission (appointed by a Conservative Government) in Canada reported,

> It is now generally recognized that imprisonment has not been effective in rehabilitating or reforming offenders, has not be shown to be strong deterrent, and has achieved only temporary public protection and uneven retribution…. The use of imprisonment as a main response to a wide variety of offences against the law is not a tenable approach in practical terms.[96]

Addressing violence within and against our communities is a far too serious, urgent, and widespread an issue to be left to a system that has proven to be an utter failure when it comes to community safety.

10. Alternatives to prisons will better prevent violence, strengthen queer and trans communities, and foster social, economic, and racial justice.

Prison abolition is not a call to suddenly fling open the prison doors without enacting alternatives. Nor is it an appeal to a utopian ideal. Abolition is a broad-based, practical vision for building models today that practice how we want to live in the future. Practicing alternatives requires different starting points, questions, and assumptions than those underlying the current system. The existing criminal justice model poses two main questions in the face of social harm: Who did it? How can we punish them? (And increasingly, how can we make money from it?). Creating safe and healthy communities requires a different set of questions: Who was harmed? How can we facilitate healing? How can we prevent such harm in the future?[97] Developing alternatives with these latter goals in mind prioritizes the needs of people who have been harmed and emphasizes more holistic, prevention-oriented responses to violence. Such frameworks not only reduce the need for prisons, but also work to strengthen communities by reducing oppression and building community capacity more broadly.

Abolitionist strategies differ from reformist tactics by working to reduce, rather than strengthen, the power of the prison industrial complex.[98] Prison reforms, however well-intentioned, have tended to extend the life and scope of prisons. So-called "gender-responsive" prisons are a prime example; reforms intended to address the needs of women have led to increased punishment and imprisonment of women, not less. By contrast, abolitionist strategies embrace tactics that undermine the prison system rather than feed it.

There are many different approaches to abolition, some of which are outlined in the classic "Instead of Prisons Handbook."[99] To highlight a few:

- *Starve the system.* Abolition means starving the prison industrial complex to death—depriving it of financial resources, human resources, access to fear-mongering, and other sustaining rhetoric.[100] Enacting a moratorium on prison expansion is one key strategy; this means preventing governments and private companies from building any new prisons, jails, or immigration detention spaces; prohibiting increases in police and prison budgets; and boycotting companies that make a profit from imprisonment. Starving the prison system means fighting new laws that increase prison time or create new criminal offenses (for example, hate crimes laws and mandatory minimum sentences), and redirecting money and resources into community-based alternatives.

- *Stop using cages.* Prisons are just one of the many cages that harm our communities. Racism, colonialism, capitalism, and ableism are other kinds of cages, which both sustain the prison system and give it force. Dismantling the prison industrial complex means working to eliminate all cages that foster violence and oppression. Taking this broad approach is especially important when developing alternatives, since some strategies (like electronic tagging or surveillance cameras) simply replace old cages with new ones. Getting people out of cages and preventing people from being put in those cages—even one person at a time—is a key abolitionist strategy.

- *Develop effective alternatives.* Dismantling the prison industrial complex is impossible without developing alternative community protocols for addressing violence and harm. Creating abolitionist alternatives means encouraging non-punitive responses to harm, · enacting community-based mechanisms of social accountability, and prioritizing prevention. Such alternatives include restorative/ transformative justice initiatives, community-based restitution projects, social and economic support networks, affordable housing, community education projects, youth-led recreational programs, free accessible healthcare services, empowerment-based mental health, addiction and harm reduction programs, quality employment opportunities, anti-poverty measures, and support for self-determination struggles.[101]

• *Practice everyday abolition.* Prison abolition is not simply an end goal but also an everyday practice. Being abolitionist is about changing the ways we interact with others on an ongoing basis and changing harmful patterns in our daily lives. Abolitionist practice mean questioning punitive impulses in our intimate relationships, rethinking the ways that we deal with personal conflicts, and reducing harms that occur in our homes, workplaces, neighborhoods, and schools. In this way, "living abolition" is part of the daily practice of creating a world without cages.

Conclusion

Among the many strengths of queer and trans communities is an acute ability to challenge social norms that discipline dissident bodies. As an institution whose violent effects cause massive damage to bodies both inside and beyond its walls, the prison should be a key target for queer/trans analysis and action. At the same time, abolishing the prison industrial complex is not only about getting rid of prisons; it is about integrating abolitionist analysis and practice into broader social, economic, and racial justice struggles. Whether fighting for trans access to housing and welfare, demanding the decriminalization of sex work, engaging in antiviolence work, or campaigning for free accessible healthcare, all our politics must be infused with an abolitionist analysis. Likewise, prison activism that does not consider the gender/sexuality dimensions of imprisonment will be unable to undo the roots of our cage-obsessed cultures. The task then is to engage in social change using strategies that bring a queer/trans analysis to the prison industrial complex and bring a prison abolition analysis to queer/trans struggles. Without integrating both, we'll neglect the very cages that prevent us from working toward broader social justice goals.

Acknowledgements: I am grateful to the Prisoners Justice Action Committee in Toronto, especially Peter Collins and Giselle Dias for contributing so much to my understanding and practice of prisoner solidarity and anti-prison work. I also want to acknowledge the many lessons I learned from working with people imprisoned in Central East Correctional Center in Lindsay, Ontario, Canada. Much inspiration also comes from work by Critical Resistance, INCITE!, the Prisoner Correspondence Project in Montreal, and the Sylvia Rivera Law Project. Thanks also to Stacy Douglas, Greygory Glass, Toni Johnson, George Lavender, Dean Spade, Mike Upton, and the book editors for very helpful feedback and discussion.

NOTES

1. Queer Kids of Queer Parents Against Gay Marriage, "Resist the Gay Marriage Agenda!" *Queer Kids of Queer Parents Against Gay Marriage* Blog, Oct. 9, 2009. http://queerkidssaynomarriage.wordpress.com, accessed Oct. 10, 2009.

2. When referring to prisons, I include all forms of forced or coerced state custody, such as jails, prisons, children's detention centers, immigration detention centers, "secure" hospital beds and psychiatric facilities, prisoner of war camps, and secret jails.

3. Recognizing the inability of a single term to encapsulate the fluidity and specificity of people's gender and sexual identities, and noting both the overlapping and distinct dimensions of these identities, I use gender and sexual identity terms in the following ways: By *queer*, I refer to people whose sexual desires, identities, and practices do not conform to heterosexual norms (including, but also going beyond, lesbian, gay, bisexual, transgender, transsexual, intersex, two-spirit, and queer people). By *trans*, I refer to people who identify or express gender differently than what is traditionally associated with the sex they were assigned at birth (e.g. transgender, transsexual, two-spirit, male-to-female, female-to-male). By *gender-non-conforming*, I refer to people whose gender presentation or identity does not conform to gender norms or expectations (e.g. women who present in a masculine way but nonetheless identify as women, as well as androgynous, gender-fluid, and gender ambiguous people).

4. Critical Resistance and INCITE! Women of Color Against Violence, "Gender Violence and the Prison Industrial Complex," in *Color of Violence: The INCITE! Anthology*, ed. INCITE! Women of Color Against Violence (Cambridge, Mass.: South End Press, 2006).

5. The *prison industrial complex* is the network of governmental and private interests that use prison as a response to social, political, and economic problems. The prison industrial complex (PIC) includes all institutions, government

branches, agencies, and businesses that have a financial, organizational, or political interest in maintaining the prison system. See ibid.

6.   See Pew Center on the States, "One in 100: Behind Bars in America 2008,"
     2008. http://stage.pewcenteronthestates.org/uploadedFiles/Onepercent20inper
     cent20100.pdf, accessed Jan. 29, 2009; Pew Center on the States, "One in 31:
     The Long Reach of American Corrections," 2009. http://www.pewcenteron-
     thestates.org/uploadedFiles/PSPP_1in31_report_FINAL_WEB_3-26-09.pdf,
     accessed Oct. 3, 2009; US Department of Justice, "One in Every 31 US Adults
     Were in Prison or Jail or on Probation or Parole in 2007," [press release] 2008.
     http://www.ojp.usdoj.gov/bjs/pub/press/p07ppuspr.htm, accessed Jan. 29,
     2009.

7.   Though originally launched by the Labour Government, these prison-building
     plans are also being pursued by the Conservative-Liberal Democratic Coali-
     tion Government. British Ministry of Justice and British National Offender
     Management Service, "New Prisons Consultation Response," April 27, 2009.
     http://www.justice.gov.uk/consultations/docs/new-prisons-response-paper.pdf,
     accessed Sept. 1, 2009.

8.   Walter S. DeKeseredy, "Canadian Crime Control in the New Millennium: The
     Influence of Neo-Conservative US Policies and Practices," *Police Practice and
     Research: An International Journal,* 2009; Joanna Smith, "Federal Prison Bill to
     Cost a Billion Dollars a Year," *Toronto Star,* June 22, 2010. http://www.thestar.
     com/news/canada/article/826778--tory-crime-bill-to-cost-extra-618m-per-
     year-report-finds, accessed Sept. 9, 2010.

9.   Jessi Gan, "'Still at the Back of the Bus': Sylvia Rivera's Struggle," *Centro Jour-
     nal* XIX, No. 1, 2007. http://redalyc.uaemex.mx/redalyc/pdf/377/37719107.
     pdf, accessed Feb. 8, 2009; Regina Kunzel, "Lessons in Being Gay: Queer En-
     counters in Gay and Lesbian Prison Activism," *Radical History Review,* No. 100,
     2008.

10. See, for example, Paul Mason, "Lies, Distortion and What Doesn't Work: Moni-
     toring Prison Stories in the British Media," *Crime, Media, Culture* 2, No. 3,
     2006.

11. In particular, I want to thank Peter Collins, whose everyday activism from in-
     side the prison walls continues to inspire, provoke, and shape my work in pro-
     found ways.

12. See for example, Gary Kinsman, *The Regulation of Desire: Homo and Hetero
     Sexualities,* 2nd ed. (Montreal: Black Rose Books, 1996); Regina Kunzel, *Crimi-
     nal Intimacy: Prison and the Uneven History of Modern American Sexuality* (Chi-
     cago and London: University of Chicago Press, 2008); Leslie J. Moran, *The
     Homosexual(Ity) of Law* (London: Routledge, 1996).

13. While Canada, the United States, and Britain have decriminalized private, con-
     sensual, same-sex acts among adults, the colonial legacy of British anti-sodomy
     laws persists elsewhere. See Human Rights Watch, "This Alien Legacy: The Ori-
     gins of 'Sodomy' Laws in British Colonialism," 2008. http://www.hrw.org/sites/
     default/files/reports/lgbt1208web.pdf, accessed Jan. 30, 2009.

14. M. Somjen Frazer, "Some Queers Are Safer Than Others: Correlates of Hate
     Crime Victimization of Lesbian, Gay, Bisexual and Transgender People in Brit-
     ain," paper presented at the American Sociological Association Annual Meeting:
     Philadelphia, Pennsylvania, 2005.

15. Amnesty International, "Stonewalled: Police Abuses against Lesbian, Gay, Bi-
     sexual and Transgender People in the USA," 2006. http://www.amnestyusa.org/
     outfront/stonewalled/report.pdf, accessed Jan. 30, 2009; Sam Dick and Stone-
     wall, "Homophobic Hate Crime: The Gay British Crime Survey," 2008. http://
     www.stonewall.org.uk/documents/homophobic_hate_crime__final_report.pdf,
     accessed Jan. 29, 2009; INCITE! Women of Color Against Violence, "Law
     Enforcement Violence against Women of Color and Trans People of Color: A
     Critical Intersection of Gender Violence and State Violence," 2008. http://www.
     incite-national.org/media/docs/3696_TOOLKIT-FINAL.pdf, accessed Feb. 9,
     2009.

16. Such killings include both direct and indirect forms of state violence, such as the
     death penalty; killings by law enforcement agents; deaths in custody that arise
     from abuse and medical neglect; significantly lower life-expectancy rates among
     prisoners and ex-prisoners; and state indifference to violence against particular
     groups of people. These deaths are targeted because they affect some groups dis-
     proportionately more than others. Consider, for example, the high rates of black
     deaths in custody, the well-documented class and racial bias in the application
     of the death penalty, the disproportionate number of lesbians on death row, and
     the 520 missing and murdered Aboriginal women in Canada.

17. Barbara Findlay, "Transsexuals in Canadian Prisons: An Equality Analysis,"
     1999. http://www.barbarafindlay.com/articles/45.pdf, accessed July 18, 2007;
     Jody Marksamer, "And by the Way, Do You Know He Thinks He's a Girl? The
     Failures of Law, Policy, and Legal Representation for Transgender Youth in Juve-
     nile Delinquency Courts," Sexuality Research and Social Policy: Journal of NSRC
     5, No. 1, 2008; Beth Ritchie, "Queering Antiprison Work: African American
     Lesbians in the Juvenile Justice System," in Global Lockdown: Race, Gender, and
     the Prison Industrial Complex, ed. Julia Sudbury (New York: Routledge, 2005);
     Stephen Whittle and Paula Stephens, "A Pilot Study of Provision for Transsexual
     and Transgender People in the Criminal Justice System, and the Information
     Needs of Probation Officers," 2001. http://www.pfc.org.uk/files/legal/cjsprov.

pdf, accessed Feb. 9, 2009.

18. Ann Cammett, "Queer Lockdown: Coming to Terms with the Ongoing Criminalization of LGBTQ Communities," *The Scholar and Feminist Online* 7, No. 3, 2009. http://www.barnard.columbia.edu/sfonline/sexecon/cammett_01.htm, accessed Oct. 3, 2009; Alexander Lee, "Prickly Coalitions: Moving Prison Abolitionism Forward," in *Abolition Now! Ten Years of Strategy and Struggle against the Prison Industrial Complex*, ed. Critical Resistance (Oakland, Calif.: AK Press, 2008): p. 109.

19. Marksamer, "Failures of Law"; Ritchie, "Queering Antiprison Work"; Sylvia Rivera Law Project, "'It's War in Here': A Report on the Treatment of Transgender and Intersex People in New York State Men's Prisons," 2007. http://www.srlp.org/files/warinhere.pdf, accessed Jan. 30, 2009.

20. Amnesty International, "Stonewalled"; INCITE! Women of Color Against Violence, "Law Enforcement Violence."

21. FIERCE!, "Transgender Youth and the Prison Industrial Complex: Disrupt the Flow," 2004. http://www.fiercenyc.org/media/docs/5166_transyouthPICflowchart.pdf, accessed Oct. 29, 2009.

22. Marksamer, "Failures of Law."

23. INCITE! Women of Color Against Violence, "Law Enforcement Violence."

24. Nicholas Ray, *Lesbian, Gay, Bisexual and Transgender Youth: An Epidemic of Homelessness* (New York: National Gay and Lesbian Task Force Policy Institute and the National Coalition for the Homeless, 2006).

25. FTM Safer Shelter Project, "Invisible Men: FTMs and Homelessness in Toronto," 2008. http://wellesleyinstitute.com/files/invisible-men.pdf, accessed Oct. 29, 2009; Dean Spade, "Compliance Is Gendered: Struggling for Gender Self-Determination in a Hostile Economy," in *Transgender Rights*, ed. Paisley Currah, Richard M. Juang, and Shannon Price Minter (Minneapolis: University of Minnesota Press, 2006).

26. On August 18, 2006, seven young African American lesbians were walking down the street, when a male bystander assaulted them with sexist and homophobic comments. When the women tried to defend themselves, a fight broke out and the seven were arrested. Three subsequently accepted plea bargains and four were given prison sentences ranging from 3 ½ to 11 years. For information on their campaign, see the "Free the New Jersey 4 Campaign" at: http://freenj4.wordpress.com/. See also INCITE! Women of Color Against Violence and FIERCE!, "Re-Thinking 'the Norm' in Police/Prison Violence and Gender Violence," *Left Turn*, Oct. 1, 2008. http://www.leftturn.org/?q=node/1236, accessed Jan. 30, 2009.

27. A transwomen recently won her case against the Ministry of Justice, who had

refused to transfer her to a women's prison even though she held a Gender Recognition Certificate identifying her as female. The High Court judge ruled that it was a breach of Article 8 of the European Convention on Human Rights for the woman to be held in a men's prison. See "Human Rights," *Law Society Gazette*, Oct. 1, 2009. http://www.lawgazette.co.uk/node/52502, accessed Oct. 20, 2009.

28. Sydney Tarzwell, "The Gender Lines Are Marked with Razor Wire: Addressing State Prison Polices and Practices for the Management of Transgender Prisoners," *Columbia Human Rights Law Review* 36, No. 1, 2006.

29. Angela Y. Davis, *Are Prisons Obsolete?* (Toronto: Seven Stories Press, 2003); Kelly Hannah-Moffat, *Punishment in Disguise: Penal Governance and Federal Imprisonment of Women in Canada* (Toronto: University of Toronto Press, 2001); Nicole Hahn Rafter, "Gender, Prisons, and Prison History," *Social Science History* 9, No. 3, 1985.

30. Alan Travis, "Sexes Equal at Prison – But Women Do the Porridge," *The Guardian* March 10, 2005. http://www.guardian.co.uk/uk/2005/mar/10/gender.uk-crime/print, accessed Jan. 30, 2009.

31. Cassandra Shaylor, "Neither Kind nor Gentle: The Perils of 'Gender Responsive Justice'," in *The Violence of Incarceration*, ed. Phil Scraton and Jude McQulloch (London & New York: Routledge, 2009).

32. Rose Braz, "Kinder, Gentler, Gender Responsive Cages: Prison Expansion Is Not Prison Reform," *Women, Girls and Criminal Justice*, October/November 2006. http://criticalresist.live.radicaldesigns.org/downloads/WG_Gender_Responsive_Cages, accessed Nov. 20, 2009.

33. Joe Sim, "Tougher Than the Rest? Men in Prison," in *Just Boys Doing Business? Men, Masculiniities and Crime*, ed. Tim Newburn and Elizabeth Stanko (London: Taylor and Francis, 1994).

34. Stop Prisoner Rape, "In the Shadows: Sexual Violence in US Detention Facilities," 2006. http://www.justdetention.org/pdf/in_the_shadows.pdf, accessed Feb. 8, 2009; Stop Prisoner Rape and American Civil Liberties Union, "Still in Danger: The Ongoing Threat of Sexual Violence against Transgender Prisoners," 2005. http://www.spr.org/pdf/stillindanger.pdf, accessed Jan. 30, 2009; Sylvia Rivera Law Project, "'It's a War in Here.'"

35. Juliet Cohen, "Safe in Our Hands?: A Study of Suicide and Self-Harm in Asylum Seekers," *Journal of Forensic and Legal Medicine* 15, No. 4, 2008; Colleen Anne Dell and Tara Beauchamp, "Self-Harm among Criminalized Women – Canadian Center of Substance Abuse Fact Sheet," 2006. http://www.addictionresearchchair.com/wp-content/uploads/Self-Harm-Among-Criminalized-Women.pdf, accessed Oct. 10, 2009; Alison Liebling, "Prison Suicide and Pris-

oner Coping," *Crime and Justice* 26, 1999.

36. Precise numbers vary according to how offenses are defined and categorized, but the assumption that prisons are filled with dangerous murderers and rapists is simply not true. See Gabriel Arkles, "Safety and Solidarity across Gender Lines: Rethinking Segregation of Transgender People in Detention," *Temple Political and Civil Rights Law Review* 18, No. 2, 2009.

37. Inquest, "Inquest Policy Webpage." http://inquest.gn.apc.org/policy.html, accessed Sept. 9, 2010.

38. Thomas Gabor, "Deaths in Custody: Final Report to the Office of the Correctional Investigator," Government of Canada, 2007: p. 5.

39. This figure includes deaths from suicide (1,172), homicide (299), drug/alcohol intoxication (213), accident (180), AIDS (1,154), other illnesses (15,335), and other/unknown (197). Although some illness-related deaths may result from "natural causes," almost 63 percent of these deaths were of prisoners under the age of 55, indicating the denial of adequate healthcare in prison as well as the detrimental health impact of imprisonment. The figure excludes deaths in local jails (7,008 total deaths between 2000 and 2006) as well as those in juvenile custody (43 total deaths between 2002 and 2005). US Bureau of Justice Statistics, "Deaths in Custody Statistical Tables," 2008. http://www.ojp.usdoj.gov/bjs/dcrp/dcst.pdf, accessed Feb. 8, 2009.

40. US Bureau of Justice Statistics, "Arrest-Related Deaths in the United States, 2003–2005," 2007. http://www.ojp.usdoj.gov/bjs/pub/pdf/ardus05.pdf, accessed Feb. 8, 2009.

41. JUSTICE, et al., "Corporate Manslaughter and Corporate Homicide Bill – Suggested Amendments for House of Lords," 2007. http://www.justice.org.uk/images/pdfs/JointamendmentsReportstage.pdf, accessed Feb. 9, 2009.

42. Stop Prisoner Rape, "In the Shadows"; Sylvia Rivera Law Project, "'It's a War in Here.'"

43. In England and Wales, for example, the Home Office stated in 1997 that it was "currently engaged in drawing up guidelines for issue to establishments on the care, management, and treatment of prisoners with gender dysphoria," yet such guidelines have yet to materialize more than twelve years later. See Stephen Whittle, Lewis Turner, and Maryam Al-Alami, "Engendered Penalties: Transgender and Transsexual People's Experiences of Inequality and Discrimination," 2007. http://www.pfc.org.uk/files/EngenderedPenalties.pdf, accessed Jan. 30, 2009.

44. Giselle Dias and Glenn Betteridge, "Hard Time: HIV and Hepatitis C Prevention Programming for Prisoners in Canada," Prisoners' HIV/AIDS Support Action Network (PASAN) and Canadian HIV/AIDS Legal Network, 2007. http://

www.pasan.org/Publications/Hard_Time.pdf, accessed Oct. 20, 2009.

45. Ann V. Scott and Rick Lines, "HIV/AIDS in the Male-to-Female Transsexual and Transgender Prison Population: A Comprehensive Strategy," Prisoners' HIV/ AIDS Support Action Network, 1999. http://www.pasan.org/Publications/T-S_&_T-G_in_Prison_99.pdf, accessed Oct. 20, 2009.

46. Arkles, "Safety and Solidarity."

47. Arkles, "Safety and Solidarity."

48. Prison Reform Trust, "Bromley Briefings: Prison Fact File," July 2010. http:// www.prisonreformtrust.org.uk/uploads/documents/FactFileJuly2010.pdf, accessed Sept. 5, 2010.

49. Peter Collins, "The Continuing Horror Story of Spiegelgrund: Mental Health, Compassion, Awareness and Incarceration," *Journal of Prisoners on Prisons* 17, No. 2, 2008; M. Grayson L. Taylor, "Prison Psychosis," *Social Justice* 27, No. 3, 2000.

50. Prison Reform Trust, "Bromley Briefings," December 2008.

51. Biko Agozino, *Counter-Colonial Criminology: A Critique of Imperialist Reason* (London: Pluto Press, 2003); Scott Christianson, *With Liberty for Some: 500 Years of Imprisonment in America* (Boston: Northeastern University Press, 2000); Michael Hallett, *Private Prisons in America: A Critical Race Perspective* (Urbana, Ill.: University of Illinois Press, 2006).

52. Davis, *Are Prisons Obsolete?*

53. Prison Reform Trust, "Bromley Briefings: Prison Fact File," June 2009, http:// www.prisonreformtrust.org.uk/documents/download.asp?lvid=1164&id=1782, accessed Oct. 5, 2009.

54. U.K. Ministry of Justice, "Statistics on Race and the Criminal Justice System – 2006/2007," 2008. http://www.justice.gov.uk/docs/stats-race-criminal-justice. pdf, accessed Jan. 30, 2009.

55. Prison Reform Trust, "Bromley Briefings: Prison Fact File," June 2008. http:// www.prisonreformtrust.org.uk/documents/download.asp?lvid=892&id=1389, accessed Jan. 29, 2009.

56. Native Women's Association of Canada, "Federally Sentenced Aboriginal Women Offenders – An Issue Paper," *Conference paper presented at National Aboriginal Women's Summit*, 2007. http://www.nwac-hq.org/en/documents/nwac-federally.pdf, accessed Oct. 22, 2009.

57. Pew Center on the States, "One in 100."

58. Canadian Association of Elizabeth Fry Societies, "Fact Sheets," 2008. http:// www.elizabethfry.ca/eweek08/factsht.htm, accessed Jan 29, 2009; Pew Center on the States, "One in 100"; Prison Reform Trust, "Bromley Briefings," December 2008; Marta Russell and Jean Stewart, "Disablement, Prison and Historical

Segregation," *Monthly Review* 53, No. 3, 2001.

59. Phillip Beatty, Amanda Petteruti, and Jason Ziedenberg, "The Vortex: The Concentrated Racial Impact of Drug Imprisonment and the Characteristics of Punitive Counties," 2007. http://www.justicepolicy.org/images/upload/07-12_REP_Vortex_AC-DP.pdf, accessed Jan. 30, 2009.

60. Amanda Petteruti and Nastassia Walsh, "Moving Target: A Decade of Resistance to the Prison Industrial Complex," 2008. http://www.justicepolicy.org/images/upload/08-09_REP_MovingTargetCR10_AC-PS.pdf, accessed Jan. 30, 2009.

61. Canadian Association of Elizabeth Fry Societies, "Fact Sheet on Criminalized & Imprisoned Women," (2008), http://www.elizabethfry.ca/eweek08/pdf/crm-women.pdf, accessed Jan. 29, 2009.

62. Jessica Hoffmann, "On Prisons, Borders, Safety, and Privilege: An Open Letter to White Feminists," *Make/shift* (Republished on *Alternet*) No. 3, 2008. http://www.alternet.org/reproductivejustice/81260/, accessed Oct. 29, 2009.

63. Prison Reform Trust, "Bromley Briefings," July 2010.

64. Ira Basen, "Close Look at Conditional Sentencing," Canadian Broadcasting Corporation. http://www.cbc.ca/news/canadavotes/realitycheck/2008/09/close_look_at_conditional_sent.html, accessed Sept. 5, 2010.

65. Pew Center on the States, "One in 100."

66. British House of Commons, "Prisoners: Food," *Hansard Written Answers*, No. 10, September 2008 – Column 1978W, 2008. http://www.publications.parliament.uk/pa/cm200708/cmhansrd/cm080910/text/80910w0044.htm, accessed Oct. 22, 2009; H.M. Inspectorate of Prisons (U.K.), "H.M. Inspectorate of Prisons Website," 2008. http://inspectorates.homeoffice.gov.uk, accessed Jan. 30, 2009.

67. Prison Reform Trust, "Bromley Briefings," December 2008.

68. Petteruti and Walsh, "Moving Target."

69. Pew Center on the States, "One in 100."

70. Prison Reform Trust, "Bromley Briefings," December 2008.

71. David Downes and Kirstine Hansen, "Welfare and Punishment: The Relationship between Spending and Imprisonment," *Crime and Society Foundation Briefing 2*, November 2006. http://www.crimeandjustice.org.uk/opus303/Welfare_and_Punishment_webversion.pdf, accessed Sept. 9, 2010.

72. Sharon Detrick, et al., "Violence against Children in Conflict with the Law: A Study on Indicators and Data Collection in Belgium, England and Wales, France and the Netherlands," 2008. http://www.dci-is.org/db/nl/up_files/Violence_Against_Children_in_Conflict_with_the_Law_DCI_HLPR_EN.pdf, accessed Feb. 9, 2009.

73.   Prison Reform Trust, "Bromley Briefings," July 2010.

74.   Loïc Wacquant, "Deadly Symbiosis: When Ghetto and Prison Meet and Mesh," *Punishment & Society* 3, No. 1, 2001.

75.   Julia Sudbury, "Feminist Critiques, Transnational Landscapes, Abolitionist Visions," in *Global Lockdown: Race, Gender, and the Prison Industrial Complex*, ed. Julia Sudbury (New York: Routledge, 2005).

76.   Ashley Nellis and Ryan S. King, "No Exit: The Expanding Use of Life Sentences in America," The Sentencing Project, 2009. http://www.sentencingproject.org/doc/publications/publications/inc_noexitseptember2009.pdf, accessed Oct. 22, 2009.

77.   Ibid; U.K. Ministry of Justice, "Story of the Prison Population 1995–2009 England and Wales," (London: Ministry of Justice, 2009).

78.   Petteruti and Walsh, "Moving Target."

79.   Nigel Morris, "More Than 3,600 New Offenses under Labor," *The Independent*, 2008.

80.   Introduced by a Republican senator, the death penalty amendment was included in the version of the bill passed by the US Senate on July 23, 2009. The death penalty amendment was subsequently removed in October 2009 when the House and Senate versions of the bill were amalgamated, and the final legislation was signed into law by President Obama on October 28, 2009. Despite its title, the act is not prevention oriented, but rather prosecution driven. See the Matthew Shepard and James Byrd, Jr. Hate Crimes Prevention Act of 2009.

81.   See for example, Leadership Conference on Civil Rights, "Oppose the Session Amendment to the Matthew Shepard Hate Crime Prevention Act" [advocacy letter], July 20, 2009. http://www.civilrights.org/advocacy/letters/2009/oppose-the-sessions.html, accessed Oct. 5, 2009; National Gay and Lesbian Task Force, "Task Force Action Fund Urges for Removal of Death Penalty Amendment from the Department of Defense Authorization Bill" [press release], July 20, 2009. http://www.thetaskforce.org/press/releases/prAF_072009, accessed Oct. 5, 2009.

82.   For two excellent critiques of hate crimes law, see Andrea Smith, "Unmasking the State: Racial/Gender Terror and Hate Crimes," *Australian Feminist Law Journal* 26, No. 47, 2007; Dean Spade and Craig Willse, "Confronting the Limits of Gay Hate Crimes Activism: A Radical Critique," *Chicano-Latino Law Review* 21, 2000.

83.   Chris Hedges, "War as Hate Crime," *Pacific Free Press* 26, October 2009. http://www.pacificfreepress.com/news/1/4947-war-as-hate-crime.html, accessed Oct. 28, 2009.

84.   A. M. Agathangelou, M. D. Bassichis, and T. L. Spira, "Intimate Investments:

Homonormativity, Global Lockdown, and the Seductions of Empire," *Radical History Review*, No. 100, 2008; Jin Haritaworn, Tamsila Tauqir, and Esra Erdem, "Gay Imperialism: Gender and Sexuality Discourse in the 'War on Terror,'" in *Out of Place: Interrogating Silences in Queerness/Raciality*, ed. Adi Kuntsman and Esperanza Miyake (York, England: Raw Nerve Books, 2008).

85. See Critical Resistance and INCITE! Women of Color Against Violence, "Gender Violence."

86. Dick and Stonewall, "Homophobic Hate Crime."

87. Frazer, "Some Queers Are Safer," p.14.

88. Prison Reform Trust, "Bromley Briefings," June 2008.

89. Canadian Association of Elizabeth Fry Societies, "Fact Sheet on Criminalized Women"; US Bureau of Justice Statistics, "Criminal Offender Statistics – Recidivism." http://www.ojp.usdoj.gov/bjs/crimoff.htm#recidivism, accessed Oct. 22, 2009.

90. Emily Dugan, "Re-Offending Rates Rise as the Prison Population Expands," *The Independent* July 20, 2008. http://www.independent.co.uk/news/uk/crime/reoffending-rates-rise-as-the-prison-population-expands-872411.html, accessed Oct. 22, 2009; Carol Hedderman, "Building on Sand: Why Expanding the Prison Estate Is Not the Way to 'Secure the Future," *Center for Crime and Justice Studies Briefing*, No. 7, July 2008. http://www.crimeandjustice.org.uk/opus733/Builtonsandbriefing.pdf, accessed Oct. 22, 2009.

91. Anthony N. Doob and Carla Cesaroni, *Responding to Youth Crime in Canada* (Toronto: University of Toronto Press, 2004); Lonn Lanza-Kaduce, et al., "Juvenile Transfer to Criminal Court Study: Final Report," 2002. http://www.prisonpolicy.org/scans/juveniletransfers.pdf, accessed Oct. 29, 2009; Anthony Petrosino, Carolyn Turpin-Petrosino, and James O. Finckenauer, "Well-Meaning Programs Can Have Harmful Effects! Lessons from Experiments of Programs Such as Scared Straight," *Crime Delinquency* 46, No. 3, 2000.

92. James Austin, et al., "Unlocking America: Why and How to Reduce America's Prison Population," 2007. http://www.jfa-associates.com/publications/srs/UnlockingAmerica.pdf, accessed Feb. 8, 2009.

93. Dugan, "Re-Offending Rates Rise."

94. See for example, Joan McCord, "Cures That Harm: Unanticipated Outcomes of Crime Prevention Programs," *Annals of the American Academy of Political and Social Science* 587, 2003; Petrosino, Turpin-Petrosino, and Finckenauer, "Well-Meaning Programs."

95. Steve Aos, Robert Barnoski, and Roxanne Leib, "Preventing Programs for Young Offenders: Effective and Cost-Effective," *Overcrowded Times* 9, No. 2, 1998; David J. Smith, "The Effectiveness of the Juvenile Justice System," *Criminal*

Justice 5, No. 2, 2005.

96. David Daubney, *Taking Responsibility: Report of the Standing Committee on Justice and Solicitor General on Its Review of Sentencing, Conditional Release, and Related Aspects of Corrections* (Ottawa: Supply and Services Canada, 1988).

97. Ruth Morris, *Stories of Transformative Justice* (Toronto: Canadian Scholars' Press, 2000).

98. Taking an abolitionist stance does not mean refusing to engage in incremental change, nor does it mean abandoning efforts to improve conditions inside prisons. Rather, abolitionists engage in "abolitionist reforms" or "non-reformist reforms." These are reforms that either directly undermine the prison industrial complex or provide support to prisoners through strategies weaken, rather than strengthen, the prison system itself. For example, rather than lobbying for bigger prison health budgets to care for elderly prisoners, an abolitionist reform strategy would aim to get elderly prisoners out on compassionate release to obtain healthcare in the community. See Critical Resistance, *A World without Walls*.

99. Prison Research Education Action Project and Critical Resistance, "Instead of Prisons: A Handbook for Abolitionists," in *Instead of Prisons*, ed. Mark Morris (New York: Prison Research Education Action Project, 2005). http://www.prisonpolicy.org/scans/instead_of_prisons/, accessed Jan. 29, 2009.

100. Rachel Herzing and Trevor Paglen, "Abolishing the Prison Industrial Complex," *Recording Carceral Landscapes Project*, 2005. http://www.paglen.com/carceral/pdfs/herzing.pdf, accessed Jan. 29, 2009.

101. For an excellent set of community accountability resources, particularly for dealing with violence against women and trans people, see INCITE! Women of Color Against Violence, "Community Accountability Resources." http://www.incite-national.org/index.php?s=114, accessed Sept. 6, 2010.

MAKING IT HAPPEN, MAMA:

A Conversation with Miss Major

Jayden Donahue

We are at an important moment in the anti-prison industrial complex movement. The largest prison expansion bill (AB 900) in the history of the world is currently being implemented in California. We are experiencing increased policing of our communities through gang injunctions and the collaboration of local police agencies with the federal government through ICE and Secure Communities as continued fear-mongering bolstered by mainstream media urges us to become more dependent on state-sponsored solutions to social problems and less reliant on the skills, tools, and knowledge that we already have to create and support self-determined communities. History tells us that trans people and transwomen of color in particular have played and continue to play a foundational role in this fight. The Trans, Gender Variant, and Intersex Justice Project is one of a handful of organizations around the country that are providing leadership, eking out victories, and exploring strategies to help us reach our goals and the challenges presented in the struggle. As part of this conversation with Miss Major, we tried to tease out some of these points to serve as a tool for organizers and individuals in recognizing places of entry into the work as well as pitfalls or places where we get stuck. We also take some time to celebrate the triumphs, an important part of reflecting on our work.

The Trans, Gender Variant, and Intersex Justice Project's (TGIJP) mission is to challenge and end the human rights abuses committed against transgender, gender-variant/genderqueer, and intersex people in California prisons and beyond. TGIJP was founded in 2003 by Alex Lee through a Soros Justice Advocacy fellowship and his work as part of the Trans in Prison Committee (TIP) at California Prison Focus. From the beginning, the organization has been volunteer-directed and currently has two staff positions: a legal director and a community organizing director. TGIJP has chosen to center trans women of color, particularly women who are currently inside and those who have been recently released, as an overall strategy to both build leadership among and empower people most affected by the PIC.

Miss Major is a black, formerly incarcerated, male-to-female transgender elder. A veteran activist born and raised on the south side of Chicago, she participated in the Stonewall rebellion in 1969 and was politicized in the wake of the Attica prison rebellion. She has worked at HIV/AIDS organizations throughout California, was an original member of the first all-transgender gospel choir, and is a father, mother, grandmother, and grandfather to her own children and to many in the transgender community. Currently, Miss Major is the executive director of TGIJP. I wanted to talk to Miss Major about some of the core elements of TGIJP and its structure, campaigns, and future work. I also wanted to take a look at some of the contradictions inherent in identity-based organizing and how TGIJP works to navigate in that space. We explore notions of political unity in a broad-based and diffuse movement as well as questions around what it means to be an ally and effectively take leadership from people most affected by the PIC.

Jayden Donahue: Can you introduce yourself and tell me a little bit about the Trans, Gender Variant, and Intersex Justice Project (TGIJP) and its mission?

Miss Major Griffin-Gracy: OK, I am Miss Major, none of this Ms. shit. I am not a liberated woman. I'm a transgendered woman and I'm working on being liberated as we speak. So, as far as TGIJP—Transgender, Gender Variant, Intersex Justice Project—we're a nonprofit organization working under the guise of Justice Now as our fiscal sponsor, that is interested in promoting the well-being and mental health and stability of transgendered women of color that are housed in the prison industrial complex (PIC). We help those that are currently housed or recently released maintain their civil rights and help them fight—basically that's the start to finish kind of a thing. We have a lawyer to help legally represent them; should their cases get an opportunity or a chance to go to court, we help them work with that and help to find suitable legal representation through the lawyer we have working here. We also help with cases here in San Francisco and push for alternative sentencing, which may or may not work, but it's something we do push toward, making sure that the judges and the district attorneys have credible and viable information that pertains to the community itself and not this hyped up bullshit that's floating around about us, about who we are and how we exist.

So, a part of us used to be the Transgender in Prison Committee (TIP), which was a part of TGIJP. TIP was like their organizing fist of action, I guess you could call it. They worked together simultaneously with the same objectives and goals except that TIP was more of the grassroots kind of a thing with organizers and allies who believed in the same mission and helped us work toward establishing those things that we chose as part of our mission. In that vein, one of the things that I think is a *major* coup for us was when Alexis Giraldo got a chance to actually sue the fucking prison system and we assisted her in getting her documentation, her legal records at the time, and stuff like that. Alex Lee helped to coordinate and organize the information that she had and helped her find an attorney and work with them so that she could go to court. We did go to court on it. And then the organizing arm of us, that would be me (naturally I would be the fist), helped to pull together over a hundred people in a day to appear outside the courtroom at seven o'clock in the morning with signs protesting about what they're doing to transgendered people, how we are always getting abused and stepped over and mutilated and raped and walked on and ignored. And so we blocked the front of the court house, but we didn't stop people from going in. All four corners of that block—Polk and McAllister—had people on them with signs, so folks had to walk around us to cross the fucking street, so that was just a little goose-bumpy, it just made you feel so good to look out there and see that. And it was allies and some of the girls came out and carried the signs. We made signs on the bumper of my car and taped and stapled and nailed them to wood, you know. It was an event; somebody ran and got bagels and donuts. So it was a good thing, it was a really good thing. She originally lost in court, but, the good thing is it went to the higher court, and they sent it back down to the lower court telling them that she can have another trial now, so that bullshit that they went through is null and void. So now we're working on helping her piece it together so that she can have another trial. So hopefully that will come to fruition.

JD: When did TGIJP start? Were you around then?

MM: I came here a little bit after it started. Alex (Alex Lee) started it, primarily by his little two-gun-shooting self. He had just gotten out of law school, he was working with TIP and he wanted to help to organize something to help defend and stand up for the rights of transgendered women that are in the prison system. So, through that he got TGIJP started and then they worked with TIP. TGIJP was doing prison visits and he was doing legal stuff to help the girls from the letters that were being sent in to Prison Focus. And from there it grew into this mammoth that we're working on building and taking to the next phase. It's an exciting thing.

JD: Could you talk a little bit about some of the challenges that TIP faced in the beginning, especially around membership and power dynamics?

MM: A sprinkle, I can talk about that a sprinkle. As usual, there were definitely a lot of transmen involved in this in the beginning, in TIP. For some reason a lot of the trans guys are really more politically aware and astute than my transwomen are. There doesn't seem to be this vanity floating through the fellas that simply butters itself up and down us transwomen. We're just bathed in it. Having to be beautiful and this and that. It will drive you crazy. You'll lose your hair trying to keep all of this shit together. So, our particular involvement as transgendered women is often minimal compared to the involvement of most trans guys. Usually they're white trans guys and they've been to college and they have an idea of how the system works and how to deal with it. With a lot of the white privilege and the education that they've got there's this tendency for them to step up and take charge and lead the way and say, "Follow me, I'll protect you," without educating people about what's going on. Of course, there are the little differences and petty things that get involved over personalities. Before I got heavily involved, there were a lot of little personality clashes and the testosterone egos bumping into each other here and there. It was a lot of the "pissing contests" the guys go through. It calmed down and the dust settled and TIP got to rise up and TGIJP was a calmer space.

JD: TGIJP has a few different committees. Can you talk about them and the work you are currently doing?

MM: Well the structure has changed from when I initially got involved and so a lot of the membership also changed. My getting on board made it a more comfortable and I think a more relaxed space in terms of meetings. The feel of everything changed and through that restructuring and getting everything to be more suitable to who we are as a different organization with the influx of more women of color and more transgendered female participants. It developed into teams. There's the legal team, which is run by our lawyer. There's the fundraising team, which is grassroots fundraising. We have a separate person who helps with the grants and that kind of annoying stuff that you have to do to survive. And then there's the Make It Happen Mamas (MIHM), which of course happens to be mine since I'm the mama. And the three of them function independently but under the same guise. We're a collective. And so, even though we function independently, there's this common rule that directs everything. The legal team of course works on getting the girls the information that they need and helping them fight in court, and writing letters to the judges and district attorneys about sentencing and stuff. And in writing to the parole officers and advocating for our clients, which are primarily transgender women of color housed in these kinds of situations. Not that we ignore white transgendered women, but our focus is primarily transgendered women of color since we're at the very bottom of the pile. We help everybody, but concentrate on transgendered women of color. The grassroots fundraising team, currently, is working on developing outside funds so that we can become self-sustaining and not need the grant money that we have to sustain us. So we're working on building up a database of funders. The team is working to get us to the point where we can be self-sustained and we can function on our own using the technology of today, which is the computer and Facebook shit and that kind of thing.

MIHM is driving itself and me crazy. We are working on revamping the organization and coming up with a new focus and direction for TGIJP since merging with TIP and becoming one organization. We've attempted to change the name and create a logo for us and ran into a brick wall, or impasse as they call it, and are sorting that out. So, we set that aside to concentrate on what the structure's going to be, where the direction is, and the aim that we're going to be taking.

One of the things that we're working on right now is developing a mentorship program so that we can help to establish and empower transgender women that have been in prison to realize that they have a voice and that their stories are important and they need to be told. We are also working with Sylvia Rivera Law Project and twelve other agencies across the United States through Transforming Justice, which was the conference that we had in 2007 in San Francisco to build a network, national network. It was attended by 250 from around the country. For our community, the male-to-female transgendered community, one of the things that works best with us in getting us to realize the things that are going on politically and socially and realize that we have to fight for social justice with folks who are not transgendered and deal with the Transgendered 101 that you have to give every time you go to pee because someone's going to ask you a question in the bathroom taking care of your business: Well, why are you in here, and how long have you been that way, and you know. A part of this mentorship program is helping the girls to understand how to deal with that, gracefully. And then getting them to take these things on and then to mentor to young girls, just one or two girls, so you don't drive yourself crazy. Help to set up boundaries and stuff like that. The mentorship program will help work on the newsletter that we send into the prison system to the girls, or work on our database and keep up on who is in there and who isn't, making things like that more current. And then working with them on establishing the pen-pal program, not just getting it up and running, but getting it functioning because it was running before but it lost wind—but like a sailboat, child, it's running along and then all of a sudden it stops. But now we have a motor on the damn boat so we won't get stuck, we can go forward.

In thinking about it and mapping it out as we are doing right now, it's an exciting thing. I mean, it's just really wonderful to think about how we can affect stuff. It feels good, and I think the comfortable thing about it for me is that I've been doing it all along and that I'm pretty good and also as an older person I don't run into a lot of walls. People give me respect, getting to be 60 years old, it's like, "Well, we better listen to what this bitch has to say," and then once I get their ear, I got 'em. And so I think it's better for us, and better for the younger girls. And the reason why we're going through all of that restructuring of stuff and trying to sort out a different direction to take us—for me, a lot of times what I've noticed in reading about stuff is that TGIJP has built something and then lost momentum or became fractioned and whatever the goal was, it disappeared on us. In trying to refocus this and keep this going I think this is something that we can take small steps on, and then after it grows we'll be able to take bigger steps, get more involved, see what other things we have, and encompass more things. And then we can reach outside of ourselves to get involved with agencies that are not specifically transgendered-geared but that can help us say, sort out what the social justice movement is, how do we become a part of that, because, to me, none of these things are going to succeed if they don't involve everybody, which means, this community has to become involved. And it can't just be the transmen, we can't be you know, off to the side being all glamour-pinning on the fence, child, our size 12 feet in size 6 shoes, so we can't walk anywhere, we just have to stand and be pretty and leave this on your back; we can't do that. We *have* to become involved.

JD: You've talked a little bit about the newsletter that TGIJP sends to people inside and the pen-pal project. Can you talk a little bit about why it's important to stay connected to people who are inside?

MM: First of all, being in prison is filled with absolute, complete hell. Not a moment's peace. You have no sanity and no safety and no safe haven and no spots to think and sort out how you deal with shit that you have to go through, just from being in prison as a transgendered woman. The reason why the things that we do, like fighting to get bras inside, are important is that people are forgetting that these are women housed in a men's prison. They're not giving any recognition to the fact that a majority of these people have breasts and oddly enough, they need to be cupped in a bra, for their safety, for them to maintain who they are and for them to hold on to their sense of self. And it's not like it's a luxury in there but you know, if women have bras in the women's prison, then the women in the men's prison should have them. It's not that they want anything special; it's just something to keep their breasts safe; to keep them from having to suffer the indignity of making them run around without that particular protection, because that's what it is for them. Every now and then we get some in and it's a major accomplishment. It's like, let's go out and throw a party. It becomes something that helps give the girls strength to sustain themselves while they are in there.

The reason we have the pen-pal program is when you're in there you're feeling so isolated and cut off and desolate and depressed and lonely. There's nowhere to turn for anything. So, if you happen to get a letter from somebody who's outside the damn wall to just say how are you doing, what can I do to help, this is what's going on here, I've seen your old friend so-and-so, it keeps you connected to your life and who you are and what you stand for. This can make a big difference in how you relate to stuff and how you get though your bid. You gotta do the time; you can't let the time do you. And without that connection to what's going on outside that wall, the time winds up doing you. When I was in there, not getting a letter from people I knew or friends, it got to the point where I'd take a postcard from a stranger saying "hey, girl," you know, just something to connect me to who I am. One of things that happens is that you lose yourself in there. All of a sudden you become Number 449632-C, and that's not who you are; that's just what you happen to be wearing at the time. Those things are awfully, awfully important.

JD: Can you talk about some of the challenges facing women coming home from prison?

MM: Talk about Mission Impossible II? I mean, it's unbelievable. It's bad enough for everybody else. It isn't just us suffering; everybody coming home is suffering. The reason why it's horrible for our community is you have a transgendered woman coming out of prison who hasn't had a moment to put her lotion on, keep herself feminine, stay in that mindset, portray the woman that she is inside. Then if they try to get a job, they're not going to hire *Barbara* because *Barbara* hasn't shaved in two days.

I've had girls who have gone up to work in the Castro area and are told, "Oh, you're so cute, it would be nice to have you working here," thinking that it's a lesbian they are talking to. And of course, she shows her ID and it says Fred Schwartz. "Ooh, well, you can't work here. I can't have people coming in here and questioning or looking at you like you're a, well, you know." Well, you want to hire me. They might come in here and like talking to me. You think I'm going to have my license pinned on my chest? "Hi, I'm Fred. Call me Gladys." And if you don't laugh at it, it will kill you. You have to have a sense of humor about this and then, in that, work on getting at the change.

And then when you go to report to your parole officer, and you do manage to run into one of your old girlfriends, so you go and stay with her and you get a chance to bathe and put lotion on and get a bra that fits and throw together a little androgynous outfit because you can't go to parole in your shit and you can't go there looking like the woman that you are. And you go in there and you get hassled: "You're a sissy and you're this and you're that and you're not going to find no fucking work and I'm not going to help you get a job and the moment you do something, I'm going to throw your ass back in jail." So, you're on the merry-go-round and you're trying to figure out: Should I reach for that brass ring or not? Well, no because that brass ring is stuck and you're going back to jail, you know. So, how do you find a job? How do you find a place to live that they're going to approve of? How do you find a way to manipulate and use the things around you so that you can be OK and get off that merry-go-round of recidivism where you're back in jail within ten months? And it gets to the point where jail becomes like an old home. That's not exactly something that you're thinking about when you realize that you are a transgendered person and that you want to make this transition. It's not like you are thinking, *All my best friends are going to be behind bars and I'm going to visit them frequently from time to time, only on the inside, so I can hug them.* That's not what the hell I want, but that's the reality, as frightening as that is.

And it takes the work of agencies and people that want to help and commit to doing this despite the reaction that they're going to get when they offer to help. People forget that we've been abused and kicked in the stomach and stepped on for so fucking long. So you say, "Hi, my name is *Don*, I want to help," and you get, "Yeah, fuck you. You're not going to do shit for me, punk-ass motherfucker; you're not going to be there. Kiss my ass." And off you go. Well, *Don* needs to get his shit together and approach them again. You need to be consistent, you need to keep pushing. If this is what you really want to do, then you're going to have to climb up the mountain with roller skates on. Because the abuse has been so long, so tumultuous, that there isn't the room. Most of the girls don't have the time to believe in everyone that comes along wanting to help because prior to them coming into our lives, someone else came along saying that very same thing and then kicked us in the ass. Or we reached for their hand and they said, "Oh, you're too heavy, I can't hold you, girl," or "Oops, sorry, I missed you by just that much." Don't matter how much, bitch: You missed me. So, in order to deal with this you come up with this shell. The shell protects you; I love my shell, where would I be without you, hug me mama. Other people don't have to have a shell.

JD: This question came up for me in the last bit that you said different groups of people feeling like they are at the bottom. It occurred to me that that this says a lot about identity politics and competition for who is most oppressed. Can you talk a little bit about this and how it plays into your work?

MM: It's like going over to one of your friend's houses and they are in the middle of the biggest pity party that they've ever thrown. And instead of trying to help them feel better, you aren't invited to their party. So you're going to throw a party of your own. As an older person, when I go to one of the senior centers to get help, like for my taxes, and I'm in there and people are saying hi to me and greeting me then they'll ask you, "How do you feel?" Well, for older people, they really want to know how you feel, how your health is. "Oh, well, I had kidney surgery and I have this scar." "Girl, I fell and broke this leg and this hip over here." What is this, a competition? When you're younger it has more to do with what you're income is or how you have been denied an income and so it turns into being so devastated that you feel you don't even deserve to breathe. Well, how do you go forward if that's your attitude, if you are living to be worse off than somebody else? Complaining about it doesn't get anything done. So, in the social justice movement I have found that the things that some people are working on and pushing toward are not more important than what everybody else is working on. All of it is important. Because with the resources that are available to us we can make sure that nobody has to go through any of this. All we had to do, for a mere moment, is to step back and realize that the sun doesn't revolve around me; it revolves around a world that has other people in it. That's too hard for people to commit to. That's why all the wealth is in, what, 6 percent of the population, and the rest of us are struggling like hell.

JD: I consider TGIJP to be a radical organization. Can you talk a little bit about where your priorities differ from mainstream gay politics?

MM: I eventually do want to get married, to the right person, pet, tree. At this point, I don't care, but I don't want to assimilate myself into a group of people who think that my very existence is abominable. Why do I want to do what they want to do? Why do I have to have a ring on my finger? Why do I have to pass? Why can't I just be recognized and acknowledged for who I am. *Well, he's pretty, the man's gorgeous.* This society is not at that level and so that makes it hard to maintain. It makes it hard to go forward. It makes it hard to sit and just accept your damn self. They say, "We're here to help." You don't know what help is. Try walking a mile in my shoes. Fuck walking a mile—why not wear my shoes, throw on my hair, wear this tight-ass dress, tuck my dick and balls into a gaff, child, and then run in front of police, jump over cars, and then snatch off your hair, put on different clothes, change your shoes and then walk down that same street past the motherfucker that was looking for you in the first place. Then you can give me some shit about who the fuck I am.

JD: Some of the things that you are talking about seem to be indirectly related to the prison industrial complex and maybe address some of the root causes of imprisonment for transgendered women of color.

MM: The thing is, it's hard to see that there is a connection, but there is a *definite* connection between that kind of stuff and the prison industrial complex. One of the things that happens for a girl getting involved in the PIC is we already, from the moment we decide to be a transgendered person, are living outside the law. The moment this dick-swinging motherfucker wants to put a dress on and head on down the street to go to the store or something like that, they have broken the law. Because it's not a legal thing that we're doing. We can be beaten, attacked, and killed, and it's OK "Oh, well, who gives a shit about that motherfucker, he's confused." You are already a convict for just how you express yourself and you might start to live a lifestyle of a person that is living outside of the law. Because you can't get a legitimate job, you can't get a chance in school, you can't get a chance to function and survive as a part of mainstream society. So, immediately, once you've done this, you're part of the PIC. Whether you get there right away or you slowly build toward it, but every step that you take, takes you another step closer to it. Now depending upon what star you were born under, you may or may not have it happen right away. But eventually, it happens most transgendered women have had some involvement with police. And this is directly related to the PIC, from my way of thinking. Because if you don't have a sense of self and you don't have a way to learn how to protect and live your life, you're on your way to prison. So, for me, I'm working at it in the best way I feel I can to make sure that the girls don't get there. If they don't get there then society can't put a number on them; they can't be labeled, they can't be marketed or targeted by the PIC.

JD: Can you talk about where you see TGIJP going and its future work?

MM: Why would you do that to me? I don't have a crystal ball. I hate that question, but I can answer it. I see us growing and getting into a position to whereby we're not only helping the girls that are in the prison system but we're holding meetings and classes in there to talk to the girls, to let them know what their rights are while they are in there, helping them with the charges they get while they're in prison doing stuff, and alleviating sentences. Because you can go to jail, get arrested inside the jail for doing something else, and then go to jail in the jail as punishment for what you did. I can see us being in a position to help to alleviate that. We could train somebody to be one of those legal representatives within the prison to help the girls with charges and papers and that kind of stuff inside. And then outside to develop a system to work with the women who are coming out, job training, organizing, and doing what they need to do to survive. Get the girls involved in school, teach them trades so if they don't want to work a 9–5 job, they can sew, help girls make gowns, learn computers, do data-entry, paint, draw, artistic stuff. Get them to express themselves in ways that are appropriate to what they've gone through. There's art inside that so many of the girls never get the opportunity to present and have it appreciated. And help families, friends, and lovers adapt to situations because it's hard to explain to people what it means to be a transgendered woman, what we go through on hormones. We need to help families understand that this person that you happen to have raised is now 16 and wants to wear a dress and they still stand up to pee; it's their choice. We need to help negotiate that so that the animosity that usually occurs doesn't.

JD: Is TGIJP an abolitionist organization?

MM: I wonder how I knew that word was going to come up when talking to you. Yes, we are definitely an abolitionist organization. The thing about trying to get rid of the system, we can't just snap our fingers and the bitches are gone. While we tear down the walls and let everybody go we have to figure out what we can do to make society accept this and figure out how to negotiate a co-existence. One of the questions that usually pops up is the idea that there are some evil, crazy, wild, stupid-ass motherfuckers who need to be behind bars. Well, it isn't that they need to be behind bars; it's that they need to be held accountable for what they do and we need to sort out a way to do that without putting them behind bars. Because when you put them behind bars, technically, you're putting all of us behind bars. It's like telling people they have to get off drugs; you have to give them some alternatives. We have to show society that their protection is still ensured by our other system. We are working on dismantling this system from the inside out, to show how it's not working, to show how it's hurting everybody and at the same time, building toward something else. My hope is that in the future, there won't be any prisons.

gender wars:

state changing shape, passing to play, and body of our movements

Vanessa Huang[1]

The alarm clock wakes me at 6:30 in the morning—early, given that I'm not preparing for a prison visit. After snoozing once or twice, I reconnect with the sustained struggle and resilience of people in California's women's prisons who cannot make the day's trip with me. While not knowing the experience of personally having been locked up, my bodymemory breathes quietpresent with the rupture of immigration, heartbreak of family missing, close and far.

> We believe in home all home all beautiful home enough bellies breathe
> and sigh
> enough skin rest dance free enough courage carry all life this a home no
> landlord

281

tenant bank imagine
no passport jail shelter claim

It's connecting across a chorus of activist spirit—amid break and toward something more safe, more whole, more true and free—that pulls me out of bed to shower and dress myself.

I pull on what I explain to housemates as my policy *disfraz*: a stern striped femme suit, the texture smoothed out of my hair, and the sturdy leather bag, usually in the bottom of my closet, slung over shoulder. Once at the office, I settle more into this suit shape containing my queer, Chinese-American, female-assigned/identified and gender-fluid, college-educated, "able" body. I check online for the morning roundup of capitol gossip. I review talking points for all twenty seconds that the committee chair will likely afford me come hearing time, when I'll say again—in suit voice—that it's a bad idea to build more prisons and that calling them "gender responsive," "community-based alternatives," or "homeless shelters" wasn't gonna cut it. I shuffle a stack of papers into my bag, roll a 30-foot-long petition into a tube, and begin the drive north from Oakland to Sacramento.

gender heartbreak, fraud tag

The once uncomfortable routine of shape change and code switching to play policy in service of containing the prison industrial complex became more and more practiced for me from the late 2005–2006 California legislative session through the first half of the 2007–2008 legislative session. I was serving as the campaign and communications director for anti-prison organization Justice Now. We were knee-deep in a contentious battle over words, ideas, jobs, moneys, ego—most significantly, the names, bodies, and lives of gender-oppressed people imprisoned and targeted for lockup in California prisons. At the heart of our quickly escalated fight response was the vital need to give shape and sound to what our movement body had held for too long: the break and tire from the feeling of unending fight against more and more criminalization, more and more stolen, more and more disappeared, more and more prematurely dying.[2]

The specific proposal our pushback targeted was California's proposal for a near 40 percent expansion of California's women's prison system in the shape of a new system of mini prisons—"Female Rehabilitative Community Correctional Centers" (FRCCCs)—throughout the Central Valley and beyond. Originally packaged as part of a portfolio of so-called reentry facilities in what would later become the single-largest prison construction package to pass in US history, according to the *New York Times*, California's FRCCCs and a broader "Female Offender Reform Master Plan" were not unique.[3]

These policy proposals were part of a coordinated and growing movement pushing prison expansion in new form: "gender responsiveness." The state changing shape in this way enabled white cisgender liberal feminists, the face of this policy trend, to blend with policy speak for "good for 'women'" while colluding with the state's ever-growing need to manage more and more communities exploited and broken by empire. "Gender responsiveness" enabled policymakers and criminologist academics to present as so-called feminist while continuing to play and stay in the policy game by keeping a "tough on crime" card amid a shifting political landscape, where our movements have labored to sound the voice of premature death from communities of resistance in prisons such that they could no longer ignore it. Notably, proposals for "gender responsive" prisons administered and staffed by prison guards was dressed in language of "community-based alternatives" and "closer to home," speaking back to longstanding desire from families and communities surviving the break of imprisonment for our loved ones to return home.

Given what was inside their frame of "gender responsiveness," the most immediate threat that Justice Now and our allies inside and out experienced was at, in, and around "women's" prisons and who most often gets stolen and hidden here: cisgender women, female-assigned, and gender-variant people, and people on the transmasculine spectrum. We also feared that in response to growing "Trans 101" training and integration across our movements, the slow trickle to state institutions would reframe "gender responsiveness"—and the specialized prison expansion policy trend more generally—over time to more intentionally collude with trans misogyny—and trans/gender oppression more generally—by way of trans-specific prisons.

Regardless of whether, when, and how the state might continue to change the shape of "gender responsiveness" over time, we were clear on the empty promise in its echo of desire for home, safe, free. Evading state accountability for past and current harm and threatening to further grow the edges of gender oppression and state violence against communities of color and poor communities, proponents' nebulous gesture of "gender responsiveness" proposed an array of so-called new "gender responsive" programming useful to people of all genders (i.e. job training and mental health support) and services and regulations steeped in rigid gender training.

Cookie Concepcion, one activist leader we worked with at Central California Women's Facility (CCWF), speaks to the fraud of "gender responsiveness" in a Feministing.com blog post dated May 13, 2008. Explaining how the prison doesn't allow female-assigned prisoners to wear boxers, Cookie writes, "Lately a lot of time and money has been spent on mandatory 'Gender Responsive' training for all officers and staff. The objective of this training is to define differences between female and male inmates. The basic ideology is that females commit crimes because they are victims, whereas males are just bad and mean. This must be where they learned how dangerous it is for females to wear boxers."

In mid-2006, Justice Now and our allies successfully lobbied Assembly member Jackie Goldberg (an original bill co-author and key policymaker promoting "gender responsive" prison expansion policy in California) to remove her name and leadership from the bill. Goldberg told the press that after listening to prisoner rights advocates' concerns and following our media hits, she realized that the proposal was a "fraud," pointing to a contract bid proposal "filled with problems that would almost certainly result in a reduction of services, less family visitation, and countless other custodial issues," and its expansion of an "already mammoth prison system."[4]

Throughout the campaign, I witnessed bill author Assembly member Sally Lieber's rallying cry to peers and lobbyists from Sacramento policy organizations without bases or constituents overlapping with people in women's prisons: *Shame on us for leaving women out of the picture.* Lobby visit after lobby visit, my heart broke at the empty promise of "gender responsiveness": while Lieber, the governor, and other state actors' reasoning for these prisons and programming relied on references to the needs of women in prison, "they did not stop to ask what we need or want, even if they care," according to Misty Rojo, an activist leader then imprisoned at CCWF and board member of Justice Now. Rojo wrote Justice Now that the plan for "gender responsive" prisons "is not truly aimed at helping us, but serves as a ploy to make prison expansion politically agreeable." My heart broke when the governor's prison proposals confirmed this fear, explicitly stating that the 4,500 prison beds vacated by prisoners for the mini-prisons would be filled by additional people.[5]

Hearing after hearing, my heart broke when proponents' language presenting as care for women in prison morphed into conversation about and with the labor lobby and who would get to fill new jobs playing "good cop" in these "good prisons," public safety committee shape changing to jobs committee.

In the hallways of the capitol, my heart broke when Mary Wiberg, director of Committee on the Status of Women, responded to Justice Now interns carrying a petition against "gender responsive" prisons on behalf of over 3,300 people in women's prisons by saying that *anyone could have gotten thousands of women in prison to sign anything.*

And in a crowded office, my heart broke when a staffer burst into tears mid-meeting after declining my invitation for her to join Justice Now on a prison visit, or to accept some collect calls, to hear directly from people inside about why they opposed these prisons.

first writing since[6]

The process of writing this essay trailed me several years since the height of the campaign; finishing the writing required a distance of time to just feel, to sleep, these two years punctuated by many prior attempts to open, many leavings, being in the direct work, later returns to page.

During this time, my partner and fellow activists were unexpectedly targeted, harassed, and beaten by police at a protest. They were arrested and charged with felonies and misdemeanors, some with terrorist enhancements, each and together held at atypically high bail. That weekend and in the weeks and months following, I learned in new ways, through body, more about how the persistence of state-sponsored crisis has shaped our movements than I ever would have wished. Here in our organizing for loved ones to return and stay home—fundraising for bail and bond, building community pressure to drop their charges—here where my edge as family of loved ones fighting back blended with the edge of their community's response after attack, I re-encountered some of my own movements: the shape of organizations and people whose labor over time has fed and raised me, a prison abolitionist attempting to wrestle the terror of police and prison violence disarming resistance of each and all where empire, racism, gender oppression, queerphobia, and silencing meet.

Here my "personal" reopened my "political"; the layered secondary traumas in my "political" further intensified my "personal." I tracked the shape and sound of my body's fight response. In this moment, in my first year outside of organizing within a full-time nonprofit framework, I understood more about collective bodymemory and shaping than in the last five years that I've actively been in practice expressing my commitment to prison industrial complex abolition and continuing to explore the politics and principles guiding that commitment. I learned about how our movements have learned to react, survive, and keep safe over time to the crisis of a state military in its stalwart growing of violence and control over more and more of our communities. My bodymemory recognized the exhaustion and safekeeping practices of our elders, OG organizers still standing after FBI infiltration and targeting of our lineages of resistance.

> *this steadfast heart/ keep safe from their watching*
> *heart/ be heart/ be heart/ beat that quiets baton*
> *heart/ beat code of ethics in crumble*

I woke to and grew empathy for the experience of chronic tire after break. I found new empathy for how mentors have labored to renew and reshape possibility and promise from this place, coaxing and feeding our movement body to grow new muscle. I located my political development inside this movement body's longing to rebuild safety to return to the fierceness of vision and strategy that our communities and movements so urgently need to contain in order to dismantle the prison industrial complex.

And I reconnected with the real body fear driving our fightback against California's threat to grow a new arm of its prison empire by way of so-called gender responsiveness. In this remembering, I understood on the body level how the state's growing trend of specialized prisons is its reaction to the real power arising from communities of resistance, the real ways we've shaken up the conditions through the tremendous labor of so many to amplify the collective voice of more and more stolen and disappeared.

> *each door forced open, each left ajar still chanting*
> *each stomach caressing ground still chanting*
> *each muscle fight back still chanting*

glimpse of fire, this slow breath home

Ultimately, Justice Now, activists inside, and our allies outside successfully defeated "gender responsive" prison construction in California's 2005–2006 and 2007–2008 legislative sessions as presented in several legislative vehicles: Assembly Bill 2066 (AB2066), ABX2-1, AB76. AB2066 gave way to ABX2-1 amid the then-California governor's call for a "special session" pushing a broader expansion package in which ABX2-1 failed, likely more because of political conditions in Sacramento and with other parties than because of our efforts. Between the 2005–2006 and 2007–2008 legislative sessions, Justice Now was able to clarify and solidify our campaign demands and targets, strategies and tactics, and messaging for our 2007 campaign, in which we successfully defeated AB76. Due to a legislative loophole, the Assembly Public Safety Committee granted the bill author a courtesy revote in which she pressured a legislator who'd abstained from voting in favor of a revised bill in which they removed the prison construction language.

Our path to successfully remove bill language authorizing "gender responsive" prison construction included weekly one-on-ones throughout the summer of 2006 with people imprisoned at Central California Women's Facility (CCWF) and Valley State Prison for Women (VSPW)—alongside conversations with allies—in an ongoing conversation about moving from reformist/expansionist responses to current conditions of confinement toward responses that speak both to conditions and open strategic opportunity to squeeze out imprisonment. Over the course of the campaign, Justice Now engaged and deepened relationships with a dozen or so activist leaders inside, strategizing with and supporting those leaders in activating over 3,300 people at CCWF, VSPW, and some other lockups in a collective demand that California not expand prisons in their name. We worked with these activists to publish letters in California dailies and submit a petition serving as a collective letter of opposition for bill analyses. And we deepened relationships with existing allies and cultivated new alliances to grow opposition statewide.[7]

Through the campaign, California's anti-prison and prisoner-rights movements grew our muscle for future policy fights, having exposed more activists to engagement in Sacramento for our overlapping goals. Through this, we demanded and won some institutional accountability where the key players expected to give none and establish our ability for oversight of the policy process. We shifted the terms of the game, escalating against our campaign target over time while continuing to negotiate and build relationships with strategic and tactical allies in and outside of the capitol building. We saw the state take on a defensive move in beginning to influence gender-oppressed prisoners via invite-only "gender responsive" training classes targeting some of the activists leaders we worked with. Over time, we saw state actors and secondary targets beginning to reflect our messaging against prison expansion, including bringing on two key policymakers as spokespeople. And in responding to a conversation framed around "gender" as code for cisgender women through alliance across

287

experiences of gender oppression, we deepened our movement body's grounding and practice toward possibility for gender liberation.

Between the lines of these victories, my bodymemory still holds the cost of passing to play. During the campaign, my face had become enough part of the capitol landscape that upon returning to Sacramento a year later, post-campaign, to emcee a press conference, a familiar photojournalist greeted me, asking where I'd been. The answer I didn't give was that I'd retreated home to recover. During this fight, my policy body tried on its growing understanding of capitol culture and its code of ethics, my heartbody prayed for its quiet of chorus to stay accountable to movement body, movement heart across prison walls. I hold the tire from bridging Sacramento's demand to make nice, make compromise, and make friends with each and all with our movement body's demand for accountability from institutional decision-makers, accountability to our communities; from learning to scurry the pecking order across three- and four-digit room assignments and internal to each office, to counting votes for hearing while cultivating tactical relationships and occasional longer-term relationships.

Simultaneous with retreat from Sacramento, Justice Now continued to engage organizationally as the legislative fight shifted into a local site fight. While our campaign successfully removed bill language authorizing "Female Rehabilitative Community Correctional Center" (FRCCC) construction, the state continued to push its agenda, seeking requests for proposals from corporations and nonprofits to build and run the FRCCCs, including them in the 2007 budget bill. I spent some time between Oakland and Fresno, backing local anti-prison organizers there waging battle against the state and local officials colluding to build an FRCCC. In many ways, this moment of campaign shift brought me present in new ways with questions about our movement body—the thousands of prisoners mobilizing against the proposal an exception; most of us who were able to show up and engage in campaign activity in Sacramento were paid staff of anti-prison and prisoner-rights organizations, and my body was the most consistent, employed by an anti-prison organization providing immense leadership because of both commitment to this fight and the resources to do so.

you eye rest my heart
shoulder in fire blink
heat of silent smolder
where body brave sleep

Today my bodymemory still holds the breaks. It holds the break in being labeled "bold broad" by a white cisgender lesbian-identified state commissioner after testifying against a prison system leader for her lack of leadership amid a "gender responsiveness" meeting where a subcommittee proposed to offer "elective" sterilization to people in prison during labor and delivery as "medically necessary"; the break in not knowing what to make of this commissioner likening my testimony to her witnessing of ACT UP days. My bodymemory holds the break still from dodging what one campaign intern observed as "looks of death" from the office housing our campaign target. It holds the break in a Republican consultant, saying that I "must have come from a nice family" (not black, brown, drug-addicted, violent).

And deep, deep inside it still holds tender so many collectively ungrieved sorrows of mass imprisonment, in layer upon layer of secondary trauma in the stories we'd been asked to receive in refusing to lose touch with growing numbers of loved ones stolen by the state.

These punctuations in memory, the still chronic tire from shape changing, are part of the discomfort in returning here to reflection. I'm left with the gift of question, where I will leave you: How has our increased engagement in state-centered organizing influenced our individual and collective visions and shaping? How do we change shape to blend with external conditions while remaining centered with our principles and building and strengthening connection between each part we bring in? How have our campaigns and actions weakened the prison industrial complex, and how might they have strengthened it?

When attacked by the state with the threat of its building more prisons, how might we stretch our hearts and build new muscle to move from automatic reaction toward grounded and timely response aligned with our truest vision and principles? How do we escalate on a timeline and tenor responsive to what external conditions demand and to internal capacity and scale? Can we wage campaigns targeting the state that strengthen and grow the resilience muscle of our movement body, account for differing locations and entries, care for each and all parts and range of ability, and stay open to transformation toward the movement body that we want to inhabit? How do we account for individual and collective tire and break in changing shape, in continuing amid attack? The anti-prison and prisoner-rights movements face particular challenges in facilitating mass-based organizing, given that our constituency is under direct attack by the state—how do we account for and meet these challenges?

How do we build the muscle, patience, and resources we need to hold meaningful, sustained, and accountable collaboration across the many surfaces that we negotiate within and across the prison and non-profit industrial complexes? How might we better open possibility and overcome the limitations in leveraging 501(c)3 nonprofit structures and current conditions of our organizing to build and strengthen our movement body while demanding accountability from external threats? How do we maintain presence, connection, and accountability with each and all we bring closer in? How do we return the body to our movements after and within crisis?

This essay has taken a few years time—including opening in the heartbreak following a partner's arrest and defense campaign—to be present in disorganization, reshaping, and articulate these questions; rewrite between the lines of what I've written and sounded ten times over through hearings, policy briefs, press releases, op-eds—to rewrite from body, outside my more practiced organizational and journalistic voices, into reflection of this time that I contributed leadership, participation, and witness from inside one organization's leadership in movement fightback to the state changing shape. This here what's distilled after slow boil of freewriting and rewriting around unanswered questions, notes to self, the space of questions we don't yet know to shape or sound. Some edges I've grown to know, some I trust to unfold with time. I'm leaving sentences unfinished, this here offering to move us closer to learning, closer to implication for our work moving forward.

NOTES

1. Thank you to Morgan, Alex, Em, Lily, Cara, Reina, and Miss Major for comradeship, love, and learnings along this journey; Hakim, Cookie, and each comrade still inside for continuing; Direct Action for Rights and Equality, Justice Now, Critical Resistance, Californians United for a Responsible Budget, Transforming Justice, Transgender, Gender Variant, and Intersex Justice Project, and all who refuse the disappearance of each stolen, each lost; the Mesa Refuge for first sleep and where the beginnings of this were written; Elmaz and Suheir for movement in finishing this writing; Eric and Nat for your patience and encouragement; generationFIVE for renewal, reshaping, and patience in learning the body of our movements; and Sins Invalid for continuing to feed a vision of movements that care for and can be led by each and all.

2. Ruth Wilson Gilmore defines racism as "the state-sanctioned or extralegal production and exploitation of group-differentiated vulnerability to premature death."

3. Also see http://www.californiaprogressreport.com/site/node/2612

4. For more see the Californians United for a Responsible Budget (CURB) report http://curbprisonspending.org/wpcontent/uploads/2010/05/curb_report_v5_all_hi_res.pdf

5. See the Governor's July 2006 "Inmate Population, Rehabilitation and Housing Management Plan" CALIFORNIA DEPARTMENT OF CORRECTIONS AND REHABILITATION, INMATE POPULATION, REHABILITATION, AND HOUSING MANAGEMENT PLAN 5 (2006) (Released in conjunction with the Governor's August 2006 Special Session, this plan proposes the explicit expansion of the women's prison system, filling the 4,500 beds vacated by those transferred to Female Rehabilitative Community Correctional Centers until fiscal year 2020/2021, at which point "CDCR will convert added capacity to men's beds").

6. Section heading "First Writing Since" after poem by same name by Suheir Hammad, written after 9/11.

7. Primarily we helped build power among organizations working with people in women's prisons (California Coalition for Women's Prisoners, Free Battered Women, Legal Services for Prisoners with Children), trans and gender-variant prisoners (Transgender, Gender Variant, and Intersex Justice Project), people returning home from prison (A New Way of Life Reentry Project, All of Us or None), and anti-prison coalitions and organizations (Californians United for a Responsible Budget, Critical Resistance, Prison Moratorium Project)—as well as nationally by strengthening our movement-building with reproductive justice, trans/gender liberation, and anti-violence organizations.

MAROON ABOLITIONISTS:

Black Gender-Oppressed Activists in the Anti-Prison Movement in the US and Canada

Julia Sudbury AKA Julia C. Oparah

Since the 1970s, the exponential growth in incarceration in the US, combined with racial targeting in the use of state surveillance and punishment, has marked the prison as a primary site of contemporary struggles for racial and economic justice. At the same time, US-style penal politics have migrated across the border, generating resistance by disenfranchised communities in Canada (Roberts et al. 2002; Prisoners Justice Action Committee 2007). There are very significant differences in the scale and practice of imprisonment in the US and Canada. The US currently incarcerates approximately 2.3 million people, or 762 per 100,000, compared to approximately 35,000, or 108 per 100,000 in Canada (International Centre for Prison Studies 2008). Moreover, whereas "tough-on-crime" reforms over the past decades have led to the widespread construction of "warehouse" prisons (Irvin and Austin 1997), a range of alternatives—from "community corrections" to restorative justice—have limited prison expansion in Canada (Pate 1999). However, there are also important and growing synergies between sentencing and penal policy in both nations. At a provincial level, conservative politicians have vigorously pursued a neoliberal, tough-on-crime approach, leading to the emergence of "no frills" provincial superjails, some built or managed by US corporations. At a federal level, critics have predicted a US-style prison building boom as the Harper government has begun to fulfill its promise to "turn around" thirty to forty years of "soft" criminal justice policy (Roslin 2007; Whittington 2008). In both countries, anti-prison activists have developed an analysis and critique of the prison industrial complex, its role in producing and maintaining racial inequalities and the need for abolition rather than reform, indicating the existence of an anti-prison movement that crosses national borders (Sudbury 2004a).

The contemporary anti-prison movement is made up of a wide range of organizations with diverse goals. These include ending the war on drugs; advocating for prisoners' health needs; spiritual freedom; family integrity and basic human rights; challenging sexual violence in prisons; working for women, queer, and trans prisoners; releasing "war on terror" detainees; ending the criminalization and detention of immigrants; protesting police brutality and racial profiling; working for the freedom of political prisoners and exiles; opposing construction of new prisons; divesting from prison construction and prison privatization; ending the death penalty; and building community-based alternatives to incarceration. This article examines the experiences of black gender-oppressed activists[1] in the anti-prison movement in the US and Canada.[2]

During the past decade, I have developed a body of scholarship that seeks to elucidate the articulation of race, gender, and punishment through the lens of women of color's imprisonment and resistance.[3] In this new work, I have expanded that focus to include transgender and gender-non-conforming people.[4] In so doing, I aim to mirror the reality of gender complexity and multiplicity both within the prison and in anti-prison organizing, and to reject the unquestioned compliance with the binary gender system in most feminist research on prisons, including my own. At the same time, I have chosen to focus on *black* activists rather than on activists of color in order to foreground the ways in which often overlooked African diasporic cultural and political legacies inform and undergird anti-prison work. The article explores the activists' motivations for involvement and barriers to participation, and explores spirituality as a source of resilience and guidance. It examines the participants' political analysis and abolitionist visions, and explores the possibility of "non-reformist reforms" that take up the challenge of a radical anti-racist gender justice perspective. The article posits the existence of a unique abolitionist vision and praxis, centered on the participants' direct experience of gender oppression and racialized surveillance and punishment and rooted in African diasporic traditions of resistance and spirituality.[5]

My research methodology draws from the insights of feminist action research and participatory action research. The research is grounded in ten years of activist ethnography in the anti-prison movement in the US and Canada.[6] In addition, I interviewed eight black[7] women and transgender activists between the ages of twenty and thirty-two from the US and Canada during 2007. The participants had been involved in anti-prison activism in Ottawa, Vancouver, Toronto and environs, New York, the San Francisco Bay Area, Chicago, and Lagos, Nigeria.[8] Most had been involved in more than one anti-prison organization, and several had held both volunteer and paid positions, although the paid positions were seldom full-time or well-remunerated and tended to grow out of prior volunteer work. Participants represented considerable diversity in terms of gender and sexual orientation: four described their gender as woman or female, and four chose the following gender-non-conforming labels: transsexual/trans-guy, trans/gender-variant/faggot, gender-queer, and two-spirited.[9] Three identified their sexual orientation as hetero(sexual), with the remainder identifying as queer, gay, faggot, free-loving, bisexual, or fluid. Participants also had diverse experiences of class, social mobility, and the criminal justice system; two had personal experience of imprisonment, and all had family members or loved ones who had been in conflict with the law.

"Love and Anger": Reasons for Resistance

The 1960s and 70s were marked by the rise of what have been labeled "new social movements" based on racial, gender, and sexual identities. Starting from these social locations, activists generated radical critiques of interlocking systems of capitalism, white supremacy, patriarchy, and compulsory heterosexuality (Melucci 1989; Combahee River Collective 1995). Despite recognizing the power of identity politics, commentators have also been critical of its tendency to promote a hierarchy of oppression and to separate oppressed groups along lines of race and gender, thus limiting possibilities for coalitional work, particularly around a common resistance to capitalist exploitation. The emergence of the global justice, anti-war, and anti-prison movements in the 1990s and 2000s marks a resurgence of movement-building based on a shared political analysis rather than on a shared social location.[10] As an ideology-based rather than an identity-based movement, the anti-prison movement engages a wide range of activists, including those with relative privilege in relation to interlocking systems of oppression. By making visible the multifaceted ways in which the prison industrial complex affects all of us, anti-prison organizations have successfully generated a wide base of support among those indirectly affected by mass incarceration, such as teachers and students, affected by swollen corrections budgets and education funding cuts. This approach has been critically important in building a mass movement to resist the prison industrial complex. At the same time, this research points to the importance of bringing social location back into ideology-based movements, in this instance by foregrounding the analysis and praxis of activists who have been *directly affected* by the prison industrial complex.[11]

All participants in this study testified that they had been directly affected by the prison industrial complex. This occurred in three ways. First, participants spoke about their experiences of policing and surveillance. For several of the participants, these experiences constituted powerful childhood memories that continued to be a source of trauma and a motivator for resistance. Jamila shared a painful memory of her father being pulled over by police in a Toronto suburb:

> I thought my Dad was going to be taken to jail; I didn't know what was going on. I remember thinking I was never going to see him again and I also remember the look on his face. He was sitting in the back of the squad car and I was on the lawn and I just remember him looking at me and there was a look of shame and embarrassment...that I will never forget. And anger too. He wasn't given a ticket and he didn't go to jail, it was just a clear-cut case of racial profiling.

As a child, Jamila had no tools with which to understand her father's humiliation at the hands of the state. As she became more politicized, she was able to put the incident into a wider perspective and to understand it as part of a collective experience of racist policing. In so doing, she channeled the pain and anger as a source for resistance. Experiences of police harassment led participants to reject common beliefs taught to children growing up with race and class privilege. Rather than believing that the police were there to protect them, and that people are arrested because they have done something wrong, the participants learned to fear the police as agents of social control and state violence.

The second way in which participants had been directly affected by the prison industrial complex is through having one or more family members imprisoned or working within the prison system. Six of the participants had had a family member in prison or on probation at some point in their life. Growing up poor and black in upstate New York, the prison was a central part of Jac's family landscape:

> My Dad had been a prison guard at Attica for about eleven years. He was hired just after the uprising because one of the things they decided to do was hire more black guards, as if that would actually make any difference.[12] And I also have another uncle who was also a guard in New York State and I had another uncle, their brother, who was imprisoned in New York. So the prison industrial complex was a huge part of our family understanding.

For Maya, the incarceration of family members was an everyday occurrence creating immense challenges for those left caring for dependents on the outside:

> Of course everyone I know has some sort of family or friend who is currently or has been incarcerated. Including myself, so I've had cousins in and out. Mainly all women and separated from their children. And seeing the impact that's had on our family has been horrific. So since very young, I've always known that there was something very wrong with this so-called correctional [system].

Maya's experience of the criminal punishment system was double-edged. At the same time that the criminal punishment system created havoc in their lives, her family also grasped at it as the only "solution" available for problems including addiction and gender violence. The solution offered, however, was, as she recognized, temporary and illusory, leaving the family further entrenched in a cycle of state and interpersonal violence:

> The same cousin, her partner was extraordinarily abusive to her and to my great aunt, and we stepped in to separate them. But the only way to provide safety for the children and my great aunt, and my cousin to a

certain extent, is to separate them, and unfortunately we ended up involving the state and he was arrested. So what are alternatives to that? So again he ends up coming out, they get back together, same thing happens all over again. Again the problem's not solved, so what do we do?

Like Jac's family, Maya's family was forced to rely for safety on the very system that was disappearing family members. Reflecting on the impact of his sister's imprisonment on his childhood experiences, Nathaniel pointed to the sometimes irreparable damage to relationships caused by these disappearances:

> You just miss this whole part of somebody's life. That to me seems like the biggest thing, it's just missing time. To me that is one of the things that I think was so disastrous within my own family. Whether you go to Memphis and somebody's just not there.... Or like with my sister, there was a significant portion of her life and of my life that we just didn't get to know each other.

When he was first exposed to anti-prison activism, Nathaniel began to view his family history through the lens of what he was learning and went back to talk to family members about their experiences of criminalization and imprisonment. This personal connection further fueled his commitment to the work.

The third way that participants had been affected was through personal experiences of arrest, prosecution, and incarceration. Two of the participants had been incarcerated. Although Bakari's father had been in prison, it was the experience of being imprisoned in the California state system for two years that s/he found radicalizing.[13] When s/he was left in a cell moaning in pain all night after guards refused requests for medical attention, Bakari was shocked and surprised. Gradually, s/he awakened to the fact that as a prisoner s/he had lost any rights as a US citizen. It was this realization that fueled a commitment to bring about change:

> It was that instinctual feeling that you guys are crazy, something's wrong for you to be treating people like this. I would say things to the police inside like: do you understand that this is a violation of my civil rights, do you understand that I'm an American citizen? Because I didn't know that when I was incarcerated, I had no civil rights, I was not viewed as a citizen.

Multiple experiences of criminalization were a powerful motivator for the participants. But gaining access to a collective movement analysis was equally important. Trey was raised by his grandmother while his mother was in and out of jail for drug use, and was sent to Spofford Juvenile Facility in upstate New York at age thirteen for fighting in school. From there, he served time for a series of property and drug-related offenses before finding the Audre Lorde project, where he served as an intern. The political education he received there led to a lifelong commitment to penal abolition fueled by his personal experiences. When asked what motivated him, Trey responded:

> My love and my anger. That I love my people and my heritage and what I know we can become too much to let it go down. And I'm angered by the oppression and the f*****g atrocities that I see every day that are committed against my people and myself. It makes me too mad to just sit down and let it happen. And it makes me too mad to just close my eyes and pretend it's not there.

The testimonies of black gender-oppressed activists reveal that even as we come together to work for social change based on our shared political analysis, rather than shared identities, we can reintroduce some of the strengths of identity politics. This is not to fetishize racialized and gendered bodies, but to tap the mobilizing force of personal experience and to rebuild some of the community power stripped by daily encounters with state violence and repression.

Maroon Abolitionism: Visions of Freedom

[W]hat makes me the most angry is that everybody's sitting there kicking it. Not knowing that they're building plantations.
—Bakari

The second distinct characteristic of anti-prison activism by black gender-oppressed activists is the development of an abolitionist vision shaped by direct confrontations with the prison industrial complex and imbued with the historical memory of slavery and rebellion. In the 1970s, political prisoners like Angela Y. Davis and Assata Shakur in conjunction with other radical activists and scholars in the US, Canada, and Europe began to shape a new anti-prison politics that combined campaigns for freedom for political prisoners with a call for the dismantling of prisons (Knopp et al. 1976). The explosion in political prisoners, fueled by the Federal Bureau of Investigation (FBI)'s Counter Intelligence Program (COINTELPRO) and targeting of black liberation, American Indian, and Puerto Rican independence movements in the US and First Nations resistance in Canada as "threats" to national security, fed into an understanding of the role of the prison in perpetuating state repression against insurgent communities (Churchill and Wall 1996; López 1996; James 2003). The new anti-prison politics were also shaped by a decade of prisoner litigation and radical prison uprisings, including the Attica Rebellion in 1971, which was brutally crushed by New York Governor Nelson Rockefeller. The "Attica Brothers"—working-class people of color imprisoned for everyday acts of survival—challenged the state's legitimacy by declaring imprisonment a form of cruel and unusual punishment and confronting the brute force of state power (Parenti 1999; Gilmore 2000).

By adopting the term "abolition," activists in the US and Canada drew deliberate links between the dismantling of prisons and the abolition of slavery. Through historical excavations, the "new abolitionists" identified the abolition of prisons as the logical completion of the unfinished liberation marked by the Thirteenth Amendment to the United States Constitution, which regulated rather than ended slavery (James 2005). Learning the truth about this "enslaving anti-enslavement document" (Gilmore 2000, xxi) was a galvanizing experience for several of the participants in this study. Maya viewed her work for freedom from persecution for political exile Assata Shakur as part of a broader struggle against penal slavery:

> The first time I found out about the Thirteenth Amendment was in Assata's book, and a lot of people didn't know that the Thirteenth Amendment had a "but" clause. So that means that people are still legally enslaved in this country. That's what inspired me also.... If you are against enslavement, how are you for prison? When legally they say that you can be enslaved.

Some scholars have critiqued the slavery–prison analogy, arguing that since work is a "privilege" coveted by and denied many prisoners, the prison should be considered a warehouse rather than a new form of slavery, subjecting its captives to incapacitation rather than forced labor (Gilmore 2007, 21). However, in focusing narrowly on slavery as a mode of labor, this critique minimizes the continuities between ideologies and practices of slavery and mass incarceration that make slavery a useful interpretive frame (Sudbury 2004b; Rodríguez 2006, 225–29). As Joy James argues:

> Prison is the modern-day manifestation of the plantation. The antebellum plantation ethos of dehumanization was marked by master–slave relations revolving about sexual terror and domination, beatings, regimentation of bodies, exploited labor, denial of religious and cultural practices, substandard food, health care and housing, forced migration, isolation in "lockdown" for punishment and control, denial of birth family and kin. That ethos is routinely practiced and reinscribed in contemporary penal sites. (James 2005, xxiii)

Participants in this study frequently referenced the institution of slavery as a framework for understanding contemporary experiences of surveillance, policing, and criminalization. Trey explained the continuing enslavement of poor black communities through the story of her birth:

> One day when my mother was in the house by herself, the police knocked on the door, and my mother…let them in and the police officer who's my father raped my mother. That's how I got here…. When we talk about slavery I don't have to go back three hundred odd years, I can go back to 1980 and have a real case of slave rape, the overseer/master raping the slave who in this case would be my mother who is a slave to the narcotics that were pushed into our community.

Trey brings our attention to the extension of state surveillance and punishment throughout poor communities of color that occurred from the late 1970s under the guise of the war on drugs.[14] Reinforced by state power, the police officer/overseer turned Trey's mother's house into a site of captivity and sexual-racial terror, marking a set of continuities among the prison, the urban 'hood, and the slave plantation.

By linking slavery and prisons, the concept of abolition also highlights the interaction of racial and economic dynamics in processes of mass incarceration. Participants were acutely aware of the role of prisons in sustaining the current mode of capitalist exploitation. Samia continued the slavery–prison analogy at a global level, pointing to the attenuated privilege awarded US blacks in comparison to black people elsewhere:

301

Globalization has created an international plantation.... I've begun to see symbolically that black people in the US represent house-slaves and that black people in the diaspora represent field-slaves. And that globalization has made that plantation of racist relationships a global one. And prisons are for the people that don't fit in the field or the house.

Samia's social location as a black woman from Canada with roots in North Africa acts as a site of epistemic privilege producing an insightful and nuanced analysis of US empire. As an African-Canadian who has moved to the US, Samia is an "outsider-within" in relation to both US global power and African American discourses of oppression and resistance (Collins 2000, 11–13). This critical lens enables her to identify the simultaneity of racial subordination and imperial privilege, suggesting that transnational solidarities must be formed not around an assumed sameness of racial oppression, but around a complex understanding of differential racisms in the context of global inequalities. These unequal positionalities rest upon both violent colonial histories and contemporary geopolitical and economic formations. This means that while black people in the US, Canada, Africa, and the Caribbean are all affected by the neoliberal economic reforms and cutbacks in spending on social welfare and education that have accompanied the globalization of capital, the impact is refracted through the particularities of local socioeconomic conditions (Steady 2002). These systemic cutbacks, coupled with inflated spending on forms of global and domestic social control, indicate the continued devaluing and dehumanization of black people and other people of color.[15] Maya pointed to this contradiction:

We have horrifically dilapidated schools with inadequate resources, no computers, no materials, teachers underpaid, we don't have health clinics. There are so many resources we need in our poor communities, communities of color. How do we have billions of dollars for this war? How do we have a million dollars to try to re-enslave a woman who fought for her political beliefs?[16]

Just as the dehumanization of captives was central to maintaining the economic system of plantation slavery, the dehumanization of people of color through racialized and criminalizing ideologies legitimates the devastation wrought by capitalist globalization. Abolition is therefore not only about ending the violence of imprisonment, but also about claiming public resources and declaring the value of human life over corporate profit.

I have chosen to name the political vision of black gender-oppressed anti-prison activists "maroon abolitionism" for two reasons. First, "maroon" serves to identify the tactics of those directly affected by slavery/incarceration. The word "maroon" refers to the communities of runaway slaves, indigenous peoples, and their descendants that formed throughout the Americas beginning in the seventeenth century (Price 1996).[17] While maroon communities existed outside of the violent social control of the slave state, they were both under threat by and at war with re-enslaving forces.[18] As maroon abolitionists, black gender-oppressed activists know that the consequences of failing to achieve abolition are that they themselves, their family members, and their loved ones will continue to be disappeared. Bakari articulated the maroon experience of constant threat from the penal/slave system: "We like the free Negroes in Alabama down South. Some of us scared because hell they going to come and get us too."

Whereas white abolitionists were guided by moral convictions, for ex-slaves and their loved ones abolition was the only avenue for liberation from the threat of captivity, torture, and social death. Hence, slaves and those who had escaped slavery rejected white abolitionists' calls for gradual emancipation through indentureship that would keep formerly enslaved African Americans tied to the land; they demanded nothing less than the immediate end of slavery. Popular histories tend to focus on formerly enslaved African Americans who sought to win white support through speeches and slave narratives, while less attention is paid to the slave rebellions, mass escapes, and maroon insurgencies that fundamentally challenged the viability and hastened the demise/restriction of chattel slavery. Twenty-first-century maroon abolitionism is also rooted in the survival imperative, guided by a sense of urgency and informed by an understanding of the prison industrial complex as a war on black communities. Samia articulated her vision of abolitionist work as a form of self-defense:

> In terms of prisons and the penal system, I think that it's at the center of a lot of our oppression. So my options are to live oppressed or to fight this. So I prefer to fight it. I think that as people of color we have no option but to fight it. It's a matter of survival. I also think that we are at war, that we are under attack, through different institutions and

cultures and social practices. And when you are at war you have no option but to fight back.

By conceptualizing state policies toward disenfranchised communities as a war, Samia implicitly refutes a prison-reform agenda, and pushes us to adopt an uncompromising position against the prison industrial complex. As Dylan Rodríguez points out, the state has long declared a series of domestic "wars"—against crime, drugs, gangs, and now terror—involving official declarations, mobilizations, and body counts, which have been waged in the streets and homes of low-income communities of color and immigrant communities (Rodríguez 2008). In claiming the language of war and mobilizing it against the state, Samia brings a radical positionality and sense of urgency common to the political visions articulated by the participants in the study.

Second, while it honors the participants' understanding of contemporary incarceration as a continuation of slavery, the concept "maroon abolitionist" avoids implying that the society outside the prison is "free." Joy James argues that we must reject the illusion that a return to civil society via parole or clemency constitutes an escape to the liberated "North" (James 2005, xxx). Instead, state penal practices exist on a continuum from the prison, the juvenile hall, and the detention center to the urban 'hood, the reservation, the school, and the welfare office where surveillance, policing, and punishment extend far beyond the prison walls. Trey's story told above is one example of the extension of captivity beyond the prison walls. Continuing her analysis, Trey argues that prison abolition involves far more than the abolition of the physical prison building:

> When I say the prisons, I mean the physical prison itself, but also the prisons we create in our communities. Whether those are physical like the projects that the government keeps building up and locking us in, and also the mental ones that we put ourselves in, all the social constructs that society projects on us…. If we have so many drug crimes and we have so many property crimes, then let's start addressing the mental health of our people and the economic development of our communities. Let's get to the root causes of why people commit crimes.

Jamila elaborated on this expansive vision of maroon abolitionist politics by distinguishing between emancipation and abolition. Rather than ending imprisonment in an otherwise unchanged society, emancipation indicates the transformation of society and an end to racism and capitalist inequality.

> We've seen abolition of slavery but the ramification of sanctioned apartheid still remains. Abolition literally means the end of something, whereas emancipation means to free or liberate. So how we understand that is critical to how we do anti-prison work. So a world without prisons would mean a world with healing, it would mean a world that had alternatives, it would mean forgiveness, it would mean justice, it would mean the eradication of poverty....

One limitation of the slavery–prison analogy is that it tends to erase the presence of non-black prisoners. This is problematic both in Canada, where First Nations prisoners suffer the most dramatic rates of incarceration, and in the US, where Latinas/os are a rapidly growing incarcerated population (Díaz-Cotto 2006).[19] While slavery was premised on the black/white binary, maroon communities rejected this racist logic. Maroon settlements incorporated resisting Indians and exiled whites as well as runaway slaves, and offered a radical multiracial alternative to North American apartheid.[20] As such, marronage offers a model for "black-brown" coalitions and reminds black activists of the value of learning from indigenous knowledges. Women from the Native Sisterhood at Grand Valley Institution for Women, for example, taught Jamila about "a form of accountability, an alternative form of justice that is grounded in the teachings from different Native nations." Although some of the participants reported not having worked with indigenous people or Latinos/as, activists like Jamila demonstrate the importance of non-black "outlyer" knowledges for contemporary abolitionist work.

Maroon abolitionism is dedicated to the creation of a world in which prison is obsolete.[21] However, the participants did not limit their activism to this long-term goal. Instead, they were involved in challenging human rights abuses and advocating for the immediate needs of prisoners. For Bakari, this meant working to challenge overcrowding and medical neglect in California women's prisons:

> Of course we have to deal with what's going on right now. So right now I want for people to live in humane conditions until we can figure out a way to get rid of prison as a form of social control. So right now what I want is all the beds off the day room. To have people

treated in a humane way. But my goal is not to have prisons. My goal is not to have capitalism.

These "non-reformist reforms" create solidarity with prisoners while paying attention to the penal system's tendency to co-opt reforms to consolidate and expand prisons. By carrying out their reformist work as part of a broader strategy of decarceration, abolition, and fundamental social transformation, maroon abolitionists address the immediate needs of captives while ultimately challenging the legitimacy of their captivity. Black gender-oppressed activists' advocacy for transgender and gender-non-conforming prisoners is one example of non-reformist reform: demands for change that challenge the logic of incarceration while simultaneously addressing prisoners' immediate needs.

Trans/forming Anti-prison Work: Beyond the Gender Binary

During the past decade, transgender and gender-non-conforming activists, both imprisoned and non-imprisoned, have worked to end the human rights abuses faced by transgender prisoners while also tackling the incarceration.[22] The participants in this study moved beyond the human rights implications of this work to generate a radical critique of the state's power to delimit and police gender. In so doing, they produced an anti-racist, gender-queer, anti-prison praxis that constitutes a challenge to the violent gender regime of the penal system and suggests new dimensions of abolitionist thought.

Penal systems are based on the premise of a rigid and fixed gender binary that, as Bakari points out, ignores the actuality of gender fluidity and multiplicity in society as a whole and within the prison in particular:

> You have male and female prisons. I ain't male or female, so which one do I get to go to? And you're housed according to your genitalia, which to me does not connote gender.

By reducing gender to biological sex represented by prisoners' genitalia, prison administrators routinely violate the right to self-determination of prisoners who do not match the narrow range of sex/gender identification allowed within the prison. This is particularly devastating for transsexual prisoners. Since many transsexuals do not choose or cannot afford gender reassignment surgery, prisoners who may have had hormone treatment and "top surgery" (to remove breasts) will be assigned to an institution according to a gender assignation based on one part of their body, which does not match the rest of their physical and emotional experience. The psychological and physical impact can be devastating, as Nathaniel shared based on his experiences of advocacy work in Ontario prisons:

> [F]or trans people depression and suicide, you can have really high risk factors for that when you're consistently being denied for who you are. When people take away your opportunity to have self-determination which happens in many ways in prison, but can be so detrimental when you're a trans woman and you're put in a men's prison, and you're denied your hormones and you're denied being called the name that you chose and you're being called he all the time.

The denial of adequate medical treatment to transgender prisoners, including but not limited to a failure to continue hormone treatment, constitutes a form of state violence enacted on prisoners' bodies and psyches (Richard 2000b).[23] In this context, the denial of adequate medical care is one method by which the state punishes gender non-conformity.

The penal system seeks to produce women's prisons inhabited by female women and men's prisons inhabited by male men, out of a population that in actuality embraces an immense range of gender diversity. In addition to transsexual prisoners who may or may not be on hormones and/or in the process of transitioning surgically, this includes butch lesbians, feminine gay men, and transgender, gender-queer, and two-spirited prisoners who identify as neither male nor female nor in transition. Since transgender and gender-non-conforming individuals are more likely to be stopped by police, both because of higher rates of homelessness and involvement in street economies arising from discrimination and familial rejection, and because of police profiling and harassment, the prison is actually a site of heightened gender variation (Amnesty International 2006). The process—and ultimately unattainable objective—of producing binary gender in the prison is one that enacts psychological, emotional, and physical violence on all transgender and gender-non-conforming prisoners. Bakari shared a critique of gender policing in the California Institution for Women:

> How they control you and mandate you to this gender binary is if you're in a women's facility you must wear whatever society says is for

women.... At CIW when I first got there, I had on boxers, they took them, said they were contraband.... Then they make you wear panties and a muumuu, an old lady housedress.... When the new people come in, all the women stand there to see if it's their friends coming in and you gotta walk by in this muumuu.

Although a relatively androgynous uniform of jeans and a t-shirt was standard issue, Bakari's masculinity was ritually stripped in front of the general population on arrival at the institution before s/he was allowed to don clothes more appropriate to the way s/he self-identified. The practice of forcing people in women's prisons to wear clothes constructed as gender-appropriate is common, and many women's prisons have rules mandating a minimum number of items of "female" attire. Policing prisoners' underwear becomes a sign of the state's power to control the most intimate aspects of prisoners' lives. In this sense, gender policing is an everyday and central part of the prison regime's brutal exercise of power over its inhabitants.

Vulnerability to physical and sexual violence is also of critical concern for transgender and gender-non-conforming prisoners. Recent research and activism has made visible the systemic and epidemic nature of sexual violence in men's prisons (Human Rights Watch 2001; Sabo et al. 2001, 109–38).[24] However, research and advocacy in this area tends to focus on gender-conforming men who have been targeted because of their perceived physical weakness or inexperience with prison life, rather than foregrounding the endemic sexual violence against transgender and gender-non-conforming prisoners. The scant research that does examine the experiences of transgender prisoners has focused on the institutional abuse and rape of transsexual MtF (male-to-female) prisoners in men's prisons, largely ignoring women's prisons (Edney 2004). The elimination of violence against gender-non-conforming prisoners in women's prisons relies on the invisibility of gender-non-conforming women and FtMs (female-to-male transgender people), as well as on erroneous gendered assumptions that women's prisons are kinder, softer environments than men's prisons. As Bakari explained, violence targeted at transgressive masculinity in women's prisons is part of a spectrum of violence fostered by the totalizing institution of the prison:

[T]he butch women are the ones who are targeted because they are the ones who are most different. And the men feel intimidated in

308

there. If they try to resist or question, they get the smackdown a lot sooner. Like they get hit, punched, thrown down to the ground.... There was one trans man in CCWF that had facial hair that was put in segregated housing for refusing to shave their facial hair.... Because it's arbitrary power in there. They can virtually do whatever it is they want unabated, unchecked, unquestioned. To your body, to your soul, to your spirit.

It is not only guards who enact this regime of violent punishment of gender non-conformity. Other prisoners are often complicit in the policing and abuse of transgender prisoners. Prisoner violence, including sexual assault, is often represented as the inevitable outcome of containing "violent criminals" in a confined space, with guards preventing the violence as best they can. This narrative leads to the common practice of placing transsexual prisoners in administrative segregation, ostensibly for their own protection, where they are isolated in highly restricted conditions otherwise used as punishment for "unruly" prisoners (Richard 2000a). However, the participants in this study argued that institutional transphobia supported violent and exploitative acts by other prisoners. Jac spoke from experience of activist work in men's prisons in California:

[P]risons create gangs because they create the need to create your own safety. But different groupings will not accept someone on the basis of some part of their identity. So for black trans women one of the black groupings will say "We don't want you." Or "We'll only have you if you sleep with all of us and give us all favors." So it means having to find a husband immediately and he's not a good one you can be out of luck. And being out of luck means being raped on a regular basis. Being harassed by guards on a regular basis...It's OK to be racist to trans women because they're "traitors to the race."

Jac points to the way in which racism and transphobia intersect within the prison to create an atmosphere of extreme vulnerability to violence for transgender prisoners of color. This interaction between racism and transphobia in the prison is the basis for an antiracist, gender-queer, anti-prison agenda promoted by black transgender and gender-non-conforming activists.

In contrast to calls to develop a "normative transgender prison order," or trans-sensitive prisons (Edney 2004, 336–37), the participants point to the systemic nature of gender violence as part of the structures of imprisonment, and reject the possibility of gender liberation under conditions of captivity. In so doing, they seek to transform anti-prison politics by calling for the abolition of gender policing as part of a broader abolitionist agenda. The following section explores the emotional costs of this radical positionality and examines the inner resources that many of the participants drew on to provide strength and resiliency in continuing the work.

Invoking the Ancestors: Spiritual Undercurrents in Anti-prison Work

Black women and transgender activists deal with personal traumas and family stresses arising from policing, criminalization, and incarceration while simultaneously confronting racist/sexist violence and gender policing. These multiple challenges constitute struggles that take place at a psychic and emotional as well as material level. In coping with the emotional toll of anti-prison work, many of the participants found strength, guidance, and solace through spiritual beliefs and practices. Following Jacqui Alexander's encouragement to "take the Sacred seriously," this research seeks to make visible the knowledge of "Sacred accompaniment" that informed the radical praxis documented here (Alexander 2005, 326–27). Anti-prison spaces are highly secularized, in part in reaction to race and class bias in early abolitionist and reform efforts based on religion. It is not surprising that none of the organizations that the participants worked with drew on religious principles. In contrast, prisons in the US and Canada are sites of both evangelist interventions and struggles over religious freedom by Muslims and indigenous people in particular, indicating the continuation of a centuries-old strategy to mold prisoners by shaping their souls and policing their relationships with the transcendent.[25] The role of religion in penal regimes mirrors its dualistic and contradictory role during slavery. The Bible's exhortation: "Slaves, obey your earthly masters with respect and fear, and with sincerity of heart, just as you would obey Christ" (Ephesians 6: 5–9) as well as the apparent justification of racial hierarchy gleaned through the story of Ham, provided the slave-owning class with a potent tool for mental colonization. At the same time, enslaved African Americans drew on both indigenous African religious practices and Old Testament stories for empowerment and liberation, finding inspiration from Moses defying "Ol' Pharaoh" and leading the slaves to freedom, or from Yoruba orishas clothed as Christian saints. Prison ministries also bring congregants an interpretation of religious teaching that erases any liberatory potential in favor of a focus on individual internal

310

transformation and accommodation to authority.[26] At the same time, the continued struggle for religious freedom within prisons indicates that many prisoners view religious practice as a powerful source of inspiration and inner strength. As Hamdiya Cooks, former Director of the California Coalition for Women Prisoners, and a formerly incarcerated activist comments: "Inside you have to have something to sustain you and fight being treated like 'things.'... My faith gave me the ability to fight, gave me the belief that I am a human being and have the right to be treated like one" (Cooks 2008). Taking a lead from imprisoned activists, this study seeks to illuminate the importance of spirituality in radical anti-prison praxis.

Six of the participants stated that spiritual beliefs played an important role in their lives, supporting their sense of self in the face of racist-sexist ideologies, lending them the strength and resiliency to keep doing insurgent work in the face of immense barriers, and guiding their activist work. Developing a personal relationship with a higher power gave Bakari the strength to give up crack cocaine and to find a calling in advocacy work with women in prison. Bakari draws our attention to the psychic brutality of the prison and the emotional strength required to continually to hear women's stories of injustice, violence, and revictimization by the state:

> Spirituality's very important for me. Spirituality stopped me from using drugs.... It helps me get up at 4:45 to drive three hours away to deal with some messed-up COs [Correctional Officers] and hold the pain of other sisters that are still there. It helps me to do that. It helps me spend all my free time doing this work.... It fills me up.

Like Bakari, Trey called on Spirit as a source of strength, but he also saw this relationship as a source of wisdom and guidance: "I do believe in a Higher Power, I'm not going to say I don't pray because I do. I'm not going to say I don't ask my grandmother for guidance because I do." Although Nathaniel was raised in Toronto, he spent summers with his grandparents in Memphis, Tennessee. There he absorbed southern black spiritual beliefs that later came to form a central but invisible foundation for his activist work, informing both his commitment to abolition and his organizing methods:

> My grandparents...were famous for saying that if they wanted to pray or speak to anything spiritual they would go into the middle of the forest because that would be the most holy place that you could go to.

I believe that. In a way that's one of the underlying beliefs as to why I believe that prisons are so wrong is just the idea that you would take someone out a natural setting, remove them from things like airflow and natural light and the energy of other living beings and deprive them of that as part of their punishment is so wrong to me.

Nathaniel's spiritual beliefs also led him to pay attention to the connection among mind, body, and spirit in his organizing, making sure that nourishing food, emotional connection and support, regular breaks, and physical movement are a part of meetings and activist work. This approach mirrors the black traditional church, where worship is embodied in food, emotional expression and comfort, movement, and song.

While spirituality was important for many of the participants, none felt that organized religion met their spiritual needs. Instead, they felt that religious institutions were complicit in punitive systems of social control. Several of the participants rejected the mainstream Christian church because of its historical role in promoting white supremacy and its complicity in slavery and colonial violence. For Bakari, there was a clear continuity between the historical and contemporary role of the church in buttressing the ideological apparatus underpinning institutions of dominance:

> The church is an institution that supported slavery, supported colonization. The history's all there but that's not what we're taught.... Religion tells you right and wrong, good and bad.... We're indoctrinated with that mentality that people are bad and they need to be punished. Christianity is a very punitive religion.

In response to racism in the mainstream church and homophobia and sexism in the black church, most of the participants turned inward to their own personal and individual relationships with Spirit. In contrast, Maya found a spiritual community in the Yoruba religion. Originating in what is now southwest Nigeria, Yoruba religious practices came to the Americas with African captives and blended with Christian practices to create syncretic Africanized religions. Contemporary African American communities have reconnected to Nigerian practitioners to re-engage with traditional Yoruba practices and to form transnational communities of practitioners that are closely linked to religious communities on the continent (Clarke 2004). Through her initiation to Oya, warrior goddess of the wind, Maya felt connected to the former prisoner and political exile Assata Shakur:

312

[T]he movie [*Eyes of the Rainbow*] was very powerful because it was very powerful to see this woman warrior both as Oya in the deity form and as a physical being in the Assata form. Defying horrific odds and fighting for justice and life and liberation.[27]

As the tempestuous goddess of upheaval and change, Oya is often represented with a machete, cutting away the old to clear a way for new growth (Gleason 1992). By invoking Oya, Maya summons ancient wisdom and power in her work with the Hands Off Assata campaign, a campaign that poses a powerful grassroots challenge to the US government's power to punish and to the legitimacy of its imperial reach. Maya's initiation to Oya enables her to channel West African encounters with the Divine Feminine to counter the "horrific odds" faced by grassroots mobilizations against and within US empire. Countering Christian conservatism rooted in Eurocentric, masculinist conceptions of the Sacred, these African diasporic spiritual practices are also evident in Nathaniel's return to black folk traditions and in Trey's reliance on her grandmother's spirit for guidance. They introduce a metaphysical component to maroon abolitionism, connecting contemporary activism to the otherworldly sources of power invoked by their maroon antecedents.[28] Calling on the ancestors and the spirit world to enliven the struggle for social justice, they represent underground spiritual currents in the anti-prison movement.

Conclusion

The activists in this study are located at the intersections of systems of dominance. The politics and subjectivity arising from this location have long been the subject of black feminist interrogation. However, our investigations have assumed that only black female subjects or other women of color experience the epistemic privilege associated with the multiple jeopardy of race, class, gender, and sexuality (Collins 1990; King 1995; Sudbury 1998). In contrast, this research finds that other gender-oppressed activists who stand at the "nexus" of systems of dominance also use an integrated antiracist, antisexist, anticapitalist analysis as a basis for their work.[29]

At the nexus of race, class, gender, and sexuality, black gender-oppressed activists bring to the anti-prison movement a unique vision of social justice based on lived experiences of racialized policing, surveillance, and imprisonment. These activists embody a tradition of marronage, the abolitionist praxis of ex-slaves and their families. In so doing, they reintroduce the Sacred as an element of anti-prison activism, indicating that liberatory African diasporic spiritual practices play a more important role in contemporary struggles for social justice than has previously been understood. This article draws on the work of black transgender and gender-non-conforming activists in order to move anti-prison praxis beyond the gender binary. While feminist anti-prison researchers and activists have worked to make imprisoned women visible, we have tended to assume that women's prisons house only women, and that all women prisoners are in women's prisons. This research demonstrates that we were wrong on both counts; many of those labeled "women offenders" by the state refuse to conform to this label, and some of those identifying as women are housed in men's prisons. This double invisibility—to prison officials and to anti-prison practitioners—creates a location of multiple marginalization and vulnerability to violence, which is compounded by racial segregation and harassment. By engaging in non-reformist reforms, black gender-oppressed activists challenge prison regimes to engage the disruptive presence of prisoners' non-conforming body politics while simultaneously working toward the dismantling of penal structures. In so doing, they place gender justice at the center of black liberation struggles.

WORKS CITED

Alexander, M. Jacqui. 2005. *Pedagogies of Crossing*. Durham, NC: Duke University Press.

Amnesty International USA. 2006. *Stonewalled: Police Abuse against Lesbian, Gay, Bisexual, and Transgender People in the US*. http://www.amnestyusa.org/outfront/stonewalled/report.pdf (accessed January 6, 2009).

Bohrman, Rebecca, and Naomi Murakawa. 2005. "Remaking Big Government: Immigration and Crime Control in the United States." In *Global Lockdown: Race, Gender and the Prison-Industrial Complex*, edited by Julia Sudbury. New York: Routledge.

Cainkar, Louise, and Maira Sunaina. 2005. "Targeting Arab/Muslim/South Asian Americans: Criminalization and Cultural Citizenship." *Amerasia Journal* 31, no. 3: 1–27.

Churchill, Ward, and Jim Vander Wall. 1996. *The COINTELPRO Papers: Documents from the FBI's Secret Wars against Dissent in the United States*. Boston: South End Press.

Clarke, Kamari Maxine. 2004. *Mapping Yoruba Networks: Power and Agency in the Making of Transnational Communities*. Durham, NC: Duke University Press.

Collins, Patricia Hill. 2000. *Black Feminist Thought: Knowledge, Consciousness, and the Politics of Empowerment*. 2nd ed. New York: Routledge.

Combahee River Collective. 1995. "A Black Feminist Statement." In *Words of Fire: An Anthology of African American Feminist Thought*, edited by Beverly Guy-Sheftall. New York: The New Press.

Cooks, Hamdiya. 2008. "Muslim Inside and Out." *The Fire Inside* 38, no. 3: 3–10.

Davis, Angela Y. 2003. *Are Prisons Obsolete?* New York: Seven Stories Press.

Demmons, Shawnna. 2007. "Race, Class and Transgender." *The Fire Inside* 35. http://www.womenprisoners.org/fire/000687.html (accessed February 2, 2009).

Díaz-Cotto, Juanita. 2006. *Chicana Lives and Criminal Justice*. Austin: University of Texas Press.

Edney, Richard. 2004. "To Keep Me Safe From Harm? Transgender Prisoners and the Experience of Imprisonment." *Deakin Law Review* 9, no. 2: 331–33.

Gaes, Gerald, and Andrew Goldberg. 2004. *Prison Rape: A Critical Review of the Literature*. Washington, DC: National Institute of Justice. http://www.nicic.org/pubs/2004/019813.pdf (accessed October 21, 2008).

Gilmore, Kim. 2000. "Slavery and Prisons—Understanding the Connections." *Critical Resistance to the Prison-Industrial Complex. Social Justice* 27, no. 3: 195–205.

Gilmore, Ruth Wilson. 2007. *Golden Gulag: Prisons, Surplus, Crisis, and Opposition in Globalizing California*. Berkeley: University of California Press.

Gleason, Judith. 1992 [1987] *Oya: In Praise of an African Goddess*. New York: Harper Collins.

Gottlieb, Karla. 2000. *The Mother of Us All: A History of Queen Nanny*. Trenton, NJ: Africa World Press.

Grant, John. 1980. *Black Nova Scotians*. Halifax: Nova Scotia Museum.

Hinds, Lennox S. 1987. "Foreword." In *Assata: An Autobiography*, by Assata Shakur. London: Zed Books.

Human Rights Watch. 2001. *No Escape: Male Rape in US Prisons*. http://www.hrw.org/reports/2001/prison/report1.html (accessed October 21, 2008).

International Centre for Prison Studies. 2008. *World Prison Brief*. http://www.kcl.ac.uk/depsta/law/research/icps/worldbrief/ (accessed October 22, 2008).

Irvin, John, and James Austin. 1997. *It's about Time: America's Imprisonment Binge*. Belmont, CA: Wadsworth Publishing.

James, Joy, ed. 2003. *Imprisoned Intellectuals: America's Political Prisoners Write on Life, Liberation, and Rebellion*. Lanham, MD: Rowman & Littlefield Publishers.

———. 2005. *The New Abolitionists: (Neo)Slave Narratives and Contemporary Prison Writings*. Albany: State University of New York Press.

King, Deborah R. 1995 [1988]. "Multiple Jeopardy, Multiple Consciousness: The Context of a Black Feminist Ideology." In *Words of Fire: An Anthology of African American Feminist Thought*, edited by Beverly Guy-Sheftall. New York: The New Press.

Knopp, Fay Honey et al. 1976. *Instead of Prisons: A Handbook for Abolitionists*. New York: Prison Research Education Action Project.

Lause, Mark A. 2002. "Borderland Visions: Maroons and Outlyers in Early American History." *Monthly Review* 54, no. 4: 38–44.

López, Jose. 1996. "Prisons as Concentration Camps: It Can't Happen Here—Or Can It?" In *Criminal Injustice: Confronting the Prison Crisis*, edited by Elihu Rosenblatt. Boston: South End Press.

Melucci, Alberto. 1989. *Nomads of the Present*. London: Hutchinson; Philadelphia: Temple University Press.

———. 1995. "The New Social Movements Revisited: Reflections on a Sociological Misunderstanding." In *Social Movements and Social Classes: The Future of Collective Action*, edited by Louis Maheu. London and Thousand Oaks, CA: Sage Publications.

Neve, Lisa, and Kim Pate. 2005. "Challenging the Criminalization of Women Who Resist." In *Global Lockdown: Race, Gender and the Prison-Industrial Complex*, edited by Julia Sudbury. New York: Routledge.

O'Connor, Thomas P., and Nathaniel J. Pallone. 2003. *Religion, the Community, and the Rehabilitation of Criminal Offenders*. Philadelphia: Haworth Press.

Parenti, Christian. 1999. *Lockdown America: Policing and Prisons in the Age of Crisis*. New York: Verso.

Pate, Kim. 1999. "Transformative Justice versus Re-entrenched Correctionalism: The Canadian Experience." In *Harsh Punishment: International Experiences of Women's Imprisonment*, edited by Sandy Cook and Susanne Davies. Boston: Northeastern University Press.

Price, Richard. 1996. *Maroon Societies: Rebel Slave Communities in the Americas*. Baltimore: John's Hopkins University Press.

Prisoners Justice Action Committee. 2007. "Tories Ram through U.S.-Style 'Justice' Laws." http://www.pjac.org (accessed August 5, 2007).

Reed, Little Rock. 2003. "American Indian Religious Freedom within the Criminal Justice Context: History, Current Status and Prospects for the Future." In *Native American Justice*, edited by Laurence Armand French. Lanham, MD: Rowman and Littlefield.

Richard, Diane. 2000a. "Trans behind Bars: Officials, Activists Struggle with Options." Contemporary Sexuality 34, no. 9: 1–5.

———. 2000b. "Trans behind Bars: Experts Sense Change, Portland Makes it Official." *Contemporary Sexuality* 34, no. 10: 4–5.

Roberts, Julian V. et al., eds. 2002. Penal Populism and Public Opinion: Lessons from Five Countries. New York: Oxford University Press.

Rodríguez, Dylan. 2006. *Forced Passages: Imprisoned Intellectuals and the U.S. Prison Regime*. Minneapolis: University of Minnesota Press.

———. 2008. "Warfare and the Terms of Engagement." In *Abolition Now! Ten Years of Struggle and Strategy against the Prison Industrial Complex*, edited by the CR10 Publications Collective. Oakland, CA: AK Press.

Roslin, Alex. 2007. "Stephen Harper Opens Door to Prison Privatization." *Georgia Straight*. November 22. http://www.straight.com/article-119340/stephen-harper-opens-door-to-prison-privatization (accessed October 22, 2008).

Sabo, Don, Terry Kupers, and Willie London. 2001. *Prison Masculinities*. Philadelphia: Temple University Press.

Smith, Christopher. 1993. "Black Muslims and the Development of Prisoners' Rights." *Journal of Black Studies* 24, no. 2: 131–46.

Steady, Filomena. 2002. *Black Women, Globalization, and Economic Justice: Studies from Africa and the African Diaspora*. Rochester, VT: Shenkman Books.

Sudbury, Julia. 1998. *Other Kinds of Dreams: Black Women's Organizations and the Politics of Transformation*. New York: Routledge.

———. 2002. "Celling Black Bodies: Black Women in the Global Prison Industrial Complex." *Feminist Review* 70: 57–75.

———. 2003. "Women of Color, Globalization, and the Politics of Incarceration." In *The Criminal Justice System and Women*, edited by Barbara Raffel Price and Natalie Sokoloff. New York: McGraw Hill.

———. 2004a. "A World without Prisons: Resisting Militarism, Globalized Punishment and Empire." *Social Justice* 31, nos. 1–2: 9–30.

———. 2004b. "From the Point of No Return to the Women's Prison: Writing Contemporary Spaces of Confinement into Diasporic Studies." *Canadian Women's Studies* 23, no. 2: 154–64.

———, ed. 2005. *Global Lockdown: Race, Gender, and the Prison-Industrial Complex*. New York: Routledge.

———. 2009. "Challenging Penal Dependency: Activist Scholars and the Anti-Prison Movement." In *Activist Scholarship: Antiracism, Feminism, and Social Change*, edited by Julia Sudbury and Margo Okazawa-Rey. Boulder, CO: Paradigm Publishers.

Whittington, Les. 2008. "PM's Plan: Life for 14 Year Olds." *The Toronto Star*. September 23. http://www.thestar.com (accessed October 22, 2008).

NOTES

1. This article is dedicated to the memory of Boitumelo "Tumi" McCallum. Her spirit is a continued inspiration in the struggle against intimate and state violence.

    This article originally appeared as, "Maroon Abolitionists: Black Gender-oppressed Activists in the Anti-Prison Movement in the US and Canada," *Meridians: feminism, race, transnationalism*—Volume 9, Number 1, 2009, pp. 1–29 (reprinted with permission).

I use "gender-oppressed" as an umbrella term to refer to women and transgender and gender-non-conforming people. The term represents a paradigm shift from prior feminist analyses of patriarchal state and interpersonal violence that are rooted in a gender binary and that therefore focus only on women's oppression. The concept is implicitly aspirational in that it both utilizes and seeks to generate a coalitional identity that might serve as a basis for solidarity.

2. I am indebted to the activists who gave generously of their time to make this research possible. As with all activist scholarship, this article is informed by the collective analysis, theorizing, and wisdom of numerous grassroots activists whom I have learned from over the years.

3. See for example, Sudbury 2002; 2003; 2005.

4. "Transgender" is an overarching term that refers to a range of people whose lived experiences do not fit the binary gender system. The term "gender-non-conforming," in keeping with usage by the Audre Lorde Project, is used as an umbrella term that includes those who may not identify as transgender but who nevertheless experience policing, discrimination, or violence based on their non-conformist gender expression. I use "transgender and gender-non-conforming" as an inclusive term throughout this article. Where the term "transsexual" is used, this refers to a smaller group of individuals whose original biological sex is at odds with their sense of self, sometimes resulting in the choice to physically alter the body through hormones or surgery (Richard 2000).

5. Although there are many organizations and individuals who seek to reform the criminal justice system and improve prison conditions, this article focuses only on activists whose work aims ultimately to abolish prisons. Drawing on histories of resistance to slavery, these activists use the term "abolition" to indicate their goal of ending the use of imprisonment as a tool of social control and as a response to deep-rooted social inequalities.

6. I was a founding member of Critical Resistance, a national organization dedicated to dismantling the prison industrial complex, and have worked with and alongside Incite!: Women of Color against Violence, the Prison Activist Resource Center, Justice Now, Legal Services for Prisoners with Children, National Network for Women in Prison, California Coalition for Women Prisoners, Arizona Prison Moratorium Coalition, the Prisoner Justice Day Committee, and the Prisoner Justice Action Committee, Toronto. For the past decade I have been based in Oakland, CA and Toronto, Canada; these two sites critically inform my activist scholarly work. For an in-depth discussion of anti-prison scholar-activist methodology, see Sudbury 2009.

7. While "black" is often treated as a unitary and homogeneous racial category, my participants, while identifying as "black," also embodied considerable ethnic and

national diversity. Participants included those who had migrated to the US and Canada as children, as well as those born and raised in the two countries. Their parents were Bajan, Grenadian, Egyptian, Palestinian, African American, white English, and Italian.

8. They were involved with the following organizations: Infinity Lifers Liaison Group, the Prison Arts Foundation, PASAN, PJAC and the Prisoners' Justice Day Committee in Canada; Critical Resistance, California Coalition for Women Prisoners, Audre Lorde Project, Prison Moratorium Project, the Trans/Gender Variant in Prison Committee of California Prison Focus, Legal Services for Prisoners with Children, Justice Now, the Hands off Assata Campaign, Incite!: Women of Color against Violence, and All of Us or None in the US; Prisoners Rehabilitation and Welfare Action in Nigeria, and the International Conference on Penal Abolition.

9. Attempts to write in ways that challenge the gender binary are complicated by our limited linguistic system. In particular, gender-non-conforming identities pose a challenge in the use of pronouns. It is extremely difficult to write an article without the use of "he" or "she." This being the case, I chose to ask participants how they preferred to be referred to. I have respected participants' requests regarding pronouns, for example, Bakari preferred s/he.

10. In the 1980s, Alberto Melucci pointed to a shift from class-based struggles over economic resources, to "new social movements" that were constitutive of new collective identities related to struggles over peace, the environment, youth, gender, and racial justice (Melucci 1989; 1995). I am arguing here that these (arguably not so) new social movements can be conceptually divided between identity-based movements in which the actors define their collectivity with reference to a shared social location in relation to systems of oppression, and ideology-based movements that unite diverse actors through a shared critical analysis. I call the contemporary anti-prison movement an "ideology-based" (rather than an identity-based or issue-based) movement because, as I demonstrate in this article, participation in it is based on a common political analysis of the prison industrial complex and a shared ideological position that draws on histories of abolitionist struggle.

11. The term "directly affected" is taken from activist spaces where it is used to highlight the importance of leadership and involvement by people from communities that have been targeted in the domestic wars allegedly against crime, drugs, and terror. This rubric makes visible the differential ways in which we are "all" affected by the prison industrial complex by distinguishing those who are indirectly affected, through the impact on state budgets for example, from those who have immediate and visceral experiences of gendered and racialized

state violence.

12. In 1971, over 1,300 prisoners led by black and Puerto Rican insurgents seized control of Attica Correctional Facility in western New York state to protest racism, brutality, and appalling conditions. Forty-three people were killed when state officials ordered an armed response to the rebellion, bringing about international censure. Recordings and documents from the McKay hearings into the rebellion can be accessed at http://www.talkinghistory.org/attica (accessed January 6, 2009).

13. See note 9.

14. The Rockefeller Drug Laws, enacted in 1973 and still in force, were at the time the toughest drug laws in the country. The laws made the penalty for selling two ounces of narcotics a Class A felony punishable by fifteen years to life in prison. See http://www.drugpolicy.org (accessed January 6, 2009).

15. For a discussion of the shift from welfare state to disciplinary state in the US and Canada, see Bohrman and Murakawa 2005; Neve and Pate 2005.

16. Maya is referring to the $1 million bounty placed on Black Panther Assata Shakur, aka Joanne Chesimard, by the US Department of Justice in May 2005. After being targeted as part of the FBI's campaign against the Black Panther Party, Shakur was found guilty by an all-white jury of killing a New Jersey state trooper, despite being incapacitated from gunshot wounds at the time of the alleged shooting. She escaped from prison in 1979 and has lived exile in Cuba since that time (Hinds 1987). For details of the current situation, see http://www.handsoffassata.org/ (accessed January 6, 2009).

17. Communities of escaped slaves and their descendants who fled via the underground railroad to settle in Ontario, Nova Scotia, and British Columbia after slavery was abolished in the British Empire in 1834 can also be seen as part of the maroon legacy.

18. For example, the maroons of Jamaica waged war with the British for 140 years before finally being deported to Halifax, Nova Scotia in 1796 (Grant 1980, 15–16). Escapees in Ontario were also at risk from slave-catchers after the passage of the Fugitive Slave Law of 1850.

19. Aboriginal people make up 2.8% of the Canadian population, but are 18% of the federal prison population. Correctional Service of Canada, "Aboriginal Community Development in Corrections: Aboriginal Offenders Overview." http://www.csc-scc.gc.ca/text/prgrm/abinit/know/7–eng.shtml (accessed February 2, 2009).

20. In the US, these rebel communities, often described as "outlyers" [sic], were found in the Great Dismal Swamp on the Virginia and North Carolina border, in the coastal marshlands of South Carolina and Georgia, and among the Semi-

noles in what was Spanish Florida (Lause 2002).

21. The work of Angela Y. Davis has been critical in envisioning this possibility (Davis 2003).

22. Organizations working on these goals include the Trans/Gender Variant in Prison Committee, the Transgender, Gender Variant & Intersex Justice Project, Human Rights Watch's LGBT Rights Program, Lambda, and the Sylvia Rivera Law Project in the US and PASAN in Canada.

23. The medical mistreatment of transgender prisoners is part of a continuum of medical neglect experienced by all prisoners. A paradigmatic case is Shumate v. Wilson, which found that endemic medical neglect in California state women's prisons constituted cruel and unusual punishment.

24. This work has been taken up by the federal government in ways that suggest, erroneously, that by deploying more policing and punishment, the state can eliminate gender violence from an institution that is constitutive of that violence. The passage of the Prison Rape Elimination Act of 2003, which mandates enhanced monitoring of incidents of sexual assault and the application of "zero tolerance" policing within prisons, does little to eradicate the culture of domination and violence that promotes and condones sexual assault (Gaes and Goldberg 2004).

25. Although indigenous prisoners' struggles to gain access to sweat-lodges and ceremonial objects have been the most visible in the fight for religious freedom in prison (Reed 2003), intensive battles were also waged for recognition of the Nation of Islam and black Muslim practices (Smith 1993; O'Connor and Pallone 2003, 96–97). The round-ups and mass detentions of Muslims in the war on terror (Cainkar and Sunaina 2005), as well as the targeting of Muslim prisoners as a potential security threat, have created new challenges for struggles for religious freedom in US and Canadian prisons and detention centers.

26. Testimony from former prisoners at "Prison Ministry or Prison Abolition? An Interfaith Conversation on Prison-Industrial Complex Abolition," Critical Resistance 10, September 27, 2008.

27. *The Eyes of the Rainbow.* 1997. Dir: Gloria Rolando. Havana, Cuba: Images of the Caribbean. Available at: http://www.afrocbaweb.com/Rainbow.htm (accessed October 18, 2008).

28. An example of the metaphysics of maroon resistance is found in the case of Queen Nanny, eighteenth-century leader and obeah woman of the Windward Maroons in Jamaica. Queen Nanny was known to use "obeah" or supernatural powers derived from Ashanti spiritual practices against the British (Gottlieb 2000).

29. See also Demmons 2007.

ABOLITIONIST IMAGININGS:

A Conversation with Bo Brown, Reina Gossett, and Dylan Rodríguez

Che Gossett

I am ever inspired and empowered by the visionary and community-centered work done by my sister Reina Gossett; ever impassioned by the intensity and sheer force of Dylan Rodríguez's abolitionist critiques; and ever oriented and grounded by Bo Brown's history and present of organizing with radical anti-prison and queer liberationist movements. At this critical juncture, this conversation offers a collective, cross-cutting dialogue about prison abolition and gender self-determination in this present era of mass incarceration and criminalization. Reina Gossett, Dylan Rodríguez, and Bo Brown have been organizing around, writing in resistance to, speaking out against and through suffering, loss, and hate violence that our communities are facing on a daily basis. This conversation highlights the ways that prison abolitionist activists and academics inform, challenge, and help nurture and develop each other. It demonstrates not only the immediate urgency of abolition and trans liberation but also the relevance of histories of community resistance and resilience to our present struggle.

Che Gosset: How were you politicized around prison abolitionism?

Dylan Rodríguez: First, let me say how important it is that we situate our biographies of politicization within our specific political-historical contexts rather than as universalizing stories of "radicalization." There is often a temptation to inhabit and perform radical political positions as if they were the inevitable result of traumatic and/or spectacular individual experiences with violence, oppression, and so forth. The fact is, we usually become radical political workers not simply because we have personal grievances with corrupt and unjust social systems, but rather because we encounter the mundane, insistent, nourishing, and contentious influences of some community of activists, teachers, survivors, and intellectuals (by which I mean people who think a lot, not just people who get paid to think and write). In this sense, I see my politicization toward prison, police, and penal abolition as a logical outcome of the people and political-intellectual traditions that I've been close to during the last two decades. There were two overlapping—really inseparable—dimensions to the process of both clarifying and (more importantly) *identifying with* an abolitionist analysis and political-intellectual position: participating in the formation of Critical Resistance as a (truly novice) activist and organizer produced an intimacy with a deep, historically specific sense of futility, urgency, and frequent desperation that I eventually realized is organic to the work of engaging liberationist and anti-racist work in a time of heightened—but no less *normalized*—warfare and institutionalized dehumanization. This is why I've spent most of my adult life trying to figure out how to conceptualize the prison and policing regimes, in their comprehensive social-institutional totality, as genocidal (or at least proto-genocidal) systems.

Let me put it this way: If our examination of the prison regime constantly leads us to the conclusion that particular populations, bodies, places, and communities are not meant to thrive or survive existing institutional arrangements, then what political practices can we conceive that directly deal with this condition *as a state of emergency*? This leads to the second major aspect of my politicization toward abolition, and that's the sometimes undervalued *activist* work of focused study, research, and analysis. Anybody who wants to contact me can ask me for my personal bibliography, and I'll be happy to send it—too many books, essays, articles, poems, and stories to name here. But let me expand on this dimension just a bit: Many of us, as activists, who are otherwise constantly thinking about and critically analyzing what we're doing, far too frequently ignore or abandon radical *intellectual* work as if it was an unaffordable luxury that's best taken up by academics, lawyers, and artists. I think this intellectual underdevelopment kills radical movements and empowers the liberal-to-conservative political circuitry that would like to see this condition of (proto-)genocide managed, reformed, and controlled rather than destroyed and transformed.

Bo Brown: I was a white working-class Butch; bar dyke on the weekends. Then I was a social prisoner due to a conviction for a less than $50 theft from the post office where I was working. I was what we now call a social prisoner in prison for less than a year in a federal prison in San Pedro, California. I was in prison in September 1971 when George Jackson was killed. In fact, I was reading *Blood in My Eye*. I was still in prison when Attica happened, a month later. So that kind of slammed open my eyes to a lot of stuff. Even though I was pretty young—23—pretty inexperienced, pretty naïve, you know, didn't know a whole lot about the rest of the world. Even though I had no real political perspective or language, I knew that was some fucked up shit that went down. It was so wrong and really outright criminal. Murders were committed. Yet they got away with it right there in front of our eyes on TV for the whole world to see.

Reina Gossett: In my life, politicization happens as a deepening process, so it was years of fermentation rather than a single event that deepened my abolitionist politics. I found out about Critical Resistance New York City the spring after the RNC. This was a time when Bush had won re-election and abolitionists in New York City had been really engaged in organizing in response to militarization in NYC and the war in Iraq. I entered during a time of reflection, burnout, and inspiration. Because of gentrification in Brooklyn, the CR office moved from Crown Heights to the West Village. What I was witnessing were people throughout different activist spaces engaging abolition, even people deeply invested in reform work.

At that moment, along with other students, I was doing creative writing and poetry workshops at Island Academy—a high school for teenagers on the Rikers Island Jail. I had strong desires for a political home to hold these experiences and make sense of them, to make my life intelligible to myself beyond the fear and shame I felt around my own trauma with the PIC.

The possibility of being involved in abolition presented a moment when traumatic experiences and shameful experiences could be transformed into the possibility of something more powerful: Yes, we have agency, yes, we are not innocent, and yes, there is something larger at work that causes ourselves and our loved to get caught up in prisons, jails, cop cars, detention centers, TSA private screenings, etc.

In that initial moment it felt like Critical Resistance NYC worked to create room for a lot of people. I felt inspired by so many queer people in a room working together and it made the Brecht Forum a space of political possibility; there were people doing childcare, and a lot of people from La Casita, the drug treatment program for women with children, came down from the South Bronx to be there. At that first meeting, people who had done a lot of work to create the space were leaving, which felt like the space didn't mandate that you stay, even if you were one of the co-creators.

Later, traveling to the Gullah Sea Islands and the Penn Center with CR deepened my connection to the spiritual/soulful aspects of this lineage of resistance and liberation. It was a powerful moment of entering a place that held such rich history of black resistance, resilience, loss, and joy. It also helped expand my understanding beyond a thinking process, meaning that the PIC doesn't just affect our material condition but also our spirits, psyches, and connection to land so any meaningful response and resistance has to be about more than our material condition.

This was all a decade after first reading George Jackson's *Blood in My Eye*, learning about Mumia, attending an Afro-centric summer and after-school program and developing a sense of wonder about my family's involvement in the black freedom movement, and many years after starting to visit my father while he was incarcerated in prison and psychiatric institutions. This makes me believe that coming into contact with the PIC or critical analysis was important, but entering a community of people committed to the process of abolition, which meant commitment to each other, was where transformation really occurred in my life.

The 2007 Transforming Justice Conference deepened and challenged my understanding of abolition politics. Many trans women, formerly incarcerated, were talking about their lives in the context of state violence and PIC abolition. Prior to that, I felt a real growing edge when it came to creating abolitionist spaces that trans people, but particularly trans women of color, could access. It challenged me to make sure I was not leaving myself at the door when I entered abolitionist spaces. This reminded me of the legacy of trans people resisting state violence and whose stories have been suppressed both in and out of abolitionist movements. So for my own politicization process it wasn't just what caught my attention, but what held and challenged me, what grew my soul and sense of somebodiness. This means to me that politicization is a sacred moment—a sacred process—and throughout my life sacred spaces have held and increased those moments and processes.

CG: "PIC abolitionism" indexes so many apparatuses of state violence, surveillance, and policing, as well as modes of resistance, healing, and accountability. How you do make the concept politically intelligible and tangible through your own work?

DR: I'll spend anything from many minutes to many hours (depending on who I'm talking to and working with) illustrating how the formation of the prison and policing regimes are inseparable from the apparatuses of racial genocide on which the United States is based. How is the prison a paradigmatically anti-black genocidal institution? Where do we find the connections between policing and the land displacement, cultural genocide, and geographic incarceration of native and indigenous peoples in and beyond North America? What is the concept of "civil death" and how does it shape a society in which 2 million people are locked up by the state? What's the critical difference between an activism that addresses "police brutality" and one that addresses "police violence" or even domestic warfare? If we ask—and begin to answer—questions like this, we can demystify the prison's apparent normalcy and political invincibility, and build a *different set of historical and political assumptions* that recast our understanding of the prison regime as a focal point of a collective, radical political creativity—abolitionism—that takes seriously the monumental challenges of freedom, liberation, self-determination, and anti-violence.

I'll put it another way: If one is willing to commit to an unapologetic, rigorous analysis of what prisons are, where they come from, and what they do, in a way that respects and challenges the intellect and sensibilities of the person or people one is engaging, the abolitionist position makes more sense than not. This is not to say that we don't need to engage in simultaneous conversations about how to deal with repressive, oppressive, and exploitative forms of structural violence that would not simply disappear with the abolition of the prison regime. Rather, it's to say that simply establishing the abolitionist concept as something that's grounded in a historical analysis and political logic results in *different sets of urgent questions* that no longer presume the existence of policing, imprisonment, or even the militarized nation-state itself.

BB: If you're about your politics, you know that all that shit comes out of the same asshole. It's all about who runs it, who profits from it: There's a medical industrial complex, a prison industrial complex, a business industrial complex—it's all about the wealthy getting wealthier. It's all connected. So you have to look at all that. I'm working toward a world in which we don't really need a prison industrial complex, a world that treats people like human beings, a world that doesn't create a War on Drugs, a world that doesn't destroy the education system and determines that the people who are somehow classified as "uneducable" or the wrong color or the wrong class will be tracked to prison, because there will be no jobs available to them, etc. A more equitable world, a more humane world, a world that's not about money—that's the primary thing—a world that's not about slavery.

RG: I've spent a lot of time wondering about how abolition is tangible in my work, and I have shifted in my practice in making abolitionist politics real. While I was involved with CR I put energy into creating a tangible abolitionist practice by challenging people to wonder if incarceration was a solution to violence by asking a lot of questions; the campaign to stop New York City from building a new jail in the South Bronx on a toxic land site, slated to be a women's jail with a nursery, fit really well into this.

Because we had been organizing to mobilize large-scale community opposition to the jail, we created a good moment to highlight how reforming and managing the prison industrial complex rather than abolition far too often leads to an expansion of state violence. In that case, the state used the fact that Rikers Island was (and is) in horrible condition and completely inaccessible for people to visit, as an excuse to build pristine new neighborhood jails so that communities could access their loved ones more easily in prison. So it became an important moment to engage the state and organize to stop this escalation of state violence.

After my involvement in the campaign and witnessing how often campaigns can make it hard for folks to not burn out, I moved into the place of wondering how to make abolition intelligible through a range of daily practices. A lot of people were really trying to incorporate principles of prevention, intervention, reparation, and transformation into how we practiced our political work. It is not enough to just be urgent and in opposition to state violence but uncritically practice it through exclusion, alienation, sexism, ableism, transphobia, and homophobia and a racist politic of policing authenticity. Prefigurative politics really resonated with me, meaning I wanted the work I did to prefigure the world or communities I wanted to live in.

A lot of the bridge or transitional space between these two ways of practicing politics was held in spaces that were not actively organizing around state violence and domestic warfare, or at least not framing it the same way. Thought a lot about Southerners on New Ground's (SONG) framework of spirits, land, labor, and bodies being both sites of violence and colonialism as well as sites of beautiful places of resistance and healing, the prison industrial complex fits really well into that framework. This marked a real shift in my politics and signaled my movement into internal practices and away from campaigns, with an emphasis on slowing down the work.

CG: How have queer, genderqueer, trans, and gender-non-conforming PIC abolitionists organized internally to foreground gender liberationist and queer politics within the abolitionist movement? How might non-trans allies address cisgender supremacy within the abolitionist movement and help to center the politics of gender self-determination?

DR: These are two of several questions that are shaping and reshaping progressive-to-radical social movements generally, and abolition particularly. You've asked related questions here—one descriptive and one speculative—and both are reflective of present-tense conditions in the prison regime that focus on gender as a site for the invention and deployment of state violence. One of the most remarkable developments in the abolitionist struggle over the last decade or so has been the emergence of a radical queer analysis of state violence that pushes our understanding of how gender (and for that matter, sexuality) is not simply one discrete axis within intersecting logics of oppression and repression, but is actually a *technology through which the state creates new forms of systemic bodily vulnerability and disintegration.* So what do we make of the prison regime if it's constantly deforming and redefining its institutionalizations of "gender" over and against the actual gender identifications of its captives, officers, and administrators?

In this sense, I think we've seen the emergence of a queer, gender-queer, trans, and gender-non-conforming *intellectual and organizational leadership* in abolitionist collectives and other social movements, including and especially those collectives and movements that don't appear at first glance to be especially focused on "gender and sexual oppression" as their primary critical engagements. My sense of this development is that this community of activists is finely attuned to the ways in which their bodies and identities are acutely vulnerable to the comprehensive, oppressive violence of the state: from being subjected to abstract normative "definitions" of their allegedly deviant sexual and gender identities—a process that leads to both reactionary, state-condoned homophobic violence and self-harm, including suicide—to their increasingly evident vulnerability, to gender-specific forms of "racial" and "class" criminalization, as is the case with the state's targeting of sex workers, black and brown "gang"-classified youth, and undocumented migrants. This sensibility can and does translate into a dense, complex, and politically explosive *political* positioning that can and must be engaged by non-queer and non-trans people. This is why I'm always a bit suspicious of and hesitant to embrace the "allies" rubric—because if we really take the queer, trans, gender-non-conforming political *position* seriously, we have to understand that to undertake the work of gender self-determination and gender liberation, we don't simply "stand alongside/behind" our queer/trans peers; we inhabit a position *with* them in absolute political intimacy.

BB: Because they [queer, genderqueer, trans, and gender-non-conforming PIC abolitionists] do the work and they bring their issues. If you don't do the work then you don't get the say. I'm a working-class person, and I believe that the product belongs to the people who do the work—not the people who wrote the theory.

We [the George Jackson Brigade] were a very integrated group, especially for our time period; there were people in the underground at that time period who said that queers could not be revolutionary and would have to be dealt with after the revolution. We were just the opposite. We were lesbian, we were gay, we were bisexual; transsexual[ity] was not necessarily an issue at that time, the way that it is now. That's who we were and then we did the work. And we did a lot of work around prisons. One of the first bombings was the Department of Corrections in support of a prison struggle, in the maximum-security prison in the state of

Washington—Walla Walla. Later there was a long, forty-seven-day lock-down or a strike by prisoners in Walla Walla, and it was the longest strike in state history and actually it might be the longest strike in prison history that we know of where the prisoners were demanding better treatment: an end to torture, better food, basic things. The mainstream press had never talked to a prisoner; they only talked to the people in charge. We did some research and found that the mainstream press was owned by the same private utility company who had workers on strike; some of the same people who were on the prison board who were on this board and that board, and there was a financial connection, and we wrote that in a communiqué and said all this shit is connected, and the demand in the communiqué was that a prisoner be interviewed.

They [non-trans allies] have to do the work to understand that it's a civil rights issue. It's not about "I want to get married so I can be accepted by mainstream society"; it's about "I would like to live my life," "I would not like to be oppressed, suppressed, beat up, and spit on on the street, whatever the fuck you as the oppressor feels like doing to us." Because everybody's not the same in this world, nor should they be.

RG: The 2007 Transforming Justice Conference in San Francisco around gender self-determination was integral to PIC abolition. It was organized primarily by trans and gender-non-conforming women who had been incarcerated or otherwise survived the PIC. Because it was organized with an understanding of how organizing against transphobia and a commitment to gender liberation and self-determination are key components in creating real safety, it really concretized a new set of possibilities within the abolitionist movement. As opposed to some of the organizing with other abolitionist spaces, this conference already began with an understanding that trans and gender-non-conforming people's lives matter. That meant that the energy it so often takes trans people to convene in other abolitionist spaces where gender self-determination is held could be used for building relationships.

The Transforming Justice Alliance continued to grow this work during Critical Resistance 10 (CR10) through plenary speakers, workshops, and film. Last April, a contingent of Transforming Justice members met with the disability justice collective here in NYC. We're expanding our understanding around sites of incarceration and policing, made a decision to gather again in 2012 in Atlanta and do it in a way that prioritizes relationships, resilience, and strategizing.

During CR10, the Gender Liberation/Self-determination working group, which was part of the CR10 planning committee, struggled with how to have gender self-determination and trans histories and communities held in that space, and it was a constant negotiation. However, we successfully engaged all of the planning process and ensured gender liberation throughout the entire weekend: from childcare, to plenaries, as well as logistics like bathrooms access and pre-conference prioritizing outreach to trans and gender-non-conforming communities.

CG: In thinking about the legacy of trans activism against prisons and policing and the bio and necropolitical dimensions of incarceration—be they the regulation of gender expression and hormonal access, or the outing of HIV status and denial of care—what are ways in which the inside/outside struggle against the PIC has been shaped by trans and queer liberationist movements—especially by people of color?

DR: These movements have initiated a decisive altering of the ways in which we "do" and "think" political work against the PIC, aiming toward abolition. These critical interventions, in my experience, are spurred by major discursive, theoretical, analytical, and conceptual disruptions and transformations of formerly prevalent and heteronormative activist assumptions: For example, when we speak of "medical neglect," "medical abuse," or "lack of access to care," we can no longer assume a normative, prototypical, male or female body as the object of racist and gender-oppressive state violence. Instead, we need to understand how it is often precisely when the prison medical and psychiatric apparatuses are "working well" that they are mobilizing some of their most fundamental violence against people's already fragile sense of bodily integrity and emotional well-being. In other words, what trans and queer liberation politics teaches us is that there is really no such thing as a "good" or "humane" imprisonment regime within our historical conditions—there are only differing capacities and political/juridical tolerances of a range of physiological destructiveness against people held captive. So by focusing on the peculiar and acute ways that trans and queer people are *actually imprisoned*, we get a far deeper insight into the institutional logics of the prison in its deadly totality.

BB: Well, you have to go back to Stonewall: Wasn't that about queer and trans people in a bar in the Village, in New York? And then you have Kuwasi Balagoon, a black liberation army member. It took people a long time to time to be able to say that, and now they can say that he was a black gay man and that he was a revolutionary. Of course he did his part in that part of the struggle and in his community and remained who he was, true to himself. And I think that the formation of TIP in San Francisco—Trans In Prison—and those kinds of organizations that are specific, that work within the context of the broader prison industrial complex, are essential.

RG: I think this question requires deep reflection on the real importance of trans history within anti-authoritarian and abolitionist spaces and how these trans legacies are passed on to people or not and held or not within the larger left/activist world.

Too often, in abolitionist movements, we imagine that trans lives have just started to exist, that there is no legacy of trans people engaging abolition. We often do not know or retell how trans people organized around state violence and the PIC, like the Street Transvestite Action Revolutionaries organizing against police violence alongside the Black Panthers and the Young Lords. We forget that, until recently, organizing led by trans people was in resistance to violence from the police. We fail to remember that in the year following Stonewall, the first gay march in New York City ended—on purpose—at the Women's House of Detention, which held Panther 21 members Joan Bird and Afeni Shakur. We hardly like to share that trans activists like Sylvia Rivera and whole communities of trans women were kicked out of burgeoning gay and lesbian movements, feminist movements, and anti-authoritarian movements in order to consolidate power, make the movement more attractive to institutional power, and win minor concessions from the state. Least of all, we do not talk about how this violent exiling of trans women from radical spaces continues to happen to this day.

If we ignore the way this legacy and history of trans and gender-non-conforming people being pushed out of and marginalized within abolitionist movements shapes current trans and gender-non-conforming struggles, then we're only getting part of the story and are perpetuating historical exile and isolation; we are perpetuating violence.

That said, I don't believe it is enough to nostalgically and uncritically call upon STAR, the leadership of trans people during the Stonewall Rebellion or the Compton's Cafeteria Riot, each time we talk about trans people resisting the PIC. When recalling STAR and trans leadership in the anti-state violence movement, we often don't have enough understanding of the social history to name not only the amazing accomplishments but equally important the moments in which more growth and development was needed: What compromises should not have been made? What ethics could have been better foregrounded? This tendency makes our history less dimensional and more flattened, and ultimately diminishes our ability to make connections and see political patterns.

Right now I am grieving the exile of our political lineage and lives from abolitionist spaces; I am longing for my history and struggling to piece it together. As a black trans woman who is queer and an abolitionist, I want to know more about how trans people have supported or rejected abolitionism and gender self-determination within a range of political movements. More than any compiling of organizations or individual activist names within a general abolitionist history, I want a fuller scope of our social history that extends beyond when we were simply only oppressed or acted incredibly exceptional. I really believe in order for this to happen we have to challenge the hierarchy of intelligible abolitionist history that keeps our stories as trans and gender-non-conforming people from ever surfacing in the first place. Rather than simply reclaiming our lineage, let's start to change the context.

Trans people and trans resistance against the PIC have existed for a very long time, and our movements deserve a more complex understanding of the way we have shaped these movements. Reproductive justice work—particularly done by and on behalf of incarcerated trans and gender-non-conforming people and supported by trans people on the outside—is an exciting piece of work I want to hold.

Gabriel Arkles, formerly a staff attorney at the Sylvia Rivera Law Project, gave a brilliant talk at Critical Resistance 10 on reproductive justice and trans people in providing a real framework to challenge the eugenicist underpinnings of the PIC. Gabriel reminded the abolitionist audience that trans people's access to different treatments or interventions like hormones and surgery are real and legitimate medical needs—most of which do not permanently end our ability to physically reproduce—and not getting them can damage trans people's health and ability to function in the world. Gabriel then goes on to name six ways that prisons act as forces of reproductive injustice and carry out eugenicist practices. These include:

- Isolation from partners: "Simply locking up huge numbers of trans people during the years when they could be having children,"

- Isolation from families: "Keeping trans people away from raising their children when they are incarcerated and have their convictions used against them in custody and visitation cases; abuse, neglect, and termination of parental rights cases; and in adoption proceedings,"
- Conditioning safety on trans people giving up their ability to have children: "The only way that trans people are put into facilities that match their gender is by having a type of surgery that may or may not be right for them, that is nearly impossible to get, and results in sterilization,"
- Denying medical care: "Denials are not only profoundly damaging the physical and mental health of trans people in prisons and robbing them of the ability to make intimate decisions about their own bodies and to self-determine their own gender, but they can also lead to loss of reproductive capacity in another way,"
- Keeping incarcerated people from having children together: "Explicitly a part of the agenda of prison officials to make sure that trans women and non-trans women in prisons, who are mostly women of color and disproportionately disabled, cannot have children together, and to make sure that trans men and non-trans men in prisons, who are mostly men of color and disproportionately disabled, cannot have children together,"
- "The final way that the prison industrial complex interferes with the ability of trans people to have children and limits the population of trans people is by literally killing trans people."

Trans and queer liberationist movements expand and transform the conversation around incarceration and reproductive justice and deeply impact the struggle against the PIC. Trans and queer liberationist movements continue to push reproductive justice spaces to remember that there are women who are incarcerated in men's prisons and that reproductive justice conversations need to expand to center trans women and gender-non-conforming people.

CG: What are ways in which the abolitionist movement needs to change and adapt in order to address current realities facing incarcerated and ICE-detained trans and gender-non-conforming people, especially women and people of color?

DR: To begin, I would largely defer on this question to people who are much more deeply enmeshed in the political and intellectual work around the specificity of these conditions of imprisonment. I think I still have a lot to learn from the experiences and analyses being generated by people who are closely and rigorously engaging this form of state violence, and perhaps this is the best way to respond to the question you've posed. I don't know that the thing we're naming as the abolitionist movement has calcified to the point that it has developed a truly parochial, common set of political paradigms and protocols—at least, not in its current rendition as a late–twentieth- and early–twenty-first-century radicalism (one could say there were at least two predominant, contradictory understandings of "abolition" during the middle-to-late part of the nineteenth century, as it was taken up by white abolitionists and enslaved and non-enslaved black abolitionists).

I'm not saying that there aren't some persistent assumptions guiding this emerging movement that reproduce oppressive racial, gender, sexual, and class logics; rather, what I'm getting at is that the field of abolitionist politics and discourses is contingent, fragile, and flexible enough at this moment that it may not be a question of whether it needs to "change and adapt" to accommodate the material and historical truths of imprisoned/detained trans and gender-non-conforming people. Instead, the issue may be one of whether and how *multiple abolitionisms* can articulate with each other in a way that poses a legitimate threat to transform the current condition. What we'd be talking about is a conception of political struggle that visualizes the abolition/transformation of various, specific, perhaps non-comparable forms of imprisonment that are sometimes lumped together within the same institutional designation: "prison." It may be the case that we can't and shouldn't attempt to compare (or conflate) the sometimes drastically different forms of policing and imprisonment targeting different bodies and populations, and instead engage them as relatively specific, but structurally connected forms of state violence. This, I think, might give the work of abolition a rich set of political tools as well as organizing strategies. With all respect to my colleagues who've spent much time and energy constructing them, I don't think there can be such a thing as a *singular* or *definitive* "abolitionist mission statement." We need many of them, and each needs to rigorously understand what its mission is attempting to engage.

BB: One thing that I think the prison movement doesn't have is a lot of information about this group. People need to make the information available; once people know the facts, I think it's pretty self-explanatory. That's what I think could happen with this in this age of computers, is that Web sites that are about prison abolition should be linked or somebody needs to be coming up with numbers and concepts and stories—like what is happening. I don't see that stuff too much on the Web. [At] Prison Activist Resource Center (PARC), where I do my prison abolitionist work, we have a resource directory and we have a pretty large LGBT section that goes in to prisoners, about somewhere between 5,000 and 10,000 of those a year go in to prisoners, and based on the replies that we get back, prisoners tell us on average they share this with fifteen other prisoners. We're trying to solicit their stories and we're trying to create a blog page where we can excerpt stories from prisoners letters and put that up, so people out here in the free world can understand, because they cannot understand, because they don't know. If you want to support prisoners, you don't take over the movement; you encourage prisoners to create their own movement and you support that movement. You can't run that from out here, but you have to make a way available to them for them to have a voice, and you can do support work on a daily basis just like you do all your other support work. You live your politics by supporting your work and making a way for others to support their own.

RG: (A lot of the information in this answer can be found in the Welfare Warriors Research Collaborative publication *A Fabulous Attitude,* which I co-authored.) Last spring, NYC-based members of Transforming Justice, including the Audre Lorde Project, Queers for Economic Justice, and the Sylvia Rivera Law Project met with two members of the Disability Justice Collective, Mia Mingus and Sebastian Margaret, to talk about the overlapping ways that ableism, poverty, transphobia, and racism construct the prison industrial complex. We talked a lot about expanding our understanding of places of incarceration to include psych hospitals, group homes, and homeless shelters, but also we talked about how we can intentionally do abolitionist work in a way that centers the disabled people within Transforming Justice and our communities. The conversation really depended on our commitment to disability justice as an abolitionist process, not just a principle that we hold.

According to the US Census, 54.4 million people in the US live with disabilities, and a recent study by the Center for Economic and Poverty Research found that half of adults who experience poverty are disabled. This is something that the Welfare Warriors Research Collaborative found when asking our community members about their experiences with poverty and disability. We also found that a substantial number of low-income queer and trans people dealt with police violence because of the NYPD's ableist racism and homophobia/transphobia. We weren't surprised when we learned that the percentage of people who named they dealt with police violence because of policing of disability was the same as the percentage of people who said they dealt with police violence because of policing of sex work. Of course, we also understood that it wasn't just disability or sex work that the police were regulating, but also that the folks who were disabled or sex workers were most often low-income, homeless, and people of color who were queer and trans.

The experiences of shame and isolation when navigating police violence are central issues for trans and gender-non-conforming people, especially people who are people of color, immigrants, low-income, and disabled. When we asked people how they navigate, 71 percent of people said they rely only on themselves when dealing with immigration issues; nearly half said they rely only on themselves when dealing with legal issues.

If we want to create an abolitionist movement that faces the realities of people navigating the prison industrial complex, then we must create strategies to generate safety and connection. So many low-income trans and gender-non-conforming people in New York City are not leaving their homes or their shelters as a proactive way of navigating transphobia and other forms of violence. If we're trying to build a grassroots movement that encompasses all of us, we need to make sure shame and isolation are challenged and incorporated into our organizing. Of course we are also not victims; we are fighting back and navigating state violence all the time, and trans people are doing incredible work around the shame and isolation that the prison industrial complex creates. When the Welfare Warriors Research Collaborative asked our community, low-income queer and trans people, how we healed from discrimination and violence, 114 community members answered: We tell others what happened (54 percent); we write in journals (40 percent); we have fun (35 percent); we exercise (30 percent); we meditate (31 percent); we make art (25 percent); and we pray (58 percent).

CG: How might the abolitionist movement speak to the demands and needs of categories of labor excluded from mainstream union politics such as sex work and incarcerated work? How do these labor politics fit into configurations of class struggle by low-income LGBTQ communities of color fighting campaigns for economic justice in both the neoliberal city and rural areas?

DR: This is crucial and difficult work because it has to address an intense confluence of unions' internal political hegemonies, late-neoliberal capital's repression and disposal of entire categories of workers, and the particular forms of criminalization reserved for laborers who are already presumed to be destined for some form of early death or imprisonment: Here I'm thinking of prison labor, undocumented workers, sex workers, and young (urban and rural) black and brown people whose only access to a real income is through the underground economy. So, there has to be an alternative to mainstream union politics, since the structural conditions confronting these kinds of "workers" are quite literally not legible to a conventional union membership or agenda. In other words, when you're focusing on workers who are not only fighting for basic economic survival (what we often call "economic justice"), but are simultaneously engaging the systemic violence of criminalization and policing, as well as the spectrum of institutionalized violence formed around the disciplining and enforcement of normative genders and sexualities, you are transcending and really obliterating the parameters of a "union politics." So I have no programmatic thoughts for how abolitionist struggles might adequately address this state of crisis, but I do think that an immediate step would be to develop a more multilayered, dynamic, and complex understanding of what "criminalization" is, how it works, when and where it's mobilized, why its technologies change and don't change, and so forth. To adequately comprehend the sites of struggle your question lays out is to build an understanding of how the technologies of criminalization not only lead to people being policed and locked up, but also lead to the most hyper-vulnerable workers being excluded or marginalized from entire categories of political advocacy. Criminalization is a violence of the social imagination that constantly creates the prison and policing regime, and works to eliminate certain people from the realm of "legitimate" politics. Abolitionism is uniquely positioned to illuminate and expound on this.

BB: You have to do the work, you have to put the information out there, you have to form a group that builds respect in the movement by being there, and then you have to demand a voice. We're queers, we know, we have to take a space for ourselves, that's the only way we'll ever get any space. And we can't just go "fuck that" and walk away. It's a process; we have work to do to earn it, we have to do it based on our politics. The thing you learn in prison is everybody's a number, anybody can say anything, but not everybody can do anything; anybody can talk the talk but not everybody walks the walk, and if we want people to pay attention to us and take us seriously, we have to walk the walk. We have to do work and then we have a right to demand, and we should be strong in those demands. And we all know that organized queers have never been known to be the quiet ones.

RG: When the Welfare Warrior Research Collaborative, a research and activist group made up of low-income queer and trans people, mostly of color, interviewed our community about interactions with the police, the people who identified as trans and the people who identified as currently homeless had the highest rate of interactions with the police. Of seven people who identified as sex workers, five of people had been strip-searched more than once. Nine people reported policing targeting based on gender expression, five of these nine people said they had been strip-searched more than once. Thirty people reported that police stereotype and target them based on sexual identity, and of these thirty people, fourteen said they have been strip-searched at least once.

As Angela Davis explains, the abolitionist movement and radical feminist movements must understand strip searches performed by police and prison guards as a form of sexual violence, "if uniforms are replaced with civilian clothes—the guards and the prisoners—then the act of strip searching would look exactly like the sexual violence that is experienced by the prisoner who is ordered to remover her clothing, stoop and spread her buttocks."

Some imagine that if you stretch the politics of large unions to include everyone, all "workers," then that will garner the greatest amount of protection for people. Some might imagine that this would protect queer and trans folks who consistently navigate this kind of sexual violence from the police. Personally, I have great doubt that mainstream union politics will ever expand enough to encompass the priorities of low-income trans people within informal and underground economies, as well as the quite formalized system of incarcerated labor. Abolition is relevant for people excluded from unions and union politics because people and communities are already taking care of and protecting themselves. For people who are doing work that is criminalized, an abolitionist politic supports relevant questions such as *How do we protect ourselves, each other, and practice justice without getting the state involved?*

CG: What kinds of political alternatives does the abolitionist movement offer in the face of current prevailing "post-racial" and neoliberal ideology?

DR: I can speak in a very incomplete way to what abolitionism *can* offer in terms of a radical racial, anti-racist politics. In my interpretation of it, the logic of an abolitionist position is that it is a direct and radical historical confrontation with the living legacies of anti-black racial slavery, racial colonialism, white supremacist nation-building, as they've differently converged in a nation-building project. So one of the most compelling political alternatives abolition can offer is a *pedagogical commitment* to learning and teaching how these systems are central to our everyday, historical present. The fraudulence of a "post-racial" (or even "post-racist") society is not hard to show—you can just go to the US government's own socioeconomic and criminal justice data to demystify the bullshit—but what's far more difficult is building a *racial/anti-racist politics* that is about liberation rather than reform and the abolition of genocide rather than genocide management.

BB: We are not post-racial; we have racism that occurs every fucking day. I think they should not be fooled by the hype: Who owns the media? It's not people of color. I would say the media takes this and that and says this movement [Obama's election] means we're past race; this in itself is a new chapter of racism. It's a way of saying, we don't have to worry about that anymore, even though we know that racism occurs every day in our lives and all around us. Don't be fooled by the bullshit. They'll [the big money that owns media] take any opportunity, they pay people millions of dollars to figure out how to talk to us and convince us that things are different than how they are. If racism had ended, there wouldn't be more than two million, gazillion, however many people of in prison; 60 to 70 percent of them are people of color. Who gets jobs? Who has the highest unemployment rates? All the numbers are there: We are not past racism. It took us 500 and however many years to get us where we are; it's not gonna change in a day or in one election. We made a step maybe, which they'll try and take away from us as soon as they can. But I mean what the fuck is the Tea Party about? It's not about "tea"; it ain't about "trans," either.

RG: We are neither post-racial nor post-racism. I think that abolitionist movements center and respond to the incredible amount of racist state violence and warfare that people every day have to navigate, and make clear links between the prison industrial complex and chattel slavery, colonialism, white supremacy, and anti-black racism. But it is unclear how an abolition movement operates as a political alternative beyond holding up the lie of post-racial ideology and promoting a politic, like Dylan said, "that is about liberation rather than reform, and the abolition of genocide rather than genocide management."

TOOLS/RESOURCES

Critical Resistance's Introduction to the Prison Industrial Complex
Picturing the PIC Exercise

WHAT YOU NEED:

For Part 1: Flip chart/Big Paper
For Part 2: Concentric Circles drawn on big paper minus the list of PIC element terms, terms sticky notes, blank sticky notes, copies of CR LA Concentric Circles Handout (see below for more)

WHAT YOU DO:

This section of the workshop has two parts: 1) a PIC brainstorm, and 2) the PIC Concentric Circles.

Part 1: PIC shout out

<u>Set up:</u> Have a piece of big paper up, and some markers. Shout out any and all parts of the prison industrial complex that you can think of.

<u>How it works:</u>

1. As you shout out parts of the PIC, write them up on the big paper. Be specific, and don't use language that empowers the PIC (i.e. don't use crime, use harm instead; don't use criminal/inmate, use people in prison instead. For CR's Thoughts on Language, go to their website.

2. After about **10 minutes**, end the brainstorm and take a look at the board. What connections do you see?

Make sure there is a good range of parts of the PIC up. It should cover policing, imprisonment, and surveillance, for example. It should have structures (**white supremacy**, **patriarchy**), and institutions (**courts**, **corporate media**) and interests (**investment banks, politicians**).

Part 2: Concentric Circles

It can also be helpful to look at all these parts of the PIC in a more systematic way. To do that, CR's LA chapter developed the following concentric circle exercise.

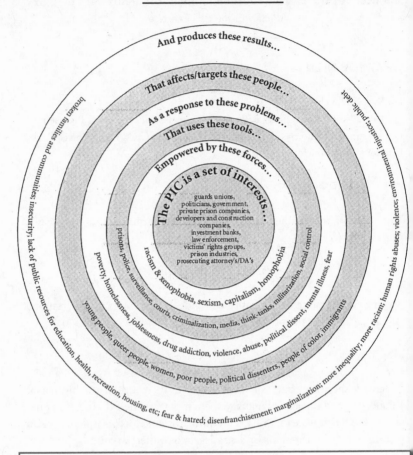

And produces these results...

That affects/targets these people...

As a response to these problems...

That uses these tools...

Empowered by these forces...

The PIC is a set of interests...

guards unions, politicians, government, private prison companies, developers and construction companies, investment banks, law enforcement, victims' rights groups, prison industries, prosecuting attorney's/DA's

racism & xenophobia, sexism, capitalism, homophobia

prisons, police, surveillance, courts, criminalization, media, think-tanks, militarization, social control

poverty, homelessness, joblessness, drug addiction, violence, abuse, political dissent, mental illness, fear

young people, queer people, women, poor people, political dissenters, people of color, immigrants

young people, health, recreation, housing, etc; fear & hatred; disenfranchisement; marginalization; more inequality; more racism; human rights abuses; violence; environmental injustice; public debt

broken families and communities; insecurity; lack of public resources for education, health, recreation, housing, etc

---

What Goes in Which Circle?

It is helpful to have (at least) one way to rephrase what each circle is about. Some ways to talk about them are:

- **"The PIC is a set of interests"** *means* "Who benefits from the PIC?"
- **"Underpinned by these systems of oppression"** *means* "What systems of power create and are supported by imprisonment, policing and surveillance?"
- **"That uses these tools"** *means* "How does the PIC keep itself going?"
- **"As a response to these problems"** *means* both the real harms we face as well as the problems people who use the PIC say it addresses.
- **"That affects/targets these people"** *means* "Who gets caught up by the PIC?"
- **"And produces these results"** *means* "What happens when we rely on imprisonment, policing, and surveillance as solutions to social, political, and economic problems?"

Source: Critical Resistance

<u>Set up</u>: **Prepare Beforehand and Bring**: Draw the concentric circles on big paper without the lists of PIC element terms (but with the sentence fragments). Create sticky notes that have those terms listed, one term per sticky note.

<u>How it works:</u>

1. The Concentric circles are a model used to assist in defining the PIC by filling in the blanks of a fragmented defining sentence.

2. Read through the fragments of the sentence aloud: ("The PIC is a set of interests...empowered by these forces...").

3. Participants should come up to the circles, one at a time, pick an element of the PIC sticky note, place it where it belongs in the circle, and explain to the group why that is so. Start with the inner circle first and work your way out, placing 2–3 sticky notes in each circle.

4. After each sticky note is placed and explained, comment on the choice of item, find out what questions there are, and see if anyone else has something brief to add.

5. After the outer-most circle is filled in, each participant should either write a new element of the PIC on a blank sticky note and place it, and/or move a sticky note from one concentric circle to another, explaining how it fits in both (or more) circles.

6. Distribute the filled in CR LA Concentric Circle Handout.

POLITICAL POINTS:

Some points you might want to think about:

- Both the brainstorm and the circles show the same thing in different ways. The brainstorm might be a better way to see how much is part of the PIC, or to search for new connections between elements of the PIC. The circles help us highlight how elements of the PIC do particular kinds of work to keep the PIC moving and growing.
- The circles show really well that the PIC is not broken—in many

ways, the interests at the center are more powerful than ever, and the results at the end are being produced more abundantly than ever

- Where are PIC reformers and abolitionists? When picturing the PIC, it might be useful to point out our place(s) in it.
- Of the three words in the phrase "PIC," "Complex" might be the most important—these models show that the PIC is broad, deep, and intertwined within itself.
- The PIC encompasses our entire society—is there anything that can't be related to punishment, imprisonment, policing, or surveillance?

WHAT MATERIALS YOU NEED:

Handout: 7 Easy Steps

WHAT YOU DO:

This section has one part: going through the "7 Easy Steps" document and discussing how you can use it to evaluate your work and plan new projects, and to use this section as an opportunity to think about how specific parts of your current work tie into one or more of these steps

<u>Set Up:</u> Pass around the 7 Easy Steps handout.

<u>How It Works:</u>

This is basically a talking piece—which means it's really important to check for understanding and draw out questions from the participants.

There are a number of points to hit:
1. 7 Easy Steps comes from Critical Resistance's Abolitionist Toolkit, and was designed to be a way for people to think through how a wide variety of projects can fit into an abolitionist practice and vision. The first part of the handout has the steps broken down really basically and the second has the same steps but with a little more detail added.
2. Read through each step and then take a minute to talk through what it means, offer an example from your work or that of other work happening, and ask for questions.
3. Use the following main political points to shape your reading and thinking about the handout.

Step 1: Life and Scope

It's really important to emphasize that we don't think abolition includes anything that makes the PIC reach further into our lives, or hang onto power longer. Campaigns to make prison more livable are an example here. A campaign that supports the building of newer cells to deal with crowding is not abolitionist, while campaigns to release the people who will fill those cells, or a campaign to decriminalize activities are (see Step 4 to ensure you are not pitting said group of activities against another). Use the third exercise to think of other examples.

Step 2: Where are you working?

It's important to emphasize here that we try to build leadership development work into our project and campaigns, not make it something separate. It's also good to mention here that we try to go after big, central parts of the PIC, not "low hanging fruit."

Step 3: Coalitions

You can't win this fight on your own. Build stronger relationships with your allies and start new relationships, in every phase of your work.

Step 4: No to NIMBY

NIMBY means "Not In My Back Yard." It's really easy to look out for NIMBY-ism in terms of prison and jail construction—making sure you aren't saying "don't build a jail here, build it there." But NIMBY also applies to the rest of the PIC. Abolition can't win if we pit groups of prisoners ("women" vs. "men," or "nonviolent" vs. "violent") against each other. We can make specific claims to eliminate specific parts of the PIC without implying that other parts are ok to let stand.

Step 5: Healthy solutions?

We have to create an active, dynamic balance between tearing down the things we don't want, and building up the things we do.

Step 6: Whose words are you using?

We all need to help each other learn new ways of talking about the world, whether it's saying "people in prison" instead of "criminals," or "inmates," or working openly to combat white supremacy, sexism, or gender violence in how we talk to each other. Building a new language takes time, but is essential to building the new world we want to live in, and it can bring to light and work to counteract the manipulative ways in which the PIC defines itself and/or co-opts the words we use.

Step 7: Short-to-Long-Term

Everything Critical Resistance does today is a short-term step to abolish the PIC, but it is also all connected to a long-term vision and strategy. It's really important that you practice laying out what those connections are, and explaining them so that people who participate in one event or project can see the connection between that and a long-term struggle for abolition.

POLITICAL POINTS:

- **Analytical work is work.** We need to constantly be evaluating if our work is getting us closer to our goal, or if we've been thrown off track. It's especially important for people new to organizing to ask questions about how the work they are doing fits into an abolitionist practice, and not assume that because an element of the PIC is being challenged that it is abolitionist work.
- **Lots of different work can be abolitionist**. There's a huge variety of work that can help abolish the PIC. The point of the tools is not to limit or restrict the type of work we take on, but to guide you in thinking really seriously and creatively about what you can do.

SEVEN EASY STEPS IDEAS & QUESTIONS FOR EVERYDAY ABOLITIONIST ORGANIZING

WHEN WE USE ABOLITION AS AN ORGANIZING TOOL, it can be confusing how exactly to support abolition on a day-to-day level, especially when we work in coalition with people who aren't sold on abolition (yet). These are some guidelines, questions, and ideas to think about as you plan and evaluate your campaigns.

1. LIFE AND SCOPE

THE CRITICAL RESISTANCE MISSION STATEMENT SAYS "Because we seek to abolish the PIC, we cannot support any work that extends its life or scope."

What we mean by not "extending the life" is that the work doesn't try to make the PIC less harmful, or to fix it, but to make it less possible for the PIC to continue.

What we mean by not "extending the scope," is that any work we take up doesn't support cages that aren't clearly prisons (like mental hospitals or prison hospices) instead of prisons; it doesn't make it easier to feed people into prisons (by putting cops in schools, for example); and it doesn't validate any part of the PIC. So even when we interact with state agencies like courts or legislatures, it's done strategically and in a way that weakens those systems, not by appealing to them as potential sources of justice.

2. WHERE ARE YOU WORKING?

We organize in different ways and places, and we have to use different levers of power to undo the PIC. And while we have to work in as many ways and places as possible, we need to give the most emphasis, presence, and support to fighting the most harmful aspects of the PIC—especially within our groups. This can mean things like insisting on leadership from people of color, challenging heterosexism within your group, or highlighting white supremacy in your literature. It can also mean taking the time to work through how a campaign will connect the communities doing the campaign to the communities being targeted, and thinking about how fighting a specific part of the PIC can make the whole system weaker.

EXAMPLE It can be hard to tell when you're using state agencies strategically and when your appeal to a court or legislature confirms its power. For example, pressuring state legislatures to decrease funding for state corrections departments during budget crunches is a useful way to challenge PIC expansion. However, it's important to make clear that (most) legislators do support prisons and police, and that opposing the PIC isn't just a matter of balanced state budgets, and that while we might be able to force legislatures to support our work sometimes, it is always going to be a matter of political force (instead of a matter of faith in democracy or the idealism of a representative). Otherwise you might find yourself in some tricky situations (in one instance, activists in California pushing for cuts to the corrections budget recently were told that if they wanted to see a decrease in funding they should support cuts to prisoner education and job training programs). Sometimes you can work against this just by saying it: telling the media and people you're working with that a campaign is appealing to such-and-such state power strategically—not because you have faith in the government—can go a long way toward changing how people inside and outside your campaign understand that work.

3. COALITIONS

As abolitionists, figuring out whom to work with might seem hard when not very many identify as abolitionist. At the same time, abolitionist politics helps you see broad connections throughout the PIC, making coalitions more necessary and more exciting. But in coalition work it can be especially hard to sort out the "life and scope" questions. Some things to think about are:

- Is the coalition's work abolitionist even if the members aren't?
- How do you relate to the non-abolitionists in your coalition? How are you working to shift their goals from reform to abolition?
- Who's indirectly involved in your coalition? Who funds the groups you're working with? What other coalitions are those groups in?

4. NO TO NIMBY

Not-In-My-BackYard (NIMBY) organizing tries to prevent something harmful from happening in one community by directly or indirectly suggesting it should happen somewhere else (someone else's backyard). A good example would be a group that organizes against a prison proposed for their community not by saying the prison shouldn't be built, but that it needs to be built in another place. NIMBY campaigns are sometimes easier to "win," because the project can still be completed, so all it really does is move the problem temporarily out of sight. Effective abolitionist work means saying "no" to the PIC anywhere and everywhere.

5. HEALTHY SOLUTIONS?

Part of building toward abolition is building other institutions and practices to maintain and create self-determination for communities and individuals. This doesn't mean that every campaign against a part of the PIC has to offer an exact alternative, but we should be thinking about those things—if you're fighting a new prison, what do you want done with that money and land instead? If you're fighting

against education and health care cuts, where from state funding of the PIC could you get money (e.g. replacing cuts to education with cuts to the prison or police budget).

6. WHOSE WORDS ARE YOU USING?

What are the ways you frame the problem, your work, your demands, and your solutions? Do they rely on the PIC's categories of criminals, fear, and punishment, or do they help us to build a world where we are accountable to each other and adress harm by providing for our collective and individual needs? Does your language help broaden people's general vision of fighting the PIC, or does it only spotlight a particular problem?

7. SHORT- TO LONG-TERM

How does your current project contribute to abolition? Does it offer immediate support to people harmed by the PIC? Is it a movement-building or educational tool? Does it connect issues that seem separate? What is it going to make possible down the line?

> I think that as we develop prison abolitionism, we also need to build on the visions of communities that have organized around the basis of identity. By that I'm not saying that we need to go back to this narrow identity politics where we can't work together unless we come from the same racial group, or sexual group or whatever, but I do think that sometimes the prison abolitionist language begins to erase the language of race and identity and sexuality, and to a lesser extent gender. And if we do that, then it becomes less—it doesn't seem so relevant to communities of color that are very much used to organizing within a framework of anti-racist, African-American, Latino language. So I think that we need to develop an abolitionism and an abolitionist statement and vision that is totally infused with the cultures of the peoples who are incarcerated.
>
> JULIA SUDBURY

Supporting Abolition
A Quick Guide to the Questions

Here's a shorter version of our questions about supporting abolition. They aren't intended as a checklist, but rather as a quick guide to some of the questions we think it's most useful to ask. They're things to think about as your work develops to make it stronger, not an entrance test for the abolition club.

|Life and Scope|
DOES YOUR WORK SEEK TO MAKE THE PIC A LESS WORKABLE SOLUTION TO PROBLEMS, AND TO LIMIT ITS REACH OVER OUR LIVES?

|Where Are You Working?|
DOES YOUR WORK TAKE ON ASPECTS OF THE PIC THAT ARE MOST HARMFUL? DO YOU WORK TO FIGHT FORMS OF HARM LIKE WHITE SUPREMACY, HETEROSEXISM AND CLASS PREJUDICE BOTH IN YOUR CAMPAIGNS AND WITHIN YOUR GROUP?

|Coalitions|
ARE YOU WORKING IN COALITIONS WITH ABOLITIONIST GOALS? ARE YOU WORKING TO HELP OTHER COALITION MEMBERS UNDERSTAND ABOLITION?

|No to NIMBY|
DOES YOUR WORK REJECT THE PIC EVERYWHERE?

|Healthy Solutions|
DOES YOUR WORK SUGGEST WORKABLE WAYS TO MAINTAIN SELF-DETERMINATION, MEANINGFUL SAFETY, AND COLLECTIVE HEALTH?

|Whose words are you using?|
DOES THE LANGUAGE YOU USE CHALLENGE COMMONLY ACCEPTED NOTIONS OF SAFETY, RESPONSIBILITY, AND JUSTICE?

|Short- to Long-term|
DOES YOUR IMMEDIATE WORK MAKE FUTURE CHALLENGES TO THE PIC POSSIBLE?

Addressing the Prison Industrial Complex: Case Studies

The following is a list of campaigns, policies and changes both past and present that address the prison industrial complex.
Review a few, discuss the results and ask the following questions:

- In what ways has this change hurt our communities and/or made the prison industrial complex stronger?

- In what ways has this change supported our communities and/or made the prison industrial complex weaker?

- Is it possible to have achieved the stated goal without hurting our communities? If so, what does this mean about the strategy of abolition?

- Any lessons learned from efforts to "fix" versus efforts to weaken/eliminate the prison industrial complex?

Goal: End domestic violence
Strategy: Create more/harsher sentences for people who abuse others
Result: Has domestic violence decreased and/or ended?

Goal: End returns to imprisonment (recidivism) by people with substance dependencies
Strategy: Legislation that forces treatment instead of imprisonment
Result: Has recidivism decreased and/or ended?

Goal: End violence against lgbtqq (queer) communities
Strategy: Hate crime legislation that gives harsher sentences for people who have caused harm against those communities
Result: Has this violence decreased and/or ended?

Goal: End returns to prison (recidivism) due to the poverty of joblessness
Strategy: "Ban the Box" campaigns that eliminate the question on city and county job applications that asks if the applicant has been convicted of a felony.
Result: Are/Will more former prisoners (be) able to apply and get jobs?

Goal: Provide safe space for transgender people in prison
Strategy: Send all transgender prisoners to a transgender only prison
Result: Did this happen/is this happening and are transgender people in prison safer now?

Goal: Decrease individual to individual (interpersonal) violence
Strategy: Increase public police presence
Result: Has violence in our neighborhoods, families, communities decreased?

Goal: Bring people in women's prisons home to be with their families
Strategy: Create more, smaller prisons located in more places
Result: Will this bring people in women's prisons home?

Goal: End violence against youth in prison in Louisiana
Strategy: Shut down the Tallulah Youth Prison
Result: The prison was closed. Did violence in this prison stop?

Goal: Decrease the number of people in prison
Strategy: "Compassionate Release" which allows for the release of terminally ill prisoners.
Result: Does this decrease the number of people in prison?

Goal: End abuses by prison officials who determine at will sentence length
Strategy: Introduce mandatory sentencing minimums for specific charges
Result: Are people in prison facing shorter sentences? Are individuals able to get shorter sentences based on individual circumstance surrounding charges with mandatory minimums?

Goal: Support people in prison who have survived violence, including sexual violence, harassment and other abuses
Strategy: Use administrative segregation as protective custody
Result: Are survivors of violence safer, cared for and/or supported and is trauma addressed in protective custody?

Goal: End imprisonment violence against youth in prison in California
Strategy: Build multiple, smaller facilities throughout the state
Result: Is there/will there be less imprisonment of youth, and is there/will there be less violence generally against youth who are locked up?

Goal: End abuses against marginalized people (people of color, transpeople, queer people) by police and prison staff
Strategy: Mandatory sensitivity trainings, already done for most of California's police force.
Result: Has/will harassment, abuse and violence against these communities by staff and police decrease(d)?

Goal: End medical neglect and crowding in prisons
Strategy: Build more prisons
Result: Has this ended medical neglect and crowding?

Can you think of more? How about ending the death penalty and replacing it with life in prison, or decreasing recidivism (see above) by decreasing parole and probation time or decreasing violence by creating curfews or fighting police violence by convicting individual police officers?

RESOURCE LIST

All Of Us Or None
1540 Market Street Suite 490
San Francisco, CA 94102
415.255.7036 ext 308, 315, 311, 312
info@allofusornone.org
www.allofusornone.org

ACT UP Philadelphia
P.O. Box 22439, Land Title Station
Philadelphia, PA 19110-2439
actupp@critpath.org
www.actupphilly.org

Audre Lorde Project
85 South Oxford St.
Brooklyn, NY 11217
718.596.0342
www.alp.org

Bent Bars Project
P.O. Box 66754
London, WC1A 9BF
United Kingdom
bent.bars.project@gmail.com

Black and Pink
c/o Community Church of Boston
545 Boylston St.
Boston, MA 02116
www.blackandpink.org

BreakOUT!
1600 Oretha C. Haley Blvd.
New Orleans, LA 70113
www.jpla.org

Critical Resistance
For more info, write to Jay Donahue
1904 Franklin St, Suite 504
Oakland, CA 94612
510.444.0484
www.criticalresistance.org

FIERCE!
437 W. 16th St, Lower Level
New York, NY 10001
646.336.6789
www.fiercenyc.org

generationFIVE
P.O. Box 1715
Oakland, CA 94604
510.251.8552
www.generationfive.org

Gay Shame
San Francisco, CA
gayshamesf@yahoo.com
www.gayshamesf.org

Hearts On A Wire
(for folks incarcerated in PA)
PO Box 36831
Philadelphia, PA 19107
heartsonawire@gmail.com

INCITE! Women of Color
Against Violence
P.O. Box 226
Redmond, WA 98073
484.932.3166
www.incite-national.org

Justice Now
1322 Webster Street, Suite 210
Oakland, CA 94612
510.839.7654
www.jnow.org

LAGAI—Queer Insurrection
lagai_qi@yahoo.com
www.lagai.org
Prison Activist Resource Center
PO Box 70447
Oakland CA 94612
510.893.4648
www.prisonactivist.org

Prisoner Correspondence Project
QPIRG Concordia c/o Concordia
University
1455 de Maisonneuve O
Montreal, QC H3G 1M8
Canada
www.prisonercorrespondenceproject.com

Prisoner's Justice Action Committee
Toronto, Ontario, Canada
pjac_committee@yahoo.com
www.pjac.org

Sylvia Rivera Law Project
322 8th Ave, 3rd Floor
New York, NY 10001
212.337.8550
www.srlp.org

Tranzmission Prison Project
P.O. 1874
Asheville, NC 28802
tranzmissionprisonproject@gmail.com

Transgender, Gender Variant, and
Intersex Justice Project
342 9th St., Suite 202B
San Francisco, CA 94103
415.252.1444
www.tgijp.org

Write to Win Collective
2040 N. Milwaukee Ave.
Chicago, IL 60647
writetowincollective@gmail.com
www.writetowin.wordpress.com

CONTRIBUTORS

Ralowe T. Ampu: the mysterious maiden from suburban California. Yes, Ralowe T. Ampu: a living testament to the activist ideal. Yes, Ralowe T. Ampu: the seductive fragrance wafting through milieus of unbridled danger and intrigue. Yes, whether it be outing gay Castro realtors as AIDS profiteers with ACT UP and GAY SHAME, or trying to free the New Jersey 4, or preventing the nonprofit management company in her SRO from killing her neighbors, Ralowe is there. Who is she? What is she? If adventure has a name: Ralowe T. Ampu. Yes.

Bo (r.d.brown) is a 63-year-old white working-class BUTCH dyke feminist who prefers female pronouns. She is an anti-authoritarian, anti-imperialist, ex-political prisoner who did eight years in federal prisons during the 1980s for several bank robberies claimed by the George Jackson Brigade in Seattle, Washington. She has been a prison abolitionist for more than thirty-five years. Bo is also a founding mother of Out of Control: Lesbian Committee to Support Women Political Prisoners. She is a proud member of All of Us or None. Bo is a board member as well as a worker at the Prison Activist Resource Center in Oakland, California. Bo works with many other prison abolition groups in the San Francisco Bay Area. You can reach her at bo@prisonactivist.org.

Morgan Bassichis lives in San Francisco and organizes for queer and trans liberation, transformative justice, and prison abolition with Community United Against Violence (CUAV), the Transgender, Gender Variant, and Intersex Justice Project (TGIJP), and the Transforming Justice Coalition. Morgan's writing has been featured in the *Radical History Review* and *The Revolution Starts at Home* (South End Press).

Stephen Dillon is a Ph.D. candidate in American Studies at the University of Minnesota, Twin Cities. His academic work focuses race, gender, terror, and the formation of the neoliberal carceral state in the 1970s United States.

Jayden Donahue is a member of the Oakland, California, chapter of Critical Resistance and believes that abolishing the Prison Industrial Complex is central to building strong, self-determined communities. He has also volunteered with the Prison Activist Resource Center and the Transgender in Prison Committee. If you don't find him organizing, he's probably out training for his next marathon. He currently lives in Oakland with his partner and a variety of animals.

Lori B. Girshick is an activist and a sociologist. She has worked extensively in the area of LGBT domestic and sexual violence, and with people in prison. She is the author of *Woman-to-Woman Sexual Violence: Does She Call It Rape?*, *Soledad Women: Wives of Prisoners Speak Out,* and *No Safe Haven: Stories of Women in Prison*. After writing the book *Transgender Voices: Beyond Women and Men*, she sought to combine her experiences by speaking with masculine-identified people in women's prisons. She teaches sociology at Chandler-Gilbert Community College in Chandler, Arizona. Lori can be reached at lgirshick@cox.net.

Che Gossett is an activist who has been involved in prison abolitionist political formations and LGBTQ struggles for self-determination. Che is part of the Hearts on a Wire collective in Philadelphia and is working on a book project on black radicalism, queer and trans resistance, and the politics of history, loss, and liberation.

Reina Gossett lives in Brooklyn and works at the Sylvia Rivera Law Project supporting SRLP's membership and community organizing work. She believes that creativity and imagination are crucial for growing strong communities and practicing self-determination. Right now she's asking herself and others a lot of questions about shame and isolation, and, relatedly, loves making collages, watching reruns of *Battlestar Galactica* and reading anything illustrated by Diane and Leo Dillon.

Nadia Guidotto, MA, LLM, is a doctoral candidate in political science at York University in Toronto, working primarily in the area of gender identity and sexual orientation. Her current research analyzes intersex and how authoritative discourses like medicine and law support each another in maintaining a hierarchy of bodies. She is also interested in exposing how silence, violence, and exclusion can result from this process.

Vanessa Huang is a poet, writer, and community organizer whose practice draws on a history of collaboration with the anti-prison, gender liberation, anti-violence, immigrant rights, reproductive justice, and disability justice movements. Vanessa is a member of generationFIVE's leadership team and Sins Invalid's advisory board; has staffed Justice Now as campaign and communications director and Transgender, Gender Variant, and Intersex Justice Project as interim grassroots fundraising coordinator; and was a founding member of Transforming Justice.

Kris is a honey black gender-non-conforming lesbian. Kristopher loves music, poems, intellectual conversations, museums and traveling around the world. Kris has worked for convalescent hospitals and with youth as a youth. Kris loves to cook and looking to also fulfill that dream. Dreams can come every day, but which ones stay? People are invited to write to Kristopher "Krystal" at Kris Shelley, W89861, VSPW, C1-30-1L, P.O. Box 92, Chowchilla, CA 93610-0092.

S. Lamble has been involved in social justice, antipoverty and prisoner solidarity work in Ontario, Canada and London, England. Lamble currently teaches at Birkbeck Law School, University of London and is a founding member of the Bent Bars Project, a collective which coordinates a letter writing program for queer, trans and gender-non-conforming prisoners in Britain.

Alexander L. Lee is the founder and former director of the Transgender, Gender Variant, and Intersex Justice Project, which works to challenge and end human- and civil-rights abuses against transgender and gender-variant people and people with intersex conditions in California prisons and beyond. He is currently a public interest career counselor at his alma mater, UC Berkeley School of Law, helping to guide the next generation of attorneys fighting for social justice. He lives in Oakland, California, with his partner.

Miss Major is a black, formerly incarcerated, male-to-female transgender elder. She has been an activist and advocate in her community for over forty years, mentoring and empowering many of today's transgender leaders to stand tall, step into their own power, and defend their human rights, from coast to coast. Miss Major was at the Stonewall uprisings in '69 and became politicized in the aftermath of Attica, has worked at HIV/AIDS organizations throughout California, was an original member of the first all-transgender gospel choir, and is a father, mother, grandmother, and grandfather to her own children and to many in the transgender community. Currently, Miss Major is the executive director of the TGI Justice Project where she instills hope and a belief in a better future to the girls that are currently incarcerated and those coming home.

Tommi Avicolli Mecca is a radical queer activist, writer, and performer whose work has appeared in almost forty anthologies. He is editor of *Smash the Church, Smash the State: The Early Years of Gay Liberation*, and co-editor of *Avanti Popolo: Italian American Writers Sail Beyond Columbus* and *Hey Paesan: Writings by Lesbians and Gay Men of Italian Descent*. His Web site is www.avicollimecca.com.

Erica R. Meiners teaches, writes, and organizes in Chicago. She has written about her ongoing labor and learning in anti-militarization campaigns, educational justice struggles, prison abolition and reform movements, and queer and immigrant rights organizing in *Flaunt It! Queers Organizing for Public Education and Justice* (2009), *Right to Be Hostile: Schools, Prisons and the Making of Public Enemies* (2007), and articles in *Radical Teacher*, *Meridians*, *Academe*, and *Social Justice: A Journal of Crime, Conflict, and World Order*. Her day job is teaching at an open-access public university, Northeastern Illinois University, where she is a member of UPI/Local 4100, and she also teaches at a free high-school program for formerly incarcerated men and women, and at a number of other popular education sites in Chicago. A 2010 Lillian J. Robinson Scholar at the Simone de Beauvoir Institute, a beekeeper, errant fruit canner, haphazard nun-fan, and non-US citizen, she enjoys long-distance running and most kinds of engagement. She can be contacted at e-meiners@neiu.edu.

Yasmin Nair is a Chicago-based writer, activist, academic, and commentator. Her work has appeared in publications like *Windy City Times*, *Discourse*, *GLQ*, *make/shift*, *Time Out Chicago*, *Bitch* magazine and *Maximum Rock'n'Roll*. She is part of the collective Against Equality (againstequality.org) and a member of the Chicago grassroots organization Gender JUST (Justice

United for Societal Transformation, www.genderjust.org). Nair is currently working on a book about affect and neoliberalism. Her work can be found at www.yasminnair.net.

blake nemec has paid the rent as a health care worker throughout his adult life, while actively providing/trading harm reduction based medicines for activists and family. Calling for the decriminalization of prostitution, he's worked with national/international groups, most recently being HOOK and COSWAS. A dilettante artist, he is most known for his short stories and is currently pursuing an MFA at the University of El Paso Texas where he can be reached at: blakej.nemec@yahoo.com.

Michelle C. Potts lives in Oakland, CA and works at the Haight Ashbury Free Medical Clinic in San Francisco. Michelle recently graduated from UC Santa Cruz with a degree in Feminist Studies and is currently a Ph.D. student in Rhetoric at UC Berkeley. Her work is interested in affective labor, anxiety, and race. She can be reached at michellepotts9@gmail.com.

Dylan Rodríguez is Professor and Chair of the Department of Ethnic Studies at UC Riverside, where he began his teaching career in 2001. He is the author of two books: *Forced Passages: Imprisoned Radical Intellectuals and the US Prison Regime* (Minneapolis: University of Minnesota Press, 2006) and *Suspended Apocalypse: White Supremacy, Genocide, and the Filipino Condition* (Minneapolis: University of Minnesota Press, 2009). His essays have appeared in such scholarly journals as *Radical History Review*; *Social Identities: Journal for the Study of Race, Nation, and Culture*; *Critical Sociology*; *The Review of Education, Pedagogy, and Cultural Studies*; *Social Justice: A Journal of Crime, Conflict, and World Order*; and *Scholar and Feminist Online*.

Lori A. Saffin received her Ph.D. in American Studies from Washington State University and currently teaches in and chairs the Sociology Department at Bellevue College. She has a passion for teaching and a general love of empowering students to act toward social change. Lori is actively involved in a variety of social justice initiatives, though is particularly invested in building coalitions within the queer community across race/ethnicity, class, gender, and nationality. She lives with her wife in Seattle.

Dean Spade is an Assistant Professor at the Seattle University School of Law. In 2002 he founded the Sylvia Rivera Law Project, a collective that provides free legal help to trans, intersex and gender-non-conforming people who are low-income and/or people of color and works to build racial and economic justice centered transresistance. He is the author of *Normal Life: Administrative Violence, Critical Trans Politics and the Limits of Law* (South End Press, 2011).

Julia Sudbury aka Julia C. Oparah is an activist scholar and Professor of Ethnic Studies Department at Mills College. She is editor of *Global Lockdown: Race, Gender and the Prison Industrial Complex* (Routledge 2005), co-editor of *Outsiders Within: Writing on Transracial Adoption* (South End 2006) and *Activist Scholarship: Antiracism, Feminism and Social Change* (Paradigm Publishers 2008), and author of *Other Kinds of Dreams: Black Women's Organisations and the Politics of Transformation* (Routledge 1998). Julia has been involved in the racial and gender justice and anti-prison movements in the US, U.K., and Canada for two decades and has worked with numerous social justice organizations including Critical Resistance, Incite! Women of Color Against Violence, and the Prisoner Justice Action Committee, Toronto. Julia is involved in spiritual, meditation and healing communities in Oakland, CA and is committed to radical womanist mothering of her daughter Onyekachi.

Clifton Goring/Candi Raine Sweet is a transgender black woman who loves writing poetry and many types of music, singing and rapping, reading vampire and serial killer fiction. Candi is best known for her voice and has 6 talent show titles and counting. Candi is smart, considerate, affable and is a joker yet loving and caring person at heart. She is simply 44 cents away from you so forever stamp her, will you J? People are invited to write to Candi at: Clifton Goring 02A2252, Sullivan Correctional Facility, PO Box 116, Fallsburg, New York 12733-0116.

Wesley Ware is the founder of BreakOUT!, a project of the Juvenile Justice Project of Louisiana (JJPL) that fights for justice for lesbian, gay, bisexual, transgender, and queer/questioning youth in the juvenile justice system and the author of the recently released report, *Locked Up & Out: Lesbian, Gay, Bisexual, and Transgender Youth in Louisiana's Juvenile Justice System*. Wes serves on the Advisory Board for the Equity Project, a national initiative to bring fairness and equity to LGBT youth in juvenile delinquency courts. At JJPL, he coordinated the investigation for a class-action lawsuit on behalf of youth detained in an abusive youth jail in New Orleans and monitors the conditions of three state-run youth prisons in Louisiana.

Paula Rae Witherspoon is a Transsexual Woman incarcerated in the Texas Dept. of Criminal Justice and is thankful for the opportunity to tell "my story," voice the cruel and unusual punishments transsexuals face in prisons throughout Texas and try my best to do my part to case CHANGE in the USA.

Jennifer Worley is a professor of English, Women's Studies, and LGBT Studies and director of the Queer Resource Center at City College of San Francisco. She is the author of "Pulpitations: The Lesbian Pulp Novel and the Imagining of Lesbian Community" (in *Invisible Suburbs*, ed. Josh Lukin, [Jackson, Miss.: University of Mississippi Press, 2009]) and the director of *Sex On Wheels*, a short film about sex-worker history that premiered in 2010 at Frameline LGBT Film Festival. She is currently at work on a feature-length version of the film and a monograph on lesbian literary cultures.

Support AK Press!

AK Press is one of the world's largest and most productive anarchist publishing houses. We're entirely worker-run and

democratically managed. We operate without a corporate structure—no boss, no managers, no bullshit. We publish close to twenty books every year, and distribute thousands of other titles published by other like-minded independent presses from around the globe.

The Friends of AK program is a way that you can directly contribute to the continued existence of AK Press, and ensure that we're able to keep publishing great books just like this one! Friends pay a minimum of $25 per month, for a minimum three month period, into our publishing account. In return, Friends automatically receive (for the duration of their membership), as they appear, one free copy of every new AK Press title. They're also entitled to a 20% discount on everything featured in the AK Press Distribution catalog and on the website, on any and every order. You or your organization can even sponsor an entire book if you should so choose!

There's great stuff in the works—so sign up now to become a Friend of AK Press, and let the presses roll!

Won't you be our friend? Email friendsofak@akpress.org for more info, or visit the Friends of AK Press website: www.akpress.org/programs/friendsofak